BEST OF
Betty Crocker®

2010

BEST OF Betty Crocker 2010

For more great recipes and ideas, go to bettycrocker.com

PUBLISHED BY
Taste of Home Books
Reiman Media Group, Inc.
5400 S. 60th St., Greendale WI 53129
www.tasteofhome.com

Printed in the U.S.A.

Taste of Home® is a registered trademark of Reiman Media Group, Inc.

The trademarks referred to herein are trademarks of General Mills, Inc., or its affiliates, except as noted.

All recipes were originally published in different form by Betty Crocker® Magazines and Betty Crocker® Most Requested Recipes™, both trademarks of General Mills, Inc.

International Standard Book Number (10):
0-89821-473-4

International Standard Book Number (13):
978-0-89821-473-4

International Standard Serial Number:
1947-234X

CREDITS

Generals Mills, Inc.

EDITORIAL DIRECTOR: Jeff Nowak
PUBLISHING MANAGER: Christine Gray
COOKBOOK EDITOR: Grace Wells
DIGITAL ASSETS MANAGER: Carrie Jacobson
PRODUCTION MANAGER: Michelle Tufts
RECIPE DEVELOPMENT AND TESTING:
Betty Crocker Kitchens
PHOTOGRAPHY: General Mills Photography Studio

Reiman Media Group, Inc.

EDITOR: Heidi Reuter Lloyd
SENIOR EDITOR/BOOKS: Mark Hagen
ART DIRECTOR: Gretchen Trautman
CONTENT PRODUCTION SUPERVISOR: Julie Wagner
LAYOUT DESIGNER: Kathy Crawford
PROOFREADER: Vicki Soukup Jensen
COVER PHOTOGRAPHY:
Reiman Publications Photo Studio
PHOTOGRAPHER: Jim Wieland
FOOD STYLIST: Diane Armstrong
SET STYLIST: Dee Dee Jacq

CREATIVE DIRECTOR: Ardyth Cope
CREATIVE DIRECTOR/CREATIVE MARKETING:
James Palmen
VICE PRESIDENT, EXECUTIVE EDITOR, BOOKS:
Heidi Reuter Lloyd
VICE PRESIDENT/BOOK MARKETING: Dan Fink
CHIEF MARKETING OFFICER: Lisa Karpinski
EDITOR IN CHIEF: Catherine Cassidy
PRESIDENT, FOOD & ENTERTAINING:
Suzanne M. Grimes
PRESIDENT & CHIEF EXECUTIVE OFFICER:
Mary G. Berner

Front Cover Photographs, clockwise from top:
Deep Dark Mocha Torte, p. 228, Double-Chocolate Cherry Cookies, p. 287, Curried Turkey Stir-Fry, p. 90, Asian Chicken Roll-Ups, p. 167 and Italian Chicken Noodle Soup, p. 169.

Back Cover Photographs, clockwise from upper left:
Chicken Stew, p. 131, Triple-Chocolate Brownies, p. 317, Small-Batch Lemon-Blueberry Muffins, p. 15 and African Groundnut Stew with Chicken, p. 135.

table
OF CONTENTS

35

49

72

101

113

142

152

181

217

251

281

320

336

Betty Crocker Shares Her Best Recipes!
NEW ANNUAL COOKBOOK SERIES MAKES YOUR COOKING EVEN BETTER

For generations, Betty Crocker has been the name to trust in kitchens across America. Home cooks knew they'd find success with Betty, whether they were using her grocery products, her recipes or both.

That statement holds especially true today, because Betty Crocker has not only kept up with the times; she remains a step ahead. She's a modern-day leader in home cooking, offering top-quality recipes, wholesome ingredients and helpful kitchen success hints for all occasions.

With Betty's help, a birthday party becomes an event to remember, and a holiday dinner becomes a fun-filled gathering that no one will forget.

That's why we're so excited about this brand-new cookbook! *Best of Betty Crocker 2010* features the most-requested recipes from a year of Betty's popular cooking magazines. This edition is the first in a series of annual cookbooks we look forward to bringing you year after year.

In this big, colorful book, we've compiled 307 family-pleasing recipes, all of them tested in the Betty Crocker Kitchens. Every recipe has a mouth-watering color photo plus a helpful tip—or even two or three. Betty's cooking experts have added handy how-to hints plus simple ingredient substitutions and practical suggestions for rounding out meals. That means you can get your family's meal on the table quicker and easier than ever before!

AT-A-GLANCE ICONS

We've added at-a-glance icons so you'll know which recipes best fit your family's needs. If you're strapped for time, we've got you double-covered. The **EASY** icon means the dish preps in just 15 minutes or less. (Then it cooks while you do other things.) The **QUICK** icon means the recipe goes together from start to finish in 30 minutes or less.

Check out the "Quick Starters" chapter on page 41 for rave-worthy appetizers for your next party. Each of the 16 recipes is ready to eat in only 10 to 20 minutes. The "Easy Weeknight Entrees" chapter on page 85 contains 24 tasty recipes that go together in a snap. A chapter of 21 "Slow Cooker Main Dishes" on page 125 offers set-it-and-forget-it convenience.

p. 96   p. 328

If you or someone in your family is watching fat or calorie intake, the **LOW FAT** icon will help. It identifies main dishes with 10 grams of fat or less and side dishes and desserts with 3 grams of fat or less. Because nutritional information is offered with every recipe in this cookbook, it's easy to plan a menu that meets any health concerns.

If you're looking for recipes for entertaining family and friends, you've got the right cookbook. In addition to two big chapters of appetizers and three chapters of main dishes, there are 119 desserts that showcase Betty's wonderful ability to create sweets that look as good as they taste. You can too; just follow the numbered steps.

The desserts range from cookies and bars to cakes and tortes, and from crisps and cobblers to fun cakes and cupcakes that will make everyone smile. For a taste of the excitement, check out the Roller Coaster Cake on page 246 or Teddy-at-the-Beach Cupcakes on page 257.

Whether you're making a weeknight dinner such as Nacho Chicken Casserole (page 87) or an easy and elegant party cake like Banana Turtle Torte (page 230), Betty Crocker is here with great recipes that help you make the most of your time with loved ones.

A general index and an alphabetical index at the back of the book will help you find just what you're looking for...for any occasion and every occasion.

BREAKFAST&BRUNCH

p. 17

21

23

6

apple breakfast wedges

Prep Time: 15 Minutes
Start to Finish: 40 Minutes
Servings: 6

EASY LOW FAT

- 1/4 cup packed brown sugar
- 1/4 teaspoon ground cinnamon
- 2 medium cooking apples, peeled, thinly sliced (about 2 cups)
- 1/3 cup water

- 2 tablespoons butter or margarine
- 1/2 cup Original Bisquick® mix
- 2 eggs

Maple-flavored syrup, if desired

1 Heat oven to 400°F. Generously grease 9-inch glass pie plate with shortening or cooking spray. In medium bowl, mix brown sugar and cinnamon. Add apples; toss and set aside.

2 In 2-quart saucepan, heat water and butter to boiling; reduce heat to low. Add Bisquick mix; stir vigorously until mixture forms a ball. Remove from heat; beat in eggs, one at a time. Continue beating until smooth.

3 Spread batter in bottom of pie plate. Arrange apples on top to within 1 inch of edge of pie plate.

4 Bake about 23 minutes or until puffed and edges are golden brown. Serve immediately. Drizzle with syrup.

High Altitude (3500-6500 ft): Heat oven to 450°F.

Nutritional Info: 1 Serving: Calories 160 (Calories from Fat 60); Total Fat 7g (Saturated Fat 3.5g, Trans Fat 0.5g); Cholesterol 80mg; Sodium 170mg; Total Carbohydrate 20g (Dietary Fiber 0g, Sugars 13g); Protein 3g. % Daily Value: Vitamin A 4%; Vitamin C 0%; Calcium 4%; Iron 4%. Exchanges: 1 Starch, 1/2 Other Carbohydrate, 1 Fat. Carbohydrate Choices: 1.

Betty's Kitchen Tips

Success Hint: Use slightly tart apples with a crisp texture, such as Haralson apples. For a sweeter apple, choose Fuji, Prairie Spy or Gala.

Special Touch: Sprinkle with powdered sugar, and serve with warm maple syrup.

mixed-berry butter crunch parfaits

Prep Time: 20 Minutes
Start to Finish: 50 Minutes
Servings: 6 parfaits

- -

1	cup Gold Medal® all-purpose flour
1/2	cup packed brown sugar
1/3	cup coarsely chopped pecans or walnuts
1/2	cup cold butter or margarine
1-1/2	cups Fiber One® cereal
1/3	cup flaked coconut
6	containers (6 oz each) Yoplait® Original 99% Fat Free red raspberry yogurt
1-1/2	cups blackberries, blueberries and raspberries

- -

1 Heat oven to 400°F. In large bowl, mix flour, brown sugar and pecans. Cut in butter, using pastry blender (or pulling 2 table knives through ingredients in opposite directions), until mixture is crumbly. Stir in cereal and coconut. Spread in ungreased 13x9-inch pan.

2 Bake 15 minutes, stirring once. Remove from oven; stir and cool 10 to 15 minutes.

3 In each of 6 parfait glasses, layer 1 to 2 tablespoons cereal mixture, 1/2 container of yogurt and 2 tablespoons berries; repeat layers. Top each with 1 tablespoon cereal mixture. If desired, garnish with additional berries. Store remaining cereal mixture in refrigerator.

High Altitude (3500-6500 ft): No change.

Nutritional Info: 1 Parfait: Calories 590 (Calories from Fat 210); Total Fat 24g (Saturated Fat 12g, Trans Fat 0.5g); Cholesterol 50mg; Sodium 260mg; Total Carbohydrate 86g (Dietary Fiber 10g, Sugars 49g); Protein 9g. % Daily Value: Vitamin A 30%; Vitamin C 15%; Calcium 30%; Iron 20%. Exchanges: 1 Starch, 1/2 Fruit, 4 Other Carbohydrate, 1/2 Skim Milk, 4-1/2 Fat. Carbohydrate Choices: 6.

Betty's Kitchen Tips

Variation: Feel free to use whatever berries are your favorite. Choose a combo or stick with one kind. It's up to you.

Do-Ahead: Make the cereal mixture ahead, but wait until serving to assemble the parfaits to keep the cereal mixture crunchy.

heart smart cheddar and potatoes breakfast bake

Prep Time: 10 Minutes
Start to Finish: 55 Minutes
Servings: 12

EASY

- 4 cups frozen potatoes O'Brien with onions and peppers (from 28-oz bag), thawed
- 1-1/2 cups shredded reduced-fat Cheddar cheese (6 oz)
- 5 slices fully cooked turkey bacon, chopped
- 1 cup Bisquick Heart Smart® mix
- 3 cups fat-free (skim) milk
- 1 cup fat-free egg product
- 1/2 teaspoon pepper

Italian (flat-leaf) parsley, if desired

1 Heat oven to 375°F. Spray 13x9-inch (3-quart) glass baking dish with cooking spray. In medium bowl, mix potatoes, 1 cup of the cheese and the bacon. Spread in baking dish.

2 In same bowl, stir Bisquick mix, milk, egg product and pepper until blended. Pour over potato mixture. Sprinkle with remaining 1/2 cup cheese.

3 Bake 30 to 35 minutes or until light golden brown around edges. Let stand 10 minutes before serving. Garnish with Italian parsley.

High Altitude (3500-6500 ft): Bake 35 to 40 minutes.

Nutritional Info: 1 Serving: Calories 140 (Calories from Fat 30); Total Fat 3.5g (Saturated Fat 1g, Trans Fat 0g); Cholesterol 10mg; Sodium 430mg; Total Carbohydrate 17g (Dietary Fiber 0g, Sugars 5g); Protein 10g. % Daily Value: Vitamin A 8%; Vitamin C 0%; Calcium 20%; Iron 6%. Exchanges: 1 Starch, 1 Lean Meat. Carbohydrate Choices: 1.

Betty's Kitchen Tips

Purchasing: O'Brien potatoes are diced potatoes, with chopped onions and pimientos or red or green bell peppers that are fried until they are golden and crispy. Frozen O'Brien potatoes have not been fried.

Variation: Using turkey bacon and reduced-fat cheese helps keep the fat and calories low. Your kids will never know the difference.

peachy mimosas

Prep Time: 5 Minutes
Start to Finish: 5 Minutes
Servings: 12 (2/3 cup each)

EASY QUICK LOW FAT

. . . .

2 cups orange juice, chilled

2 cups peach nectar, chilled

1 bottle (1 liter) regular or nonalcoholic dry champagne or sparkling wine, chilled

. . . .

1 In 1-1/2-quart pitcher, mix orange juice and peach nectar.

2 Pour champagne into glasses until half full. Fill glasses with juice mixture.

High Altitude (3500-6500 ft): No change.

Nutritional Info: 1 Serving: Calories 100 (Calories from Fat 0); Total Fat 0g (Saturated Fat 0g, Trans Fat 0g); Cholesterol 0mg; Sodium 10mg; Total Carbohydrate 11g (Dietary Fiber 0g, Sugars 9g); Protein 0g. % Daily Value: Vitamin A 4%; Vitamin C 30%; Calcium 0%; Iron 2%. Exchanges: 1/2 Fruit, 1 Fat. Carbohydrate Choices: 1.

Betty's Kitchen Tips

Did You Know? A traditional mimosa is made with orange juice. The addition of peach nectar makes this drink a bit sweeter and slightly less acidic.

Purchasing: Look for bottles of peach nectar in the juice aisle of your grocery store.

sausage oven pancake square

Prep Time: 20 Minutes
Start to Finish: 50 Minutes
Servings: 6

- 1 package (12 oz) bulk pork sausage
- 1 cup shredded American-Cheddar cheese blend (4 oz)
- 1 egg
- 1/4 cup milk
- 2 tablespoons maple-flavored syrup

- 1 tablespoon vegetable oil
- 1/2 cup Gold Medal® all-purpose flour
- 1 teaspoon baking powder
- 1/8 teaspoon salt
- 3/4 cup maple-flavored syrup

1 Heat oven to 350°F. In 10-inch skillet, cook the sausage over medium-high heat 5 to 7 minutes, stirring frequently, until no longer pink. Drain the sausage on paper towels. In ungreased 8-inch or 9-inch square pan, spread cooked sausage. Sprinkle cheese over sausage.

2 In large bowl, beat egg, milk, 2 tablespoons maple syrup and the oil with wire whisk until well blended. Beat in flour, baking powder and salt. Pour batter evenly over sausage and cheese.

3 Bake uncovered 25 to 30 minutes or until golden brown. Serve topped with 3/4 cup maple syrup.

High Altitude (3500-6500 ft): No change.

Nutritional Info: 1 Serving: Calories 390 (Calories from Fat 160); Total Fat 18g (Saturated Fat 7g, Trans Fat 0g); Cholesterol 75mg; Sodium 740mg; Total Carbohydrate 44g (Dietary Fiber 0g, Sugars 19g); Protein 12g. % Daily Value: Vitamin A 6%; Vitamin C 0%; Calcium 15%; Iron 6%. Exchanges: 1 Starch, 2 Other Carbohydrate, 1-1/2 High-Fat Meat, 1 Fat. Carbohydrate Choices: 3.

Betty's Kitchen Tip

- If you don't have American-Cheddar cheese blend on hand, you can easily substitute shredded Cheddar, Colby or Colby-Monterey Jack.

orange pancakes with raspberry sauce

Prep Time: 30 Minutes
Start to Finish: 30 Minutes
Servings: 8

QUICK LOW FAT

Raspberry Sauce

3	tablespoons sugar
1	tablespoon cornstarch
2/3	cup orange juice
1	box (10 oz) frozen raspberries in syrup, thawed, undrained

Pancakes

2	eggs
1-1/2	cups milk
1/4	cup vegetable oil
2	cups Gold Medal® all-purpose flour
2	tablespoons sugar
2	teaspoons baking powder
2	teaspoons grated orange peel
1	teaspoon vanilla
1/4	teaspoon salt

1 In 1-quart saucepan, mix 3 tablespoons sugar and the cornstarch. Stir in orange juice and raspberries. Cook over medium heat, stirring constantly, until mixture thickens and boils. Boil and stir 1 minute. Remove from heat.

2 Heat griddle or skillet over medium-high heat or to 375°F. If necessary, brush the griddle with vegetable oil before batter for pancakes is added (or spray with cooking spray before heating).

3 In large bowl, beat eggs with wire whisk until well beaten. Beat in remaining ingredients just until smooth.

4 For each pancake, pour slightly less than 1/4 cup batter from cup or pitcher onto hot griddle. Cook pancakes 1 to 2 minutes or until bubbly on top, puffed and dry around edges. Turn; cook other sides 1 to 2 minutes or until golden brown. Serve with sauce.

High Altitude (3500-6500 ft): No change.

Nutritional Info: 1 Serving: Calories 300 (Calories from Fat 80); Total Fat 9g (Saturated Fat 2g, Trans Fat 0g); Cholesterol 55mg; Sodium 230mg; Total Carbohydrate 49g (Dietary Fiber 3g, Sugars 20g); Protein 7g. % Daily Value: Vitamin A 4%; Vitamin C 10%; Calcium 15%; Iron 10%. Exchanges: 2 Starch, 1-1/2 Other Carbohydrate, 1-1/2 Fat. Carbohydrate Choices: 3.

Betty's Kitchen Tip

• Once the pancakes are cooked, place them in a pan and transfer them to a warm oven until all the pancakes are cooked and ready to be served.

almond-tres leches muffins

Prep Time: 20 Minutes
Start to Finish: 50 Minutes
Servings: 12 muffins

- -

1/2	cup butter or margarine, softened
2/3	cup sugar
1/2	teaspoon almond extract
2	eggs
2	cups Gold Medal® all-purpose flour
2	teaspoons baking powder

1/3	cup (from 14-oz can) sweetened condensed milk (not evaporated)
1/3	cup whipping cream
1/3	cup milk
3/4	cup sliced almonds

Additional sweetened condensed milk (1/4 cup)

- -

1 Heat oven to 400°F. Grease 12 regular-size muffin cups with shortening or cooking spray, or line with paper baking cups.

2 In large bowl, beat butter and sugar with electric mixer on medium speed until smooth. Beat in almond extract and eggs. Stir in flour, baking powder, 1/3 cup condensed milk, the whipping cream, milk and 1/2 cup of the almonds just until flour is moistened. Divide batter evenly among muffin cups (3/4 full). Sprinkle remaining 1/4 cup almonds evenly over batter in cups.

3 Bake 15 to 20 minutes or until light golden brown. Immediately remove muffins from pan to cooling rack. Cool 10 minutes. Drizzle 1 teaspoon additional condensed milk over top of each muffin. Serve warm.

High Altitude (3500-6500 ft): Line muffin cups with paper baking cups. Decrease baking powder to 1-1/2 teaspoons. Bake 20 to 25 minutes.

Nutritional Info: 1 Muffin: Calories 310 (Calories from Fat 140); Total Fat 15g (Saturated Fat 8g, Trans Fat 0.5g); Cholesterol 70mg; Sodium 170mg; Total Carbohydrate 37g (Dietary Fiber 1g, Sugars 20g); Protein 6g. % Daily Value: Vitamin A 8%; Vitamin C 0%; Calcium 10%; Iron 8%. Exchanges: 1-1/2 Starch, 1 Other Carbohydrate, 3 Fat. Carbohydrate Choices: 2-1/2.

Betty's Kitchen Tips

Success Hint: Depending on the type of muffin pan you use, you may get 15 muffins.

Did You Know? The phrase "tres leches" means "three milks," referring to the three different kinds of milk in the muffins.

canadian bacon and potato quiche

Prep Time: 20 Minutes
Start to Finish: 1 Hour 5 Minutes
Servings: 8

1	refrigerated pie crust (from 15-oz package)
1	cup frozen country-style shredded potatoes, thawed
1	cup 1/2-inch pieces fresh asparagus
1	cup diced Canadian-style bacon
1-1/2	cups shredded Havarti cheese (6 oz)
4	eggs
1	cup milk
1/2	teaspoon dried marjoram leaves
1/4	teaspoon salt

1 Heat oven to 375°F. Place pie crust in 9-inch glass pie plate as directed on package for one-crust filled pie. Bake about 8 minutes or until light golden brown.

2 Layer potatoes, asparagus, bacon and cheese in partially baked crust. In medium bowl, beat eggs, milk, marjoram and salt with wire whisk until well blended. Pour over mixture in pie plate.

3 Bake 45 to 50 minutes or until knife inserted in center comes out clean. Let stand 5 minutes before cutting.

High Altitude (3500-6500 ft): In step 1, bake about 10 minutes.

Nutritional Info: 1 Serving: Calories 290 (Calories from Fat 170); Total Fat 19g (Saturated Fat 8g, Trans Fat 2g); Cholesterol 140mg; Sodium 640mg; Total Carbohydrate 15g (Dietary Fiber 1g, Sugars 3g); Protein 15g. % Daily Value: Vitamin A 10%; Vitamin C 4%; Calcium 20%; Iron 6%. Exchanges: 1 Starch, 2 High-Fat Meat, 1/2 Fat. Carbohydrate Choices: 1.

Betty's Kitchen Tip

• Partially baking the pie crust before adding the filling prevents the crust from getting soggy.

pepperoni breakfast pizza

Prep Time: 20 Minutes
Start to Finish: 25 Minutes
Servings: 8

QUICK

- -

1-1/2	cups Original Bisquick® mix
1/3	cup hot water
8	eggs
1/4	cup milk
1/8	teaspoon pepper
1	cup diced pepperoni (from 6-oz package)

2	medium green onions, sliced (2 tablespoons)
1	tablespoon butter or margarine
1/2	cup pizza sauce (from 8-oz can)
1-1/2	cups finely shredded Italian cheese blend (6 oz)
1	tablespoon sliced fresh basil leaves, if desired

- -

1 Heat oven to 425°F. Spray 12-inch pizza pan with cooking spray. In medium bowl, stir Bisquick mix and hot water until soft dough forms. Press dough in bottom and up side of pan, using fingers dipped in Bisquick mix, forming rim at edge.

2 Bake 10 to 15 minutes or until golden brown.

3 Meanwhile, in large bowl, beat eggs, milk and pepper with wire whisk or fork until blended. Stir in pepperoni and onions.

4 In 12-inch nonstick skillet, melt butter over medium heat. Add egg mixture; cook 3 to 5 minutes, stirring occasionally, until firm but still moist.

5 Spread pizza sauce over baked crust. Top evenly with egg mixture. Sprinkle with cheese. Bake 3 to 5 minutes or until cheese is melted and pizza is hot. Sprinkle with basil.

High Altitude (3500-6500 ft): No change.

Nutritional Info: 1 Serving: Calories 320 (Calories from Fat 190); Total Fat 21g (Saturated Fat 9g, Trans Fat 1g); Cholesterol 245mg; Sodium 790mg; Total Carbohydrate 18g (Dietary Fiber 1g, Sugars 3g); Protein 16g. % Daily Value: Vitamin A 15%; Vitamin C 0%; Calcium 25%; Iron 10%. Exchanges: 1 Starch, 2 Medium-Fat Meat, 2 Fat. Carbohydrate Choices: 1.

Betty's Kitchen Tips

Variation: As with any pizza, it's easy to swap the toppings for your family's favorite. Cooked sausage, olives, or plain cheese are just a few options you may want to try.

How-To: Basil leaves cut into thin strips are called "chiffonade." Stack the leaves on top of each other, then roll up like a cigar. Slice across the roll to form long shreds.

small-batch lemon-blueberry muffins

Prep Time: 10 Minutes
Start to Finish: 25 Minutes
Servings: 4 muffins

EASY QUICK

1/2	cup Bisquick Heart Smart® mix
1/4	cup fat-free egg product
1	tablespoon sugar
2	tablespoons fat-free sour cream
1	teaspoon grated lemon peel
2	teaspoons vegetable oil
1/4	teaspoon vanilla
1/4	cup fresh or frozen (do not thaw) blueberries
1	teaspoon sugar

1 Heat oven to 400°F. Place paper baking cup in each of 4 regular-size muffin cups; spray insides of paper baking cups with cooking spray.

2 In small bowl, stir all ingredients except blueberries and 1 teaspoon sugar just until moistened. Stir in blueberries. Spoon batter into muffin cups. Sprinkle 1 teaspoon sugar over tops.

3 Bake 12 to 13 minutes or until toothpick inserted in center comes out clean.

High Altitude (3500-6500 ft): Bake 13 to 14 minutes.

Nutritional Info: 1 Muffin: Calories 110 (Calories from Fat 30); Total Fat 3.5g (Saturated Fat 0g, Trans Fat 0g); Cholesterol 0mg; Sodium 170mg; Total Carbohydrate 17g (Dietary Fiber 0g, Sugars 7g); Protein 3g. % Daily Value: Vitamin A 4%; Vitamin C 0%; Calcium 8%; Iron 4%. Exchanges: 1 Starch, 1/2 Fat. Carbohydrate Choices: 1.

Betty's Kitchen Tips

Special Touch: For more texture and interesting tops, sprinkle muffins with coarse sugar instead of granulated sugar.

Variation: For a different flavor, swap the lemon peel with orange peel.

apple coffee cake

Prep Time: 15 Minutes
Start to Finish: 1 Hour
Servings: 8

EASY

Streusel Topping

2/3	cup Original Bisquick® mix
2/3	cup packed brown sugar
1	teaspoon ground cinnamon
1/2	teaspoon ground nutmeg
1/4	cup cold butter or margarine

Coffee Cake

2	cups Original Bisquick® mix
2/3	cup milk or water

3	tablespoons granulated sugar
1	egg
2	medium cooking apples, peeled and thinly sliced (2 cups)
2	tablespoons chopped nuts

Glaze

1/2	cup powdered sugar
2	to 3 teaspoons milk

1. Heat oven to 400°F. Spray 9-inch square pan with cooking spray. In small bowl, mix 2/3 cup Bisquick mix, brown sugar, cinnamon and nutmeg. Cut in butter, using pastry blender (or pulling 2 knives through the ingredients in opposite directions), until crumbly; set aside.

2. Stir together 2 cups Bisquick mix, 2/3 cup milk, the granulated sugar and egg; beat vigorously 30 seconds. Spread half of the batter in pan. Arrange apple slices on batter; sprinkle with half of the streusel topping. Spread with remaining batter; sprinkle with remaining topping. Sprinkle with nuts.

3. Bake about 25 minutes or until toothpick inserted in center comes out clean; cool 20 minutes. Stir glaze ingredients until smooth enough to drizzle. Drizzle glaze over warm coffee cake.

High Altitude (3500-6500 ft): Bake about 30 minutes.

Nutritional Info: 1 Serving: Calories 380 (Calories from Fat 120); Total Fat 13g (Saturated Fat 6g, Trans Fat 2g); Cholesterol 45mg; Sodium 550mg; Total Carbohydrate 61g (Dietary Fiber 1g, Sugars 35g); Protein 5g. % Daily Value: Vitamin A 6%; Vitamin C 0%; Calcium 10%; Iron 10%. Exchanges: 1-1/2 Starch, 2-1/2 Other Carbohydrate, 2-1/2 Fat. Carbohydrate Choices: 4.

Betty's Kitchen Tips

Variation: For 7 grams fat, 320 calories and 390 mg sodium per serving, use Bisquick Heart Smart® mix and fat-free (skim) milk. Substitute 1/4 cup fat-free egg product for the egg. Decrease butter in Streusel Topping to 2 tablespoons.

Purchasing: Some common cooking apples are Cortland, Northern Spy, Rome Beauty, Winesap, Golden Delicious and Granny Smith.

chocolate-cherry muffins

Prep Time: 15 Minutes
Start to Finish: 50 Minutes
Servings: 6 jumbo or 12 regular-size muffins

EASY

1	cup milk
1/2	cup vegetable oil
1	egg
1-1/2	cups Gold Medal® all-purpose flour
3/4	cup granulated sugar
1/2	cup unsweetened baking cocoa

2-1/2	teaspoons baking powder
1/2	teaspoon salt
3/4	cup chopped maraschino cherries, well drained, reserving 2 tablespoons cherry juice
1	cup powdered sugar

1 Heat oven to 375°F. Grease bottoms only of 6 jumbo muffin cups (3-1/2 x 1-3/4 inches) or 12 regular-size muffin cups with the shortening, or line with paper baking cups.

2 In medium bowl, beat milk, oil and egg with fork. Stir in remaining ingredients except cherries, juice and powdered sugar just until flour is moistened. Stir in the cherries. Divide batter evenly among muffin cups. (For 12 regular-size muffins, cups will be almost full.)

3 Bake jumbo muffins 23 to 25 minutes, regular-size muffins 18 to 20 minutes, or until toothpick inserted in center comes out clean. Cool jumbo muffins 10 minutes or regular-size muffins 5 minutes; remove from pan.

4 In small bowl, mix powdered sugar and reserved 2 tablespoons cherry juice with spoon; drizzle over warm muffins. Serve warm.

High Altitude (3500-6500 ft): Add an additional 1 tablespoon flour to batter.

Nutritional Info: 1 Jumbo Muffin: Calories 560 (Calories from Fat 190); Total Fat 21g (Saturated Fat 4g, Trans Fat 0g); Cholesterol 40mg; Sodium 430mg; Total Carbohydrate 84g (Dietary Fiber 4g, Sugars 55g); Protein 7g. % Daily Value: Vitamin A 2%; Vitamin C 0%; Calcium 20%; Iron 15%. Exchanges: 2 Starch, 3-1/2 Other Carbohydrate, 4 Fat. Carbohydrate Choices: 5-1/2.

Betty's Kitchen Tips

Serve-With: Serve with Confetti Egg Bake, page 28, and fresh fruit.

Did You Know? Baking cocoa is dried chocolate liquor, with the cocoa butter removed, and ground into unsweetened baking cocoa. Cocoa drink mixes have powdered milk and sugar added and should not be used for baking cocoa.

special raspberry punch

Prep Time: 25 Minutes
Start to Finish: 2 Hours 25 Minutes
Servings: 24 (1/2 cup each)   **LOW FAT**

- 4 boxes (10 oz each) frozen raspberries, thawed, undrained
- 1/2 can (12-oz size) frozen lemonade concentrate, thawed
- 1 bottle (2 liters) ginger ale, chilled

1 In 4-quart Dutch oven, cook raspberries over medium heat 10 minutes, stirring frequently; cool slightly. Push through strainer with large spoon to remove seeds. Refrigerate raspberry juice at least 2 hours.

2 In punch bowl or large pitcher, mix the raspberry juice and lemonade concentrate. Stir in ginger ale. Serve immediately over ice.

High Altitude (3500-6500 ft): No change.

Nutritional Info: 1 Serving: Calories 100 (Calories from Fat 0); Total Fat 0g (Saturated Fat 0g, Trans Fat 0g); Cholesterol 0mg; Sodium 10mg; Total Carbohydrate 25g (Dietary Fiber 2g, Sugars 22g); Protein 0g. % Daily Value: Vitamin A 0%; Vitamin C 15%; Calcium 0%; Iron 2%. Exchanges: 1/2 Fruit, 1 Other Carbohydrate. Carbohydrate Choices: 1-1/2.

Betty's Kitchen Tips

Variation: Use frozen strawberries and limeade concentrate in place of the raspberries and lemonade. There's no need to strain the cooked strawberries.

Special Touch: An ice ring in a punch bowl will last longer than ice cubes. Be sure the size of the ice ring will fit the punch bowl.

ginger-carrot-nut bread

Prep Time: 15 Minutes
Start to Finish: 3 Hours 25 Minutes
Servings: 1 loaf (16 slices)

EASY

2	eggs		2	teaspoons baking powder
3/4	cup packed brown sugar		1	teaspoon ground ginger
1/3	cup vegetable oil		1/2	teaspoon salt
1/2	cup milk		1	cup shredded carrots (about 2 medium)
1	teaspoon vanilla		1/2	cup chopped nuts
2	cups Gold Medal® all-purpose flour			

1 Heat oven to 350°F. Grease bottom only of 8x4-inch loaf pan with shortening; lightly flour (or spray bottom of pan with baking spray with flour).

2 In large bowl, beat eggs and brown sugar with electric mixer on medium speed until creamy. Beat in oil, milk and vanilla. On low speed, beat in flour, baking powder, ginger and salt until smooth. Stir in carrots and nuts. Spread in pan.

3 Bake 50 to 60 minutes or until toothpick inserted in center comes out clean. Cool in pan 10 minutes; remove from pan to cooling rack. Cool completely, about 2 hours.

High Altitude (3500-6500 ft): Decrease baking powder to 1-1/2 teaspoons. Bake about 1 hour.

Nutritional Info: 1 Slice: Calories 180 (Calories from Fat 70); Total Fat 8g (Saturated Fat 1g, Trans Fat 0g); Cholesterol 25mg; Sodium 150mg; Total Carbohydrate 24g (Dietary Fiber 1g, Sugars 11g); Protein 3g. % Daily Value: Vitamin A 25%; Vitamin C 0%; Calcium 6%; Iron 6%. Exchanges: 1 Starch, 1/2 Other Carbohydrate, 1-1/2 Fat. Carbohydrate Choices: 1-1/2.

Betty's Kitchen Tips

Serve-With: Serve slices of this fragrant loaf with whipped cream cheese.

How-To: The reason only the bottom of the pan is greased is to keep the loaf from sinking around the edges.

chocolate chip pancakes

Prep Time: 20 Minutes
Start to Finish: 20 Minutes
Servings: 5 (3 pancakes each)

QUICK

· ·

2	cups Original Bisquick® mix
1	cup milk
2	eggs
1/2	cup miniature semisweet chocolate chips

Maple-flavored syrup, if desired

· ·

1 In medium bowl, stir Bisquick mix, milk and eggs with wire whisk or fork until blended. Stir in chocolate chips.

2 Brush nonstick griddle or nonstick skillet with vegetable oil; heat griddle to 350°F or heat skillet over medium-low heat.

3 For each pancake, pour slightly less than 1/4 cup batter onto hot griddle. Cook until edges are dry. Turn; cook other sides until golden brown. Serve with syrup.

High Altitude (3500-6500 ft): No change.

Nutritional Info: 1 Serving: Calories 340 (Calories from Fat 130); Total Fat 14g (Saturated Fat 6g, Trans Fat 2g); Cholesterol 90mg; Sodium 630mg; Total Carbohydrate 44g (Dietary Fiber 2g, Sugars 13g); Protein 8g. % Daily Value: Vitamin A 4%; Vitamin C 0%; Calcium 10%; Iron 10%. Exchanges: 2 Starch, 1 Other Carbohydrate, 2-1/2 Fat. Carbohydrate Choices: 3.

Betty's Kitchen Tip

• For a change of pace, use peanut butter chips instead of chocolate chips.

double-streusel coffee cake

Prep Time: 15 Minutes
Start to Finish: 1 Hour 15 Minutes
Servings: 6

EASY

- -

Streusel

2/3 cup Original Bisquick® mix
2/3 cup packed brown sugar
1 teaspoon ground cinnamon
3 tablespoons cold butter or margarine

Coffee Cake

2 cups Original Bisquick® mix
1/2 cup milk or water
2 tablespoons granulated sugar
1-1/2 teaspoons vanilla
1 egg

- -

1 Heat oven to 375°F. Spray bottom and side of 9-inch round cake pan with cooking spray. In small bowl, mix 2/3 cup Bisquick mix, the brown sugar and cinnamon. Cut in butter, using pastry blender (or pulling 2 table knives through ingredients in opposite directions), until crumbly; set aside.

2 In medium bowl, stir coffee cake ingredients until blended. Spread about 1 cup of the batter in pan. Sprinkle with about 3/4 cup of the streusel. Drop remaining batter over top of streusel; spread carefully over streusel. Sprinkle remaining streusel over top.

3 Bake 20 to 24 minutes or until golden brown. Let stand 30 minutes before serving. Serve warm or cool.

High Altitude (3500-6500 ft): No change.

Nutritional Info: 1 Serving: Calories 410 (Calories from Fat 120); Total Fat 14g (Saturated Fat 6g, Trans Fat 2.5g); Cholesterol 50mg; Sodium 720mg; Total Carbohydrate 64g (Dietary Fiber 1g, Sugars 30g); Protein 5g. % Daily Value: Vitamin A 6%; Vitamin C 0%; Calcium 10%; Iron 10%. Exchanges: 1-1/2 Starch, 3 Other Carbohydrate, 2-1/2 Fat. Carbohydrate Choices: 4.

Betty's Kitchen Tip

• A drizzle of almond glaze adds a nice finishing touch. Stir together 3/4 cup powdered sugar, 1 tablespoon milk and 1/2 teaspoon almond extract until thin enough to drizzle. Drizzle glaze over warm coffee cake.

do-ahead breakfast bake

Prep Time: 15 Minutes
Start to Finish: 5 Hours
Servings: 12

EASY

- 1   cup diced cooked ham
- 2   boxes Betty Crocker® (5.2 oz each) hash brown skillet potatoes
- 1   medium green bell pepper, chopped (1 cup)
- 1   tablespoon dried chopped onion
- 2   cups shredded Cheddar cheese (8 oz)
- 1   cup Original Bisquick® mix
- 1/2 teaspoon pepper
- 3   cups milk
- 4   eggs

1 Spray 13x9-inch (3-quart) glass baking dish with cooking spray. In baking dish, mix ham, potatoes, bell pepper, onion and 1 cup of the cheese; spread evenly.

2 In medium bowl, stir Bisquick mix, pepper, milk and eggs with wire whisk or fork until blended. Pour over potato mixture. Sprinkle with remaining cheese. Cover; refrigerate at least 4 hours but no longer than 24 hours.

3 Heat oven to 375°F. Uncover and bake 30 to 35 minutes or until light golden brown around edges and cheese is melted. Let stand 10 minutes before serving.

High Altitude (3500-6500 ft): No change.

Nutritional Info: 1 Serving: Calories 280 (Calories from Fat 110); Total Fat 12g (Saturated Fat 6g, Trans Fat 0.5g); Cholesterol 100mg; Sodium 870mg; Total Carbohydrate 29g (Dietary Fiber 2g, Sugars 4g); Protein 14g. % Daily Value: Vitamin A 8%; Vitamin C 8%; Calcium 20%; Iron 6%. Exchanges: 2 Starch, 1 Medium-Fat Meat, 1 Fat. Carbohydrate Choices: 2.

Betty's Kitchen Tips

Variation: Try different types of cheeses in this recipe. Swiss and Monterey Jack work well, but so do seasoned cheeses, such as shredded taco-seasoned cheese or pepper Jack cheese.

Do-Ahead: Preparing this dish the night before makes it a fast breakfast choice for a hectic day.

whole wheat-granola waffles

Prep Time: 55 Minutes
Start to Finish: 55 Minutes
Servings: 6 (two 4-inch waffles, 1/4 cup berries and 2 tablespoons syrup each)

2 cups Original Bisquick® mix	2 tablespoons vegetable oil
1/2 cup Gold Medal® whole wheat flour	1 egg
1/2 cup granola	1-1/2 cups mixed fresh berries (raspberries, blueberries, sliced strawberries)
1-1/2 cups milk	3/4 cup maple-flavored syrup
2 tablespoons packed brown sugar	

1 Heat waffle iron. (Waffle irons without a nonstick coating may need to be brushed with vegetable oil or sprayed with cooking spray.) In medium bowl, stir all ingredients except berries and syrup with wire whisk or fork until blended.

2 For each waffle, pour batter onto center of hot waffle iron. (Check manufacturer's directions for recommended amount of batter.) Close lid of waffle iron. Bake 3 to 5 minutes or until steaming stops.

3 Carefully remove waffle. Serve waffles with berries and syrup.

High Altitude (3500-6500 ft): No change.

Nutritional Info: 1 Serving: Calories 470 (Calories from Fat 120); Total Fat 13g (Saturated Fat 3.5g, Trans Fat 1.5g); Cholesterol 40mg; Sodium 560mg; Total Carbohydrate 80g (Dietary Fiber 3g, Sugars 28g); Protein 8g. % Daily Value: Vitamin A 4%; Vitamin C 15%; Calcium 15%; Iron 10%. Exchanges: 2-1/2 Starch, 3 Other Carbohydrate, 2 Fat. Carbohydrate Choices: 5.

Betty's Kitchen Tips

Do-Ahead: Get a head start by making a batch of waffles for the freezer. Wrap cooled waffles in foil or in a resealable freezer plastic bag, and freeze up to 1 month. To serve, place frozen waffles on cookie sheet and reheat in 350°F oven 10 minutes, or pop them in a toaster.

Special Touch: For a breakfast to remember, arrange the berries on your child's waffle to form a face.

pumpkin smoothies

Prep Time: 5 Minutes
Start to Finish: 5 Minutes
Servings: 2 (1 cup each)

EASY QUICK LOW FAT

1-1/4	cups vanilla-flavored soymilk
1/4	cup cold canned pumpkin (not pumpkin pie mix)
1	container (6 oz) Yoplait® Original 99% Fat Free French vanilla yogurt
1	tablespoon honey
1/2	teaspoon pumpkin pie spice
1/4	teaspoon vanilla

1 Place all ingredients in blender or food processor. Cover; blend on high speed about 1 minute or until smooth.

2 Pour into 2 chilled glasses. Serve immediately.

High Altitude (3500-6500 ft): No change.

Nutritional Info: 1 Serving: Calories 190 (Calories from Fat 25); Total Fat 3g (Saturated Fat 1g, Trans Fat 0g); Cholesterol 5mg; Sodium 150mg; Total Carbohydrate 35g (Dietary Fiber 1g, Sugars 30g); Protein 7g. % Daily Value: Vitamin A 110%; Vitamin C 2%; Calcium 30%; Iron 6%. Exchanges: 1-1/2 Other Carbohydrate, 1 Skim Milk. Carbohydrate Choices: 2.

5 TIPS FOR HOSTING A SUCCESSFUL BRUNCH

1 Set the dining table and/or buffet table the day before your brunch, if possible.

2 Set out serving dishes and utensils the day before, or plan which ones to use.

3 Make two shopping trips: the first one for all ingredients that will not perish (this can be done a week ahead) and the second one a day or two before the brunch to pick up perishables.

4 Bake and freeze recipes ahead of time. Most coffee cakes, muffins, quick breads and yeast breads can be baked ahead and stored tightly wrapped in the freezer for up to three months.

5 Serve main dishes that can be prepared the day before, such as Do-Ahead Breakfast Bake (p. 23) or Overnight French Toast Bake with Berry Topping (p. 32).

make-ahead sausage and mushroom scrambled eggs

Prep Time: 30 Minutes
Start to Finish: 1 Hour
Servings: 12 (3/4 cup each)

8 oz bulk pork sausage

1 package (8 oz) sliced fresh mushrooms (3 cups)

1/4 cup finely chopped red bell pepper

1/4 cup finely chopped green bell pepper

3 tablespoons butter or margarine

16 eggs

1 cup half-and-half or milk

1/2 teaspoon dried thyme leaves

1/2 teaspoon salt

1/4 teaspoon pepper

1 can (10-3/4 oz) condensed reduced-sodium cream of mushroom soup

2 cups shredded Cheddar cheese (8 oz)

1 In 12-inch nonstick skillet, cook sausage over medium-high heat 5 to 7 minutes, stirring occasionally, until no longer pink. Add mushrooms and bell peppers; cook 4 to 5 minutes, stirring frequently, until vegetables are tender. Remove mixture from skillet; drain. Wipe skillet clean with paper towel.

2 In same skillet, melt butter over medium heat. Meanwhile, in large bowl, beat eggs. Stir half-and-half, thyme, salt and pepper into eggs. Add egg mixture to butter in skillet. Cook over medium heat about 7 minutes, stirring constantly, until mixture is firm but still moist. Stir in soup.

3 Spray 3- to 4-quart slow cooker with cooking spray. In cooker, place half of egg mixture. Top with half each of the sausage mixture and cheese. Repeat layers.

4 Cover; cook on Low heat setting 30 minutes or until cheese is melted. Mixture can be kept warm on Low heat setting up to 2 hours.

High Altitude (3500-6500 ft): No change.

Nutritional Info: 1 Serving: Calories 280 (Calories from Fat 200); Total Fat 22g (Saturated Fat 10g, Trans Fat 0g); Cholesterol 325mg; Sodium 490mg; Total Carbohydrate 5g (Dietary Fiber 0g, Sugars 3g); Protein 16g. % Daily Value: Vitamin A 15%; Vitamin C 8%; Calcium 15%; Iron 8%. Exchanges: 1/2 Other Carbohydrate, 2-1/2 High-Fat Meat. Carbohydrate Choices: 1/2.

Betty's Kitchen Tip

• Try using Italian-style soy-protein crumbles in place of the sausage for a vegetarian variation. In nonstick skillet, cook mushrooms and bell peppers in 1 teaspoon oil until tender. Stir in crumbles; cook until warm. Remove mixture from skillet; continue with step 2.

mocha muffins

Prep Time: 10 Minutes
Start to Finish: 30 Minutes
Servings: 12 muffins

EASY QUICK

2	cups Gold Medal® all-purpose flour
2	tablespoons unsweetened baking cocoa
2-1/2	teaspoons baking powder
1/2	teaspoon salt
1/3	cup packed brown sugar
1	cup milk
1/3	cup vegetable oil
1	tablespoon powdered instant coffee (dry)
1	egg
1	cup semisweet chocolate chunks or chips

1 Heat oven to 400°F. Grease bottoms only of 12 regular-size muffin cups with shortening or cooking spray, or line muffin cups with paper baking cups.

2 In medium bowl, mix flour, cocoa, baking powder and salt; set aside. In large bowl, beat brown sugar, milk, oil, coffee and egg with fork or wire whisk. Stir in flour mixture just until flour is moistened. Fold in chocolate chunks. Divide batter evenly among muffin cups.

3 Bake 18 to 20 minutes or until toothpick inserted in center comes out clean. Immediately remove muffins from pan to cooling rack.

High Altitude (3500-6500 ft): No change.

Nutritional Info: 1 Muffin: Calories 240 (Calories from Fat 100); Total Fat 11g (Saturated Fat 4g); Cholesterol 20mg; Sodium 220mg; Total Carbohydrate 33g (Dietary Fiber 2g); Protein 4g. Exchanges: 1 Starch, 1 Fruit, 2 Fat.

Betty's Kitchen Tips

Special Touch: Drizzle muffins with a mixture of a teaspoon or two of brewed coffee and a spoonful of Betty Crocker® Rich & Creamy chocolate frosting.

Success Hint: Be sure to use unsweetened baking cocoa, not hot chocolate mix. It is not the same.

confetti egg bake

Prep Time: 15 Minutes
Start to Finish: 55 Minutes
Servings: 12

EASY

- 1 bag (20 oz) refrigerated cooked shredded hash brown potatoes
- 1 tablespoon butter or margarine
- 2 medium green onions, sliced (2 tablespoons)
- 1 package (8 oz) sliced fresh mushrooms (3 cups)

- 1 cup Green Giant® frozen mixed vegetables, thawed
- 12 eggs
- 2 cups shredded Cheddar cheese (8 oz)
- 1/2 cup milk
- 1 teaspoon salt
- 1/4 teaspoon pepper

1 Heat oven to 350°F. Spray 13x9-inch (3-quart) glass baking dish with cooking spray. Pat hash brown potatoes in bottom of baking dish.

2 In 10-inch skillet, melt butter over medium heat. Add onions and mushrooms; cook 5 to 7 minutes, stirring occasionally, until mushrooms are tender. Stir in mixed vegetables.

3 In large bowl, beat eggs, cheese, milk, salt and pepper with wire whisk until well mixed. Stir in mushroom mixture. Carefully pour into baking dish.

4 Bake uncovered about 40 minutes or until eggs are set in center.

High Altitude (3500-6500 ft): No change.

Nutritional Info: 1 Serving: Calories 235 (Calories from Fat 115); Total Fat 13g (Saturated Fat 6g); Cholesterol 235mg; Sodium 390mg; Total Carbohydrate 16g (Dietary Fiber 2g); Protein 13g. Exchanges: 1 Starch. Carbohydrate Choices: 1.

Betty's Kitchen Tips

Substitution: Other types of cheese can be used in place of the Cheddar. Monterey Jack, Colby, Havarti and Gruyère are good choices.

How-To: You can remove the 1 cup of frozen vegetables from the bag the night before, and cover and thaw in the refrigerator, or you can quickly thaw frozen vegetables under cool running water.

brunch eggs on english muffins

Prep Time: 25 Minutes
Start to Finish: 25 Minutes
Servings: 4

QUICK

- 1   teaspoon butter or margarine
- 2   teaspoons all-purpose flour
- 1/2 cup milk
- 1/4 cup shredded Cheddar cheese (1 oz)
- 2   teaspoons grated Parmesan cheese
- 1   teaspoon chopped fresh or 1/4 teaspoon dried basil leaves

Dash of ground red pepper (cayenne)
- 2   English muffins, split
- 4   thin slices fully cooked Canadian-style bacon (2 oz)
- 8   eggs, beaten

Freshly ground pepper

1 In 1-quart nonstick saucepan, melt the butter over low heat. Stir in flour; remove from heat. Gradually stir in milk. Heat to boiling, stirring constantly. Boil and stir 1 minute; remove from heat. Stir in cheeses, basil and red pepper; keep warm.

2 Toast English muffins. In 10-inch nonstick skillet, cook bacon over medium heat until brown on both sides. Remove from skillet; keep warm.

3 Heat same skillet over medium heat. Pour eggs into skillet. As mixture begins to set at bottom and side, gently lift cooked portions with spatula so that thin, uncooked portion can flow to bottom. Avoid constant stirring. Cook 3 to 4 minutes or until eggs are thickened throughout but still moist.

4 Place 1 slice bacon on each muffin half. Top with eggs. Spoon about 2 tablespoons sauce over eggs. Sprinkle with pepper.

High Altitude (3500-6500 ft): No change.

Nutritional Info: 1 Serving: Calories 300 (Calories from Fat 150); Total Fat 16g (Saturated Fat 6g, Trans Fat 0g); Cholesterol 445mg; Sodium 520mg; Total Carbohydrate 17g (Dietary Fiber 0g, Sugars 7g); Protein 21g. % Daily Value: Vitamin A 15%; Vitamin C 0%; Calcium 20%; Iron 10%. Exchanges: 1/2 Starch, 3 Medium-Fat Meat. Carbohydrate Choices: 1.

Betty's Kitchen Tips

Health Twist: Try reduced-fat cheese for a lower-fat sauce.

Serve-With: Round out this hearty dish with fresh fruit, coffee and fresh-squeezed orange juice.

heart smart banana bread

Prep Time: 10 Minutes
Start to Finish: 2 Hours 50 Minutes
Servings: 1 loaf (16 slices)

EASY LOW FAT

1-1/3	cups mashed very ripe bananas (about 2 large)
2/3	cup sugar
3/4	cup fat-free egg product
1/4	cup fat-free (skim) milk
2	tablespoons vegetable oil
1/2	teaspoon vanilla
3	cups Bisquick Heart Smart® mix

1 Heat oven to 350°F. Spray bottom only of 9x5-inch loaf pan with cooking spray. In large bowl, stir bananas, sugar, egg product, milk, oil and vanilla until blended. Stir in Bisquick mix. Pour into pan.

2 Bake 55 to 60 minutes or until toothpick inserted in center comes out clean.

3 Cool 10 minutes. Run knife or metal spatula around sides of pan to loosen bread; remove from pan to cooling rack. Cool completely, about 1 hour 30 minutes, before slicing.

High Altitude (3500-6500 ft): Heat oven to 375°F.

Nutritional Info: 1 Slice: Calories 150 (Calories from Fat 30); Total Fat 3g (Saturated Fat 0g, Trans Fat 0g); Cholesterol 0mg; Sodium 210mg; Total Carbohydrate 28g (Dietary Fiber 0g, Sugars 13g); Protein 3g. % Daily Value: Vitamin A 4%; Vitamin C 0%; Calcium 10%; Iron 6%. Exchanges: 1 Starch, 1 Other Carbohydrate, 1/2 Fat. Carbohydrate Choices: 2.

Betty's Kitchen Tip

• The best bananas to use for baking have skins turning brown with black spots, and they are soft to the touch. Overripe bananas can be put in the freezer, unpeeled, for later use. When you're ready to use them, just thaw them, cut off the top of the peel, and squeeze the banana into your measuring cup.

overnight french toast bake with berry topping

Prep Time: 20 Minutes
Start to Finish: 4 Hours 50 Minutes
Servings: 8

French Toast Bake

12	cups cubed (1 inch) soft French bread (about 13 oz)
8	eggs
3	cups half-and-half
1/4	cup sugar
1	teaspoon ground cinnamon
1/2	teaspoon salt

2	teaspoons vanilla

Berry Topping

1	cup sugar
1	tablespoon cornstarch
1/4	cup orange juice
1	bag (12 oz) frozen unsweetened mixed berries
3	cups fresh strawberries, cut into quarters

1 Spray bottom and sides of 13x9-inch (3-quart) glass baking dish with cooking spray. Place bread cubes in dish. In large bowl, beat eggs, half-and-half, 1/4 cup sugar, the cinnamon, salt and vanilla with wire whisk until smooth; pour over bread cubes. Cover tightly; refrigerate at least 4 hours but no longer than 24 hours.

2 Heat oven to 400°F. Uncover dish; bake 25 to 35 minutes or until golden brown and knife inserted in center comes out clean.

3 Meanwhile, in 2-quart saucepan, stir together 1 cup sugar and the cornstarch. Stir in orange juice until smooth. Stir in mixed berries. Heat to boiling over medium heat, stirring constantly. Cook about 6 minutes, stirring constantly, until topping is slightly thickened. Remove from heat.

4 Just before serving, stir strawberries into topping. Serve warm over French toast bake.

High Altitude (3500-6500 ft): No change.

Nutritional Info: 1 Serving: Calories 510 (Calories from Fat 150); Total Fat 17g (Saturated Fat 8g, Trans Fat 0g); Cholesterol 245mg; Sodium 550mg; Total Carbohydrate 74g (Dietary Fiber 3g, Sugars 47g); Protein 15g. % Daily Value: Vitamin A 15%; Vitamin C 50%; Calcium 15%; Iron 15%. Exchanges: 2 Starch, 3 Other Carbohydrate, 1 Medium-Fat Meat, 2 Fat. Carbohydrate Choices: 5.

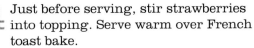

Betty's Kitchen Tip

• Use a serrated bread knife to easily cut through the bread slices. Slice off and discard the loaf ends so each slice will readily soak up the egg mixture.

apple-sausage-cheddar breakfast bake

Prep Time: 25 Minutes
Start to Finish: 1 Hour 10 Minutes
Servings: 12

- 1-1/2 lb bulk pork sausage
- 1 can (21 oz) apple pie filling with more fruit
- 2 medium apples, peeled, chopped (about 2 cups)
- 2 cups shredded sharp Cheddar cheese (8 oz)
- 1-1/2 cups Original Bisquick® mix
- 1-1/2 cups milk
- 1/4 teaspoon salt
- 1/8 teaspoon pepper
- 6 eggs

1 Heat oven to 375°F. Spray 13x9-inch (3-quart) glass baking dish with cooking spray. In 12-inch skillet, cook sausage over medium-high heat 5 to 7 minutes, stirring occasionally, until no longer pink; drain. Stir in pie filling and apples. Spread the mixture evenly in baking dish. Top with 1 cup of the cheese.

2 In large bowl, stir Bisquick mix, milk, salt, pepper and eggs with wire whisk or fork until blended. Pour evenly over cheese.

3 Bake 30 to 37 minutes or until knife inserted in center comes out clean. Top with remaining 1 cup cheese. Bake 3 to 5 minutes longer or until cheese is melted. Let stand 5 minutes before serving.

High Altitude (3500-6500 ft): Chop apples very finely if using firm ones.

Nutritional Info: 1 Serving: Calories 340 (Calories from Fat 170); Total Fat 19g (Saturated Fat 8g, Trans Fat 1g); Cholesterol 150mg; Sodium 590mg; Total Carbohydrate 28g (Dietary Fiber 1g, Sugars 16g); Protein 15g. % Daily Value: Vitamin A 8%; Vitamin C 0%; Calcium 15%; Iron 8%. Exchanges: 1 Starch, 1 Other Carbohydrate, 1-1/2 High-Fat Meat, 1 Fat. Carbohydrate Choices: 2.

Betty's Kitchen Tips

Special Touch: If the timing is right, plan a trip to a nearby apple orchard with your family. Not only is it a great way to spend time together; your kids will get a lesson in how apples are grown.

Substitution: You can use turkey sausage as a substitute for the pork sausage.

strawberry shortcake coffee cake

Prep Time: 25 Minutes
Start to Finish: 1 Hour 25 Minutes
Servings: 12

2	cups Gold Medal® all-purpose flour		1	teaspoon almond extract
1/2	cup granulated sugar		1	egg, slightly beaten
2	teaspoons baking powder		1	cup whipping cream
1/2	teaspoon salt		2	packages (3 oz each) cream cheese, softened
1	cup cold butter or margarine		1/3	cup powdered sugar
1/2	cup milk		1	lb fresh strawberries, sliced (3 cups)

1 Heat oven to 450°F. In medium bowl, mix flour, granulated sugar, baking powder and salt. Cut in butter, using pastry blender (or pulling 2 table knives through mixture in opposite directions), until mixture looks like fine crumbs. Stir in milk, almond extract and egg just until blended. Spread in ungreased 13x9-inch pan.

2 Bake 11 to 13 minutes or until golden brown. Cool completely, about 1 hour.

3 In small bowl, beat whipping cream with electric mixer on high speed until soft peaks form; set aside. In medium bowl, beat cream cheese and powdered sugar on medium speed until well blended. Fold in whipped cream. Frost top of cooled cake with whipped cream mixture. (Frosted cake can be refrigerated up to 6 hours.)

4 Just before serving, top cake with the strawberries. (Cake topped with strawberries can be refrigerated up to 2 hours.)

High Altitude (3500-6500 ft): Decrease baking powder to 1-1/2 teaspoons. Bake 15 to 17 minutes.

Nutritional Info: 1 Serving: Calories 400 (Calories from Fat 260); Total Fat 29g (Saturated Fat 16g, Trans Fat 1.5g); Cholesterol 100mg; Sodium 340mg; Total Carbohydrate 32g (Dietary Fiber 2g, Sugars 15g); Protein 5g. % Daily Value: Vitamin A 20%; Vitamin C 20%; Calcium 10%; Iron 8%. Exchanges: 1 Starch, 1 Other Carbohydrate, 5-1/2 Fat. Carbohydrate Choices: 2.

Betty's Kitchen Tip

• Whipping cream will whip up much faster if you chill the beaters and bowl first.

maple-nut-raisin muffins

Prep Time: 20 Minutes
Start to Finish: 45 Minutes
Servings: 12 muffins

• •

Topping

2	tablespoons packed brown sugar
1	tablespoon Original Bisquick® mix
1	teaspoon butter or margarine, softened

Muffins

2	cups Original Bisquick® mix
1/3	cup raisins
1/3	cup chopped pecans
1/4	cup packed brown sugar
2/3	cup milk
2	tablespoons vegetable oil
1	teaspoon maple flavor
1	egg

• •

1 Heat oven to 400°F. Grease bottoms only of muffin cups with shortening or cooking spray or place paper baking cup in each of 12 regular-size muffin cups. In small bowl, stir topping ingredients until crumbly; set aside.

2 In large bowl, stir muffin ingredients just until moistened. Spoon batter evenly into muffin cups. Sprinkle evenly with topping.

3 Bake 15 to 18 minutes or until golden brown. Cool slightly; remove from pan to cooling rack. Serve warm.

High Altitude (3500-6500 ft): No change.

Nutritional Info: 1 Muffin: Calories 180 (Calories from Fat 70); Total Fat 8g (Saturated Fat 2g, Trans Fat 1g); Cholesterol 20mg; Sodium 270mg; Total Carbohydrate 24g (Dietary Fiber 1g, Sugars 10g); Protein 3g. % Daily Value: Vitamin A 0%; Vitamin C 0%; Calcium 4%; Iron 6%. Exchanges: 1 Starch, 1/2 Other Carbohydrate, 1-1/2 Fat. Carbohydrate Choices: 1-1/2.

Betty's Kitchen Tips

Special Touch: Jazz up these muffins by using brightly colored or patterned paper liners. Visit fancyflours.com for examples.

How-To: To avoid soggy muffins, take them out of the pan immediately after removing them from the oven.

peach melba pancakes

Prep Time: 25 Minutes
Start to Finish: 25 Minutes
Servings: 9

QUICK LOW FAT

2	eggs
2	cups Gold Medal® all-purpose flour
1-1/2	cups milk
1/4	cup vegetable oil
2	tablespoons sugar
3	teaspoons baking powder

1/2	teaspoon salt
1/2	cup chopped canned (drained) or frozen (thawed and drained) sliced peaches
1/2	cup fresh or frozen (thawed and well drained) raspberries

Additional peaches and raspberries, if desired

Raspberry syrup, if desired

1 Heat griddle or skillet over medium heat or to 375°F. If necessary, brush griddle with vegetable oil before batter for pancakes is added (or spray with cooking spray before heating).

2 In medium bowl, beat eggs with wire whisk until well beaten. Beat in remaining ingredients except fruit and syrup just until smooth. Stir in 1/2 cup each peaches and raspberries.

3 For each pancake, pour slightly less than 1/4 cup batter onto hot griddle. Cook until bubbly on top, puffed and dry around edges. Turn; cook other sides until golden brown. Serve with additional peaches and raspberries and syrup.

Nutritional Info: 1 Serving: Calories 110 (Calories from Fat 40); Total Fat 4g (Saturated Fat 1g, Trans Fat 0g); Cholesterol 25mg; Sodium 160mg; Total Carbohydrate 14g (Dietary Fiber 0g, Sugars 3g); Protein 3g. % Daily Value: Vitamin A 2%; Vitamin C 6%; Calcium 8%; Iron 4%. Exchanges: 1 Starch, 1/2 Fat. Carbohydrate Choices: 1.

Betty's Kitchen Tip

• Adding fruit to your pancakes adds flavor, color, variety and most of all, extra nutrition. Experts now recommend at least 5 servings of fruits and vegetables per day, and scientists are still uncovering important benefits of those nutrient powerhouses.

ham and pineapple bake

Prep Time: 10 Minutes
Start to Finish: 40 Minutes
Servings: 6

EASY

- 1-1/2 cups chopped fully cooked ham
- 1 can (8 oz) crushed pineapple in juice, drained
- 4 medium green onions, sliced (1/4 cup)
- 1 cup Original Bisquick® mix
- 1 cup milk
- 2 eggs
- 2 teaspoons yellow mustard
- 1 cup shredded Colby-Monterey Jack cheese (4 oz)

1 Heat oven to 400°F. Spray 9-inch glass pie plate with cooking spray. Sprinkle ham, pineapple and onions in pie plate.

2 In medium bowl, stir Bisquick mix, milk, eggs and mustard until blended; pour over ham mixture.

3 Bake uncovered about 25 minutes or until knife inserted in center comes out clean. Sprinkle with cheese. Bake 3 to 4 minutes longer or until cheese is melted.

High Altitude (3500-6500 ft): Bake uncovered about 30 minutes.

Nutritional Info: 1 Serving: Calories 290 (Calories from Fat 150); Total Fat 16g (Saturated Fat 7g, Trans Fat 0.5g); Cholesterol 115mg; Sodium 770mg; Total Carbohydrate 21g (Dietary Fiber 0g, Sugars 10g); Protein 17g. % Daily Value: Vitamin A 8%; Vitamin C 4%; Calcium 25%; Iron 10%. Exchanges: 1-1/2 Starch, 1-1/2 Medium-Fat Meat, 1-1/2 Fat. Carbohydrate Choices: 1-1/2.

Betty's Kitchen Tips

Substitution: Any cheese, or a combination of cheeses, can be used in this casserole. Try Swiss, smoked Gouda or Cheddar.

Time-Saver: To save a step, look for chopped ham at the salad bar of your grocery store.

blueberry-orange pancakes with blueberry-orange sauce

Prep Time: 35 Minutes
Start to Finish: 35 Minutes
Servings: 7

LOW FAT

Blueberry-Orange Sauce

1/4	cup sugar
1-1/2	teaspoons cornstarch
2	tablespoons orange juice
1/4	teaspoon grated orange peel
2	cups fresh or frozen unsweetened blueberries

Pancakes

2	cups Original Bisquick® mix
1	cup milk
2	eggs
1	teaspoon grated orange peel
1/4	teaspoon ground nutmeg
1	cup fresh or frozen unsweetened blueberries

1 In 1-1/2-quart saucepan, mix sugar, cornstarch, orange juice and 1/4 teaspoon orange peel until smooth. Stir in 2 cups blueberries. Heat to boiling over medium heat, stirring constantly. Boil about 2 minutes, stirring occasionally, until thickened. Keep warm.

2 Heat griddle or skillet over medium heat or to 375°F. If necessary, brush griddle with vegetable oil before pancake batter is added (or spray with cooking spray before heating).

3 In medium bowl, stir all pancake ingredients except blueberries with spoon until blended. Fold in 1 cup blueberries.

4 For each pancake, pour slightly less than 1/4 cup batter onto hot griddle. Cook until edges are dry. Turn; cook other sides until golden. Serve with warm sauce.

Nutritional Info: 1 Serving: Calories 250 (Calories from Fat 60); Total Fat 7g (Saturated Fat 2g, Trans Fat 1g); Cholesterol 65mg; Sodium 520mg; Total Carbohydrate 40g (Dietary Fiber 2g, Sugars 18g); Protein 6g. % Daily Value: Vitamin A 4%; Vitamin C 6%; Calcium 10%; Iron 8%. Exchanges: 2 Starch, 1/2 Fruit, 1-1/2 Fat. Carbohydrate Choices: 2-1/2.

Betty's Kitchen Tip

• When using frozen blueberries in the pancakes, be sure to blot them with paper towels to keep the juice from staining the batter.

bacon & swiss quiche

Prep Time: 15 Minutes
Start to Finish: 55 Minutes
Servings: 8

EASY

- 1-1/4 cups Original Bisquick® mix
- 1/4 cup butter or margarine, softened
- 2 tablespoons boiling water
- 1 package (6 oz) sliced Canadian-style bacon, chopped
- 1 cup shredded Swiss cheese (4 oz)
- 4 medium green onions, thinly sliced (1/4 cup)
- 1-1/2 cups half-and-half
- 3 eggs
- 1/2 teaspoon salt
- 1/4 teaspoon ground red pepper (cayenne)

1 Heat oven to 375°F. Spray 9-inch glass pie plate with cooking spray. In medium bowl, stir Bisquick mix and butter until mixed. Add boiling water; stir vigorously until soft dough forms. Press dough in bottom and up side of pie plate, forming edge on rim of pie plate.

2 Sprinkle bacon, cheese and green onions over crust. In medium bowl, beat half-and-half, eggs, salt and red pepper with wire whisk until well mixed. Pour into crust.

3 Bake uncovered 35 to 40 minutes or until edge is brown and knife inserted in center comes out clean.

High Altitude (3500-6500 ft): Bake about 40 minutes.

Nutritional Info: 1 Serving: Calories 300 (Calories from Fat 190); Total Fat 21g (Saturated Fat 10g, Trans Fat 1g); Cholesterol 135mg; Sodium 800mg; Total Carbohydrate 15g (Dietary Fiber 0g, Sugars 4g); Protein 13g. % Daily Value: Vitamin A 15%; Vitamin C 0%; Calcium 25%; Iron 6%. Exchanges: 1 Starch, 1-1/2 High-Fat Meat, 1-1/2 Fat. Carbohydrate Choices: 1.

Betty's Kitchen Tips

Do-Ahead: Break out of the sandwich rut and try a slice of this cheesy quiche for lunch. Make it a day ahead, then pull it out of the refrigerator and warm it up in the microwave. It even tastes great cold!

Special Touch: Dress up this baked egg dish with tomato wedges arranged in a pinwheel pattern on top of the quiche.

streusel-topped peach coffee cake

Prep Time: 10 Minutes
Start to Finish: 1 Hour 25 Minutes
Servings: 12

EASY

Streusel

1	cup Original Bisquick® mix
2/3	cup packed brown sugar
1-1/2	teaspoons ground cinnamon
3	tablespoons cold butter or margarine

Coffee Cake

1	can (15 oz) peach slices in juice, drained (reserving 1/4 cup juice)
3	cups Original Bisquick® mix
1/4	cup granulated sugar
1	teaspoon vanilla
1/4	teaspoon ground nutmeg
1	egg

1 Heat oven to 350°F. Spray bottom and sides of 13x9-inch pan with cooking spray. In small bowl, stir 1 cup Bisquick mix, the brown sugar and cinnamon. Cut in butter, using pastry blender (or pulling 2 table knives through ingredients in opposite directions), until crumbly; set aside.

2 Add enough water to 1/4 cup reserved peach juice to measure 2/3 cup. In large bowl, beat juice mixture, 3 cups Bisquick mix, the granulated sugar, vanilla, nutmeg and egg with electric mixer on low speed until blended. Pour batter into pan; spread evenly. Place the peach slices on batter. Sprinkle streusel over top.

3 Bake 25 to 30 minutes or until toothpick inserted in center comes out clean. Cool 45 minutes. Serve warm or cool.

High Altitude (3500-6500 ft): Bake 30 to 35 minutes.

Nutritional Info: 1 Serving: Calories 280 (Calories from Fat 80); Total Fat 8g (Saturated Fat 3.5g, Trans Fat 1.5g); Cholesterol 25mg; Sodium 520mg; Total Carbohydrate 46g (Dietary Fiber 1g, Sugars 20g); Protein 3g. % Daily Value: Vitamin A 4%; Vitamin C 0%; Calcium 6%; Iron 8%. Exchanges: 1 Starch, 2 Other Carbohydrate, 1-1/2 Fat. Carbohydrate Choices: 3.

Betty's Kitchen Tips

Serve-With: Serve this sweet coffee cake with scrambled eggs, crispy slices of bacon and cut-up fresh fruit for a special breakfast.

Variation: Top this warm-from-the-oven coffee cake with ice cream for a wonderful dessert.

quick STARTERS

p. 49

52

44

57

layered mediterranean tuna spread

Prep Time: 15 Minutes
Start to Finish: 15 Minutes
Servings: 16 (1/4 cup spread and 3 crackers each)

EASY QUICK

- 1 container (8 oz) chives-and-onion cream cheese spread
- 1 shallot, finely chopped
- 1 teaspoon Italian seasoning
- 1/2 cup pitted niçoise or kalamata olives, cut in half

- 1 can (6 oz) albacore tuna, well drained, broken into chunks
- 1 medium tomato, seeded, coarsely chopped
- 1 hard-cooked egg, finely chopped
- 1 tablespoon chopped fresh parsley
- 48 crackers

1 In small bowl, mix cream cheese, shallot and Italian seasoning until well blended. Spread in 8-inch circle on serving plate.

2 Top with olives, tuna, tomato, egg and parsley. Serve with crackers.

High Altitude (3500-6500 ft): No change.

Nutritional Info: 1 Serving: Calories 110 (Calories from Fat 60); Total Fat 7g (Saturated Fat 3g, Trans Fat 0g); Cholesterol 30mg; Sodium 220mg; Total Carbohydrate 7g (Dietary Fiber 0g, Sugars 0g); Protein 5g. % Daily Value: Cholesterol 10%; Vitamin A 6%; Vitamin C 2%; Calcium 2%; Iron 6%. Exchanges: 1/2 Starch, 1/2 Lean Meat, 1 Fat. Carbohydrate Choices: 1/2.

Betty's Kitchen Tips

Time-Saver: Save time by purchasing the hard-cooked egg from your grocery store's deli.

Substitution: Herbes de Provence can be substituted for the Italian seasoning.

hummus and cucumber bites

Prep Time: 15 Minutes
Start to Finish: 15 Minutes
Servings: 16 appetizers

EASY QUICK LOW FAT

2	pita (pocket) breads (6 inch)
2/3	cup roasted red pepper hummus (from 7-oz container)
1/3	English (seedless) cucumber (about 4 inches)
1/2	teaspoon smoked Spanish paprika
16	fresh dill weed sprigs

1 Cut each pita bread into 8 wedges. Spread about 1 teaspoon hummus on each wedge.

2 Score cucumber peel lengthwise with tines of fork. Cut cucumber in half lengthwise. Cut each half crosswise into 16 thin slices. Place 2 half-slices cucumber on hummus on each bite.

3 Sprinkle with paprika. Garnish with dill weed.

High Altitude (3500-6500 ft): No change.

Nutritional Info: 1 Appetizer: Calories 40 (Calories from Fat 10); Total Fat 1g (Saturated Fat 0g, Trans Fat 0g); Cholesterol 0mg; Sodium 70mg; Total Carbohydrate 6g (Dietary Fiber 0g, Sugars 0g); Protein 1g. % Daily Value: Cholesterol 0%; Vitamin A 0%; Vitamin C 0%; Calcium 0%; Iron 4%. Exchanges: 1/2 Starch. Carbohydrate Choices: 1/2.

Betty's Kitchen Tips

Substitution: Smoked Spanish paprika has a smoky, spicy flavor. Regular paprika can be substituted for it, if you like.

Success Hint: Hummus comes in a variety of flavors; try these bites with your favorite.

apricot-chipotle-cream cheese star

Prep Time: 15 Minutes
Start to Finish: 15 Minutes
Servings: 16 (2 tablespoons spread and 3 crackers each)

EASY QUICK

- 12 oz cream cheese (from two 8-oz packages), softened
- 1 cup shredded sharp white Cheddar cheese (4 oz)
- 1/2 teaspoon onion powder
- 1/2 teaspoon ground mustard
- 1/2 cup chopped pecans
- 1/2 cup apricot preserves
- 2 teaspoons finely chopped gingerroot
- 2 teaspoons chopped chipotle chiles in adobo sauce (from 7-oz can)
- 48 crackers

1 In food processor, place cream cheese, Cheddar cheese, onion powder and mustard. Cover; process, scraping side of bowl if necessary, until well mixed. Add pecans. Cover; process with on-and-off pulses 2 or 3 times until mixed.

2 Using the star pattern on p. 352, trace and cut out a star from parchment paper. Spoon the cheese spread evenly onto the shape, using a table knife to shape the star. Turn onto a serving plate; remove the parchment paper.

3 In small bowl, mix preserves, gingerroot and chiles. Spoon over cheese star. Serve with crackers.

High Altitude (3500-6500 ft): No change.

Nutritional Info: 1 Serving: Calories 200 (Calories from Fat 130); Total Fat 15g (Saturated Fat 7g, Trans Fat 0g); Cholesterol 30mg; Sodium 190mg; Total Carbohydrate 14g (Dietary Fiber 0g, Sugars 6g); Protein 4g. % Daily Value: Cholesterol 10%; Vitamin A 8%; Vitamin C 0%; Calcium 6%; Iron 4%. Exchanges: 1/2 Starch, 1/2 Other Carbohydrate, 3 Fat. Carbohydrate Choices: 1.

Betty's Kitchen Tip

- Chipotle chiles in adobo sauce can be found in the ethnic-foods section of the grocery store. Pour the remaining chiles and sauce into a freezer container and freeze for future use.

pimiento-cheese spread appetizers

Prep Time: 15 Minutes
Start to Finish: 15 Minutes
Servings: 16 appetizers

EASY QUICK

2/3	cup small whole pimiento-stuffed green olives (from 10-oz jar)
1	cup shredded Cheddar cheese (4 oz)
1/4	cup mayonnaise or salad dressing
1	package (3 oz) cream cheese, softened

Dash ground red pepper (cayenne)

16	slices cocktail rye bread

1 Reserve 16 whole olives for garnish. Chop remaining olives; place in medium bowl. Add Cheddar cheese, mayonnaise, cream cheese and red pepper; beat with electric mixer on medium speed until well blended.

2 Spread about 2 tablespoons cheese mixture on 8 of the bread slices. Top with the remaining bread slices. Cut each sandwich diagonally in half.

3 Garnish each appetizer with 1 whole olive secured with a toothpick or decorative pick.

High Altitude (3500-6500 ft): No change.

Nutritional Info: 1 Appetizer: Calories 130 (Calories from Fat 80); Total Fat 8g (Saturated Fat 3.5g, Trans Fat 0g); Cholesterol 15mg; Sodium 290mg; Total Carbohydrate 9g (Dietary Fiber 1g, Sugars 0g); Protein 3g. % Daily Value: Cholesterol 5%; Vitamin A 4%; Vitamin C 0%; Calcium 6%; Iron 4%. Exchanges: 1/2 Starch, 2 Fat. Carbohydrate Choices: 1/2.

Betty's Kitchen Tips

How-To: To quickly soften cream cheese, use your microwave. Remove foil wrapper and place cream cheese in a microwavable bowl. Microwave uncovered on Medium (50%) 45 to 60 seconds for a 3-ounce package of cream cheese.

Substitution: If cocktail rye bread isn't available, spread cheese mixture on low-fat rye crackers instead.

greek salad kabobs

Prep Time: 15 Minutes
Start to Finish: 15 Minutes
Servings: 24 (1 kabob and 1/2 tablespoon dip each)

EASY QUICK LOW FAT

Dip

3/4	cup plain yogurt
2	teaspoons honey
2	teaspoons chopped fresh dill weed
2	teaspoons chopped fresh oregano leaves
1/4	teaspoon salt
1	small clove garlic, finely chopped

Kabobs

24	cocktail picks or toothpicks
24	pitted kalamata olives
24	small grape tomatoes
12	slices (1/2 inch) English (seedless) cucumber, cut in half crosswise

1 In small bowl, mix dip ingredients; set aside.

2 On each cocktail pick, thread 1 olive, 1 tomato and 1 half-slice cucumber. Serve kabobs with dip.

High Altitude (3500-6500 ft): No change.

Nutritional Info: 1 Serving: Calories 15 (Calories from Fat 5); Total Fat 0.5g (Saturated Fat 0g, Trans Fat 0g); Cholesterol 0mg; Sodium 70mg; Total Carbohydrate 2g (Dietary Fiber 0g, Sugars 1g); Protein 0g. % Daily Value: Cholesterol 0%; Vitamin A 0%; Vitamin C 2%; Calcium 2%; Iron 0%. Exchanges: Free. Carbohydrate Choices: 0.

Betty's Kitchen Tips

Success Hint: A regular cucumber can be substituted. If the skin is thick or has been coated with a vegetable coating, you may want to peel it.

Substitution: Small pitted ripe olives can be substituted but will lack some of the flavor kalamata olives impart.

fresh mozzarella in tomato cups

Prep Time: 15 Minutes
Start to Finish: 15 Minutes
Servings: 12 appetizers

EASY QUICK LOW FAT

12	large cherry tomatoes
2	oz fresh mozzarella cheese, cut into 1/2-inch cubes
1/4	cup Italian dressing
12	small basil leaves

1 Cut top off each cherry tomato. With melon baller or measuring spoon, scoop out seeds from each tomato, leaving enough for a firm shell. If necessary, cut small slice from bottom so tomato stands upright. Place tomatoes on serving plate or tray.

2 In small bowl, toss cheese and dressing. Place 1 cheese cube in each tomato; top each with basil leaf.

High Altitude (3500-6500 ft): No change.

Nutritional Info: 1 Appetizer: Calories 35 (Calories from Fat 20); Total Fat 2.5g (Saturated Fat 0.5g, Trans Fat 0g); Cholesterol 0mg; Sodium 115mg; Total Carbohydrate 2g (Dietary Fiber 0g, Sugars 1g); Protein 1g. % Daily Value: Cholesterol 0%; Vitamin A 4%; Vitamin C 4%; Calcium 4%; Iron 0%. Exchanges: 1/2 Fat. Carbohydrate Choices: 0.

Betty's Kitchen Tips

Did You Know? Fresh mozzarella is made with whole milk, is white colored and has a delicate, sweet, milky flavor. This soft cheese is packed in water or whey and is often formed into balls or slices.

Variation: If enough tiny basil leaves are not available, shred 3 to 4 large leaves for the garnish.

mediterranean nachos

Prep Time: 10 Minutes
Start to Finish: 10 Minutes
Servings: 6

EASY QUICK

- 2 tablespoons finely chopped kalamata olives
- 2 tablespoons finely chopped sun-dried tomatoes in oil (from 7-oz jar)
- 2 teaspoons oil from jar of sun-dried tomatoes

- 1 small plum (Roma) tomato, finely chopped, drained
- 1 medium green onion, thinly sliced (1 tablespoon)
- 4 oz restaurant-style corn tortilla chips (about 30 chips)
- 1 package (4 oz) crumbled feta cheese, finely crumbled

1 In small bowl, mix olives, sun-dried tomatoes, oil, plum tomato and onion; set aside.

2 On large microwavable plate, arrange tortilla chips in single layer. Top evenly with cheese. Microwave uncovered on High 1 minute. Rotate plate 1/2 turn; microwave 30 to 60 seconds longer or until cheese is melted and bubbly.

3 Spoon tomato mixture evenly over chips and cheese.

High Altitude (3500-6500 ft): No change.

Nutritional Info: 1 Serving: Calories 170 (Calories from Fat 100); Total Fat 11g (Saturated Fat 3.5g, Trans Fat 0g); Cholesterol 15mg; Sodium 360mg; Total Carbohydrate 14g (Dietary Fiber 1g, Sugars 2g); Protein 4g. % Daily Value: Cholesterol 6%; Vitamin A 4%; Vitamin C 6%; Calcium 10%; Iron 6%. Exchanges: 1 Starch, 2 Fat. Carbohydrate Choices: 1.

Betty's Kitchen Tips

Variation: For an extra flavor boost, look for sun-dried tomatoes in oil with herbs.

Special Touch: Feta cheese is available plain or flavored. You can use cheese with garlic, basil or herbs.

curried chicken salad cups

Prep Time: 15 Minutes
Start to Finish: 15 Minutes
Servings: 24 appetizers

EASY QUICK

- 1 can (12.5 oz) white chicken breast, drained
- 1/3 cup diced celery
- 1/3 cup mayonnaise or salad dressing
- 1/4 cup chopped cashews
- 1 tablespoon mild curry paste (from 10 oz jar)
- 24 frozen mini fillo shells (from two 2.1-oz packages)
- 24 fresh parsley leaves

1 In medium bowl, stir together all the ingredients except fillo shells and parsley.

2 Just before serving, spoon about 1 tablespoon chicken mixture into each fillo shell. Garnish with parsley.

High Altitude (3500-6500 ft): No change.

Nutritional Info: 1 Appetizer: Calories 60 (Calories from Fat 35); Total Fat 4g (Saturated Fat 0g, Trans Fat 0g); Cholesterol 5mg; Sodium 85mg; Total Carbohydrate 3g (Dietary Fiber 0g, Sugars 0g); Protein 3g. % Daily Value: Cholesterol 2%; Vitamin A 0%; Vitamin C 2%; Calcium 0%; Iron 0%. Exchanges: 1/2 Lean Meat, 1/2 Fat. Carbohydrate Choices: 0.

Betty's Kitchen Tips

Did You Know? Curry paste is a blend of clarified butter, curry powder, vinegar and other seasonings. It can be found in the Asian-foods section of the supermarket.

Success Hint: There's no need to thaw the fillo shells before filling them. They'll be thawed by the time you serve them.

ham and asparagus rolls

Prep Time: 20 Minutes
Start to Finish: 20 Minutes
Servings: 12 appetizers

- -

12 fresh asparagus spears (about 1 lb)	1 teaspoon chopped fresh thyme leaves
1/4 cup mayonnaise or salad dressing	6 slices (1/16-inch thick) cooked ham (from deli; about 10 oz)
1 tablespoon Dijon mustard	

- -

1 Fill 13x9-inch (3-quart) glass baking dish half full with water and ice; set aside.

2 In 12-inch skillet, heat 1 inch water to boiling over high heat. Snap or cut off tough ends of asparagus spears and discard. Add asparagus to boiling water; cook uncovered 2 to 3 minutes or until crisp-tender. Remove asparagus from skillet; place in baking dish with ice water. Let stand 3 to 5 minutes or until chilled. Drain; pat dry with paper towels. Set aside.

3 Meanwhile, in small bowl, mix mayonnaise, mustard and thyme.

4 Spread about 1 teaspoon mayonnaise mixture over each ham slice to within 1 inch of edges. Cut each ham slice in half lengthwise. Roll 1 ham strip tightly around each asparagus spear. Store tightly covered in refrigerator.

High Altitude (3500-6500 ft): No change.

Nutritional Info: 1 Appetizer: Calories 70 (Calories from Fat 45); Total Fat 5g (Saturated Fat 1g, Trans Fat 0g); Cholesterol 15mg; Sodium 340mg; Total Carbohydrate 1g (Dietary Fiber 0g, Sugars 0g); Protein 5g. % Daily Value: Cholesterol 5%; Vitamin A 4%; Vitamin C 0%; Calcium 0%; Iron 4%. Exchanges: 1/2 Lean Meat, 1 Fat. Carbohydrate Choices: 0.

Betty's Kitchen Tips

Do-Ahead: These appetizers can be prepared a day ahead. Refrigerate them tightly covered.

Substitution: Prosciutto can be substituted for the ham.

creamy salsa dip

Prep Time: 10 Minutes
Start to Finish: 10 Minutes
Servings: 14 (2 tablespoons dip and 6 tortilla chips each)

EASY QUICK

- 1/2 cup sour cream
- 1/2 cup mayonnaise or salad dressing
- 3/4 cup chipotle salsa or Old El Paso® Thick 'n Chunky salsa
- 1/4 cup lightly packed chopped fresh cilantro
- 8 oz round tortilla chips or crackers

1 In small bowl, mix all ingredients except tortilla chips.

2 Serve immediately with tortilla chips, or cover and refrigerate 1 to 2 hours to blend flavors.

High Altitude (3500-6500 ft): No change.

Nutritional Info: 1 Serving: Calories 160 (Calories from Fat 110); Total Fat 12g (Saturated Fat 2.5g, Trans Fat 0g); Cholesterol 10mg; Sodium 230mg; Total Carbohydrate 12g (Dietary Fiber 0g, Sugars 1g); Protein 1g. % Daily Value: Cholesterol 3%; Vitamin A 4%; Vitamin C 0%; Calcium 0%; Iron 4%. Exchanges: 1/2 Starch, 2-1/2 Fat. Carbohydrate Choices: 1.

Betty's Kitchen Tips

Health Twist: To make this dip more healthful, use reduced-fat sour cream and mayo, and serve it with bell pepper strips and carrot sticks as dippers.

Purchasing: Look for chipotle salsa in the Mexican-foods section, refrigerated section or condiment section of most grocery stores.

grilled mediterranean bread crisps

Prep Time: 15 Minutes
Start to Finish: 15 Minutes
Servings: 6 (2 crisps each)

EASY QUICK

- -

  3   tablespoons butter or margarine, softened
  3   tablespoons crumbled feta cheese
 12 thin slices French bread
  3   tablespoons chopped kalamata olives
Fresh oregano leaves, if desired

- -

1 Heat gas or charcoal grill. In small bowl, mix butter and cheese; set aside.

2 Place bread on grill over medium heat. Cover grill; cook 3 to 5 minutes or until lightly toasted.

3 Spread cheese mixture over toasted sides of bread. Sprinkle with olives. Place bread, olive sides up, on grill. Cover; cook 3 to 5 minutes or until cheese is melted. Garnish with oregano leaves.

High Altitude (3500-6500 ft): Cook covered over medium-low heat.

Nutritional Info: 1 Serving: Calories 120 (Calories from Fat 70); Total Fat 8g (Saturated Fat 4.5g, Trans Fat 0g); Cholesterol 20mg; Sodium 250mg; Total Carbohydrate 11g (Dietary Fiber 0g, Sugars 2g); Protein 3g. % Daily Value: Cholesterol 6%; Vitamin A 4%; Vitamin C 0%; Calcium 4%; Iron 4%. Exchanges: 1/2 Starch, 1-1/2 Fat. Carbohydrate Choices: 1.

Betty's Kitchen Tips

Variation: To bake the crisps in the oven, place the bread slices on an ungreased cookie sheet, top as directed and bake at 400°F for 10 minutes or until crisp.

Substitution: If you prefer, you can substitute ripe olives or green olives for the kalamata olives.

smoked salmon pâté

Prep Time: 15 Minutes
Start to Finish: 15 Minutes
Servings: 24 (1 tablespoon pâté and 1 bread slice each)

EASY QUICK LOW FAT

4 oz smoked salmon (lox)	1-1/2 teaspoons lemon-pepper seasoning
1 container (8 oz) chives-and-onion cream cheese spread	1 teaspoon chopped fresh dill weed
1/4 cup finely chopped red bell pepper	3 tablespoons chopped fresh parsley
	24 slices cocktail pumpernickel bread

1 Line 2-cup bowl with plastic wrap. In medium bowl, beat all ingredients except parsley and bread with electric mixer on medium speed until smooth. Spoon into lined bowl; press with rubber spatula. Cover; refrigerate until ready to serve.

2 To unmold, place 8-inch plate upside down on bowl, then turn plate and bowl over; remove bowl and plastic wrap. Sprinkle parsley over top of pâté and on rim of plate. Serve with bread.

High Altitude (3500-6500 ft): No change.

Nutritional Info: 1 Serving: Calories 50 (Calories from Fat 30); Total Fat 3g (Saturated Fat 2g, Trans Fat 0g); Cholesterol 10mg; Sodium 170mg; Total Carbohydrate 4g (Dietary Fiber 0g, Sugars 0g); Protein 2g. % Daily Value: Cholesterol 3%; Vitamin A 4%; Vitamin C 4%; Calcium 0%; Iron 2%. Exchanges: 1/2 High-Fat Meat. Carbohydrate Choices: 0.

Betty's Kitchen Tip

• Lox is salmon that is brine-cured, then cold-smoked.

spanish fruit and cheese stacks

Prep Time: 15 Minutes
Start to Finish: 15 Minutes
Servings: 24 appetizers

EASY QUICK LOW FAT

1   container (10 oz) quince paste
6   oz Manchego or Parmesan cheese
2   large pears
Grated peel from 4 lemons (about 3 tablespoons)

1 Remove quince paste from container. Cut paste crosswise into 12 equal slices; cut each slice diagonally in half for total of 24 slices.

2 Cut cheese into 24 equal slices. Cut each pear in half lengthwise and remove core. Cut each half into 6 equal wedges for total of 24 wedges.

3 To serve, place pear wedges on serving plate; top each wedge with quince paste slice and cheese slice. Sprinkle with lemon peel.

High Altitude (3500-6500 ft): No change.

Nutritional Info: 1 Appetizer: Calories 50 (Calories from Fat 15); Total Fat 2g (Saturated Fat 1g, Trans Fat 0g); Cholesterol 0mg; Sodium 115mg; Total Carbohydrate 5g (Dietary Fiber 1g, Sugars 3g); Protein 2g. % Daily Value: Cholesterol 0%; Vitamin A 0%; Vitamin C 6%; Calcium 8%; Iron 0%. Exchanges: 1/2 Other Carbohydrate, 1/2 Fat. Carbohydrate Choices: 1/2.

Betty's Kitchen Tips

Did You Know? Quince is a fruit that tastes like a cross between an apple and a pear. It usually comes in cans or plastic tubs. Often you can find it near the cheese section or in the deli department of your grocery store.

Variation: Next time, for a change of flavor, use apple slices instead of the pear slices.

caribbean layered dip

Prep Time: 20 Minutes
Start to Finish: 20 Minutes
Servings: 24 (2 tablespoons dip and 3 chips each)

QUICK

1	package (8 oz) cream cheese, softened
1/2	cup sour cream
1	tablespoon Old El Paso® taco seasoning mix (from 1-oz package)
1	can (15 oz) Progresso® black beans, drained, well rinsed

1/2	cup chopped red bell pepper
1/2	cup chopped mango
2	tablespoons chopped fresh cilantro
1	to 2 teaspoons finely chopped jalapeño chiles

Lime-flavored or plain tortilla chips

1 In small bowl, mix cream cheese, sour cream and taco seasoning mix with spoon or electric mixer on medium speed until well mixed. Spread on 10-inch round serving plate.

2 Top cream cheese mixture with remaining ingredients except tortilla chips. Serve immediately, or refrigerate until serving. Serve with tortilla chips.

High Altitude (3500-6500 ft): No change.

Nutritional Info: 1 Serving: Calories 120 (Calories from Fat 60); Total Fat 7g (Saturated Fat 3g, Trans Fat 0g); Cholesterol 15mg; Sodium 120mg; Total Carbohydrate 11g (Dietary Fiber 2g, Sugars 1g); Protein 2g. % Daily Value: Cholesterol 5%; Vitamin A 6%; Vitamin C 8%; Calcium 2%; Iron 4%. Exchanges: 1 Other Carbohydrate, 1-1/2 Fat. Carbohydrate Choices: 1.

Betty's Kitchen Tips

Health Twist: Trim fat to 4.5 grams and calories to 100 per serving by using fat-free sour cream and reduced-fat cream cheese (Neufchâtel).

Do-Ahead: Save on last-minute fussing. Make this layered dip up to 4 hours ahead; cover tightly and refrigerate.

crab gazpacho cocktails

Prep Time: 15 Minutes
Start to Finish: 15 Minutes
Servings: 8

EASY QUICK LOW FAT

- 1   can (14.5 oz) Muir Glen® organic fire-roasted diced tomatoes, undrained
- 1/2   cup tomato juice
- 1   slice (1/4 inch thick) red onion
- 1   tablespoon cider vinegar
- 1   tablespoon olive or vegetable oil
- 1/2   teaspoon salt
- 3   drops red pepper sauce
- 1   small cucumber, peeled, diced (3/4 cup)
- 1   can (6-1/2 oz) special white crabmeat, drained (about 1 cup)
- 2   teaspoons coarsely chopped fresh dill weed

1 In food processor, place all ingredients except cucumber, crabmeat and dill weed. Cover; process with on-and-off pulses until mixture is coarsely pureed. Stir in cucumber.

2 Spoon about 1/3 cup tomato mixture into each of 8 martini or wine glasses. Spoon about 1 heaping tablespoon crabmeat onto center of each cocktail. Sprinkle dill weed over top.

High Altitude (3500-6500 ft): No change.

Nutritional Info: 1 Serving: Calories 50 (Calories from Fat 20); Total Fat 2g (Saturated Fat 0g, Trans Fat 0g); Cholesterol 15mg; Sodium 320mg; Total Carbohydrate 3g (Dietary Fiber 0g, Sugars 2g); Protein 4g. % Daily Value: Cholesterol 5%; Vitamin A 2%; Vitamin C 15%; Calcium 4%; Iron 4%. Exchanges: 1/2 Other Carbohydrate, 1/2 Lean Meat. Carbohydrate Choices: 0.

Betty's Kitchen Tips

Purchasing: Canned crabmeat comes in different styles and varieties, including lump (most expensive), white and claw (least expensive). We chose the white for the best appearance in this elegant appetizer. Frozen crabmeat can be used instead of the canned, if desired.

Do-Ahead: Nothing is more refreshing than chilled gazpacho on a hot summer evening! If desired, chill the tomato-cucumber mixture up to 1 hour before spooning into glasses. A bonus is that the flavors will have blended more.

spicy corn guacamole

Prep Time: 15 Minutes
Start to Finish: 15 Minutes
Servings: 16 (2 tablespoons guacamole and 3 chips each)

EASY QUICK

- 1/2 cup Green Giant® Niblets® frozen whole kernel corn, thawed
- 2 ripe avocados, pitted, peeled and diced
- 1/4 cup diced red onion
- 1/4 cup Old El Paso® pickled jalapeño slices (from 12-oz jar), drained, diced

- 2 tablespoons fresh lime juice
- 2 tablespoons mayonnaise or salad dressing
- 1/2 teaspoon salt
- 48 tortilla chips

1 In 8-inch nonstick skillet, cook corn over medium-high heat 5 to 8 minutes, stirring occasionally, until lightly toasted.

2 Meanwhile, in medium bowl, mix remaining ingredients except tortilla chips with fork, mashing avocados. Stir in corn. Serve with tortilla chips.

High Altitude (3500-6500 ft): No change.

Nutritional Info: 1 Serving: Calories 90 (Calories from Fat 60); Total Fat 6g (Saturated Fat 1g, Trans Fat 0g); Cholesterol 0mg; Sodium 170mg; Total Carbohydrate 9g (Dietary Fiber 1g, Sugars 0g); Protein 1g. % Daily Value: Cholesterol 0%; Vitamin A 0%; Vitamin C 4%; Calcium 0%; Iron 2%. Exchanges: 1/2 Starch, 1 Fat. Carbohydrate Choices: 1/2.

Betty's Kitchen Tips

How-To: To easily dice avocados, cut lengthwise around the avocado and twist to separate halves. Hold the half with the pit in one hand. Tap pit firmly with edge of sharp knife and twist to remove pit. Score avocado flesh lengthwise and crosswise with tip of knife, making little cubes. Scoop out with a spoon.

Success Hint: The acidic nature of lime juice prevents the avocado from darkening.

party
APPETIZERS

p. 69

79

84

74

spicy chicken nachos

Prep Time: 15 Minutes
Start to Finish: 3 Hours
Servings: 24 (1/4 cup topping and 7 chips each)

EASY

  1   loaf (16 oz) Mexican prepared cheese product with jalapeño peppers, cut into cubes
3/4   cup Old El Paso® Thick 'n Chunky salsa
  1   can (15 oz) Progresso® black beans, drained, rinsed
  1   package (9 oz) frozen cooked chicken breast strips, thawed, cubed

  1   container (8 oz) sour cream
  1   medium red bell pepper, chopped (1 cup)
  3   medium green onions, sliced (3 tablespoons)
Large tortilla chips

1 Spray 3- to 4-quart slow cooker with cooking spray. In cooker, place cheese, salsa, beans and chicken.

2 Cover; cook on Low heat setting 2 hours, stirring once halfway through cooking.

3 Stir in sour cream, bell pepper and onions. Increase heat setting to High. Cover; cook about 45 minutes longer or until mixture is hot.

4 Serve with tortilla chips. Topping can be kept warm on Low heat setting up to 2 hours; stir occasionally.

High Altitude (3500-6500 ft): No change.

Nutritional Info: 1 Serving: Calories 200 (Calories from Fat 100); Total Fat 11g (Saturated Fat 4.5g, Trans Fat 0g); Cholesterol 25mg; Sodium 400mg; Total Carbohydrate 17g (Dietary Fiber 2g, Sugars 3g); Protein 9g. % Daily Value: Vitamin A 10%; Vitamin C 8%; Calcium 10%; Iron 6%. Exchanges: 1 Starch, 1 High-Fat Meat, 1/2 Fat. Carbohydrate Choices: 1.

Betty's Kitchen Tips

Substitution: In place of the frozen cooked chicken, use rotisserie or deli chicken.

Variation: Use flavored or multicolored tortillas for these nachos.

mascarpone and pistachio toasts

Prep Time: 10 Minutes
Start to Finish: 25 Minutes
Servings: 18 appetizers

EASY QUICK LOW FAT

4	oz mascarpone cheese (about 1/2 cup), softened
18	slices (1/4 inch thick) baguette French bread
1/3	cup pistachio nuts (about 2 oz), coarsely chopped
2	tablespoons honey
2	tablespoons thinly sliced fresh basil leaves

1 Heat oven to 350°F. Spread cheese on each bread slice. Place in single layer in ungreased 15x10x1-inch pan. Sprinkle nuts over cheese.

2 Bake 10 to 12 minutes or until edges of bread are light golden.

3 Drizzle honey over top of each toast. Garnish with basil.

High Altitude (3500-6500 ft): No change.

Nutritional Info: 1 Appetizer: Calories 60 (Calories from Fat 30); Total Fat 3g (Saturated Fat 1.5g, Trans Fat 0g); Cholesterol 5mg; Sodium 40mg; Total Carbohydrate 7g (Dietary Fiber 0g, Sugars 3g); Protein 1g. % Daily Value: Cholesterol 2%; Vitamin A 0%; Vitamin C 0%; Calcium 0%; Iron 0%. Exchanges: 1/2 Starch, 1/2 Fat. Carbohydrate Choices: 1/2.

Betty's Kitchen Tips

Substitution: If mascarpone isn't available, you can still make these tasty toasts. Use 4 ounces of cream cheese, softened, instead.

Success Hint: Spray your tablespoon with cooking spray to keep the honey from sticking when you measure it.

meatball mini burgers

Prep Time: 45 Minutes
Start to Finish: 45 Minutes
Servings: 32 appetizers

- -

Tiny Buns

1 can (16.3 oz) Pillsbury® Grands!® Flaky Layers refrigerated buttermilk or original biscuits (8 biscuits)

1 egg

1 tablespoon water

2 tablespoons sesame seed

Meatballs

2 teaspoons vegetable oil

1/2 cup chopped onion (1 medium)

3/4 cup chili sauce

1/4 cup water

1/4 cup yellow mustard

2 teaspoons chili powder

32 frozen plain meatballs (from 28-oz package; about 3 cups), thawed

8 slices (3/4 oz each) American cheese, cut into quarters

- -

1 Heat oven to 350°F. On ungreased cookie sheet, place biscuits 1 to 2 inches apart. Cut each biscuit into quarters, but do not separate pieces. In small bowl, beat egg and 1 tablespoon water. Brush egg mixture over tops of biscuits; sprinkle with sesame seed.

2 Bake 14 to 17 minutes or until golden brown. Cool slightly; separate biscuit quarters.

3 Meanwhile, in 2-quart saucepan, heat oil over medium-high heat. Add onion; cook, stirring frequently, until onion is tender.

Stir in chili sauce, 1/4 cup water, mustard and chili powder. Cook 3 to 5 minutes, stirring frequently, until slightly thickened.

4 Add meatballs to chili sauce mixture. Cover; cook over medium heat 8 to 10 minutes, stirring occasionally, until the meatballs are hot.

5 Split each biscuit quarter to make a tiny bun. Fill each bun with 1 cheese piece, 1 meatball and some of the sauce. Secure with toothpick.

High Altitude (3500-6500 ft): No change.

Nutritional Info: 1 Appetizer: Calories 150 (Calories from Fat 70); Total Fat 8g (Saturated Fat 3g, Trans Fat 1g); Cholesterol 40mg; Sodium 470mg; Total Carbohydrate 11g (Dietary Fiber 1g, Sugars 3g); Protein 8g. % Daily Value: Cholesterol 13%; Vitamin A 4%; Vitamin C 0%; Calcium 6%; Iron 6%. Exchanges: 1/2 Starch, 1 High-Fat Meat. Carbohydrate Choices: 1.

Betty's Kitchen Tip

• Experiment with different cheeses such as Cheddar, Gouda or Monterey Jack with jalapeño peppers, to create a new taste sensation.

mojito melon kabobs

Prep Time: 20 Minutes
Start to Finish: 1 Hour 20 Minutes
Servings: 12 appetizers

LOW FAT

2	limes
1-1/2	lb assorted melons, cut into 1-inch cubes (about 5 cups)
1/3	cup sugar
1/3	cup dark rum, if desired
3	tablespoons finely chopped fresh mint leaves
12	bamboo skewers (5 or 6 inch)

1 Grate 2 tablespoons peel from limes. Cut each lime in half crosswise; squeeze halves over small bowl to remove 6 tablespoons juice.

2 Place melon cubes in 1-gallon resealable food-storage plastic bag. Sprinkle lime peel and pour lime juice over melon. Add sugar, rum and mint. Seal bag; turn to coat melon.

3 Refrigerate at least 1 hour to blend flavors but no longer than 24 hours. To serve, thread 4 or 5 melon cubes on each skewer. Discard marinade.

High Altitude (3500-6500 ft): No change.

Nutritional Info: 1 Appetizer: Calories 50 (Calories from Fat 0); Total Fat 0g (Saturated Fat 0g, Trans Fat 0g); Cholesterol 0mg; Sodium 10mg; Total Carbohydrate 13g (Dietary Fiber 1g, Sugars 11g); Protein 0g. % Daily Value: Cholesterol 0%; Vitamin A 25%; Vitamin C 35%; Calcium 0%; Iron 0%. Exchanges: 1 Other Carbohydrate. Carbohydrate Choices: 1.

Betty's Kitchen Tips

Did You Know? "Mojito" typically refers to a cocktail made with lime juice, sugar, mint leaves and rum. We've taken those same flavors and turned them into a refreshing appetizer.

Substitution: One-third cup frozen (thawed) limeade concentrate can be substituted for the rum.

green beans with peanut-ginger dip

Prep Time: 20 Minutes
Start to Finish: 50 Minutes
Servings: 20 (5 beans and 1 teaspoon dip each)

LOW FAT

1	lb fresh green beans, trimmed
1/4	cup creamy peanut butter
1	tablespoon sugar
2	tablespoons rice vinegar
2	tablespoons soy sauce

1	tablespoon vegetable oil
1/4	teaspoon crushed red pepper flakes
1	piece (1 inch) gingerroot, peeled, finely chopped (2 tablespoons)
1	clove garlic, finely chopped

Chopped peanuts, if desired

1 In 3-quart saucepan, heat 6 cups water to boiling over high heat. Add beans to boiling water. Cook 4 to 6 minutes or until crisp-tender; drain. Rinse with cold water; drain. Cover; refrigerate while making dip.

2 In medium bowl, beat the remaining ingredients except peanuts with wire whisk until smooth. Cover; refrigerate at least 30 minutes to blend flavors. Stir before serving. Garnish with peanuts. Serve beans with dip.

High Altitude (3500-6500 ft): No change.

Nutritional Info: 1 Serving: Calories 40 (Calories from Fat 20); Total Fat 2.5g (Saturated Fat 0g, Trans Fat 0g); Cholesterol 0mg; Sodium 105mg; Total Carbohydrate 3g (Dietary Fiber 1g, Sugars 2g); Protein 1g. % Daily Value: Cholesterol 0%; Vitamin A 4%; Vitamin C 4%; Calcium 0%; Iron 0%. Exchanges: 1/2 Vegetable, 1/2 Fat. Carbohydrate Choices: 0.

Betty's Kitchen Tips

Did You Know? Fresh gingerroot resembles a gnarled tan-colored root. It adds a distinctive pungency and aroma to foods and is used extensively in dishes of the Far East. To prepare, use a small sharp knife to peel the tough skin and then finely chop the gingerroot into pieces.

Success Hint: Cooking the beans in boiling water and then rinsing them in cold water will bring out their bright color.

grilled spicy chili-glazed riblets

Prep Time: 25 Minutes
Start to Finish: 7 Hours 25 Minutes
Servings: 30 appetizers

- -

3	lb pork baby back ribs (ask butcher to cut ribs in half horizontally)
1	tablespoon garlic-pepper blend
1/3	cup maple-flavored syrup
1/4	cup Dijon mustard
3	tablespoons hot chili paste
3	tablespoons molasses
1	tablespoon cider vinegar

- -

1 Spray inside of 3- to 4-quart slow cooker with cooking spray. Cut ribs between bones into individual pieces. Place riblets in slow cooker. Sprinkle garlic-pepper blend over top; stir to coat evenly.

2 Cover; cook on Low heat setting 7 to 8 hours.

3 In large bowl, mix remaining ingredients. Using slotted spoon, remove riblets from slow cooker and add to the maple syrup mixture. Toss riblets to coat.

4 Heat gas or charcoal grill. Spray grill basket (grill "wok") with cooking spray. Place riblets in basket; place basket on grill over medium heat. Cover grill; cook 10 to 12 minutes, stirring ribs or shaking basket after 5 minutes, until the ribs are well glazed.

High Altitude (3500-6500 ft): No change.

Nutritional Info: 1 Appetizer: Calories 100 (Calories from Fat 60); Total Fat 7g (Saturated Fat 2.5g, Trans Fat 0g); Cholesterol 25mg; Sodium 115mg; Total Carbohydrate 5g (Dietary Fiber 0g, Sugars 4g); Protein 6g. % Daily Value: Cholesterol 9%; Vitamin A 2%; Vitamin C 0%; Calcium 0%; Iron 4%. Exchanges: 1/2 Other Carbohydrate, 1 Medium-Fat Meat. Carbohydrate Choices: 1/2.

Betty's Kitchen Tips

How-To: To bake riblets, prepare as directed in steps 1 and 2. Heat oven to 450°F. Place riblets in 15x10x1-inch pan lined with foil. Bake 10 to 12 minutes, without turning, until ribs are well glazed.

Success Hint: The heat level among brands of chili paste varies a lot. If you want spicier ribs, add 1 to 2 tablespoons more chili paste.

grilled honey-herb shrimp

Prep Time: 35 Minutes
Start to Finish: 1 Hour 35 Minutes
Servings: 8

LOW FAT

1/3 cup honey

1/4 cup vegetable oil

1/4 cup finely chopped green onions (4 medium)

3 tablespoons chopped fresh parsley

2 tablespoons chopped fresh thyme leaves

2 teaspoons grated fresh lemon or lime peel

1 tablespoon fresh lemon or lime juice

1/2 teaspoon salt

24 uncooked medium shrimp (about 1 lb), peeled, deveined

Lemon or lime slices, halved, if desired

8 bamboo skewers (5 or 6 inch)

1 In 1-gallon resealable food-storage plastic bag, mix all ingredients except shrimp and skewers. Add shrimp to bag. Seal bag; turn to coat shrimp. Place bag in large bowl. Refrigerate at least 1 hour to marinate but no longer than 8 hours.

2 Soak skewers in water for 30 minutes to prevent burning. Meanwhile, heat gas or charcoal grill.

3 Drain shrimp; discard marinade. Thread 3 shrimp and 3 lemon slices on each skewer, leaving 1/4-inch space between each shrimp.

4 Place shrimp on grill over medium heat. Cover grill; cook 5 to 7 minutes, turning once, until shrimp are pink. Serve warm.

High Altitude (3500-6500 ft): Cook covered over medium-low heat.

Nutritional Info: 1 Serving: Calories 60 (Calories from Fat 20); Total Fat 2g (Saturated Fat 0g, Trans Fat 0g); Cholesterol 55mg; Sodium 100mg; Total Carbohydrate 4g (Dietary Fiber 0g, Sugars 4g); Protein 5g. % Daily Value: Cholesterol 18%; Vitamin A 2%; Vitamin C 0%; Calcium 0%; Iron 6%. Exchanges: 1/2 Other Carbohydrate, 1/2 Lean Meat. Carbohydrate Choices: 0.

Betty's Kitchen Tips

How-To: For an alternative method to the skewers, place the shrimp and lime wedges in a grill basket (grill "wok"). Grill as directed above. Transfer the grilled shrimp and lime to a platter and guests can use decorative picks to serve themselves.

Time-Saver: You can shave several minutes off the prep time by purchasing shrimp already peeled and deveined.

cheesy stars

Prep Time: 25 Minutes
Start to Finish: 40 Minutes
Servings: 16 appetizers

- 1/2 cup finely chopped sweet onion (such as Walla Walla or Maui)
- 1/2 cup shredded Swiss cheese (2 oz)
- 1/2 cup diced yellow bell pepper
- 1/2 cup mayonnaise or salad dressing
- 16 slices firm white bread

1 Heat oven to 375°F. In small bowl, stir together all ingredients except bread.

2 Spray cookie sheet with cooking spray. Cut star shape from each bread slice with 3- or 4-inch star-shaped cookie cutter. Spread about 1 tablespoon cheese mixture on each bread star; place on cookie sheet.

3 Bake 12 to 15 minutes or until cheese is melted and bottoms of bread stars are golden brown.

High Altitude (3500-6500 ft): No change.

Nutritional Info: 1 Appetizer: Calories 100 (Calories from Fat 60); Total Fat 7g (Saturated Fat 1.5g, Trans Fat 0g); Cholesterol 5mg; Sodium 140mg; Total Carbohydrate 8g (Dietary Fiber 0g, Sugars 1g); Protein 2g. % Daily Value: Cholesterol 2%; Vitamin A 0%; Vitamin C 8%; Calcium 6%; Iron 4%. Exchanges: 1/2 Starch, 1-1/2 Fat. Carbohydrate Choices: 1/2.

Betty's Kitchen Tip

• Serve these cute canapés at your Memorial Day or 4th of July get-together.

cashew-chicken firecrackers

Prep Time: 25 Minutes
Start to Finish: 45 Minutes
Servings: 20 (1 appetizer and 2 teaspoons sauce each)

LOW FAT

- 1 cup finely chopped cooked chicken
- 1/2 cup red bell pepper strips (1x1/4x1/4 inch)
- 1/2 cup shredded carrots (2 small)
- 1/3 cup coarsely chopped cashews
- 4 medium green onions, thinly sliced (1/4 cup)
- 3 tablespoons orange marmalade
- 1 teaspoon garlic-pepper blend
- 1 package (16 oz) frozen phyllo (fillo) dough sheets (40 sheets; 14x9 inch), thawed
- Olive oil cooking spray or 2 tablespoons olive oil
- 1/4 cup hoisin sauce
- 1/4 cup orange juice

1 Heat oven to 375°F. Spray cookie sheets with cooking spray. In medium bowl, mix chicken, bell pepper, carrots, cashews, onions, marmalade and garlic-pepper blend; set aside.

2 Work with 2 phyllo sheets at a time. Cover remaining sheets with plastic wrap and damp towel. On work surface, stack 2 phyllo sheets. Spray with cooking spray (2 seconds). Cut in half crosswise, forming 2 (9x7-inch) rectangles.

3 Spoon 1 rounded tablespoon chicken mixture on short end of each rectangle. Roll up; twist about 1 inch from each end, sealing tube and forming firecracker shape. Place seam side down on cookie sheet.

4 Repeat with remaining phyllo sheets and chicken mixture. Spray tops of appetizers with cooking spray (1 second for 2 appetizers).

5 Bake 18 to 20 minutes or until crisp and brown. Meanwhile, in small bowl, mix hoisin sauce and orange juice for dipping sauce. Serve sauce with warm "firecrackers."

High Altitude (3500-6500 ft): No change.

Nutritional Info: 1 Serving: Calories 120 (Calories from Fat 25); Total Fat 3g (Saturated Fat 0.5g, Trans Fat 0g); Cholesterol 5mg; Sodium 140mg; Total Carbohydrate 19g (Dietary Fiber 1g, Sugars 3g); Protein 4g. % Daily Value: Cholesterol 2%; Vitamin A 10%; Vitamin C 6%; Calcium 0%; Iron 6%. Exchanges: 1/2 Starch, 1 Other Carbohydrate, 1/2 Fat. Carbohydrate Choices: 1.

Betty's Kitchen Tip

• Phyllo (fillo) pastry sheets vary in size depending on the brand. Cut sheets so they are about the size given in the recipe.

roast beef bruschetta

Prep Time: 30 Minutes
Start to Finish: 30 Minutes
Servings: 30 appetizers

QUICK

- 1 loaf (1 lb) baguette French bread, cut into 30 (1/4-inch) slices
- 2 tablespoons olive or vegetable oil
- 1/2 cup chives-and-onion cream cheese spread
- 1/2 lb thinly sliced cooked roast beef
- 1/4 teaspoon coarsely ground pepper
- 8 cherry tomatoes, thinly sliced
- 8 medium green onions, sliced (1/2 cup)

1 Heat oven to 375°F. Brush both sides of bread slices with oil; place on ungreased cookie sheet.

2 Bake about 5 minutes or until crisp. Cool 5 minutes.

3 Spread cream cheese over each slice. Top with beef; sprinkle with pepper. Top each with tomato slice and onions.

High Altitude (3500-6500 ft): No change.

Nutritional Info: 1 Appetizer: Calories 80 (Calories from Fat 30); Total Fat 3.5g (Saturated Fat 1.5g, Trans Fat 0g); Cholesterol 10mg; Sodium 130mg; Total Carbohydrate 9g (Dietary Fiber 0g, Sugars 2g); Protein 4g. % Daily Value: Cholesterol 3%; Vitamin A 2%; Vitamin C 2%; Calcium 0%; Iron 4%. Exchanges: 1/2 Starch, 1/2 Medium-Fat Meat. Carbohydrate Choices: 1/2.

Betty's Kitchen Tips

Do-Ahead: Toast the bread slices a day ahead of time, and store loosely covered at room temperature. Top them up to 1 hour ahead, then cover and refrigerate until serving.

Did You Know? The leftover cream cheese is a great spread for summer sandwiches. Use it with beef, turkey or vegetable sandwiches.

the big game chex® mix

Prep Time: 15 Minutes
Start to Finish: 30 Minutes
Servings: 24 (1/2 cup each)

- 3 cups Corn Chex® cereal
- 3 cups Rice Chex® cereal
- 3 cups Wheat Chex® cereal
- 2 cups honey mustard flavor small pretzel twists, pieces or nuggets
- 1 cup smoked almonds

- 1/4 cup butter or margarine
- 2 tablespoons yellow mustard or hot and spicy mustard
- 2 tablespoons honey
- 1 teaspoon seasoned salt

1 In large microwavable bowl, mix cereals, pretzels and almonds.

2 In microwavable measuring cup, microwave butter, mustard, honey and seasoned salt uncovered on High 1 to 2 minutes or until butter is melted and mixture is hot; stir. Pour over cereal mixture, stirring until evenly coated. Microwave uncovered on High 5 to 6 minutes, stirring every 2 minutes, until mixture begins to brown.

3 Spread on waxed paper or foil to cool, about 15 minutes. Store in airtight container.

Oven Directions: Heat oven to 250°F. In ungreased large roasting pan, mix cereals, pretzels and almonds. In 1-quart saucepan, heat butter, mustard, honey and seasoned salt over medium heat, stirring frequently, until butter is melted and mixture is hot. Pour over cereal mixture, stirring until evenly coated. Bake uncovered about 45 minutes, stirring every 15 minutes, until mixture begins to brown. Spread on waxed paper or foil to cool, about 15 minutes. Store in airtight container.

High Altitude (3500-6500 ft): No change.

Nutritional Info: 1 Serving: Calories 130 (Calories from Fat 45); Total Fat 5g (Saturated Fat 1.5g, Trans Fat 0g); Cholesterol 5mg; Sodium 290mg; Total Carbohydrate 18g (Dietary Fiber 2g, Sugars 3g); Protein 3g. % Daily Value: Vitamin A 6%; Vitamin C 2%; Calcium 6%; Iron 25%. Exchanges: 1 Starch, 1 Fat. Carbohydrate Choices: 1.

Betty's Kitchen Tips

Special Touch: Colorful paper cups make great holders for snack mixes. Look for them at paper and discount stores. Or, wrap clear plastic cups with fun paper.

How-To: Store any additional mix in an airtight container. The snack is great to serve at football-game-watching parties.

barbecued bacon-chicken skewers

Prep Time: 25 Minutes
Start to Finish: 40 Minutes
Servings: 15 appetizers

LOW FAT

- -

15 bamboo skewers (6 inch)
3 large boneless skinless chicken breasts (about 1 lb)
4 large green onions

1 package (2.1 oz) refrigerated fully cooked bacon (15 pieces)
1/2 cup barbecue sauce

- -

1 Soak skewers in water at least 30 minutes to prevent burning. Meanwhile, cut each chicken breast in half lengthwise, then cut crosswise to make 10 (about 1-inch) pieces. Cut onions into 2-inch pieces (30 pieces total). Cut bacon slices in half crosswise.

2 Heat gas or charcoal grill. Push 1 skewer through end of 1 bacon piece, then through middle of 1 chicken piece and back through other end of bacon piece;

add 2 onion pieces, then repeat with another bacon piece and chicken piece. Place on large plate or tray. Repeat to make remaining kabobs.

3 Place kabobs on grill over medium heat. Cover grill; cook 5 minutes. Turn kabobs; brush with half of the barbecue sauce. Cover; cook 5 minutes. Turn kabobs; brush with remaining sauce. Cover; cook about 1 minute longer or until chicken is no longer pink in center. If desired, serve with additional barbecue sauce for dipping.

High Altitude (3500-6500 ft): No change.

Nutritional Info: 1 Appetizer: Calories 70 (Calories from Fat 25); Total Fat 2.5g (Saturated Fat 1g, Trans Fat 0g); Cholesterol 25mg; Sodium 180mg; Total Carbohydrate 4g (Dietary Fiber 0g, Sugars 3g); Protein 8g. % Daily Value: Cholesterol 8%; Vitamin A 0%; Vitamin C 0%; Calcium 0%; Iron 2%. Exchanges: 1/2 Other Carbohydrate, 1 Lean Meat. Carbohydrate Choices: 0.

Betty's Kitchen Tips

Variation: To bake: Heat oven to 400°F. Line large cookie sheet with foil; spray with cooking spray. Make kabobs as directed; place on cookie sheet. Drizzle or brush barbecue sauce over all sides of kabobs. Bake 10 minutes. Turn kabobs. Bake 5 to 10 minutes longer or until chicken is no longer pink in center.

Success Hint: Keep pieces of bacon at the tip of the skewer while threading to keep bacon tight.

chili-cheese twists

Prep Time: 15 Minutes
Start to Finish: 40 Minutes
Servings: 28 appetizers

EASY

- 1   sheet frozen puff pastry (from 17.3-oz package)
- 1   egg
- 1   tablespoon water
- 1/2   cup finely shredded Cheddar cheese (2 oz)
- 1   tablespoon chili powder

1   Thaw pastry sheet at room temperature 30 minutes. Meanwhile, in small bowl, beat egg and water until well blended; set aside. In another small bowl, mix cheese and chili powder.

2   Heat oven to 400°F. Spray large cookie sheet with cooking spray.

3   On lightly floured surface, roll thawed pastry sheet with rolling pin into 14x10-inch rectangle; cut in half lengthwise. Brush egg mixture over both rectangles; reserve remaining egg mixture. Spread cheese mixture evenly over 1 rectangle; top with the second rectangle, egg side down. Gently roll pastry to seal.

4   Cut pastry crosswise into 28 (1/2-inch) strips. Twist strips; place 2 inches apart on cookie sheet, pressing ends down. Brush with remaining egg mixture.

5   Bake 10 to 12 minutes or until golden brown. Serve warm or at room temperature.

High Altitude (3500-6500 ft): No change.

Nutritional Info: 1 Appetizer: Calories 60 (Calories from Fat 40); Total Fat 4.5g (Saturated Fat 1.5g, Trans Fat 0g); Cholesterol 20mg; Sodium 40mg; Total Carbohydrate 4g (Dietary Fiber 0g, Sugars 0g); Protein 1g. % Daily Value: Cholesterol 7%; Vitamin A 2%; Vitamin C 0%; Calcium 0%; Iron 2%. Exchanges: 1 Fat. Carbohydrate Choices: 0.

Betty's Kitchen Tips

Special Touch: Serve the twists in glass tumblers to add height to the appetizer buffet table.

Do-Ahead: These cheesy twists can be made up to a month ahead and frozen until ready to bake. Increase bake time to 15 minutes.

Success Hint: Store the twists refrigerated in an airtight container up to one week.

chicken-filled lettuce wraps

Prep Time: 30 Minutes
Start to Finish: 30 Minutes
Servings: 12 appetizers (1 wrap and 1/12 of toppings each)

QUICK

1/3	cup orange marmalade
1	tablespoon fresh lime juice
1	tablespoon soy sauce
1/2	teaspoon grated gingerroot
1/3	cup Thai peanut sauce
2	cups small bite-size strips cooked chicken breast

12	leaves Boston lettuce (about 1-1/2 heads)
1	cup diced fresh mango (about 1 mango)
1	medium red bell pepper, cut into bite-size strips (about 1 cup)
1	cup diagonally sliced fresh snow pea pods (strings removed)
1/2	cup coarsely chopped peanuts

1 In small bowl, mix marmalade, lime juice, soy sauce and gingerroot; set aside.

2 In medium bowl, mix peanut sauce and 1 tablespoon of the marmalade mixture. Stir in chicken until coated.

3 Spoon about 2 tablespoons chicken mixture onto center of each lettuce leaf; place on large platter. Top with mango, bell pepper, pea pods, peanuts and marmalade mixture. To eat, wrap lettuce around the chicken mixture and toppings.

High Altitude (3500-6500 ft): No change.

Nutritional Info: 1 Appetizer: Calories 140 (Calories from Fat 50); Total Fat 6g (Saturated Fat 1g, Trans Fat 0g); Cholesterol 20mg; Sodium 130mg; Total Carbohydrate 12g (Dietary Fiber 1g, Sugars 7g); Protein 10g. % Daily Value: Cholesterol 6%; Vitamin A 20%; Vitamin C 35%; Calcium 2%; Iron 4%. Exchanges: 1 Other Carbohydrate, 1-1/2 Lean Meat. Carbohydrate Choices: 1.

Betty's Kitchen Tips

Purchasing: Look for Thai or Asian peanut sauce in the ethnic-foods section of the grocery store.

Variation: Other tender leaf lettuce can be used in this recipe. Or use small pieces of iceberg lettuce to make lettuce cups instead of wraps.

Substitution: Rotisserie chicken or refrigerated cooked chicken breast strips, cut into small strips, work well in this recipe, too.

blt crostini

Prep Time: 15 Minutes
Start to Finish: 30 Minutes
Servings: 12 appetizers

EASY QUICK

- 1/2 cup shredded Swiss cheese (2 oz)
- 1/4 cup mayonnaise or salad dressing
-   2 medium green onions, thinly sliced (2 tablespoons)
- 12 slices (1/4 inch thick) baguette French bread
-   6 slices refrigerated fully cooked bacon (from 2.1-oz package), cut in half
- 1/4 cup finely shredded iceberg lettuce
-   4 cherry tomatoes, each cut into 3 slices

1 Heat oven to 375°F. In small bowl, mix cheese, mayonnaise and onions. Spread about 1 teaspoon cheese mixture on each bread slice; place on ungreased cookie sheet. Top each with half slice of bacon.

2 Bake 10 to 12 minutes or until edges of bread are golden brown and cheese is melted.

3 Garnish each crostini with lettuce and tomato slice.

High Altitude (3500-6500 ft): No change.

Nutritional Info: 1 Appetizer: Calories 80 (Calories from Fat 50); Total Fat 6g (Saturated Fat 2g, Trans Fat 0g); Cholesterol 10mg; Sodium 120mg; Total Carbohydrate 5g (Dietary Fiber 0g, Sugars 0g); Protein 3g. % Daily Value: Cholesterol 3%; Vitamin A 2%; Vitamin C 0%; Calcium 4%; Iron 0%. Exchanges: 1/2 Starch, 1 Fat. Carbohydrate Choices: 1/2.

Betty's Kitchen Tips

Did You Know? Crostini are simply small, thin slices of toasted bread that are brushed with olive oil. For extra flavor, try rubbing these crostini with garlic cloves before spreading them with the cheese mixture.

Purchasing: Look for bags of shredded lettuce in the produce section of your supermarket. Or, you can use small pieces of torn leaf lettuce instead of the shredded lettuce.

potato salad bites

Prep Time: 30 Minutes
Start to Finish: 2 Hours 20 Minutes
Servings: 24 appetizers

LOW FAT

12	small red potatoes (1-1/2 to 1-3/4 inches in diameter)
1	teaspoon salt
1	hard-cooked egg, finely chopped
1/4	cup chopped celery
3	tablespoons dill pickle relish

2	tablespoons mayonnaise or salad dressing
1	teaspoon yellow mustard
1/4	teaspoon pepper
2	medium green onions, thinly sliced (2 tablespoons)
3	radishes, thinly sliced (1/4 cup), if desired

1 Heat oven to 400°F. Place potatoes in ungreased 15x10x1-inch pan. Bake 30 to 40 minutes or until tender. Cool 10 mintues or until cool enough to handle.

2 Cut potatoes in half. With melon baller, scoop out insides of potatoes into medium bowl, leaving 1/4-inch lining of potato flesh around edges of shells. Sprinkle shells with 1/2 teaspoon of the salt. To potato flesh in bowl, add remaining 1/2 teaspoon salt and remaining ingredients except onions and radishes; mix well, breaking up potatoes.

3 Cut very thin slice off bottom of each potato shell so potatoes will stand upright. Fill each potato shell with about 1 tablespoon filling mixture. Top with onions. Cover; refrigerate about 1 hour or until chilled. Garnish with radish slices.

High Altitude (3500-6500 ft): No change.

Nutritional Info: 1 Appetizer: Calories 30 (Calories from Fat 10); Total Fat 1g (Saturated Fat 0g, Trans Fat 0g); Cholesterol 10mg; Sodium 140mg; Total Carbohydrate 5g (Dietary Fiber 0g, Sugars 0g); Protein 0g. % Daily Value: Cholesterol 3%; Vitamin A 0%; Vitamin C 6%; Calcium 0%; Iron 2%. Exchanges: 1/2 Other Carbohydrate. Carbohydrate Choices: 1/2.

Betty's Kitchen Tips

Time-Saver: Purchasing already-cooked eggs is a real time-saver. They're usually found in the deli department of the grocery store.

Success Hint: A small teaspoon can be used to scoop out the potatoes if a melon baller is not available. A small cookie scoop works well for filling the potato shells.

grilled bacon and tomato pizza wedges

Prep Time: 15 Minutes
Start to Finish: 25 Minutes
Servings: 16 appetizers

EASY QUICK

5	slices bacon, cut into 1/2-inch pieces
1/2	cup garlic-and-herbs spreadable cheese (from 6.5-oz container)
1	package (10 oz) prebaked Italian pizza crusts (two 8-inch crusts)
1	large plum (Roma) tomato, cut into 10 thin slices
1	tablespoon extra-virgin olive oil
1/4	cup chopped fresh basil leaves

1 Heat gas or charcoal grill. In 10-inch skillet, cook bacon over medium heat, stirring frequently, until crisp. Drain on paper towel; set aside.

2 Spread cheese evenly on pizza crusts. Top with tomato and bacon. Drizzle with oil.

3 Place pizzas on grill over low heat. Cover grill; cook 4 to 8 minutes or until bottoms are deep golden brown and toppings are warm. Sprinkle basil over pizzas. Cut each into 8 wedges.

High Altitude (3500-6500 ft): No change.

Nutritional Info: 1 Appetizer: Calories 90 (Calories from Fat 50); Total Fat 5g (Saturated Fat 2.5g, Trans Fat 0g); Cholesterol 10mg; Sodium 170mg; Total Carbohydrate 8g (Dietary Fiber 0g, Sugars 0g); Protein 3g. % Daily Value: Cholesterol 4%; Vitamin A 4%; Vitamin C 0%; Calcium 0%; Iron 4%. Exchanges: 1/2 Starch, 1 Fat. Carbohydrate Choices: 1/2.

Betty's Kitchen Tips

Success Hint: Watch pizzas carefully. Each grill heats and cooks differently. If the lowest setting of your grill seems too hot, move pizzas to a cooler part of the grill. You could also turn off a burner if your grill has more than one burner.

Variation: To bake pizzas, heat oven to 375°F. Place pizzas on cookie sheet. Bake 6 to 8 minutes or until toppings are warm. Sprinkle basil over the pizzas.

marinara sauce with mozzarella cheese dip

Prep Time: 5 Minutes
Start to Finish: 2 Hours 35 Minutes
Servings: 24 (2 tablespoons dip and 4 baguette slices each)

EASY

2 cups chunky marinara sauce (from 26-oz jar)

8 oz fresh mozzarella cheese, cubed

2 tablespoons chopped fresh basil leaves

2 loaves (10 oz each) baguette-style French bread, cut into 1/2-inch slices, toasted

1 Spray 1-1/2-quart slow cooker with cooking spray. Pour marinara sauce into cooker.

2 Cover; cook on Low heat setting about 2 hours or until hot.

3 Stir in cheese and basil. Cover; cook on Low heat setting about 30 minutes longer or until cheese is just starting to melt. Serve with baguette slices. Dip can be kept warm on Low heat setting up to 2 hours; stir occasionally.

High Altitude (3500-6500 ft): No change.

Nutritional Info: 1 Serving: Calories 110 (Calories from Fat 30); Total Fat 3.5g (Saturated Fat 1.5g, Trans Fat 0g); Cholesterol 5mg; Sodium 290mg; Total Carbohydrate 16g (Dietary Fiber 0g, Sugars 2g); Protein 5g. % Daily Value: Vitamin A 4%; Vitamin C 0%; Calcium 10%; Iron 6%. Exchanges: 1 Starch, 1/2 Fat. Carbohydrate Choices: 1.

Betty's Kitchen Tips

Variation: For a change of flavor, try using goat cheese instead of the fresh mozzarella.

Special Touch: Garnish the warm appetizer with fresh basil leaves.

grilled brie with mango and raspberries

Prep Time: 25 Minutes
Start to Finish: 55 Minutes
Servings: 10

1	untreated cedar plank (about 15x6 inches)
1	small round (4-1/2 oz) Brie cheese
1/2	cup diced mango
1/2	cup fresh raspberries
1/2	teaspoon kosher (coarse) salt
2	tablespoons honey
10	slices (1/4 inch thick) baguette French bread

1 Soak the cedar plank in water at least 30 minutes. Meanwhile, heat gas or charcoal grill.

2 Remove plank from water. Place cheese (in rind) on plank. Spoon mango and raspberries over cheese. Sprinkle with salt.

3 Place plank with cheese on grill over medium heat. Cover grill; cook 15 to 20 minutes or until cheese is warm.

4 Remove plank from grill. Transfer cheese and fruits to serving plate. Drizzle honey over cheese and fruits. Serve with bread slices.

High Altitude (3500-6500 ft): No change.

Nutritional Info: 1 Serving: Calories 80 (Calories from Fat 35); Total Fat 3.5g (Saturated Fat 2.5g, Trans Fat 0g); Cholesterol 15mg; Sodium 180mg; Total Carbohydrate 9g (Dietary Fiber 0g, Sugars 5g); Protein 3g. % Daily Value: Cholesterol 4%; Vitamin A 2%; Vitamin C 6%; Calcium 2%; Iron 2%. Exchanges: 1/2 Other Carbohydrate, 1/2 High-Fat Meat. Carbohydrate Choices: 1/2.

ABOUT PLANK
GRILLING

• Plank grilling is the technique of cooking food on an untreated presoaked wood plank over a gas or charcoal grill. The wood plank infuses food with a subtle smoky flavor or seasoning, depending on the type of wood used.

• Preparation directions for planks vary among brands but usually involve soaking the plank in water for as short as 30 minutes to as long as overnight. This makes the plank less likely to burn while on the grill.

• To soak a plank in your kitchen sink, use a heavy object to keep the wood submerged. Hot water will speed the soaking process.

• You can impart more flavor by adding white wine, beer, apple cider, fruit juice or fresh herbs to the water.

• After soaking the plank, dry it off and lightly coat the surface with olive or vegetable oil. You can rub fresh herbs, garlic or flavored oil on the plank for even more flavor.

• Look for grilling planks at your local grocery, home improvement or specialty food and kitchen store, as well as online.

artichoke-crab spread

Prep Time: 15 Minutes
Start to Finish: 1 Hour 30 Minutes
Servings: 24 (2 tablespoons spread and 2 bread slices each)

EASY

- 1 cup refrigerated flake-style imitation crabmeat (from 8-oz package)
- 1/2 cup grated Parmesan cheese
- 4 teaspoons lemon juice
- 4 medium green onions, sliced (1/4 cup)
- 1 can (14 oz) artichoke hearts, drained, coarsely chopped
- 1 package (8 oz) cream cheese, cubed
- French baguette bread or cocktail rye bread slices
- 1 red bell pepper, cut into wedges, if desired

1 Spray 1- to 1-1/2-quart slow cooker with cooking spray. In cooker, place all ingredients except bread.

2 Cover; cook on Low heat setting 1 hour to 1 hour 15 minutes. Stir until cheese is smooth.

3 Scrape down side of cooker with rubber spatula to help prevent edge of spread from scorching. Serve with bread slices. Spread can be kept warm on Low heat setting up to 3 hours; stir occasionally.

High Altitude (3500-6500 ft): No change.

Nutritional Info: 1 Serving: Calories 90 (Calories from Fat 40); Total Fat 4.5g (Saturated Fat 2.5g, Trans Fat 0g); Cholesterol 15mg; Sodium 250mg; Total Carbohydrate 9g (Dietary Fiber 1g, Sugars 0g); Protein 4g. % Daily Value: Vitamin A 4%; Vitamin C 0%; Calcium 6%; Iron 4%. Exchanges: 1/2 Starch, 1 Fat. Carbohydrate Choices: 1/2.

Betty's Kitchen Tips

Special Touch: Wrap the slow cooker in a colorful cloth to make it more festive for serving food at a party.

Success Hint: Everyone will love this delicious, rich spread. Because of the cheeses, the spread may separate and little puddles could appear. So stir occasionally, and it will look as good as new.

grilled firecracker chicken drummies

Prep Time: 35 Minutes
Start to Finish: 1 Hour 35 Minutes
Servings: 20 appetizers   **LOW FAT**

- 2 tablespoons chili powder
- 1-1/2 teaspoons dried oregano leaves
- 1-1/4 teaspoons ground red pepper (cayenne)
- 1 teaspoon garlic salt
- 1 teaspoon ground cumin
- 1 teaspoon pepper
- 2 packages (1 lb each) chicken wing drummettes

Sour cream, if desired

Paprika, if desired

1 In 1-gallon resealable food-storage plastic bag, place all ingredients except chicken, sour cream and paprika. Seal bag; shake to blend seasonings. Add chicken; seal bag and shake until chicken is coated with seasonings. Refrigerate at least 1 hour to marinate but no longer than 24 hours.

2 Heat gas or charcoal grill. Place chicken in grill basket (grill "wok"). Place basket on grill over medium heat. Cover grill; cook 20 to 25 minutes, shaking basket to turn chicken after 10 minutes, until juice of chicken is clear when thickest part is cut to bone (180°F).

3 Serve chicken with sour cream sprinkled with paprika.

High Altitude (3500-6500 ft): Cook covered over medium-low heat.

Nutritional Info: 1 Appetizer: Calories 50 (Calories from Fat 20); Total Fat 2.5g (Saturated Fat 1g, Trans Fat 0g); Cholesterol 20mg; Sodium 70mg; Total Carbohydrate 0g (Dietary Fiber 0g, Sugars 0g); Protein 6g. % Daily Value: Cholesterol 6%; Vitamin A 6%; Vitamin C 0%; Calcium 0%; Iron 4%. Exchanges: 1 Lean Meat. Carbohydrate Choices: 0.

Betty's Kitchen Tips

Variation: Purchased blue cheese dressing can be served instead of the sour cream and paprika.

Purchasing: Grill baskets (grill "woks") are available at discount stores or in kitchen specialty shops.

planked salmon platter

Prep Time: 50 Minutes
Start to Finish: 1 Hour 20 Minutes
Servings: 16 (2 tablespoons salmon, 2 bread slices and 1/16 of accompaniments each)

Salmon

1	untreated cedar plank (about 15x6 inches)
1	salmon fillet, about 1 inch thick (1 lb)
2	tablespoons mayonnaise or salad dressing
2	teaspoons Dijon mustard
1	teaspoon grated lemon peel

Accompaniments

1/2	cup sour cream
1	teaspoon chopped fresh or 1/2 teaspoon dried dill weed
1	jar (3-1/2 oz) small capers, drained
1/4	cup spicy brown mustard
2	hard-cooked eggs, finely chopped
1	cup thinly sliced cucumber
32	slices cocktail rye bread

1 Soak the cedar plank in water for 30 minutes.

2 Heat gas or charcoal grill for indirect-heat cooking as directed by manufacturer. Remove plank from water. Place salmon, skin side down, on plank. In small bowl, mix mayonnaise, mustard and lemon peel; brush generously over salmon.

3 Place the plank with salmon on grill for indirect cooking. Cover grill; cook over medium heat 25 to 30 minutes or until salmon flakes easily with fork.

4 Using large pancake turner, remove salmon from plank to serving platter, or leave salmon on plank and place on large wooden cutting board or platter.

5 In small bowl, mix sour cream and dill weed. Place remaining accompaniments except bread in individual small bowls. Place sour cream mixture and remaining accompaniments around salmon. Serve salmon and accompaniments with bread.

High Altitude (3500-6500 ft): No change.

Nutritional Info: 1 Serving: Calories 110 (Calories from Fat 50); Total Fat 5g (Saturated Fat 2g, Trans Fat 0g); Cholesterol 50mg; Sodium 320mg; Total Carbohydrate 8g (Dietary Fiber 1g, Sugars 1g); Protein 7g. % Daily Value: Cholesterol 16%; Vitamin A 2%; Vitamin C 0%; Calcium 4%; Iron 4%. Exchanges: 1/2 Other Carbohydrate, 1 Medium-Fat Meat. Carbohydrate Choices: 1/2.

Betty's Kitchen Tip

• For a primer on plank grilling, please see page 79. Wood grilling planks are often made of western red cedar, but alder, hickory, mesquite and oak grilling planks are also available.

feta cheese, lemon and chive turnovers

Prep Time: 30 Minutes
Start to Finish: 50 Minutes
Servings: 16 appetizers

- 2 oz crumbled garlic-and-herb feta cheese
- 2 tablespoons thinly sliced fresh chives
- 2 medium green onions, sliced (2 tablespoons)
- 1/2 teaspoon grated lemon peel

Flour for dusting

- 1 sheet frozen puff pastry (from 17.3-oz package), thawed

1 Heat oven to 400°F. In medium bowl, mash cheese with fork. Stir in chives, onions and lemon peel until well mixed.

2 On lightly floured surface, unfold pastry sheet; sprinkle lightly with flour. Roll pastry into 12-inch square. Cut pastry into 4 rows by 4 rows to make 16 squares. Spoon cheese mixture onto center of each square (about 1 rounded teaspoon each). If desired, cut small shape from one side of square.

3 Moisten edges of 1 square with fingertip dipped in water. Fold square over filling to form a triangle, gently pressing to remove air pockets around filling and pressing edges of pastry together. Use tines of fork to crimp and seal edges of turnover. Repeat with remaining squares. Using spatula, make edges of turnovers even if necessary; place on ungreased cookie sheet.

4 Bake 10 to 15 minutes or until puffed and golden all over. Remove from cookie sheet to cooling rack; cool 2 to 3 minutes before serving.

High Altitude (3500-6500 ft): No change.

Nutritional Info: 1 Appetizer: Calories 100 (Calories from Fat 60); Total Fat 7g (Saturated Fat 2.5g, Trans Fat 0.5g); Cholesterol 20mg; Sodium 80mg; Total Carbohydrate 7g (Dietary Fiber 0g, Sugars 0g); Protein 1g. % Daily Value: Cholesterol 7%; Vitamin A 0%; Vitamin C 0%; Calcium 2%; Iron 4%. Exchanges: 1/2 Starch, 1-1/2 Fat. Carbohydrate Choices: 1/2.

Betty's Kitchen Tips

Did You Know? Puff pastry is made of hundreds of layers of chilled butter and pastry dough. As it bakes, the moisture in the butter creates steam, causing the dough to puff and separate into hundreds of flaky layers.

Do-Ahead: Turnovers can be prepared, covered and refrigerated for up to 2 hours before baking.

hawaiian pork ribs

Prep Time: 15 Minutes
Start to Finish: 6 Hours 40 Minutes
Servings: 10

EASY

- 6 lb pork loin back ribs
- 3/4 cup ketchup
- 3/4 cup pineapple preserves
- 1/2 cup teriyaki marinade and sauce
- 2 tablespoons packed brown sugar
- 2 cloves garlic, finely chopped
- 1/2 cup cornstarch
- 1 can (20 oz) pineapple chunks in juice, drained, with 1/3 cup juice reserved
- 1 bag (1 lb) frozen bell pepper and onion stir-fry

1 Spray 6-quart slow cooker with cooking spray. Cut ribs into 2- or 3-rib portions; place in cooker. In small bowl, mix ketchup, preserves, teriyaki marinade, brown sugar and garlic; pour over ribs.

2 Cover; cook on Low heat setting 6 to 7 hours.

3 Skim fat from liquid in cooker if necessary. Remove ribs from cooker; cover to keep warm or keep warm in 200°F oven. In small bowl, mix cornstarch and reserved 1/3 cup pineapple juice until smooth; stir into liquid in cooker. Increase heat setting to High. Cover; cook about 25 minutes or until thickened.

4 Meanwhile, in large microwavable bowl, mix pineapple chunks and stir-fry vegetables. Microwave uncovered on High 5 to 7 minutes or until thoroughly heated. Drain; stir vegetable mixture into sauce in cooker. Serve vegetable mixture over ribs.

High Altitude (3500-6500 ft): In step 4, microwave uncovered on High 7 to 9 minutes.

Nutritional Info: 1 Serving: Calories 700 (Calories from Fat 360); Total Fat 40g (Saturated Fat 15g, Trans Fat 0g); Cholesterol 160mg; Sodium 820mg; Total Carbohydrate 44g (Dietary Fiber 1g, Sugars 30g); Protein 40g. % Daily Value: Vitamin A 6%; Vitamin C 20%; Calcium 8%; Iron 15%. Exchanges: 3 Other Carbohydrate, 5 High-Fat Meat. Carbohydrate Choices: 3.

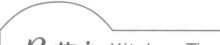

Betty's Kitchen Tips

How-To: A clever trick for skimming fat from the cooked meat mixture is to place a slice of bread on top of the mixture for a few minutes to absorb the fat.

Variation: To turn this main-dish recipe into a delicious riblet appetizer, ask the meat cutter at your supermarket to cut across the ribs horizontally.

nacho chicken casserole

Prep Time: 15 Minutes
Start to Finish: 1 Hour 25 Minutes
Servings: 5

EASY LOW FAT

2	cups diced cooked chicken
1/2	cup uncooked instant rice
1	can (14.5 oz) diced tomatoes, drained
1	can (10-3/4 oz) condensed reduced-fat reduced-sodium cream of chicken soup
1	can (11 oz) Green Giant® Mexicorn® whole kernel corn with red and green peppers, undrained
1	teaspoon Old El Paso® taco seasoning mix (from 1-oz package)
1-1/4	cups shredded reduced-fat Cheddar cheese (5 oz)
1	cup tortilla chips

1 Heat oven to 350°F. Spray 2-quart casserole with cooking spray. In casserole, stir chicken, rice, tomatoes, soup, corn, taco seasoning mix and 1 cup of the cheese until well mixed.

2 Cover and bake about 1 hour or until rice is tender and mixture is heated through. Top with tortilla chips; sprinkle with remaining 1/4 cup cheese. Bake about 10 minutes longer or until filling is bubbly and cheese is melted.

High Altitude (3500-6500 ft): No change.

Nutritional Info: 1 Serving: Calories 330 (Calories from Fat 80); Total Fat 9g (Saturated Fat 3g, Trans Fat 0g); Cholesterol 55mg; Sodium 950mg; Total Carbohydrate 34g (Dietary Fiber 2g, Sugars 6g); Protein 28g. % Daily Value: Vitamin A 4%; Vitamin C 8%; Calcium 25%; Iron 15%. Exchanges: 2 Starch, 3 Lean Meat. Carbohydrate Choices: 2.

Betty's Kitchen Tip
• This casserole makes good use of the broken pieces at the bottom of a bag of tortilla chips.

gravy pork chops with stuffing biscuits

Prep Time: 20 Minutes
Start to Finish: 45 Minutes
Servings: 4

- -

1	tablespoon butter or margarine		1/4	cup chopped onion
4	bone-in pork loin chops, about 1/2 inch thick (about 1-3/4 lb)		1	cup Original Bisquick® mix
1	jar (12 oz) home-style pork gravy		1/2	teaspoon dried sage leaves
1	medium stalk celery, thinly sliced (1/2 cup)		1/3	cup milk

- -

1 Heat oven to 375°F. Spray 13x9-inch (3-quart) glass baking dish with cooking spray.

2 In 12-inch nonstick skillet, melt butter over medium-high heat. Add pork chops; cook 8 to 10 minutes, turning once, until browned. Place pork chops in baking dish. Pour gravy over top.

3 In same skillet, cook celery and onion over medium-high heat 3 to 5 minutes, stirring frequently, until tender; remove from heat.

4 In small bowl, stir Bisquick mix, sage and milk until blended. Stir in celery and onion mixture. Drop large spoonful of dough onto each pork chop.

5 Bake 20 to 25 minutes or until biscuits are golden brown and pork chops are no longer pink in center.

High Altitude (3500-6500 ft): Bake 23 to 28 minutes.

Nutritional Info: 1 Serving: Calories 430 (Calories from Fat 180); Total Fat 20g (Saturated Fat 8g, Trans Fat 1.5g); Cholesterol 100mg; Sodium 940mg; Total Carbohydrate 26g (Dietary Fiber 1g, Sugars 3g); Protein 37g. % Daily Value: Vitamin A 4%; Vitamin C 0%; Calcium 8%; Iron 15%. Exchanges: 1-1/2 Starch, 4-1/2 Lean Meat, 1 Fat. Carbohydrate Choices: 2.

Betty's Kitchen Tips

Did You Know? Pork loin chops are one of the leanest cuts of pork. In fact, any pork item labeled "loin" is an excellent slimmed-down, lower-fat selection.

Serve-With: Serve your favorite steamed vegetables with this easy oven entrée.

easy garden bake

Prep Time: 15 Minutes
Start to Finish: 55 Minutes
Servings: 2

EASY   LOW FAT

1	small zucchini, chopped (1/2 cup)
1	large tomato, chopped (1 cup)
1/4	cup chopped onion
1/3	cup grated Parmesan cheese
1/4	cup Bisquick Heart Smart® mix
1/2	cup fat-free (skim) milk
1/2	cup fat-free egg product or 2 eggs
1/4	teaspoon salt

Dash pepper

1 Heat oven to 400°F. Lightly spray 9x5-inch (1-1/2-quart) glass loaf dish with cooking spray. Sprinkle zucchini, tomato, onion and cheese in dish.

2 In medium bowl, stir remaining ingredients until blended. Pour over vegetables and cheese.

3 Bake 30 to 35 minutes or until knife inserted in center comes out clean. Cool 5 minutes before serving.

High Altitude (3500-6500 ft): Increase Bisquick mix to 1/3 cup.

Nutritional Info: 1 Serving: Calories 210 (Calories from Fat 50); Total Fat 6g (Saturated Fat 3g, Trans Fat 0g); Cholesterol 15mg; Sodium 830mg; Total Carbohydrate 21g (Dietary Fiber 2g, Sugars 9g); Protein 17g. % Daily Value: Vitamin A 35%; Vitamin C 15%; Calcium 35%; Iron 10%. Exchanges: 1/2 Starch, 1/2 Other Carbohydrate, 1 Vegetable, 2 Lean Meat. Carbohydrate Choices: 1-1/2.

Betty's Kitchen Tips

Purchasing: Fat-free egg products are sold in the refrigerator and freezer sections of your grocery store.

Success Hint: Tomatoes and zucchini in your garden? Here's a great recipe for including them.

curried turkey stir-fry

Prep Time: 30 Minutes
Start to Finish: 30 Minutes
Servings: 4 (1-1/4 cups stir-fry and 3/4 cup rice each)

QUICK   LOW FAT

1-3/4   cups uncooked instant brown rice
2   teaspoons canola oil
1   lb turkey breast tenderloins, cut into 2x1-inch strips
1   medium red bell pepper, cut into thin strips
2   cups small broccoli florets

1-1/4   cups reduced-sodium chicken broth
4   teaspoons cornstarch
4   teaspoons curry powder
1/2   teaspoon ground ginger
1/4   teaspoon salt

1 Cook rice as directed on package, omitting butter and salt.

2 Meanwhile, in 12-inch nonstick skillet, heat oil over medium-high heat. Add turkey; cook 5 to 8 minutes, stirring frequently, until browned. Stir in bell pepper and broccoli. Cook 2 minutes.

3 In small bowl, stir together remaining ingredients. Stir into turkey and vegetables. Heat to boiling; reduce heat. Cover and cook 2 to 3 minutes or until vegetables are crisp-tender and turkey is no longer pink in center. Serve over brown rice.

High Altitude (3500-6500 ft): No change.

Nutritional Info: 1 Serving: Calories 360 (Calories from Fat 45); Total Fat 5g (Saturated Fat 0.5g, Trans Fat 0g); Cholesterol 75mg; Sodium 400mg; Total Carbohydrate 46g (Dietary Fiber 4g, Sugars 2g); Protein 33g. % Daily Value: Vitamin A 25%; Vitamin C 80%; Calcium 6%; Iron 15%. Exchanges: 2-1/2 Starch, 1 Vegetable, 3 Very Lean Meat, 1/2 Fat. Carbohydrate Choices: 3.

Betty's Kitchen Tip

• Because it's quick, instant rice is a great choice for busy cooks. When you have the time, make this stir-fry with regular brown rice. Brown rice cooks in 45 minutes and has a chewy, nutty texture. You can cook it ahead of time and refrigerate for up to three days or freeze for up to three months. Just heat and eat.

fire roasted tomato-shrimp veracruz with couscous

Prep Time: 15 Minutes
Start to Finish: 15 Minutes
Servings: 4

EASY   QUICK   LOW FAT

- 1   tablespoon olive or canola oil
- 1   lb uncooked deveined peeled medium shrimp, thawed if frozen, tail shells removed
- 4   medium green onions, sliced (1/4 cup)
- 1   medium fresh jalapeño or serrano chile, seeded, finely chopped
- 1   teaspoon grated orange peel
- 1   teaspoon chopped fresh or 1/2 teaspoon dried thyme leaves
- 1   can (14.5 oz) Muir Glen® organic fire roasted diced tomatoes, undrained
- 1-1/2   cups uncooked whole wheat couscous

1 In 12-inch skillet, heat oil over medium-high heat. Cook shrimp, green onions, chile, orange peel and thyme in oil 1 minute, stirring frequently.

2 Stir in tomatoes. Heat to boiling. Reduce heat; simmer uncovered about 5 minutes, stirring occasionally, until shrimp are pink and sauce is slightly thickened.

3 Meanwhile, make couscous as directed on package, omitting butter and salt. Serve shrimp mixture over couscous.

High Altitude (3500-6500 ft): No change.

Nutritional Info: 1 Serving: Calories 390 (Calories from Fat 50); Total Fat 5g (Saturated Fat 0.5g, Trans Fat 0g); Cholesterol 160mg; Sodium 420mg; Total Carbohydrate 58g (Dietary Fiber 7g, Sugars 4g); Protein 27g. % Daily Value: Vitamin A 20%; Vitamin C 20%; Calcium 8%; Iron 30%. Exchanges: 2-1/2 Starch, 1 Other Carbohydrate, 1 Vegetable, 2-1/2 Very Lean Meat, 1/2 Fat. Carbohydrate Choices: 4.

Betty's Kitchen Tip

• Great news! Now you can buy whole wheat couscous, which contains all parts of the grain, making it a wonderful whole-grain accompaniment to any main dish.

broccoli, ham and cheese foldovers

Prep Time: 25 Minutes
Start to Finish: 55 Minutes
Servings: 6 foldovers

- -

4-1/2   cups Original Bisquick® mix
1   cup boiling water
1   box (10 oz) Green Giant® frozen broccoli & cheese flavored sauce
2   cups finely diced cooked ham
1/2   cup cheese-flavored French-fried onions

1/2   cup shredded Cheddar cheese (2 oz)
1   egg
1   tablespoon water
1   tablespoon grated Parmesan cheese, if desired

- -

1 Heat oven to 375°F. Spray 2 cookie sheets with cooking spray. In large bowl, stir Bisquick mix and boiling water until dough forms. Place dough on surface sprinkled with Bisquick mix. Knead 20 times; divide dough into 6 balls. Return balls to bowl; cover with plastic wrap.

2 Cook broccoli & cheese sauce as directed on box; empty into medium bowl. Stir in ham, onions and Cheddar cheese; set aside. In small bowl, beat egg and water with fork or wire whisk until blended; set aside.

3 Pat or roll 1 ball of dough into 7-inch circle. Spoon about 1/2 cup ham mixture onto half of the circle; moisten edge of circle with water. Fold other half of dough circle over filling; press edge with fork to seal. Place on cookie sheet. Repeat to use up remaining dough and filling.

4 Brush tops of foldovers with egg mixture; sprinkle each with 1/2 teaspoon Parmesan cheese. Cut 3 slits in top of each for steam to escape. Bake 25 to 30 minutes or until golden brown.

High Altitude (3500-6500 ft): No change.

Nutritional Info: 1 Foldover: Calories 540 (Calories from Fat 200); Total Fat 23g (Saturated Fat 8g, Trans Fat 4g); Cholesterol 70mg; Sodium 2080mg; Total Carbohydrate 64g (Dietary Fiber 3g, Sugars 3g); Protein 21g. % Daily Value: Vitamin A 4%; Vitamin C 10%; Calcium 15%; Iron 20%. Exchanges: 3 Starch, 1 Other Carbohydrate, 1-1/2 Medium-Fat Meat, 3 Fat. Carbohydrate Choices: 4.

Betty's Kitchen Tip

- These foldovers can be served warm or cold. To reheat baked foldovers that have been frozen, microwave uncovered on High 2 to 3 minutes; let stand 1 minute. To bake, heat oven to 350°F; bake on cookie sheet 35 to 40 minutes.

impossibly easy taco pie

Prep Time: 15 Minutes
Start to Finish: 50 Minutes
Servings: 6

EASY

- 1 lb ground turkey breast
- 1 medium onion, chopped (1/2 cup)
- 1 package (1 oz) Old El Paso® taco seasoning mix
- 1 can (4.5 oz) Old El Paso® chopped green chiles, undrained
- 1/2 cup Original Bisquick® mix
- 1 cup milk
- 2 eggs
- 1/2 cup shredded Colby-Monterey Jack cheese blend (2 oz)
- 1 medium tomato, chopped (3/4 cup)
- 1-1/2 cups shredded lettuce
- 2 medium green onions, sliced (2 tablespoons), if desired

1 Heat oven to 400°F. Spray 9-inch glass pie plate with cooking spray. In 10-inch skillet, cook turkey and onion over medium-high heat, stirring occasionally, until turkey is no longer pink. Sprinkle taco seasoning mix over turkey mixture; mix well. Spread in pie plate. Top evenly with chiles.

2 In medium bowl, stir Bisquick mix, milk and eggs with wire whisk or fork until blended. Pour into pie plate.

3 Bake 25 minutes. Top with cheese and tomato. Bake 2 to 3 minutes longer or until cheese is melted. Let stand 5 minutes before serving. Sprinkle with lettuce and onions.

High Altitude (3500-6500 ft): No change.

Nutritional Info: 1 Serving: Calories 250 (Calories from Fat 100); Total Fat 11g (Saturated Fat 4.5g, Trans Fat 0.5g); Cholesterol 135mg; Sodium 880mg; Total Carbohydrate 15g (Dietary Fiber 1g, Sugars 6g); Protein 23g. % Daily Value: Vitamin A 15%; Vitamin C 20%; Calcium 15%; Iron 10%. Exchanges: 1/2 Starch, 1/2 Other Carbohydrate, 3 Lean Meat, 1/2 Fat. Carbohydrate Choices: 1.

Betty's Kitchen Tips

Variation: To make Impossibly Easy Beef Taco Pie, substitute 1 lb lean (at least 80%) ground beef for the turkey. Cook beef until thoroughly cooked. Drain and return to skillet. Continue as directed in Step 1.

Time-Saver: Keep frozen chopped onions on hand in the freezer to speed up weeknight meal preparation.

turkey and green chile stuffing casserole

Prep Time: 25 Minutes
Start to Finish: 1 Hour 40 Minutes
Servings: 6

LOW FAT

- 2 tablespoons butter or margarine
- 1 medium onion, chopped (1/2 cup)
- 1 small red bell pepper, chopped (1/2 cup)
- 4 cups seasoned cornbread stuffing mix
- 1 cup Green Giant® Niblets® frozen whole kernel corn

- 1 can (4.5 oz) Old El Paso® chopped green chiles, undrained
- 1-1/2 cups water
- 2 turkey breast tenderloins (about 3/4 lb each)
- 1/2 teaspoon chili powder
- 1/2 teaspoon peppered seasoned salt

1 Heat oven to 350°F. Spray 11x7-inch (2-quart) glass baking dish with cooking spray. In 12-inch nonstick skillet, melt butter over medium-high heat. Cook onion and bell pepper in butter 2 to 3 minutes, stirring frequently, until tender. Stir in stuffing mix, corn, chiles and water. Spread stuffing mixture in baking dish.

2 Sprinkle both sides of turkey tenderloins with chili powder and peppered seasoned salt. Place on stuffing, pressing into stuffing mixture slightly. Spray sheet of foil with cooking spray. Cover baking dish with foil, sprayed side down.

3 Bake 1 hour. Uncover and bake 10 to 15 minutes longer or until juice of turkey is no longer pink when centers of thickest pieces are cut.

High Altitude (3500-6500 ft): No changes.

Nutritional Info: 1 Serving: Calories 340 (Calories from Fat 60); Total Fat 7g (Saturated Fat 3g, Trans Fat 0g); Cholesterol 85mg; Sodium 940mg; Total Carbohydrate 38g (Dietary Fiber 3g, Sugars 5g); Protein 31g. % Daily Value: Vitamin A 20%; Vitamin C 25%; Calcium 6%; Iron 20%. Exchanges: 2 Starch, 1/2 Other Carbohydrate, 3-1/2 Very Lean Meat, 1/2 Fat. Carbohydrate Choices: 2-1/2.

Betty's Kitchen Tip

- You can reduce or eliminate the peppered seasoned salt in this recipe if you are sensitive to sodium.

old-fashioned chicken pie

Prep Time: 15 Minutes
Start to Finish: 35 Minutes
Servings: 4

EASY

- 2 cups cubed cooked chicken
- 2 cups Green Giant® frozen mixed vegetables
- 1 jar (12 oz) chicken gravy
- 1/4 teaspoon dried thyme leaves
- 1 cup Original Bisquick® mix
- 1/4 cup milk

1 Heat oven to 400°F. Spray 1-1/2-quart round casserole with cooking spray. In 2-quart saucepan, stir chicken, vegetables, gravy and thyme until well mixed. Cook over medium heat 6 to 8 minutes, stirring occasionally, until vegetables are thawed and mixture is hot and begins to bubble. Pour into casserole.

2 In medium bowl, stir Bisquick mix and milk until soft dough forms; beat vigorously 30 seconds. Place dough on surface sprinkled with Bisquick mix; roll in Bisquick mix to coat. Press or roll dough into 7-1/2-inch round (or large enough round to cover top of 1-1/2-quart casserole).

3 Place dough round on chicken mixture in casserole. Cut slits in dough to allow steam to escape.

4 Bake 15 to 20 minutes or until golden brown.

High Altitude (3500-6500 ft): No change.

Nutritional Info: 1 Serving: Calories 380 (Calories from Fat 130); Total Fat 14g (Saturated Fat 4g, Trans Fat 1.5g); Cholesterol 65mg; Sodium 950mg; Total Carbohydrate 37g (Dietary Fiber 5g, Sugars 5g); Protein 26g. % Daily Value: Vitamin A 80%; Vitamin C 2%; Calcium 10%; Iron 15%. Exchanges: 1-1/2 Starch, 1/2 Other Carbohydrate, 1 Vegetable, 3 Lean Meat, 1 Fat. Carbohydrate Choices: 2-1/2.

Betty's Kitchen Tips

Variation: To make Old-Fashioned Turkey Pie, substitute 2 cups cubed cooked turkey for the chicken.

Serve-With: Serve with a fresh green salad and tall glasses of cold milk.

Easy Weeknight Entrees **95**

stir-fried pork with mushrooms and broccoli

Prep Time: 25 Minutes
Start to Finish: 25 Minutes
Servings: 4 (1-1/2 cups stir-fry and 1 cup rice each)

QUICK

1-1/2	cups uncooked instant brown rice
1	tablespoon cornstarch
1/4	cup reduced-sodium teriyaki marinade (from 12-oz bottle)
1/2	cup water
1/2	teaspoon ground ginger
3	teaspoons canola oil
3/4	lb boneless pork loin, trimmed of fat, cut into 2-inch strips

2	cups fresh broccoli florets
1	small onion, cut into thin wedges
1	package (8 oz) sliced fresh mushrooms (3 cups)
1	medium red, yellow or orange bell pepper, cut into 1-inch pieces
2	cloves garlic, finely chopped

1 Cook rice as directed on package, omitting butter and salt. Meanwhile, place cornstarch in small bowl or cup. Gradually stir in teriyaki marinade, water and ginger.

2 In 12-inch nonstick skillet or wok, heat 2 teaspoons of the oil over medium-high heat. Add pork; cook and stir 4 to 5 minutes or until no longer pink in center. Remove pork from skillet; keep warm.

3 Add remaining 1 teaspoon oil to skillet. Add broccoli, onion, mushrooms, bell pepper and garlic; cook and stir 4 to 5 minutes or until vegetables are crisp-tender.

4 Stir cornstarch mixture into broccoli mixture. Add pork; cook and stir until sauce is thickened. Serve over rice.

High Altitude (3500-6500 ft): Add up to 1/4 cup water if sauce gets too thick.

Nutritional Info: 1 Serving: Calories 310 (Calories from Fat 100); Total Fat 11g (Saturated Fat 2.5g, Trans Fat 0g); Cholesterol 55mg; Sodium 380mg; Total Carbohydrate 30g (Dietary Fiber 3g, Sugars 7g); Protein 24g. % Daily Value: Vitamin A 25%; Vitamin C 80%; Calcium 4%; Iron 8%. Exchanges: 1 Starch, 1/2 Other Carbohydrate, 1-1/2 Vegetable, 2-1/2 Lean Meat, 1/2 Fat. Carbohydrate Choices: 2.

Betty's Kitchen Tips

Serve-With: Add a simple all-green salad to this stir-fry dinner. Mix salad greens, thinly sliced cucumber, sliced green onions and chives.

Variation: To make this delicious dish even more colorful, use 1/2 red pepper and 1/2 yellow pepper.

rotisserie turkey à la king

Prep Time: 25 Minutes
Start to Finish: 25 Minutes
Servings: 6

QUICK

2-1/2 cups Original Bisquick® mix	1/2 cup chopped red bell pepper
2 tablespoons grated Parmesan cheese	1 deli rotisserie turkey breast half (20 oz), cubed, (about 3-1/2 cups)
1/4 teaspoon dried thyme leaves	
3-2/3 cups milk	1 cup Green Giant® frozen sweet peas
1 tablespoon butter or margarine	1/2 teaspoon salt
1 small clove garlic, finely chopped	1/4 teaspoon pepper
1 cup sliced fresh mushrooms (3 oz)	

1 Heat oven to 425°F. Spray cookie sheet with cooking spray. In medium bowl, stir 2-1/4 cups of the Bisquick mix, the Parmesan cheese, thyme and 2/3 cup of the milk until dough forms. Drop dough by 6 large spoonfuls onto cookie sheet.

2 Bake 8 to 10 minutes or until golden brown.

3 Meanwhile, in 12-inch nonstick skillet, melt butter over medium-high heat. Add garlic, mushrooms and bell pepper. Cook 3 to 4 minutes, stirring occasionally, until vegetables are crisp-tender. Stir in remaining 1/4 cup Bisquick mix until blended. Stir in turkey, peas, salt, pepper and remaining 3 cups milk. Cook over medium-high heat, stirring constantly, until mixture bubbles and thickens.

4 Split biscuits, and place bottoms on individual serving plates. Spoon 1/2 cup turkey mixture over each biscuit bottom. Top with biscuit tops and remaining turkey mixture.

High Altitude (3500-6500 ft): No change.

Nutritional Info: 1 Servings: Calories 430 (Calories from Fat 120); Total Fat 13g (Saturated Fat 6g, Trans Fat 2g); Cholesterol 85mg; Sodium 1310mg; Total Carbohydrate 44g (Dietary Fiber 2g, Sugars 11g); Protein 35g. % Daily Value: Vitamin A 25%; Vitamin C 15%; Calcium 25%; Iron 20%. Exchanges: 2 Starch, 1/2 Other Carbohydrate, 1 Vegetable, 4 Lean Meat. Carbohydrate Choices: 3.

Betty's Kitchen Tip

• For a richer sauce, use 1 cup half-and-half and 2-2/3 cups milk. Fat-free half-and-half will give you the same great richness as regular but with less fat and fewer calories.

penne with spicy sauce

Prep Time: 30 Minutes
Start to Finish: 30 Minutes
Servings: 6

QUICK

- 1 package (16 oz) whole wheat penne pasta
- 1 can (28 oz) Muir Glen® organic fire roasted whole peeled plum tomatoes, undrained
- 2 tablespoons olive or canola oil
- 2 cloves garlic, finely chopped
- 1/2 to 1 teaspoon crushed red pepper flakes
- 2 tablespoons chopped fresh parsley
- 1 tablespoon tomato paste
- 1/2 cup freshly grated or shredded Parmesan cheese (2 oz)

1 Cook and drain pasta as directed on package.

2 Meanwhile, in food processor or blender, place tomatoes with juice. Cover and process until coarsely chopped; set aside.

3 In 12-inch skillet, heat oil over medium-high heat. Cook garlic, red pepper and parsley in oil about 5 minutes, stirring frequently, until garlic just begins to turn golden. Stir in chopped tomatoes and tomato paste. Heat to boiling; reduce heat. Cover and simmer about 10 minutes, stirring occasionally, until slightly thickened.

4 Add pasta and 1/4 cup of the cheese to tomato mixture. Cook about 3 minutes, tossing gently, until pasta is evenly coated. Sprinkle with remaining 1/4 cup cheese.

High Altitude (3500-6500 ft): No change.

Nutritional Info: 1 Serving: Calories 370 (Calories from Fat 70); Total Fat 8g (Saturated Fat 2.5g, Trans Fat 0g); Cholesterol 5mg; Sodium 600mg; Total Carbohydrate 59g (Dietary Fiber 7g, Sugars 5g); Protein 15g. % Daily Value: Vitamin A 8%; Vitamin C 10%; Calcium 20%; Iron 20%. Exchanges: 4 Starch, 1 Fat. Carbohydrate Choices: 4.

Betty's Kitchen Tips

Serve-With: This is a great meatless meal. Tame the fiery pepper taste with steamed broccoli.

Variation: Add 2 tablespoons chopped fresh basil and 1 teaspoon chopped fresh oregano with the parsley to enhance the herb flavor.

easy lasagna squares

Prep Time: 20 Minutes
Start to Finish: 1 Hour 5 Minutes
Servings: 6

1	lb lean (at least 80%) ground beef
1/2	teaspoon dried oregano leaves
1/2	teaspoon dried basil leaves
1	can (6 oz) tomato paste
2	cups shredded mozzarella cheese (8 oz)
1/2	cup small-curd cottage cheese

1/4	cup shredded Parmesan cheese (1 oz)
2/3	cup Original Bisquick® mix
1	cup milk
2	eggs

Cherry tomatoes, quartered, if desired
Fresh basil leaves, if desired

1 Heat oven to 400°F. In 10-inch skillet, cook beef over medium-high heat 5 to 7 minutes, stirring occasionally, until thoroughly cooked; drain. Stir in oregano, basil, tomato paste and 1/2 cup of the mozzarella cheese.

2 Spray 8-inch square (2-quart) glass baking dish with cooking spray. Layer cottage cheese and Parmesan cheese in baking dish. Spoon beef mixture evenly over top of cheese.

3 In medium bowl, stir Bisquick mix, milk and eggs with wire whisk or fork until blended. Pour into dish.

4 Bake 30 to 35 minutes or until knife inserted in center comes out clean.

5 Sprinkle remaining 1-1/2 cups mozzarella cheese over top. Bake 2 to 3 minutes longer or until cheese is melted. Let stand 5 minutes before serving. Garnish with tomatoes and basil leaves.

High Altitude (3500-6500 ft): Bake 33 to 38 minutes.

Nutritional Info: 1 Serving: Calories 400 (Calories from Fat 190); Total Fat 21g (Saturated Fat 10g, Trans Fat 1.5g); Cholesterol 145mg; Sodium 810mg; Total Carbohydrate 19g (Dietary Fiber 1g, Sugars 7g); Protein 33g. % Daily Value: Vitamin A 15%; Vitamin C 6%; Calcium 45%; Iron 15%. Exchanges: 1 Starch, 1/2 Other Carbohydrate, 4 Medium-Fat Meat. Carbohydrate Choices: 1.

Betty's Kitchen Tips

Purchasing: Tomato paste is available in tubes and cans. Look for it in the supermarket next to the canned tomato products.

Substitution: As with most recipes that call for ground beef, you can use ground turkey instead.

salsa chicken fiesta

Prep Time: 15 Minutes
Start to Finish: 45 Minutes
Servings: 8

EASY

● ●

1-1/3	cups Original Bisquick® mix
1/4	cup water
2	eggs
2-1/2	cups shredded Cheddar cheese (10 oz)
6	large boneless skinless chicken breasts, cut into 1/2-inch pieces
1	jar (16 oz) Old El Paso® Thick 'n Chunky salsa

Sour cream, if desired

Ground red pepper (cayenne), if desired

● ●

1 Heat oven to 400°F. Spray 13x9-inch baking dish with cooking spray. In medium bowl, stir Bisquick mix, water and eggs; spread in pan. Sprinkle with 2 cups of the cheese.

2 In 12-inch nonstick skillet, cook chicken over medium-high heat, stirring frequently, until no longer pink; drain. Stir in salsa; heat until hot. Spoon over batter in pan to within 1/2 inch of edges.

3 Bake about 25 to 30 minutes or until edges are dark golden brown. Sprinkle with remaining 1/2 cup cheese. Bake about 2 minutes longer or until cheese is melted; loosen from sides of pan. Top each serving with a dollop of sour cream; sprinkle with ground red pepper.

High Altitude (3500-6500 ft): No change.

Nutritional Info: 1 Serving: Calories 390 (Calories from Fat 170); Total Fat 19g (Saturated Fat 10g, Trans Fat 1g); Cholesterol 155mg; Sodium 970mg; Total Carbohydrate 19g (Dietary Fiber 0g, Sugars 3g); Protein 34g. % Daily Value: Vitamin A 15%; Vitamin C 0%; Calcium 20%; Iron 10%. Exchanges: 1 Starch, 1/2 Other Carbohydrate, 4 Lean Meat, 1-1/2 Fat. Carbohydrate Choices: 1.

Betty's Kitchen Tips

Time-Saver: To get dinner on the table quicker, use 6 cups chopped deli chicken for the chicken breast, and heat it with the salsa.

Serve-With: Serve with bowls of shredded lettuce, chopped tomatoes and sour cream.

turkey-cornbread tostadas

Prep Time: 25 Minutes
Start to Finish: 25 Minutes
Servings: 4

QUICK

1-1/4 cups Original Bisquick® mix
1/2 cup cornmeal
1/2 cup milk
1 lb lean ground turkey
1 package (1 oz) Old El Paso® 40% less sodium taco seasoning mix

2/3 cup water
1/2 cup finely shredded Mexican cheese blend (2 oz)
1 cup shredded lettuce
1/4 cup sour cream
1/4 cup Old El Paso® taco sauce

1 Heat oven to 425°F. Spray cookie sheet with cooking spray. In medium bowl, stir Bisquick mix, cornmeal and milk until soft dough forms. Drop dough into 4 mounds on cookie sheet. Pat each mound into 5-inch round, using fingers coated in Bisquick mix; pinch edges to form 1/4-inch rim. Prick bottoms with fork.

2 Bake 8 to 10 minutes or until golden brown. Place on individual serving plates.

3 Meanwhile, in 10-inch nonstick skillet, cook turkey over medium-high heat 5 to 7 minutes, stirring occasionally, until no longer pink. Stir in taco seasoning mix and water. Cook uncovered about 5 minutes, stirring occasionally, until thick and bubbly. Spoon mixture onto baked rounds. Top with cheese, lettuce, sour cream and taco sauce.

High Altitude (3500-6500 ft): Bake 10 to 12 minutes.

Nutritional Info: 1 Serving: Calories 510 (Calories from Fat 170); Total Fat 19g (Saturated Fat 8g, Trans Fat 2g); Cholesterol 100mg; Sodium 1250mg; Total Carbohydrate 50g (Dietary Fiber 2g, Sugars 4g); Protein 33g. % Daily Value: Vitamin A 15%; Vitamin C 0%; Calcium 20%; Iron 20%. Exchanges: 2-1/2 Starch, 1 Other Carbohydrate, 3-1/2 Lean Meat, 1-1/2 Fat. Carbohydrate Choices: 3.

Betty's Kitchen Tips

Did You Know? Cornmeal is simply dried and ground corn. Available in fine, medium and coarse grinds, cornmeal can be white, yellow or even blue. Most cornbreads and muffins are made with medium or coarse meal.

Serve-With: Serve with your favorite salsa to kick the flavor up a notch.

mexican macaroni and cheese

Prep Time: 25 Minutes
Start to Finish: 25 Minutes
Servings: 4

QUICK LOW FAT

- 2 cups uncooked radiatore (nugget) pasta (6 oz)
- 1/2 cup shredded reduced-fat Colby-Monterey Jack cheese blend (2 oz)
- 1/4 cup sliced ripe olives
- 1/2 cup fat-free (skim) milk
- 1 small red bell pepper, chopped (1/2 cup)
- 1 can (4.5 oz) Old El Paso® chopped green chiles, drained

Chopped fresh cilantro, if desired

1 Cook and drain pasta as directed on package.

2 Stir remaining ingredients except cilantro into pasta. Cook over low heat about 5 minutes, stirring occasionally, until cheese is melted and sauce is hot. Sprinkle with cilantro.

High Altitude (3500-6500 ft): No change.

Nutritional Info: 1 Serving: Calories 260 (Calories from Fat 45); Total Fat 5g (Saturated Fat 2g, Trans Fat 0g); Cholesterol 10mg; Sodium 850mg; Total Carbohydrate 42g (Dietary Fiber 3g, Sugars 4g); Protein 12g. % Daily Value: Vitamin A 25%; Vitamin C 30%; Calcium 15%; Iron 15%. Exchanges: 2-1/2 Starch, 1/2 High-Fat Meat. Carbohydrate Choices: 3.

Betty's Kitchen Tips

Special Touch: Top this Mexican mac and cheese with a little salsa, sliced olives and a dollop of reduced-fat sour cream.

Substitution: Radiatore is a really fun pasta that kids love, but any medium-size pasta shape, such as rotini, penne or wagon wheel, also works great.

sweet-and-sour chicken stir-fry

Prep Time: 30 Minutes
Start to Finish: 30 Minutes
Servings: 6 (1-1/4 cups each)

QUICK

1 cup Original Bisquick® mix	1 medium green bell pepper, cut into strips (1 cup)
1/2 teaspoon pepper	1 small onion, thinly sliced, separated into rings (1/3 cup)
2 eggs	1 can (20 oz) pineapple chunks, drained
1 lb boneless skinless chicken breasts, cut into cubes	1/2 cup sweet-and-sour sauce
1/4 cup vegetable oil	Cooked rice, if desired
3 medium carrots, cut diagonally into 1/4-inch slices (1-1/2 cups)	

1 In large resealable food-storage plastic bag, mix Bisquick mix and pepper.

2 In medium bowl, beat eggs slightly. Stir in chicken until coated. Using slotted spoon, remove chicken from eggs; place in bag with Bisquick mix. Seal bag; shake bag until chicken is coated.

3 In 12-inch skillet, heat 1 tablespoon of the oil over medium-high heat. Add carrots; cook 2 minutes, stirring frequently. Add bell pepper and onion; cook 2 minutes longer, stirring frequently. Remove from skillet.

4 In same skillet, heat remaining 3 tablespoons oil. Add chicken; cook, stirring frequently, until golden brown on outside and no longer pink in center. Add vegetables; cook about 2 minutes, stirring frequently, until hot. Stir in pineapple and sweet-and-sour sauce; cook until hot. Serve over cooked rice.

High Altitude (3500-6500 ft): No change.

Nutritional Info: 1 Serving: Calories 380 (Calories from Fat 150); Total Fat 17g (Saturated Fat 3.5g, Trans Fat 1g); Cholesterol 115mg; Sodium 410mg; Total Carbohydrate 35g (Dietary Fiber 3g, Sugars 19g); Protein 21g. % Daily Value: Vitamin A 110%; Vitamin C 20%; Calcium 6%; Iron 10%. Exchanges: 1/2 Starch, 1-1/2 Other Carbohydrate, 1 Vegetable, 2-1/2 Lean Meat, 2 Fat. Carbohydrate Choices: 2.

Betty's Kitchen Tips

Substitution: Red or yellow bell peppers may be substituted for the green.

Variation: Zucchini or broccoli work well in stir-fries, too.

latin-style flank steak with spicy parsley pesto

Prep Time: 20 Minutes
Start to Finish: 20 Minutes
Servings: 4

QUICK LOW FAT

1	beef flank steak (1 lb)
1/4	teaspoon pepper
1/4	teaspoon salt
1/2	cup chopped fresh Italian (flat-leaf) or curly-leaf parsley
2	teaspoons red wine vinegar
5	or 6 drops red pepper sauce
1/8	teaspoon ground cumin

1 Place oven rack in second position from the top. Set oven control to broil.

2 On rack in broiler pan, place beef. Sprinkle with pepper and half of the salt. Broil with top 4 to 6 inches from heat 10 to 12 minutes, turning once, until desired doneness.

3 In small bowl, mix parsley, vinegar, pepper sauce, cumin and remaining half of the salt.

4 Cut beef across grain into thin strips. Serve beef with parsley pesto.

High Altitude (3500-6500 ft): No change.

Nutritional Info: 1 Serving: Calories 180 (Calories from Fat 70); Total Fat 8g (Saturated Fat 3g, Trans Fat 0g); Cholesterol 50mg; Sodium 190mg; Total Carbohydrate 0g (Dietary Fiber 0g, Sugars 0g); Protein 26g. % Daily Value: Vitamin A 15%; Vitamin C 8%; Calcium 0%; Iron 15%. Exchanges: 3-1/2 Lean Meat. Carbohydrate Choices: 0.

Betty's Kitchen Tips

Time-Saver: For easy cleanup, line the broiler pan with foil.

Serve-With: Mixed vegetables are a good accompaniment to the steak, or choose your favorite roasted veggies.

chicken cordon bleu pizza

Prep Time: 10 Minutes
Start to Finish: 35 Minutes
Servings: 8

EASY

- 1-1/2 cups Original Bisquick® mix
- 2 tablespoons grated Parmesan cheese
- 1/3 cup hot water
- 1/2 cup Alfredo pasta sauce (from 16-oz jar)

- 2 cups chopped cooked chicken
- 1/2 cup chopped cooked ham
- 1-1/2 cups finely shredded Swiss cheese (6 oz)
- 3 medium green onions, sliced (3 tablespoons)

1 Heat oven to 425°F. Spray 12-inch pizza pan or cookie sheet with cooking spray. In medium bowl, stir Bisquick mix, Parmesan cheese and hot water until soft dough forms. Press dough in pizza pan, using fingers dipped in Bisquick mix; pinch edge to form 1/2-inch rim.

2 Bake 7 to 8 minutes or until light golden brown.

3 Spread Alfredo sauce over partially baked crust. Top with chicken, ham, Swiss cheese and onions.

4 Bake 10 to 15 minutes longer or until crust is golden brown and cheese is melted.

High Altitude (3500-6500 ft): No change.

Nutritional Info: 1 Serving: Calories 310 (Calories from Fat 150); Total Fat 17g (Saturated Fat 9g, Trans Fat 1.5g); Cholesterol 70mg; Sodium 560mg; Total Carbohydrate 17g (Dietary Fiber 0g, Sugars 1g); Protein 21g. % Daily Value: Vitamin A 8%; Vitamin C 0%; Calcium 25%; Iron 6%. Exchanges: 1 Starch, 2-1/2 Medium-Fat Meat, 1 Fat. Carbohydrate Choices: 1

Betty's Kitchen Tips

Did You Know? Cordon bleu is a French dish combining chicken or veal with ham or prosciutto and Swiss or Gruyère cheese. In this recipe, those flavors are simplified to produce a fantastic-tasting pizza.

Success Hint: Be sure to use hot water to make the pizza crust. It helps keep the crust from rising too high during baking and keeps it chewy and crisp.

skillet chicken parmesan

Prep Time: 25 Minutes
Start to Finish: 25 Minutes
Servings: 4

QUICK

- 3/4 cup Original Bisquick® mix
- 1 teaspoon Italian seasoning
- 2 tablespoons grated Parmesan cheese
- 1 egg
- 4 boneless skinless chicken breasts (4 oz each)
- 3 tablespoons olive or vegetable oil
- 2 cups tomato pasta sauce (from 26-oz jar)
- 1 cup shredded Italian cheese blend (4 oz)

1. In shallow dish or pie plate, mix Bisquick mix, Italian seasoning and Parmesan cheese. In another shallow dish or pie plate, beat egg. Coat chicken with Bisquick mixture, then dip into egg, and coat again with Bisquick mixture.

2. In 12-inch nonstick skillet, heat oil over medium heat. Add chicken; cook 4 to 6 minutes, turning once, until golden brown. Cover; cook 8 to 10 minutes longer, turning once, until juice of chicken is clear when center of thickest part is cut (170°F). Remove from skillet to plate.

3. Add pasta sauce to skillet. Place chicken on top of sauce. Sprinkle with Italian cheese blend. Cover; cook 2 to 3 minutes or until bubbly and cheese is melted.

High Altitude (3500-6500 ft): No change.

Nutritional Info: 1 Serving: Calories 580 (Calories from Fat 280); Total Fat 31g (Saturated Fat 10g, Trans Fat 1g); Cholesterol 145mg; Sodium 1270mg; Total Carbohydrate 39g (Dietary Fiber 2g, Sugars 14g); Protein 39g. % Daily Value: Vitamin A 15%; Vitamin C 8%; Calcium 35%; Iron 20%. Exchanges: 1 Starch, 1-1/2 Other Carbohydrate, 5 Lean Meat, 3 Fat. Carbohydrate Choices: 2-1/2.

Betty's Kitchen Tips

Serve-With: Serve this easy chicken dish with cooked spaghetti, broccoli and a tossed salad. Your family will love it.

Substitution: One cup mozzarella cheese may be used instead of the Italian cheese blend.

deep-dish taco squares

Prep Time: 25 Minutes
Start to Finish: 55 Minutes
Servings: 6

1/2 lb lean (at least 80%) ground beef

1/4 cup chopped onion

2 tablespoons Old El Paso® taco seasoning mix (from 1-oz package)

1 cup Original Bisquick® mix

1/4 cup cold water

1/2 cup sour cream

1/3 cup mayonnaise or salad dressing

1/2 cup shredded sharp Cheddar cheese (2 oz)

1 medium tomato, chopped (3/4 cup)

1 can (4.5 oz) Old El Paso® chopped green chiles

1 Heat oven to 375°F. Spray 8-inch square (2-quart) glass baking dish with cooking spray. In 8-inch skillet, cook beef and onion over medium-high heat 5 to 7 minutes, stirring occasionally, until thoroughly cooked; drain. Stir in taco seasoning mix until blended.

2 In medium bowl, stir Bisquick mix and water until soft dough forms. Using fingers dipped in Bisquick mix, pat dough in bottom and 1/2 inch up sides of baking dish.

3 In same bowl, mix sour cream, mayonnaise and cheese until blended.

4 Layer beef mixture, tomato and chiles over dough; spoon sour cream mixture over top.

5 Bake 25 to 30 minutes or until edges of dough are light golden brown.

High Altitude (3500-6500 ft): Bake 28 to 33 minutes.

Nutritional Info: 1 Serving: Calories 330 (Calories from Fat 210); Total Fat 23g (Saturated Fat 8g, Trans Fat 1.5g); Cholesterol 50mg; Sodium 820mg; Total Carbohydrate 18g (Dietary Fiber 1g, Sugars 4g); Protein 11g. % Daily Value: Vitamin A 10%; Vitamin C 15%; Calcium 10%; Iron 10%. Exchanges: 1 Starch, 1 Medium-Fat Meat, 3-1/2 Fat. Carbohydrate Choices: 1.

Betty's Kitchen Tips

Did You Know? This "one-pan" taco combines all the great ingredients of tacos, but is a snap to make and less messy to eat than regular tacos.

Time-Saver: Cut down on prep time by using frozen chopped onions.

pork fajita wraps

Prep Time: 20 Minutes
Start to Finish: 35 Minutes
Servings: 4

LOW FAT

1/4	cup lime juice
1-1/2	teaspoons ground cumin
3/4	teaspoon salt
4	cloves garlic, finely chopped
1/2	lb pork tenderloin, cut into very thin slices
1	large onion, thinly sliced
3	medium bell peppers, thinly sliced
4	flour tortillas (8 inch)

1 In shallow glass or plastic dish, mix lime juice, cumin, salt and garlic. Stir in pork. Cover; refrigerate, stirring occasionally, at least 15 minutes but no longer than 24 hours.

2 Remove pork from marinade; reserve marinade. Heat 12-inch nonstick skillet over medium-high heat. Add pork; cook 3 minutes, stirring once. Stir in onion, bell peppers and marinade. Cook 5 to 8 minutes longer, stirring frequently, until onion and peppers are crisp-tender.

3 Place one-fourth of pork mixture on center of each tortilla. Fold one end of tortilla up about 1 inch over pork mixture; fold right and left sides over folded end, overlapping.

High Altitude (3500-6500 ft): No change.

Nutritional Info: 1 Serving: Calories 260 (Calories from Fat 60); Total Fat 6g (Saturated Fat 1.5g, Trans Fat 0.5g); Cholesterol 35mg; Sodium 770mg; Total Carbohydrate 34g (Dietary Fiber 3g, Sugars 5g); Protein 18g. % Daily Value: Vitamin A 6%; Vitamin C 70%; Calcium 10%; Iron 20%. Exchanges: 2 Starch, 1 Vegetable, 1-1/2 Lean Meat. Carbohydrate Choices: 2.

Betty's Kitchen Tip
• One bell pepper packs a nutritional punch. It contains one and one-half times the vitamin C your body needs daily.

sesame shrimp stir-fry

Prep Time: 25 Minutes
Start to Finish: 1 Hour 25 Minutes
Servings: 4

LOW FAT

12	oz uncooked deveined peeled large shrimp, thawed if frozen, tail shells removed
1/4	cup teriyaki marinade
1-1/2	cups uncooked quinoa
1/2	cup water
1	tablespoon cornstarch

1	tablespoon canola oil
1	medium carrot, sliced (1/2 cup)
2	cups fresh snow pea pods, strings removed, cut in half
2	cups sliced fresh mushrooms (about 5 oz)
1	tablespoon sesame seed, toasted

1 In 8-inch square (2-quart) glass baking dish, place shrimp. Pour teriyaki marinade over shrimp. Cover and refrigerate at least 1 hour but no longer than 2 hours.

2 Rinse quinoa under cold water 1 minute; drain. Cook quinoa as directed on package.

3 Meanwhile, remove shrimp from marinade; reserve marinade. Stir water and cornstarch into remaining marinade; set aside.

4 Heat wok or 10-inch nonstick skillet over medium-high heat. Add oil; rotate wok to coat side. Add carrot; cook and stir 1 minute. Add shrimp, pea pods and mushrooms; cook and stir 3 to 5 minutes or until shrimp are pink and vegetables are crisp-tender.

5 Stir marinade mixture into shrimp mixture; heat to boiling. Cook and stir until sauce is thickened. Sprinkle with sesame seed. Serve with quinoa.

High Altitude (3500-6500 ft): After adding shrimp, pea pods and mushrooms, cook and stir 4 to 6 minutes.

Nutritional Info: 1 Serving: Calories 400 (Calories from Fat 80); Total Fat 9g (Saturated Fat 1g, Trans Fat 0g); Cholesterol 120mg; Sodium 780mg; Total Carbohydrate 53g (Dietary Fiber 5g, Sugars 8g); Protein 25g. % Daily Value: Vitamin A 60%; Vitamin C 20%; Calcium 8%; Iron 50%. Exchanges: 2 Starch, 1 Other Carbohydrate, 1 Vegetable, 2-1/2 Very Lean Meat, 1-1/2 Fat. Carbohydrate Choices: 3-1/2.

Betty's Kitchen Tip

• Instant brown rice is ready in about 10 minutes and has double the fiber compared to instant white rice.

dinner
CLASSICS

p. 121

114

117

116

halibut with potato succotash

Prep Time: 20 Minutes
Start to Finish: 45 Minutes
Servings: 4

LOW FAT

- 1   halibut fillet (1 to 1-1/2 lb)
- 1   tablespoon butter or margarine, melted
- 1   tablespoon canola oil
- 2   cups frozen diced potatoes O'Brien (from 32-oz bag)
- 1   box (9 oz) Green Giant® frozen baby lima beans

- 1   cup Green Giant® Niblets® frozen whole kernel corn
- 1/2 teaspoon garlic-pepper blend
- 1/2 teaspoon seasoned salt
- 1/2 teaspoon dried thyme leaves
- 1/8 teaspoon ground red pepper (cayenne)

1 Heat oven to 425°F. Spray 11x7-inch (2-quart) glass baking dish with cooking spray. Cut halibut into 4 serving-size pieces. Place the halibut in baking dish. Brush butter over the halibut.

2 In 10-inch nonstick skillet, heat oil over medium-high heat. Cook potatoes in oil 5 minutes, stirring occasionally. Stir in lima beans and corn. Cook 3 to 5 minutes or until vegetables are crisp-tender. Spoon mixture around halibut in baking dish. Sprinkle halibut and vegetables with the remaining ingredients; stir the vegetables slightly.

3 Bake 20 to 25 minutes or until halibut flakes easily with fork and vegetables are tender.

High Altitude (3500-6500 ft): No change.

Nutritional Info: 1 Serving: Calories 300 (Calories from Fat 70); Total Fat 8g (Saturated Fat 2.5g, Trans Fat 0g); Cholesterol 70mg; Sodium 340mg; Total Carbohydrate 30g (Dietary Fiber 5g, Sugars 3g); Protein 27g. % Daily Value: Vitamin A 8%; Vitamin C 10%; Calcium 4%; Iron 10%. Exchanges: 2 Starch, 3 Very Lean Meat, 1 Fat. Carbohydrate Choices: 2.

Betty's Kitchen Tips

Time-Saver: It's easier if you cook the halibut with the skin on. When it's done, the fish separates easily from the skin and you can discard it.

Variation: Try this colorful dish with swordfish or salmon instead of halibut.

easy beef short rib supper

Prep Time: 15 Minutes
Start to Finish: 8 Hours 40 Minutes
Servings: 6

EASY

- 3 lb beef short ribs, cut into rib sections
- 1/2 teaspoon seasoned salt
- 12 small whole red potatoes
- 1-1/2 cups ready-to-eat baby-cut carrots
- 1 can (10-3/4 oz) condensed cream of celery soup
- 1/2 cup chili sauce
- 2 tablespoons Worcestershire sauce
- 1/2 teaspoon garlic-pepper blend
- 1-1/2 cups Green Giant® frozen cut green beans, thawed

1 Spray 5- to 6-quart slow cooker and 12-inch skillet with cooking spray. Sprinkle ribs with seasoned salt. In skillet, cook ribs over medium-high heat 6 to 8 minutes, turning occasionally, until well browned.

2 Remove ribs from skillet with fork or tongs; place in cooker. Add potatoes and carrots to cooker. In small bowl, mix soup, chili sauce, Worcestershire sauce and garlic-pepper blend; pour over ribs and vegetables.

3 Cover; cook on Low heat setting 8 to 10 hours.

4 Skim fat from liquid in cooker if desired. Stir in green beans. Increase heat setting to High. Cover; cook 15 to 25 minutes longer or until beans are tender.

High Altitude (3500-6500 ft): No change.

Nutritional Info: 1 Serving: Calories 530 (Calories from Fat 150); Total Fat 16g (Saturated Fat 6g, Trans Fat 0.5g); Cholesterol 70mg; Sodium 920mg; Total Carbohydrate 71g (Dietary Fiber 11g, Sugars 10g); Protein 24g. % Daily Value: Vitamin A 110%; Vitamin C 40%; Calcium 15%; Iron 40%. Exchanges: 3 Starch, 1-1/2 Other Carbohydrate, 1 Vegetable, 2 Lean Meat, 1-1/2 Fat. Carbohydrate Choices: 5.

Betty's Kitchen Tips

Did You Know? Short ribs are trimmed from narrow beef rib and short plate sections. They're tasty but not tender, so slow cooking is great for tenderizing them.

Success Hint: Browning the short ribs before slow cooking gives the dish a rich, savory flavor and removes some of the fat.

spicy parmesan meatballs with angel hair pasta

Prep Time: 50 Minutes
Start to Finish: 50 Minutes
Servings: 4

- 3/4 cup Fiber One® cereal
- 1 lb extra-lean (at least 90%) ground beef
- 1/4 cup shredded Parmesan cheese (1 oz)
- 3/4 teaspoon Italian seasoning
- 1/4 teaspoon garlic powder
- 1 can (8 oz) tomato sauce
- 1 can (14.5 oz) diced tomatoes with green pepper and onion, undrained
- 1/8 teaspoon ground red pepper (cayenne)
- 6 oz uncooked whole wheat angel hair (capellini) pasta

Additional shredded Parmesan cheese, if desired
- 1 to 2 tablespoons chopped fresh parsley, if desired

1 Place cereal in resealable food-storage plastic bag; seal bag and finely crush with rolling pin or meat mallet.

2 In large bowl, mix cereal, beef, 1/4 cup cheese, the Italian seasoning, garlic powder and 1/4 cup of the tomato sauce until well blended. Shape into 16 (1-1/2-inch) meatballs.

3 Spray 12-inch skillet with cooking spray. Cook meatballs in skillet over medium heat 8 to 10 minutes, turning occasionally, until browned. Drain if necessary. Add remaining tomato sauce, the tomatoes and red pepper to skillet; turn meatballs to coat.

4 Cover; cook over medium-low heat 15 to 20 minutes, stirring sauce and turning meatballs occasionally, until meatballs are thoroughly cooked and no longer pink in center.

5 Meanwhile, cook and drain pasta as directed on package. Serve meatballs over pasta. Top each serving with additional Parmesan cheese and parsley.

High Altitude (3500-6500 ft): No change.

Nutritional Info: 1 Serving: Calories 460 (Calories from Fat 110); Total Fat 12g (Saturated Fat 5g, Trans Fat 0.5g); Cholesterol 75mg; Sodium 950mg; Total Carbohydrate 54g (Dietary Fiber 10g, Sugars 9g); Protein 33g. % Daily Value: Vitamin A 10%; Vitamin C 10%; Calcium 20%; Iron 40%. Exchanges: 2-1/2 Starch, 1 Other Carbohydrate, 3-1/2 Lean Meat. Carbohydrate Choices: 3-1/2.

Betty's Kitchen Tip

• You can also use ground turkey breast in this recipe with equally delicious results.

lemon-dill breaded fish

Prep Time: 20 Minutes
Start to Finish: 20 Minutes
Servings: 4

QUICK

- 1/2   cup Original Bisquick® mix
- 1/4   cup Progresso® plain bread crumbs
- 2   teaspoons grated lemon peel
- 1   teaspoon dried dill weed
- 1/2   teaspoon salt
- 1   egg
- 4   (4 oz) tilapia or other mild-flavored fish fillets, about 1/2 inch thick
- 2   tablespoons vegetable oil

1 In shallow dish, stir Bisquick mix, bread crumbs, lemon peel, dill weed and salt until blended. In another shallow dish, beat egg. Dip fish into egg, then coat with Bisquick mixture.

2 In 12-inch nonstick skillet, heat oil over medium-low heat. Add fish. Cook 8 to 10 minutes, turning once, until fish flakes easily with fork and is brown on both sides.

High Altitude (3500-6500 ft): No change.

Nutritional Info: 1 Serving: Calories 270 (Calories from Fat 110); Total Fat 12g (Saturated Fat 2.5g, Trans Fat 0.5g); Cholesterol 115mg; Sodium 640mg; Total Carbohydrate 15g (Dietary Fiber 0g, Sugars 1g); Protein 25g. % Daily Value: Vitamin A 2%; Vitamin C 0%; Calcium 6%; Iron 8%. Exchanges: 1 Starch, 3 Lean Meat, 1/2 Fat. Carbohydrate Choices: 1.

Betty's Kitchen Tips

Did You Know? Tilapia, sometimes called St. Peter's fish, is a white fish that's raised primarily on fish farms. It has a delicate flavor and slightly firm texture.

Variation: Orange roughy, perch or walleye would all be delicious choices for this dish.

grilled pork tenderloin with pineapple salsa

Prep Time: 40 Minutes
Start to Finish: 40 Minutes
Servings: 4

LOW FAT

- -

Pork

2	teaspoons canola oil
2	pork tenderloins (3/4 lb each)
1	teaspoon black pepper
1/4	to 1/2 teaspoon ground red pepper (cayenne)
1/2	teaspoon salt

Pineapple Salsa

1	can (8 oz) pineapple tidbits, drained
4	medium green onions, sliced (1/4 cup)
1/4	cup chopped red bell pepper
2	tablespoons chopped fresh or 2 teaspoons dried mint leaves
1/2	teaspoon grated lime peel
2	teaspoons lime juice
1/4	teaspoon salt

- -

1 Heat gas or charcoal grill. Rub 1 teaspoon oil onto each pork tenderloin; sprinkle with peppers and 1/2 teaspoon salt.

2 Carefully brush grill rack with oil. Place pork on grill over medium heat. Cover grill; cook 20 to 30 minutes, turning 3 times, until pork has slight blush of pink in center and meat thermometer inserted in center reads 160°F.

3 Meanwhile, in medium bowl, mix salsa ingredients. Cut pork into 1/2-inch slices. Serve with salsa.

Broil Directions: Set oven control to broil. Prepare pork as directed in step 1; place on rack in broiler pan. Broil with tops 4 to 5 inches from heat using times in recipe as a guide, turning 3 times, until pork has slight blush of pink in center and meat thermometer inserted in center reads 160°F. Continue as directed in step 3.

High Altitude (3500-6500 ft): No change.

Nutritional Info: 1 Serving: Calories 270 (Calories from Fat 80); Total Fat 9g (Saturated Fat 2.5g, Trans Fat 0g); Cholesterol 110mg; Sodium 520mg; Total Carbohydrate 8g (Dietary Fiber 1g, Sugars 7g); Protein 39g. % Daily Value: Vitamin A 10%; Vitamin C 40%; Calcium 2%; Iron 15%. Exchanges: 1/2 Other Carbohydrate, 5-1/2 Very Lean Meat, 1 Fat. Carbohydrate Choices: 1/2.

Betty's Kitchen Tip

• If you don't have a lime on hand but you do have a lemon, you can use it for the juice and peel instead.

pesto-glazed salmon fillet

Prep Time: 5 Minutes
Start to Finish: 45 Minutes
Servings: 8

EASY

• •

1	salmon fillet (2 lb)
1/3	cup mayonnaise or salad dressing
1/3	cup basil pesto

• •

1 Heat oven to 375°F. Spray 13x9-inch (3-quart) glass baking dish with cooking spray. Place salmon fillet, skin side down, in dish. In small bowl, stir together the mayonnaise and pesto; spread over salmon.

2 Bake uncovered 30 to 35 minutes or until salmon flakes easily with fork. Let stand 5 minutes. Place on serving platter. Cut into serving pieces.

High Altitude (3500-6500 ft): No change.

Nutritional Info: 1 Serving: Calories 280 (Calories from Fat 180); Total Fat 20g (Saturated Fat 3.5g, Trans Fat 0g); Cholesterol 70mg; Sodium 190mg; Total Carbohydrate 0g (Dietary Fiber 0g, Sugars 0g); Protein 24g. % Daily Value: Vitamin A 2%; Vitamin C 0%; Calcium 6%; Iron 6%. Exchanges: 3-1/2 Lean Meat, 2 Fat. Carbohydrate Choices: 0.

Betty's Kitchen Tips

Success Hint: You'll find prepared pesto, a blend of basil, garlic, olive oil and Parmesan cheese, with the fresh pasta in the refrigerated section of your supermarket.

Special Touch: Place the salmon on a serving platter, and garnish with lemon wedges, fresh basil leaves and red currants for a pretty holiday look.

grilled shrimp kabobs

Prep Time: 20 Minutes
Start to Finish: 50 Minutes
Servings: 4

LOW FAT

- -

1 lb uncooked deveined peeled large shrimp, thawed if frozen, tail shells removed

1 cup fat-free Italian dressing

1 medium red onion, cut into 8 pieces

1 medium bell pepper, cut into 8 pieces

16 medium cherry tomatoes

16 small whole mushrooms

- -

1 Place shrimp and dressing in shallow glass or plastic dish or heavy-duty resealable food-storage plastic bag. Cover dish or seal bag and refrigerate 30 minutes.

2 Heat gas or charcoal grill. Remove shrimp from marinade; reserve marinade. Thread shrimp, onion, bell pepper, tomatoes and mushrooms alternately on each of four 15-inch metal skewers, leaving 1/4-inch space between each piece.

3 Place kabobs on grill over medium heat. Cover grill; cook 6 to 8 minutes, turning frequently and brushing several times with marinade, until shrimp are pink. Discard any remaining marinade.

High Altitude (3500-6500 ft): No change.

Nutritional Info: 1 Serving: Calories 140 (Calories from Fat 15); Total Fat 1.5g (Saturated Fat 0g, Trans Fat 0g); Cholesterol 160mg; Sodium 680mg; Total Carbohydrate 12g (Dietary Fiber 2g, Sugars 8g); Protein 20g. % Daily Value: Vitamin A 20%; Vitamin C 30%; Calcium 6%; Iron 20%. Exchanges: 1/2 Other Carbohydrate, 1 Vegetable, 2-1/2 Very Lean Meat. Carbohydrate Choices: 1.

Betty's Kitchen Tip

- Leave about a 1/4-inch space between the pieces on the skewers to allow for even cooking.

tuna with avocado-kiwi salsa

Prep Time: 40 Minutes
Start to Finish: 1 Hour 10 Minutes
Servings: 6

Tuna

1-1/2	lb tuna steaks, 3/4 to 1 inch thick
1/4	cup lime juice
2	teaspoons chili oil
2	tablespoons finely chopped fresh cilantro
1	clove garlic, finely chopped
1/2	teaspoon salt

Salsa

1	small avocado, pitted, peeled and coarsely chopped (1 cup)
1	kiwifruit, peeled, chopped (1/2 cup)
3	medium green onions, chopped (3 tablespoons)
1	small jalapeño chile, seeded, finely chopped (1 tablespoon)
2	tablespoons lime juice
2	tablespoons chopped fresh cilantro
1/4	teaspoon salt

1 If tuna steaks are large, cut into 6 serving pieces. In shallow glass or plastic dish, mix remaining tuna ingredients. Add tuna; turn to coat with marinade. Cover; refrigerate, turning once, at least 30 minutes but no longer than 2 hours to marinate.

2 Meanwhile, in medium bowl, mix all salsa ingredients; refrigerate.

3 Spray grill rack with cooking spray. Heat gas or charcoal grill. Remove tuna from marinade; reserve marinade. Place tuna on grill. Cover grill; cook over medium heat 11 to 16 minutes, brushing 2 or 3 times with marinade and turning once, until tuna flakes easily with fork and is slightly pink in center. Discard any remaining marinade. Top tuna with salsa.

High Altitude (3500-6500 ft): No change.

Nutritional Info: 1 Serving: Calories 220 (Calories from Fat 100); Total Fat 11g (Saturated Fat 2.5g, Trans Fat 0g); Cholesterol 65mg; Sodium 360mg; Total Carbohydrate 6g (Dietary Fiber 2g, Sugars 2g); Protein 23g. % Daily Value: Vitamin A 4%; Vitamin C 40%; Calcium 2%; Iron 6%. Exchanges: 1/2 Other Carbohydrate, 3-1/2 Lean Meat. Carbohydrate Choices: 1/2.

Betty's Kitchen Tip

• When buying an avocado, look for skin that's free of bruises, scars and mushy areas. Ripe avocados have firm flesh but give a little with pressure.

oven-baked chicken

Prep Time: 10 Minutes
Start to Finish: 1 Hour
Servings: 5

EASY

- -

1	tablespoon butter or margarine
2/3	cup Original Bisquick® mix
1-1/2	teaspoons paprika
1	teaspoon salt or garlic salt
1	teaspoon Italian seasoning, if desired
1/4	teaspoon pepper
1	cut-up whole chicken (3 to 3-1/2 lb)

- -

1 Heat oven to 425°F. Melt butter in 13x9-inch glass baking dish in oven.

2 In medium bowl, stir together Bisquick mix, paprika, salt, Italian seasoning and pepper; coat chicken with Bisquick mixture. Place skin side down in heated dish.

3 Bake 35 minutes. Turn chicken; bake about 15 minutes longer or until chicken juice is clear when thickest piece is cut to bone (170°F for breasts; 180°F for thighs and drumsticks).

High Altitude (3500-6500 ft): Bake 40 minutes. Turn chicken; bake about 20 minutes longer.

Nutritional Info: 1 Serving: Calories 360 (Calories from Fat 180); Total Fat 20g (Saturated Fat 7g, Trans Fat 1g); Cholesterol 110mg; Sodium 780mg; Total Carbohydrate 11g (Dietary Fiber 0g, Sugars 0g); Protein 33g. % Daily Value: Vitamin A 10%; Vitamin C 0%; Calcium 4%; Iron 10%. Exchanges: 1/2 Starch, 4-1/2 Lean Meat, 1-1/2 Fat. Carbohydrate Choices: 1.

Betty's Kitchen Tip

• This chicken has a nice, slightly sweet taste to it because of the Bisquick coating. The coating keeps the chicken juicy and tender, too.

bacon-chili beef stew

Prep Time: 1 Hour 50 Minutes
Start to Finish: 1 Hour 50 Minutes
Servings: 6 (1-1/2 cups each)

4	slices bacon, cut into 1/2-inch pieces
1-1/2	lb lean beef stew meat (1/2-inch pieces)
1	medium onion, chopped (1/2 cup)
1/2	teaspoon seasoned salt
1/8	teaspoon pepper
2	cans (14.5 oz each) diced tomatoes with mild green chilies, undrained

1	jar (12 oz) home-style beef gravy
2	tablespoons chili sauce
4	unpeeled small red potatoes, diced (2 cups)
2	medium carrots, sliced (1 cup)
1	cup Green Giant® Niblets® frozen whole kernel corn

1 In 4-quart saucepan, cook bacon over medium heat 3 to 4 minutes, stirring frequently, until cooked but not crisp. Drain all but 2 tablespoons bacon fat from saucepan.

2 Add beef and onion to bacon; sprinkle with seasoned salt and pepper. Cook 4 to 6 minutes, stirring frequently, until beef is beginning to brown and onion is tender.

3 Stir in tomatoes, gravy and chili sauce. Heat to boiling. Stir in potatoes and carrots. Reduce heat to medium-low. Cover; cook 50 to 60 minutes, stirring occasionally, until beef is tender.

4 Stir in the corn. Cook uncovered 10 to 15 minutes longer, stirring occasionally, until corn is tender.

High Altitude (3500-6500 ft): If stew becomes too thick, add up to 1/2 cup hot water.

Nutritional Info: 1 Serving: Calories 430 (Calories from Fat 190); Total Fat 22g (Saturated Fat 8g, Trans Fat 0.5g); Cholesterol 80mg; Sodium 1070mg; Total Carbohydrate 28g (Dietary Fiber 5g, Sugars 9g); Protein 31g. % Daily Value: Vitamin A 90%; Vitamin C 15%; Calcium 8%; Iron 25%. Exchanges: 1 Starch, 1/2 Other Carbohydrate, 1 Vegetable, 3-1/2 Lean Meat, 2 Fat. Carbohydrate Choices: 2.

Betty's Kitchen Tips

Substitution: Like your chili spicy? Use tomatoes labeled "hot" instead of the mild variety.

Serve-With: Serve the stew with warm rolled flour tortillas or corn muffins and a tossed green salad.

graham-crusted tilapia

Prep Time: 15 Minutes
Start to Finish: 25 Minutes
Servings: 4 servings   **EASY QUICK**

- 1 lb tilapia, cod, haddock or other medium-firm fish fillets, about 3/4 inch thick
- 1/2 cup graham cracker crumbs (about 8 squares)
- 1 teaspoon grated lemon peel
- 1/4 teaspoon salt
- 1/8 teaspoon pepper
- 1/4 cup fat-free (skim) milk
- 2 tablespoons canola oil
- 2 tablespoons chopped toasted pecans

1 Move oven rack to position slightly above middle of oven. Heat oven to 500°F.

2 Cut fish fillets crosswise into 2-inch-wide pieces. In shallow dish, mix cracker crumbs, lemon peel, salt and pepper. Place milk in another shallow dish.

3 Dip fish into milk, then coat with cracker mixture. Place in ungreased 13x9-inch pan. Drizzle oil over fish; sprinkle with pecans.

4 Bake about 10 minutes or until fish flakes easily with fork.

High Altitude (3500-6500 ft): No change.

Nutritional Info: 1 Serving: Calories 230 (Calories from Fat 100); Total Fat 12g (Saturated Fat 1.5g, Trans Fat 0g); Cholesterol 60mg; Sodium 300mg; Total Carbohydrate 9g (Dietary Fiber 0g, Sugars 5g); Protein 23g. % Daily Value: Vitamin A 0%; Vitamin C 0%; Calcium 4%; Iron 4%. Exchanges: 1/2 Starch, 3 Lean Meat, 1/2 Fat. Carbohydrate Choices: 1/2.

Betty's Kitchen Tip

• Toasting nuts adds a lot of great flavor. To toast nuts, bake uncovered in ungreased shallow pan in 350°F oven 6 to 10 minutes, stirring occasionally, until light brown.

italian-style shepherd's pie

Prep Time: 20 Minutes
Start to Finish: 50 Minutes
Servings: 4 (1-1/2 cups each)

1	lb boneless beef sirloin, trimmed of fat, cut into 1-inch cubes		1/2	box (7.2-oz size) Betty Crocker® roasted garlic mashed potatoes (1 pouch)
1	medium onion, sliced (1 cup)		3/4	cup hot water
2	medium carrots, sliced (1 cup)		1-1/4	cups fat-free (skim) milk
1/4	teaspoon pepper		1	tablespoon butter or margarine
1-1/2	cups sliced fresh mushrooms (about 4 oz)		2	tablespoons shredded fresh Parmesan cheese
1	jar (14 oz) tomato pasta sauce (any variety) (1-1/2 cups)			

1 Heat oven to 375°F. Spray 2-quart casserole or 11x7-inch glass baking dish with cooking spray. Heat 12-inch nonstick skillet over medium-high heat. Add beef, onions and carrots to skillet; sprinkle with pepper. Cook 3 to 5 minutes, stirring frequently, until beef is brown.

2 Stir in mushrooms and pasta sauce. Heat to boiling. Cook over medium heat 5 minutes, stirring occasionally. Spread in casserole.

3 Make potatoes as directed on box for 4 servings, using 1 pouch Potatoes and Seasoning, water, milk and butter. Spoon into 8 mounds around edge of hot beef mixture. Sprinkle cheese over all.

4 Bake uncovered 25 to 30 minutes or until bubbly and potatoes are light golden brown.

High Altitude (3500-6500 ft): Make potatoes following High Altitude directions on package.

Nutritional Info: 1 Serving: Calories 430 (Calories from Fat 100); Total Fat 12g (Saturated Fat 4.5g, Trans Fat 0g); Cholesterol 75mg; Sodium 920mg; Total Carbohydrate 47g (Dietary Fiber 4g, Sugars 16g); Protein 35g. % Daily Value: Vitamin A 120%; Vitamin C 10%; Calcium 20%; Iron 20%. Exchanges: 1-1/2 Starch, 1 Other Carbohydrate, 1 Vegetable, 4 Lean Meat. Carbohydrate Choices: 3.

Betty's Kitchen Tips

Variation: To bump up the amount of vegetables in this recipe, add 1 cup peas, corn or mixed vegetables.

Serve-With: Ginger-Almond Biscotti cookies on page 295 would be a sweet ending to this Italian-themed dinner.

slow cooker
MAIN DISHES

p. 142

144

130

131

sweet-and-sour chicken

Prep Time: 10 Minutes
Start to Finish: 7 Hours 10 Minutes
Servings: 6

EASY

- 1-1/2 cups ready-to-eat baby-cut carrots
- 6 large boneless skinless chicken thighs (about 2 lb)
- 1/2 teaspoon crushed red pepper flakes
- 1-1/3 cups sweet-and-sour sauce

- 1 can (20 oz) pineapple chunks in juice, drained
- 1 bag (1 lb) frozen bell pepper and onion stir-fry, thawed, drained
- 2 cups uncooked regular long-grain white rice
- 4 cups water

1 Spray 3- to 4-quart slow cooker with cooking spray. Place carrots in cooker. Top with chicken; sprinkle with red pepper flakes.

2 Cover; cook on Low heat setting 6 to 7 hours.

3 Remove chicken and carrots from cooker; drain and discard liquid from cooker. Return carrots and chicken to cooker. Pour sweet-and-sour sauce over chicken; top with pineapple and stir-fry vegetables.

4 Increase heat setting to High. Cover; cook 45 to 60 minutes longer or until stir-fry vegetables are crisp-tender. Cook rice in water as directed on package. Serve chicken mixture with rice.

High Altitude (3500-6500 ft): No change.

Nutritional Info: 1 Serving: Calories 630 (Calories from Fat 130); Total Fat 14g (Saturated Fat 4g, Trans Fat 0g); Cholesterol 95mg; Sodium 1040mg; Total Carbohydrate 88g (Dietary Fiber 4g, Sugars 25g); Protein 39g. % Daily Value: Vitamin A 110%; Vitamin C 25%; Calcium 10%; Iron 35%. Exchanges: 3 Starch, 1/2 Fruit, 2 Other Carbohydrate, 1 Vegetable, 4 Lean Meat. Carbohydrate Choices: 6.

Betty's Kitchen Tips

Success Hint: Sweet-and-sour sauces come in a variety of colors, ranging from pink to golden. The golden-colored variety will give this dish the most attractive look. Some sweet-and-sour sauces turn chicken an unsightly bright pink!

Variation: Several types of rice are available. You may want to serve this dish over brown rice or jasmine rice for a change of pace.

corned beef brisket with horseradish sour cream

Prep Time: 5 Minutes
Start to Finish: 8 Hours 5 Minutes
Servings: 8

EASY

- 1 large sweet onion (Bermuda, Maui or Spanish), sliced
- 1 corned beef brisket (3 to 3-1/2 lb)
- 3/4 teaspoon crushed red pepper flakes
- 1 cup reduced-sodium chicken broth
- 1 tablespoon Worcestershire sauce
- 1/2 cup sour cream
- 1 tablespoon cream-style prepared horseradish
- 2 tablespoons chopped fresh parsley

1 Spray 5- to 6-quart slow cooker with cooking spray. Place onion in cooker. Remove beef from package; discard liquid and seasoning packet. Thoroughly rinse beef. Place beef on onion; sprinkle with red pepper flakes. In small bowl, mix broth and Worcestershire sauce; pour over beef.

2 Cover; cook on Low heat setting 8 to 9 hours.

3 In small bowl, stir sour cream, horseradish and parsley until well mixed. Serve with beef and onion.

High Altitude (3500-6500 ft): No change.

Nutritional Info: 1 Serving: Calories 300 (Calories from Fat 130); Total Fat 14g (Saturated Fat 6g, Trans Fat 0.5g); Cholesterol 85mg; Sodium 160mg; Total Carbohydrate 3g (Dietary Fiber 0g, Sugars 2g); Protein 40g. % Daily Value: Vitamin A 4%; Vitamin C 2%; Calcium 4%; Iron 20%. Exchanges: 5-1/2 Lean Meat. Carbohydrate Choices: 0.

Betty's Kitchen Tips

Did You Know? Corned beef was originally "corned," or preserved with granular salt, because there was no refrigeration. Today, the beef is cured in brine, and spices are added for a distinctive tangy flavor. Because we use crushed red pepper flakes in this recipe, there's no need to use the additional seasonings found in the seasoning packet.

Serve-With: Serve this traditional Irish dinner with steamed green cabbage and carrots.

pork chop supper

Prep Time: 15 Minutes
Start to Finish: 6 Hours 30 Minutes
Servings: 6

EASY

- 6 pork loin or rib chops, 1/2 inch thick
- 6 medium red potatoes (about 1-1/2 lb), cut into eighths
- 1 can (10-3/4 oz) condensed cream of mushroom soup
- 1 jar (4.5 oz) Green Giant® sliced mushrooms, drained
- 2 tablespoons dry white wine or chicken broth
- 1/4 teaspoon dried thyme leaves
- 1/2 teaspoon garlic powder
- 1/2 teaspoon Worcestershire sauce
- 3 tablespoons Gold Medal® all-purpose flour
- 1 tablespoon diced pimientos (from 2-oz jar)
- 2 cups Green Giant® frozen sweet peas, rinsed, drained

1 Heat a 12-inch nonstick skillet over medium-high heat. Cook pork chops in skillet 2 to 4 minutes, turning once, until brown.

2 Spray 4- to 5-quart slow cooker with cooking spray. Place potatoes in cooker. In medium bowl, mix soup, mushrooms, wine, thyme, garlic powder, Worcestershire sauce and flour. Spoon half of the soup mixture over potatoes. Place pork on potatoes; cover with remaining soup mixture.

3 Cover; cook on Low heat setting 6 to 7 hours.

4 Remove pork from cooker; keep warm. Stir pimientos and peas into cooker. Cover; cook on Low heat setting about 15 minutes longer or until peas are tender. Serve with pork.

High Altitude (3500-6500 ft): No change.

Nutritional Info: 1 Serving: Calories 350 (Calories from Fat 100); Total Fat 11g (Saturated Fat 3.5g, Trans Fat 0g); Cholesterol 65mg; Sodium 510mg; Total Carbohydrate 34g (Dietary Fiber 5g, Sugars 4g); Protein 28g. % Daily Value: Vitamin A 20%; Vitamin C 15%; Calcium 6%; Iron 20%. Exchanges: 2 Starch, 1 Vegetable, 3 Lean Meat. Carbohydrate Choices: 2.

Betty's Kitchen Tips

Success Hint: Virtually any cream soup will work in this recipe. Try golden cream of mushroom, cream of chicken or cream of celery instead of the cream of mushroom.

Substitution: Apple juice works as a substitute for the white wine.

marinara sauce with spaghetti

Prep Time: 25 Minutes
Start to Finish: 8 Hours 25 Minutes
Servings: 12

LOW FAT

- 2 cans (28 oz each) Progresso® diced tomatoes with Italian herbs, undrained
- 1 can (6 oz) tomato paste
- 1 large onion, chopped (1 cup)
- 8 cloves garlic, finely chopped
- 1 tablespoon olive or vegetable oil
- 2 teaspoons sugar
- 2 teaspoons dried basil leaves
- 1 teaspoon dried oregano leaves
- 1 teaspoon salt
- 1 teaspoon pepper
- 24 oz uncooked spaghetti

Shredded Parmesan cheese, if desired

1 Spray 3- to 4-quart slow cooker with cooking spray. In cooker, mix all ingredients except spaghetti and cheese.

2 Cover; cook on Low heat setting 8 to 10 hours.

3 Cook and drain spaghetti as directed on package. Serve sauce over spaghetti. Sprinkle with cheese.

High Altitude (3500-6500 ft): No change.

Nutritional Info: 1 Serving: Calories 320 (Calories from Fat 25); Total Fat 2.5g (Saturated Fat 0g, Trans Fat 0g); Cholesterol 0mg; Sodium 890mg; Total Carbohydrate 63g (Dietary Fiber 5g, Sugars 10g); Protein 11g. % Daily Value: Vitamin A 20%; Vitamin C 20%; Calcium 6%; Iron 20%. Exchanges: 2-1/2 Starch, 1 Other Carbohydrate, 1-1/2 Vegetable, 1/2 Fat. Carbohydrate Choices: 4.

Betty's Kitchen Tips

How-To: This all-purpose sauce is so easy to make that you'll want to make it often and keep a few extra containers in the freezer. Ladle the cooked sauce into airtight freezer containers; cover and freeze up to 1 month.

Variation: Try serving this sauce with penne, rotini or your family's favorite pasta.

asian pork stew

Prep Time: 25 Minutes
Start to Finish: 7 Hours 25 Minutes
Servings: 8 (1 cup stew and 3/4 cup rice each)

- 2 lb boneless country-style pork ribs, cut into 2-inch pieces
- 3 medium carrots, cut into 1-inch slices
- 2 medium onions, cut into 1-inch wedges
- 1 package (8 oz) fresh whole mushrooms, cut in half if large
- 1 can (8 oz) whole water chestnuts, drained
- 1 can (8 oz) bamboo shoots, drained
- 3/4 cup hoisin sauce

- 1/3 cup reduced-sodium soy sauce
- 4 large cloves garlic, finely chopped
- 1 tablespoon finely chopped gingerroot
- 4 cups water
- 2 cups uncooked long-grain white rice
- 2 tablespoons cornstarch
- 3 tablespoons water
- 1/3 cup lightly packed coarsely chopped cilantro

1 Spray 5- to 6-quart slow cooker with cooking spray. In cooker, layer pork, carrots, onions, mushrooms, water chestnuts and bamboo shoots. In small bowl, stir together 1/2 cup of the hoisin sauce, the soy sauce, garlic and gingerroot; pour into slow cooker.

2 Cover; cook on Low heat setting for 7 to 9 hours.

3 During last hour of cooking, in 3-quart saucepan, heat 4 cups water and the rice to boiling over high heat. Reduce heat to low. Cover; simmer 15 to 20 minutes or until rice is tender and water is absorbed.

4 Gently remove pork and vegetables with slotted spoon to large bowl; cover to keep warm. Skim any fat from liquid in cooker. Pour liquid into 1-quart saucepan. Stir remaining 1/4 cup hoisin sauce into liquid; heat to boiling. In small bowl, mix cornstarch and 3 tablespoons water; stir into liquid. Cook, stirring constantly, until thickened; pour over pork mixture and gently stir.

5 Sprinkle cilantro over stew. Serve over rice.

High Altitude (3500-6500 ft): No change.

Nutritional Info: 1 Serving: Calories 510 (Calories from Fat 130); Total Fat 15g (Saturated Fat 5g, Trans Fat 0g); Cholesterol 70mg; Sodium 810mg; Total Carbohydrate 63g (Dietary Fiber 3g, Sugars 5g); Protein 30g. % Daily Value: Vitamin A 80%; Vitamin C 6%; Calcium 6%; Iron 20%. Exchanges: 3 Starch, 1 Other Carbohydrate, 1 Vegetable, 2-1/2 Medium-Fat Meat. Carbohydrate Choices: 4.

Betty's Kitchen Tips

Time-Saver: Keep cleanup to a minimum by using a heat-resistant slow cooker liner in your slow cooker.

Did You Know? Hoisin sauce is often used in Chinese cuisine. The reddish brown sauce, flavored with soybeans, garlic, chiles and numerous spices, tastes spicy and sweet.

chicken stew

Prep Time: 10 Minutes
Start to Finish: 8 Hours 10 Minutes
Servings: 6 (1-2/3 cups each)   **EASY**

- 3 medium potatoes (about 1 lb), cut into 1-1/2-inch cubes
- 2 cups ready-to-eat baby-cut carrots
- 1 package (8 oz) fresh whole mushrooms, each cut in half
- 2 packages (20 oz each) boneless skinless chicken thighs
- 1/2 teaspoon salt
- 1 teaspoon dried chopped onion
- 1/4 teaspoon garlic powder
- 1-1/2 jars (12 oz each) chicken gravy (about 2-1/4 cups)
- 1 tablespoon tomato paste
- 1/2 cup dry white wine or water
- 2 tablespoons chopped fresh parsley, if desired

1 Spray 4- to 5-quart slow cooker with cooking spray. In cooker, toss potatoes, carrots and mushrooms. Arrange chicken on vegetable mixture. Sprinkle salt, onion and garlic powder over chicken. Stir together gravy and tomato paste. Pour gravy mixture and wine over all.

2 Cover; cook on Low heat setting 8 to 10 hours. Sprinkle servings with parsley.

High Altitude (3500-6500 ft): No change.

Nutritional Info: 1 Serving: Calories 460 (Calories from Fat 180); Total Fat 20g (Saturated Fat 6g, Trans Fat 0g); Cholesterol 120mg; Sodium 870mg; Total Carbohydrate 24g (Dietary Fiber 4g, Sugars 5g); Protein 44g. % Daily Value: Vitamin A 140%; Vitamin C 10%; Calcium 10%; Iron 30%. Exchanges: 1 Starch, 1/2 Other Carbohydrate, 6 Lean Meat, 1/2 Fat. Carbohydrate Choices: 1-1/2.

Betty's Kitchen Tip

- A sprinkling of fresh parsley can add spark to slow-cooked food.

country french beef stew

Prep Time: 25 Minutes
Start to Finish: 7 Hours 55 Minutes
Servings: 12

6	slices bacon, cut into 1/2-inch pieces
1	boneless beef chuck roast (3 lb), trimmed of fat, cut into 1-inch pieces
1	large onion, cut into 1/2-inch wedges
3	cups ready-to-serve baby-cut carrots
1	cup red Zinfandel wine or nonalcoholic red wine
3/4	cup beef broth
3	tablespoons Gold Medal® all-purpose flour
1	teaspoon dried basil leaves

1/2	teaspoon dried thyme leaves
1/2	teaspoon salt
1/4	teaspoon pepper
1	can (14.5 oz) diced tomatoes, undrained
1	package (8 oz) sliced fresh mushrooms (3 cups)
1/2	cup julienne-cut sun-dried tomatoes (not oil-packed)

Hot cooked egg noodles, if desired

Chopped fresh parsley or basil leaves, if desired

1 Spray 5- to 6-quart slow cooker with cooking spray. In 12-inch nonstick skillet, cook bacon over medium-high heat, stirring occasionally, until crisp. Place bacon in cooker. Discard all but 1 tablespoon bacon fat in skillet. Cook beef in bacon fat 2 to 3 minutes, stirring occasionally, until brown. Stir onion into beef. Cook 1 minute, stirring occasionally. Spoon mixture into cooker.

2 Stir carrots, wine, broth, flour, basil, thyme, salt, pepper and canned diced tomatoes into mixture in cooker.

3 Cover; cook on Low heat setting 7 to 8 hours.

4 Stir in mushrooms and sun-dried tomatoes. Cover; cook on Low heat setting 20 to 30 minutes longer or until sun-dried tomatoes are tender. Serve beef mixture over noodles; sprinkle with parsley.

High Altitude (3500-6500 ft): No change.

Nutritional Info: 1 Serving: Calories 270 (Calories from Fat 140); Total Fat 15g (Saturated Fat 6g, Trans Fat 0.5g); Cholesterol 70mg; Sodium 430mg; Total Carbohydrate 9g (Dietary Fiber 2g, Sugars 4g); Protein 25g. % Daily Value: Vitamin A 100%; Vitamin C 6%; Calcium 4%; Iron 20%. Exchanges: 1 Vegetable, 3-1/2 Lean Meat, 1 Fat. Carbohydrate Choices: 1/2.

Betty's Kitchen Tips

Success Hint: If you can't find the julienne-cut tomatoes, cut the sun-dried tomatoes with a kitchen scissors.

Substitution: If you prefer, you can use beef broth instead of the wine. To save time, you may want to use beef stew meat instead of cutting the beef roast into pieces.

chicken in red wine

Prep Time: 20 Minutes
Start to Finish: 8 Hours 50 Minutes
Servings: 8

LOW FAT

6 slices bacon	2 cloves garlic, finely chopped
8 boneless skinless chicken thighs (about 1-1/2 lb)	2 dried bay leaves
1 bag (16 oz) ready-to-eat baby-cut carrots	1-1/4 cups dry red wine or nonalcoholic red wine
8 oz tiny pearl onions	3/4 cup chicken broth
1 teaspoon salt	1 lb fresh small whole mushrooms
1/4 teaspoon pepper	2 tablespoons Gold Medal® all-purpose flour
1 teaspoon dried thyme leaves	2 tablespoons cold water
	1/4 cup chopped fresh parsley

1 Line microwavable plate with microwavable paper towel. Add bacon; cover with paper towel. Microwave on High 3 to 5 minutes or until crisp. Crumble bacon.

2 Spray 5- to 6-quart slow cooker with cooking spray. Place chicken in cooker. Add carrots, onions, bacon, salt, pepper, thyme, garlic, bay leaves, wine and broth.

3 Cover; cook on Low heat setting 8 to 10 hours.

4 Skim any fat from surface of chicken mixture. Stir in mushrooms. In small bowl, mix flour and water; stir into chicken mixture. Stir in 2 tablespoons parsley.

5 Increase heat setting to High. Cover; cook about 30 minutes longer or until mixture is thickened. Remove bay leaves before serving. Sprinkle with remaining chopped parsley.

High Altitude (3500-6500 ft): No change.

Nutritional Info: 1 Serving: Calories 230 (Calories from Fat 90); Total Fat 10g (Saturated Fat 3g, Trans Fat 0g); Cholesterol 60mg; Sodium 620mg; Total Carbohydrate 12g (Dietary Fiber 3g, Sugars 5g); Protein 23g. % Daily Value: Vitamin A 190%; Vitamin C 6%; Calcium 6%; Iron 15%. Exchanges: 1/2 Other Carbohydrate, 1 Vegetable, 3 Lean Meat. Carbohydrate Choices: 1.

Betty's Kitchen Tip

• This robust chicken dish, known as Coq au Vin in France, gets its wonderful flavor and rich color from the red wine and bacon. It is usually prepared with bone-in chicken pieces, but we found that boneless chicken thighs work best in the slow cooker. The chicken becomes very tender and will fall apart into pieces for easier serving.

african groundnut stew with chicken

Prep Time: 20 Minutes
Start to Finish: 8 Hours 20 Minutes
Servings: 8 (1-1/2 cups each)

6	boneless skinless chicken thighs (about 1 lb)
3	boneless skinless chicken breasts (about 3/4 lb)
1	medium onion, chopped (1 cup)
3/4	cup peanut butter
1	can (28 oz) Progresso® diced tomatoes, undrained
1	can (14 oz) chicken broth
2	tablespoons grated gingerroot
2	tablespoons tomato paste
2	teaspoons curry powder
1	teaspoon crushed red pepper flakes
1/2	teaspoon salt
1-1/2	lb sweet potatoes (3 medium), peeled, cubed (about 4 cups)
1	lb small red potatoes (about 12), cut into eighths (about 2-1/2 cups)

1 Spray 5- to 6-quart slow cooker with cooking spray. In cooker, layer all ingredients, spooning peanut butter in dollops.

2 Cover; cook on Low heat setting 8 to 10 hours. Break up chicken before serving.

High Altitude (3500-6500 ft): No change.

Nutritional Info: 1 Serving: Calories 420 (Calories from Fat 170); Total Fat 19g (Saturated Fat 4.5g, Trans Fat 0g); Cholesterol 60mg; Sodium 710mg; Total Carbohydrate 32g (Dietary Fiber 6g, Sugars 10g); Protein 31g. % Daily Value: Vitamin A 220%; Vitamin C 20%; Calcium 10%; Iron 25%. Exchanges: 1-1/2 Starch, 1/2 Other Carbohydrate, 1 Vegetable, 3-1/2 Lean Meat, 1 Fat. Carbohydrate Choices: 2.

Betty's Kitchen Tips

Purchasing: To save money, buy boneless skinless chicken breasts and thighs in bulk when on sale. Divide into portions and freeze until needed.

Did You Know? Peanuts are also called groundnuts or earth nuts.

new england pot roast

Prep Time: 30 Minutes
Start to Finish: 8 Hours 30 Minutes
Servings: 8

2 tablespoons vegetable oil	1 to 2 teaspoons salt
1 beef arm, blade or cross rib pot roast (4 lb)	1 teaspoon pepper
8 small potatoes, cut in half	1 cup water
8 medium carrots, cut into quarters	1/2 cup cold water
8 small onions	1/4 cup Gold Medal® all-purpose flour
1 jar (8 oz) prepared horseradish	

1 In 12-inch skillet, heat oil over medium heat. Add beef; cook about 10 minutes, turning occasionally, until brown on all sides.

2 Spray 6-quart slow cooker with cooking spray. In cooker, place potatoes, carrots and onions. Place beef on vegetables. In small bowl, mix horseradish, salt, pepper and 1 cup water; pour over beef.

3 Cover; cook on Low heat setting 8 to 10 hours.

4 Remove beef and vegetables from cooker; place on serving platter. Cover to keep warm.

5 Into 2-cup measuring cup, pour liquid from cooker; skim excess fat from liquid. Add enough water to liquid if necessary to measure 2 cups; pour into 2-quart saucepan. In tightly covered container, shake 1/2 cup cold water and the flour; gradually stir into liquid. Heat to boiling, stirring constantly. Boil and stir 1 minute. Serve gravy with beef and vegetables.

High Altitude (3500-6500 ft): In step 5, boil and stir 3 minutes.

Nutritional Info: 1 Serving: Calories 590 (Calories from Fat 170); Total Fat 19g (Saturated Fat 6g, Trans Fat 0.5g); Cholesterol 100mg; Sodium 510mg; Total Carbohydrate 48g (Dietary Fiber 8g, Sugars 9g); Protein 57g. % Daily Value: Vitamin A 21%; Vitamin C 30%; Calcium 10%; Iron 40%. Exchanges: 2 Starch, 1/2 Other Carbohydrate, 2 Vegetable, 6-1/2 Lean Meat. Carbohydrate Choices: 3.

Betty's Kitchen Tips

How-To: Carrots can vary in size and thickness. For even cooking, if the stem ends of the carrots are very thick, cut in half lengthwise.

Success Hint: Be sure you use prepared horseradish, not horseradish sauce. There is a big difference in flavor impact.

mediterranean pot roast

Prep Time: 10 Minutes
Start to Finish: 8 Hours 25 Minutes
Servings: 8-10

EASY

1	boneless beef chuck roast (3 lb)
1	teaspoon salt
1	tablespoon Italian seasoning
1	large clove garlic, finely chopped
1/3	cup sun-dried tomatoes in oil, drained, chopped
1/2	cup sliced pitted kalamata or ripe olives
1/2	cup beef broth
1/2	cup frozen small whole onions (from 1 lb bag)

1 Spray 12-inch skillet with cooking spray; heat over medium-high heat. In skillet, cook beef about 5 minutes, turning once, until brown. Sprinkle with salt, Italian seasoning and garlic; remove from heat.

2 Spray 4- to 5-quart slow cooker with cooking spray. Place beef, seasoned side up, in cooker. Spread tomatoes and olives over beef. Add broth and onions.

3 Cover; cook on Low heat setting 8 to 10 hours.

4 Remove beef from cooker; cover and let stand 15 minutes. Slice beef; serve with beef juice and onions from cooker.

High Altitude (3500-6500 ft): No change.

Nutritional Info: 1 Serving: Calories 340 (Calories from Fat 200); Total Fat 22g (Saturated Fat 8g, Trans Fat 1g); Cholesterol 100mg; Sodium 530mg; Total Carbohydrate 3g (Dietary Fiber 0g, Sugars 1g); Protein 32g. % Daily Value: Vitamin A 2%; Vitamin C 4%; Calcium 4%; Iron 25%. Exchanges: 4-1/2 Lean Meat, 2 Fat. Carbohydrate Choices: 0.

Betty's Kitchen Tips

Did You Know? Italian seasoning is a prepared blend of herbs popular in Italian cooking. The blend usually includes thyme, oregano, basil, savory, marjoram, rosemary and sage.

Serve-With: In keeping with the Mediterranean theme, try sprinkling crumbled feta cheese over the slices of beef just before serving. Pita bread triangles make yummy sides.

mango chutney-chicken curry

Prep Time: 15 Minutes
Start to Finish: 6 Hours 45 Minutes
Servings: 4

EASY LOW FAT

4	skinless bone-in chicken breast halves (about 10 oz each)
1	can (15 to 16 oz) garbanzo beans, drained, rinsed
1	small onion, thinly sliced
1	medium red bell pepper, chopped (1/2 cup)
1/2	cup water
2	tablespoons cornstarch

1	tablespoon curry powder
1/2	teaspoon salt
1/4	teaspoon pepper
1	jar (9 oz) mango chutney
1	cup fresh snap pea pods, strings removed
1	cup uncooked regular long-grain rice
2	cups water

1 Spray 3- to 4-quart slow cooker with cooking spray. In cooker, layer chicken, beans, onion and bell pepper. In small bowl, mix 1/2 cup water, the cornstarch, curry powder, salt, pepper and chutney; pour into cooker.

2 Cover; cook on Low heat setting 6 to 7 hours.

3 Increase heat setting to High. Stir in pea pods. Cover; cook 20 to 30 minutes longer or until pea pods are crisp-tender. Meanwhile, cook rice in water as directed on package. Serve chicken mixture over rice.

High Altitude (3500-6500 ft): No change.

Nutritional Info: 1 Serving: Calories 700 (Calories from Fat 90); Total Fat 10g (Saturated Fat 2.5g, Trans Fat 0g); Cholesterol 125mg; Sodium 1000mg; Total Carbohydrate 94g (Dietary Fiber 8g, Sugars 21g); Protein 58g. % Daily Value: Vitamin A 25%; Vitamin C 60%; Calcium 10%; Iron 40%. Exchanges: 4 Starch, 2 Other Carbohydrate, 1 Vegetable, 6 Very Lean Meat. Carbohydrate Choices: 6.

Betty's Kitchen Tips

Serve-With: Serve with small bowls of traditional curry dish toppers, such as toasted shredded coconut, chopped peanuts and raisins. The saltiness of the peanuts and the sweetness of the coconut and raisins enhance the flavors of the curry powder and chutney.

Did You Know? Chutney is a spicy mixture of fruit, vinegar, sugar and spices. It can vary in texture from chunky to smooth and in spiciness from mild to hot. We liked the sweetness of the mango chutney, but feel free to experiment.

cola barbecued ribs

Prep Time: 10 Minutes
Start to Finish: 9 Hours 10 Minutes
Servings: 4

EASY

- -

3-1/2	lb pork spareribs or loin back ribs
1/4	cup packed brown sugar
1/2	teaspoon hickory smoked salt
1/4	teaspoon pepper
1/2	cup cola
1-1/4	cups barbecue sauce

- -

1 Spray 4- to 5-quart slow cooker with cooking spray. Trim excess fat and remove membranes from ribs. In small bowl, mix brown sugar, hickory smoked salt and pepper; rub mixture into ribs. Cut ribs into 2- or 3-rib portions. Place ribs in cooker; pour cola around ribs.

2 Cover; cook on Low heat setting 8 to 9 hours.

3 Remove ribs from cooker; place in shallow baking pan. Drain liquid from cooker and discard. Brush both sides of ribs with barbecue sauce. Return ribs to cooker. Pour any remaining sauce over ribs.

4 Cover; cook on Low heat setting about 1 hour longer or until ribs are glazed and sauce is desired consistency. Cut into single-rib servings if desired.

High Altitude (3500-6500 ft): No change.

Nutritional Info: 1 Serving: Calories 800 (Calories from Fat 420); Total Fat 47g (Saturated Fat 17g, Trans Fat 0g); Cholesterol 190mg; Sodium 1270mg; Total Carbohydrate 49g (Dietary Fiber 0g, Sugars 42g); Protein 46g. % Daily Value: Vitamin A 4%; Vitamin C 2%; Calcium 15%; Iron 25%. Exchanges: 3 Other Carbohydrate, 6 High-Fat Meat. Carbohydrate Choices: 3.

Betty's Kitchen Tips

Serve-With: For a comforting homemade dinner, serve with coleslaw and hot-from-the-oven cornbread. Don't forget to pass the butter to top off the cornbread!

Substitution: Hickory smoked salt adds a nice hint of barbecue flavor to these ribs. If you don't have smoky-flavored salt on hand, use 1/2 teaspoon garlic salt instead.

southwestern pork burritos

Prep Time: 10 Minutes
Start to Finish: 8 Hours 10 Minutes
Servings: 12 burritos

EASY

- 1 boneless pork shoulder roast (2-1/2 lb), trimmed of fat
- 1 can (10 oz) diced tomatoes and green chiles, undrained
- 3 tablespoons tomato paste
- 1 tablespoon honey
- 3 cloves garlic, finely chopped
- 1 tablespoon chili powder
- 1/4 teaspoon salt
- 12 Old El Paso® flour tortillas for burritos (8 inch; from two 11.5 oz packages)

Assorted toppings (such as shredded Cheddar cheese, sour cream, chopped fresh cilantro, shredded lettuce, diced tomatoes), if desired

1 Spray 3- to 4-quart slow cooker with cooking spray. Place pork in cooker.

2 In blender, place tomatoes, tomato paste, honey, garlic, chili powder and salt. Cover; blend on medium-high speed 10 seconds, stopping blender frequently to scrape sides. Pour over pork.

3 Cover; cook on Low heat setting 8 to 10 hours.

4 Remove pork from cooker; place on cutting board. Shred pork with 2 forks; return to cooker and mix well.

5 Serve the pork mixture on tortillas with toppings; roll up. Pork mixture will hold on Low heat setting up to 2 hours.

High Altitude (3500-6500 ft): No change.

Nutritional Info: 1 Burrito: Calories 330 (Calories from Fat 140); Total Fat 15g (Saturated Fat 5g, Trans Fat 1g); Cholesterol 60mg; Sodium 490mg; Total Carbohydrate 24g (Dietary Fiber 0g, Sugars 3g); Protein 24g. % Daily Value: Vitamin A 6%; Vitamin C 2%; Calcium 8%; Iron 10%. Exchanges: 1 Starch, 1/2 Other Carbohydrate, 3 Lean Meat, 1 Fat. Carbohydrate Choices: 1-1/2.

Betty's Kitchen Tips

Variation: This tasty pork filling also makes great sandwiches. Spoon the filling on top of toasted bread slices. Top with shredded lettuce and shredded Monterey Jack or Cheddar cheese.

How-To: To warm tortillas, wrap them in foil and heat in a 325°F oven for about 15 minutes. Or place on a microwavable paper towel, and microwave on High for 30 seconds.

chicken cacciatore

Prep Time: 15 Minutes
Start to Finish: 8 Hours 25 Minutes
Servings: 6

EASY

2-1/2	lb boneless skinless chicken thighs (about 12)
1	jar (4.5 oz) Green Giant® sliced mushrooms, drained
2	cans (6 oz each) Italian-style tomato paste
1	can (14 oz) chicken broth
1/2	cup white wine, if desired

1-1/2	teaspoons dried basil leaves
1/2	teaspoon salt
1	dried bay leaf
12	oz uncooked linguine
1/4	teaspoon dried thyme leaves
1	tablespoon cornstarch

Shredded Parmesan cheese, if desired

1 Spray 3- to 4-quart slow cooker with cooking spray. Place chicken in cooker. Add mushrooms, tomato paste, broth, wine, basil, salt and bay leaf; gently stir to mix.

2 Cover; cook on Low heat setting 8 to 10 hours.

3 About 15 minutes before serving, cook and drain linguine as directed on package. Remove chicken from slow cooker; cover to keep warm. Stir thyme into sauce in cooker. Increase heat setting to High. In small bowl, mix 1/4 cup sauce from cooker and the cornstarch until smooth; stir into remaining sauce in cooker.

4 Cover; cook 10 minutes longer, stirring frequently. Remove bay leaf before serving. Serve chicken and sauce over linguine. Sprinkle with cheese.

High Altitude (3500-6500 ft): No change.

Nutritional Info: 1 Serving: Calories 540 (Calories from Fat 120); Total Fat 13g (Saturated Fat 4g, Trans Fat 0g); Cholesterol 85mg; Sodium 1310mg; Total Carbohydrate 63g (Dietary Fiber 6g, Sugars 8g); Protein 42g. % Daily Value: Vitamin A 20%; Vitamin C 10%; Calcium 8%; Iron 35%. Exchanges: 3 Starch, 1 Other Carbohydrate, 4-1/2 Lean Meat. Carbohydrate Choices: 4.

Betty's Kitchen Tips

Serve-With: Serve with sesame breadsticks and a simple salad of mixed greens drizzled with olive oil and balsamic vinegar.

Substitute: One 26-ounce jar of tomato pasta sauce can be substituted for the tomato paste, chicken broth and white wine.

caramelized onion pot roast

Prep Time: 25 Minutes
Start to Finish: 8 Hours 25 Minutes
Servings: 12

- 1 tablespoon olive or vegetable oil
- 1 boneless beef chuck roast (4 lb)
- 1 teaspoon salt
- 1/2 teaspoon pepper
- 6 medium onions, sliced
- 1-1/2 cups beef broth
- 3/4 cup regular or nonalcoholic beer
- 2 tablespoons packed brown sugar
- 3 tablespoons Dijon mustard
- 2 tablespoons cider vinegar

1 In 10-inch skillet, heat oil over medium-high heat. Add beef; cook about 10 minutes, turning occasionally, until brown on all sides. Sprinkle with salt and pepper.

2 Spray 4- to 5-quart slow cooker with cooking spray. Place onions in cooker. Place beef on onions. In medium bowl, mix remaining ingredients; pour over beef and onions.

3 Cover; cook on Low heat setting 8 to 10 hours.

4 Remove beef and onions from cooker, using slotted spoon. Cut beef into slices or break into pieces. Skim fat from beef juices in cooker if desired. Serve beef with juices.

High Altitude (3500-6500 ft): No change.

Nutritional Info: 1 Serving: Calories 330 (Calories from Fat 170); Total Fat 19g (Saturated Fat 7g, Trans Fat 1g); Cholesterol 85mg; Sodium 500mg; Total Carbohydrate 8g (Dietary Fiber 1g, Sugars 5g); Protein 29g. % Daily Value: Vitamin A 0%; Vitamin C 4%; Calcium 2%; Iron 20%. Exchanges: 1/2 Other Carbohydrate, 4 Lean Meat, 1-1/2 Fat. Carbohydrate Choices: 1/2.

SLOW COOKER TRAVELING TIPS

- Keep the lid in place by stretching rubber bands around the slow cooker handles and across the lid.

- Wrap the slow cooker in a towel or in newspaper to insulate it, then place it in a box to keep it steady. Or, if you transport your slow cooker often, consider purchasing an insulated slow cooker tote.

- Once you arrive at your gathering, plug the slow cooker in and set on Low. Serve food within two hours of toting it.

- Carry along an extension cord just in case there are no nearby outlets.

sweet and tangy short ribs

Prep Time: 35 Minutes
Start to Finish: 9 Hours 35 Minutes
Servings: 6

Ribs

- 1 tablespoon vegetable oil
- 4 lb beef short ribs
- 1 large sweet onion (such as Bermuda, Maui or Spanish), cut in half, halves sliced (about 3-1/2 cups)

Sauce

- 1 bottle (12 oz) chili sauce
- 3/4 cup apricot preserves
- 2 tablespoons packed brown sugar
- 2 tablespoons cider vinegar
- 2 tablespoons Worcestershire sauce
- 2 teaspoons ground mustard
- 2 cloves garlic, finely chopped

1 In 12-inch nonstick skillet, heat oil over medium-high heat. Add ribs, in batches if necessary; cook 6 to 8 minutes, turning occasionally, until brown on all sides.

2 Spray 4- to 5-quart slow cooker with cooking spray. Place onion in cooker. Top with ribs. Cover; cook on Low heat setting 8 hours.

3 In 2-quart saucepan, cook sauce ingredients over low heat 15 to 20 minutes, stirring frequently, until the sauce has thickened.

4 Drain excess liquid from cooker. Pour sauce over ribs. Increase heat setting to High. Cover; cook about 1 hour longer or until meat begins to separate from bones.

High Altitude (3500-6500 ft): No change.

Nutritional Info: 1 Serving: Calories 470 (Calories from Fat 180); Total Fat 20g (Saturated Fat 7g, Trans Fat 1g); Cholesterol 90mg; Sodium 880mg; Total Carbohydrate 47g (Dietary Fiber 4g, Sugars 32g); Protein 24g. % Daily Value: Vitamin A 8%; Vitamin C 15%; Calcium 6%; Iron 15%. Exchanges: 3 Other Carbohydrate, 3-1/2 Medium-Fat Meat, 1/2 Fat. Carbohydrate Choices: 3.

Betty's Kitchen Tips

Do-Ahead: Make the sauce a day ahead. Store covered in the refrigerator, and heat before adding to the ribs.

Serve-With: These ribs are great with steamed broccoli and warm dinner rolls.

apricot-glazed pork roast and stuffing

Prep Time: 10 Minutes
Start to Finish: 7 Hours 10 Minutes
Servings: 6

EASY

4	cups herb-seasoned stuffing cubes
3/4	cup chicken broth
1/2	cup dried apricots, chopped
1/3	cup frozen chopped onions (from 14-oz bag)
1	boneless pork loin roast (2 to 2-1/2 lb), trimmed of fat
1/3	cup apricot jam
1	tablespoon balsamic vinegar

1 Spray 3- to 4-quart slow cooker with cooking spray. In cooker, mix stuffing, broth, apricots and onions. Place pork on stuffing mixture. In small bowl, mix jam and vinegar; brush over pork.

2 Cover; cook on Low heat setting 7 to 8 hours.

3 Remove pork from cooker; place on cutting board. Stir stuffing before serving. Cut pork into slices; serve with stuffing.

High Altitude (3500-6500 ft): No change.

Nutritional Info: 1 Serving: Calories 470 (Calories from Fat 120); Total Fat 13g (Saturated Fat 4g, Trans Fat 0g); Cholesterol 95mg; Sodium 730mg; Total Carbohydrate 49g (Dietary Fiber 4g, Sugars 17g); Protein 39g. % Daily Value: Vitamin A 8%; Vitamin C 2%; Calcium 6%; Iron 20%. Exchanges: 1-1/2 Starch, 1-1/2 Other Carbohydrate, 5 Lean Meat. Carbohydrate Choices: 3.

Betty's Kitchen Tips

Success Hint: To give this tasty roast more color, brown all sides in 1 tablespoon of vegetable oil in a 12-inch skillet over medium-high heat before placing in the slow cooker and brushing with jam.

Substitute: If you don't have any balsamic vinegar, use 1 tablespoon cider or white vinegar. Also, peach jam will work if apricot jam isn't readily available on your pantry shelf.

chili mole

Prep Time: 15 Minutes
Start to Finish: 4 Hours 15 Minutes
Servings: 6 (1-1/2 cups each)

EASY

- 1 lb lean (at least 80%) ground beef
- 1 medium onion, chopped (1/2 cup)
- 1 package (1.25 oz) Tex-Mex chili seasoning mix
- 1 can (28 oz) Progresso® diced tomatoes, undrained
- 1 can (28 oz) Progresso® crushed tomatoes, undrained
- 1 can (15 oz) spicy chili beans, undrained
- 1 oz unsweetened baking chocolate, coarsely chopped

1 Spray 4- to 5-quart slow cooker with cooking spray. In 10-inch skillet, cook beef and onion over medium heat 8 to 10 minutes, stirring occasionally, until beef is thoroughly cooked; drain.

2 In cooker, mix beef mixture and remaining ingredients.

3 Cover; cook on Low heat setting 4 to 6 hours. Stir well before serving.

High Altitude (3500-6500 ft): No change.

Nutritional Info: 1 Serving: Calories 310 (Calories from Fat 110); Total Fat 12g (Saturated Fat 5g, Trans Fat 0.5g); Cholesterol 45mg; Sodium 1100mg; Total Carbohydrate 29g (Dietary Fiber 8g, Sugars 10g); Protein 20g. % Daily Value: Vitamin A 15%; Vitamin C 20%; Calcium 10%. Exchanges: 1-1/2 Starch, 1 Vegetable, 2 Medium-Fat Meat. Carbohydrate Choices: 2.

SLOW COOKER DO'S FOR FOOD SAFETY

- Refrigerate perishable ingredients that you've prepared ahead (such as meat and vegetables) in separate containers to avoid cross-contamination.

- Defrost meat or poultry before adding it to the slow cooker.

- Heat or microwave leftovers until thoroughly heated before placing in a preheated slow cooker to keep hot.

- Refrigerate leftovers in covered shallow containers within two hours after cooking is complete.

chicken alfredo stew

Prep Time: 10 Minutes
Start to Finish: 6 Hours 10 Minutes
Servings: 6

EASY

- 1 jar (16 oz) Alfredo pasta sauce
- 3/4 cup water
- 1/2 teaspoon dried basil leaves
- 1/2 teaspoon salt
- 4 cups refrigerated cooked diced potatoes with onions (from 20-oz bag)
- 1-1/4 lb boneless skinless chicken thighs, cut into 1-inch-wide strips
- 1 bag (1 lb) Green Giant® frozen mixed vegetables

1 In small bowl, mix pasta sauce, water, basil and salt.

2 Spray 3- to 4-quart slow cooker with cooking spray. In cooker, layer half each of the potatoes, chicken strips, frozen vegetables and pasta sauce. Repeat layers ending with pasta sauce.

3 Cover; cook on Low heat setting for 6 to 8 hours.

High Altitude (3500-6500 ft): No change.

Nutritional Info: 1 Serving: Calories 530 (Calories from Fat 280); Total Fat 31g (Saturated Fat 17g, Trans Fat 1g); Cholesterol 135mg; Sodium 730mg; Total Carbohydrate 33g (Dietary Fiber 5g, Sugars 3g); Protein 30g. % Daily Value: Vitamin A 80%; Vitamin C 8%; Calcium 20%; Iron 15%. Exchanges: 2 Starch, 1 Vegetable, 3 Very Lean Meat, 5-1/2 Fat. Carbohydrate Choices: 2.

Betty's Kitchen Tips

Substitute: Unbreaded chicken breast tenders can be used instead of the cut-up chicken thighs.

Variation: If you like garlic, try using garlic-flavored Alfredo pasta sauce.

SLOW COOKER DON'TS FOR FOOD SAFETY

- Never put raw ground meat in a slow cooker. It must be cooked first.

- Don't slow cook whole chickens or meat loaf because they'd cook too slowly and remain in the harmful bacteria zone too long.

- Don't fully or partially cook meat and then refrigerate it before adding it to the slow cooker.

- Don't use your slow cooker to reheat leftovers straight from the fridge.

chipotle pulled-pork sandwiches

Prep Time: 15 Minutes
Start to Finish: 7 Hours 45 Minutes
Servings: 20 sandwiches

EASY

1	tablespoon packed brown sugar
2	teaspoons salt
2	teaspoons garlic powder
1-1/2	teaspoons ground mustard
3	teaspoons chili powder
1	boneless pork shoulder (3 lb), trimmed of fat

1	can (8 oz) tomato sauce
2	canned chipotle chiles, finely chopped
1	tablespoon adobo sauce from canned chipotle chiles
20	burger buns, split
5	medium avocados, pitted, peeled and thinly sliced

1 Spray 4- to 5-quart slow cooker with cooking spray. In small bowl, mix brown sugar, salt, garlic powder, mustard and chili powder. Rub seasoning mixture over pork. Place pork in cooker. Sprinkle any remaining seasoning mixture that doesn't stick to pork over top of pork in cooker.

2 Cover; cook on Low heat setting 7 to 8 hours.

3 Remove pork from cooker; place on cutting board. Remove liquid from cooker; skim fat from liquid and reserve liquid. Cool pork slightly. With 2 forks, shred pork. Return to cooker. Stir the tomato sauce, chipotle chiles and adobo sauce into the shredded pork. If desired, stir in some of the reserved cooking liquid for desired moistness.

4 Increase heat setting to High. Cover; cook 15 to 30 minutes longer or until hot. Spoon about 1/3 cup pork mixture into each bun. Place a few slices of avocado over pork in each bun. Pork mixture can be kept warm on Low heat setting up to 2 hours; stir occasionally.

High Altitude (3500-6500 ft): No change.

Nutritional Info: 1 Sandwich: Calories 340 (Calories from Fat 150); Total Fat 17g (Saturated Fat 4.5g, Trans Fat 0g); Cholesterol 45mg; Sodium 550mg; Total Carbohydrate 27g (Dietary Fiber 4g, Sugars 4g); Protein 20g. % Daily Value: Vitamin A 4%; Vitamin C 4%; Calcium 8%; Iron 15%. Exchanges: 1 Starch, 1/2 Other Carbohydrate, 2-1/2 Lean Meat, 2 Fat. Carbohydrate Choices: 2.

Betty's Kitchen Tips

Serve-With: Complete this meal with carrot sticks and corn chips.

Did You Know? Leftover pork makes a tasty burrito filling or tostada topping.

ham and wild rice soup

Prep Time: 15 Minutes
Start to Finish: 7 Hours 30 Minutes
Servings: 6 (1-1/2 cups each)   **EASY**

- 2 cups diced cooked ham
- 1 cup purchased julienne (matchstick-cut) carrots
- 3/4 cup uncooked wild rice
- 1 medium onion, chopped (1/2 cup)
- 1 can (14 oz) chicken broth
- 1 can (10-3/4 oz) reduced-sodium cream of celery soup
- 1/4 teaspoon pepper
- 3 cups water
- 1 cup half-and-half
- 1/4 cup sliced almonds
- 2 tablespoons dry sherry, if desired
- 1/4 cup chopped fresh parsley

1 Spray 3- to 4-quart slow cooker with cooking spray. In cooker, mix all ingredients except half-and-half, almonds, sherry and parsley.

2 Cover; cook on Low heat setting 7 to 8 hours.

3 Stir in remaining ingredients. Increase heat setting to High. Cover; cook 10 to 15 minutes longer or until hot.

High Altitude (3500-6500 ft): No change.

Nutritional Info: 1 Serving: Calories 290 (Calories from Fat 110); Total Fat 12g (Saturated Fat 5g, Trans Fat 0g); Cholesterol 40mg; Sodium 1190mg; Total Carbohydrate 28g (Dietary Fiber 3g, Sugars 5g); Protein 17g. % Daily Value: Vitamin A 80%; Vitamin C 6%; Calcium 10%; Iron 10%. Exchanges: 1-1/2 Starch, 1/2 Other Carbohydrate, 2 Lean Meat, 1 Fat. Carbohydrate Choices: 2.

Betty's Kitchen Tips

Purchasing: Look for a bag of julienne-cut carrots or French-cut cooking carrots in the refrigerated vegetable section of your grocery store.

Success Hint: For best results, we don't recommend using canned or quick-cooking wild rice for this recipe.

italian beef and bean soup

Prep Time: 20 Minutes
Start to Finish: 40 Minutes
Servings: 5 (about 1-1/2 cups each)

2 teaspoons Gold Medal® all-purpose flour	1 can (15 oz) Progresso® cannellini beans, drained, rinsed
1/4 teaspoon salt	1 can (14.5 oz) diced tomatoes with basil, garlic and oregano, undrained
1/4 teaspoon pepper	2 cups frozen Italian-blend vegetables (from 1-lb bag)
1/2 lb boneless beef round steak, cut into 1/2-inch cubes	3 cups water
1 tablespoon olive or canola oil	Grated Parmesan cheese, if desired

1 In 1-quart resealable food-storage plastic bag, place flour, salt and pepper. Seal bag; shake until blended. Add beef; seal bag and shake until beef is evenly coated with flour mixture.

2 In 3-quart heavy saucepan or Dutch oven, heat oil over medium-high heat. Add beef; cook 4 to 5 minutes, stirring occasionally, until brown on all sides.

3 Stir in remaining ingredients except cheese. Heat to boiling. Reduce heat; simmer uncovered 15 to 20 minutes or until vegetables are tender. Serve with cheese.

High Altitude (3500-6500 ft): No change.

Nutritional Info: 1 Serving: Calories 220 (Calories from Fat 40); Total Fat 4.5g (Saturated Fat 1g, Trans Fat 0g); Cholesterol 25mg; Sodium 250mg; Total Carbohydrate 25g (Dietary Fiber 7g, Sugars 4g); Protein 19g. % Daily Value: Vitamin A 6%; Vitamin C 8%; Calcium 10%; Iron 30%. Exchanges: 1-1/2 Starch, 1 Vegetable, 1-1/2 Very Lean Meat, 1/2 Fat. Carbohydrate Choices: 1-1/2.

Betty's Kitchen Tips

Serve-With: Add Italian breadsticks and a bagged salad for a quick and easy meal.

Substitution: Beans are interchangeable. You can try kidney, pinto or great northern beans for the cannellini beans in this steamy soup.

mushroom-swiss veggie burgers

Prep Time: 20 Minutes
Start to Finish: 20 Minutes
Servings: 4

QUICK

- 4 frozen vegetable burgers
- 1 jar (4.5 oz) Green Giant® sliced mushrooms, drained
- 4 slices (about 1 oz each) reduced-fat Swiss cheese
- 1/4 cup fat-free mayonnaise
- 4 whole-grain hamburger buns
- 4 tomato slices
- 4 lettuce leaves

Ketchup and mustard, if desired

1 Heat gas or charcoal grill. Place vegetable burgers on grill over medium heat. Cover grill; cook 6 to 9 minutes, turning once, until thoroughly heated.

2 Divide mushrooms evenly onto patties; top with cheese. Cover grill; cook 1 to 2 minutes longer or until cheese is melted. Spread 1 tablespoon mayonnaise on each bun. Serve patties in buns with tomatoes, lettuce, ketchup and mustard.

High Altitude (3500-6500 ft): Cover and grill over medium-low heat.

Nutritional Info: 1 Serving: Calories 300 (Calories from Fat 70); Total Fat 8g (Saturated Fat 2.5g, Trans Fat 0g); Cholesterol 15mg; Sodium 930mg; Total Carbohydrate 32g (Dietary Fiber 8g, Sugars 8g); Protein 25g. % Daily Value: Vitamin A 10%; Vitamin C 4%; Calcium 40%; Iron 20%. Exchanges: 1-1/2 Starch, 1/2 Other Carbohydrate, 3 Very Lean Meat, 1 Fat. Carbohydrate Choices: 2.

Betty's Kitchen Tips

Success Hint: If you haven't had veggie burgers for a while, you're in for a treat! They come in many flavors, from Cajun-spiced to classic grilled. Choose your favorite version.

Serve-With: Team these burgers with classic picnic fare: Carrot and celery sticks, fresh-cut melon and lemonade.

peppered pork pitas with garlic spread

Prep Time: 20 Minutes
Start to Finish: 20 Minutes
Servings: 4

QUICK

- 1/3 cup fat-free mayonnaise or salad dressing
- 2 tablespoons fat-free (skim) milk
- 2 cloves garlic, finely chopped
- 1/2 lb boneless pork loin chops, cut into thin bite-size strips

- 1 tablespoon olive or canola oil
- 1 teaspoon coarsely ground pepper
- 1 jar (7.25 oz) roasted red bell peppers, drained, sliced
- 4 pita fold breads (7 inch)

1 In small bowl, mix mayonnaise, milk and garlic; set aside.

2 In medium bowl, mix pork, oil and pepper. Heat 10-inch skillet over medium-high heat. Add pork; cook 5 to 6 minutes, stirring occasionally, until pork is lightly browned and no longer pink in center. Stir in bell peppers; heat until warm.

3 Heat pita folds as directed on package. Lightly spread one side of each pita fold with garlic mixture. Spoon pork mixture over each; fold up.

High Altitude (3500-6500 ft): No change.

Nutritional Info: 1 Serving: Calories 340 (Calories from Fat 80); Total Fat 9g (Saturated Fat 2.5g, Trans Fat 0g); Cholesterol 35mg; Sodium 560mg; Total Carbohydrate 45g (Dietary Fiber 2g, Sugars 5g); Protein 19g. % Daily Value: Vitamin A 50%; Vitamin C 60%; Calcium 8%; Iron 15%. Exchanges: 2-1/2 Starch, 1/2 Other Carbohydrate, 1-1/2 Lean Meat, 1/2 Fat. Carbohydrate Choices: 3.

Betty's Kitchen Tips

Variation: Use thinly sliced chicken instead of the pork. Cook 5 to 6 minutes or until the chicken is no longer pink in center.

Health Twist: For extra fiber, texture and whole-grain goodness, use whole wheat pita bread instead of regular pita bread.

chicken-vegetable soup with dumplings

Prep Time: 10 Minutes
Start to Finish: 35 Minutes
Servings: 6 (1 cup each)

EASY

- 2 cups cut-up cooked chicken
- 4 cups reduced-sodium chicken broth (from three 14-oz cans)
- 1 tablespoon chopped fresh parsley
- 1 tablespoon chopped fresh thyme leaves
- 2 cloves garlic, finely chopped
- 1 bag (1 lb) frozen mixed vegetables, thawed, drained
- 1 cup Original Bisquick® mix
- 1/3 cup fat-free (skim) milk

1 In 3-quart saucepan, heat all ingredients except Bisquick mix and milk to boiling, stirring occasionally.

2 In small bowl, stir Bisquick mix and milk with fork until soft dough forms. Drop dough by 18 teaspoonfuls onto boiling soup. If dumplings sink into soup, carefully bring to top of broth with slotted spoon.

3 Reduce heat to medium-low; cook uncovered 10 minutes. Cover; cook 15 minutes longer.

High Altitude (3500-6500 ft): No change.

Nutritional Info: 1 Serving: Calories 230 (Calories from Fat 50); Total Fat 6g (Saturated Fat 1.5g, Trans Fat 1g); Cholesterol 40mg; Sodium 690mg; Total Carbohydrate 24g (Dietary Fiber 4g, Sugars 4g); Protein 19g. % Daily Value: Vitamin A 70%; Vitamin C 4%; Calcium 8%; Iron 10%. Exchanges: 1 Starch, 1 Vegetable, 2 Lean Meat. Carbohydrate Choices: 1-1/2.

Betty's Kitchen Tip

- Rich and hearty, this familiar chicken soup tastes as good as it looks, and the dumplings add a special touch. Use any combination of frozen vegetables your family enjoys.

chicken chili with cornbread dumplings

Prep Time: 10 Minutes
Start to Finish: 30 Minutes
Servings: 4 (1-1/2 cups each)

EASY   QUICK

Chili

3	cups cubed cooked chicken
1-1/2	cups water
1	can (10-3/4 oz) condensed cream of chicken soup
1	can (15 oz) navy beans, drained, rinsed
1	can (11 oz) Green Giant® Mexicorn® whole kernel corn with red and green peppers, undrained

1	can (4.5 oz) Old El Paso® chopped green chiles
1	teaspoon ground cumin

Dumplings

1-1/3	cups Original Bisquick® mix
2/3	cup yellow cornmeal
2/3	cup milk
1	teaspoon chili powder

1   In 5-quart nonstick Dutch oven, heat all chili ingredients over medium-high heat, stirring occasionally, until bubbly.

2   Meanwhile, in medium bowl, stir all dumpling ingredients until soft dough forms.

3   Drop dough by 8 rounded spoonfuls onto simmering chili. Reduce heat to medium-low. Cover; cook 13 to 15 minutes or until dumplings are dry.

High Altitude (3500-6500 ft): After adding dumplings, simmer covered 14 to 16 minutes.

Nutritional Info: 1 Serving: Calories 750 (Calories from Fat 180); Total Fat 20g (Saturated Fat 6g, Trans Fat 2g); Cholesterol 100mg; Sodium 1520mg; Total Carbohydrate 96g (Dietary Fiber 14g, Sugars 9g); Protein 47g. % Daily Value: Vitamin A 15%; Vitamin C 10%; Calcium 20%; Iron 40%. Exchanges: 4 Starch, 2-1/2 Other Carbohydrate, 5 Lean Meat. Carbohydrate Choices: 6-1/2.

Betty's Kitchen Tips

Did You Know? A 3-lb frying chicken, cooked, skinned and boned, will yield about 3 cups cubed chicken.

Substitution: Pinto beans may be substituted for the navy beans if you like.

grilled fish tacos

Prep Time: 20 Minutes
Start to Finish: 35 Minutes
Servings: 4

LOW FAT

- -

2	tablespoons lime juice
2	teaspoons chili powder
1	teaspoon ground cumin
2	tilapia or cod fillets (10 oz)
4	whole wheat tortillas (6 inch)
1	cup shredded lettuce
1/2	cup rinsed drained Progresso® black beans (from 15-oz can)
1/4	cup chopped seeded tomato
1/4	cup shredded reduced-fat Cheddar cheese
1/4	cup reduced-fat sour cream, if desired
2	tablespoons chopped fresh cilantro

- -

1 In pint-size heavy-duty resealable food-storage plastic bag, mix lime juice, chili powder and cumin. Add fish; seal bag. Turn bag several times to coat fish with marinade. Refrigerate 15 to 30 minutes.

2 Heat gas or charcoal grill. Carefully brush grill rack with canola oil. Place fish on grill over medium heat. Cover grill; cook 4 to 6 minutes, turning after 2 minutes, until fish flakes easily with fork.

3 Cut fish into bite-size pieces. Divide the fish between tortillas; fill with the remaining ingredients.

High Altitude (3500-6500 ft): Grill over medium heat 7 to 9 minutes, turning after 3 minutes.

Nutritional Info: 1 Serving: Calories 170 (Calories from Fat 25); Total Fat 2.5g (Saturated Fat 0.5g, Trans Fat 0g); Cholesterol 40mg; Sodium 250mg; Total Carbohydrate 18g (Dietary Fiber 4g, Sugars 1g); Protein 19g. % Daily Value: Vitamin A 10%; Vitamin C 4%; Calcium 10%; Iron 10%. Exchanges: 1 Starch, 2-1/2 Very Lean Meat. Carbohydrate Choices: 1.

Betty's Kitchen Tip

• Now you can have this popular restaurant favorite at home with fewer calories and less fat.

grilled barbecued beef and bean burgers

Prep Time: 25 Minutes
Start to Finish: 25 Minutes
Servings: 5

1/2 lb extra-lean (at least 90%) ground beef
  1 can (15 to 16 oz) great northern beans, drained, rinsed
1/4 cup finely crushed saltine crackers (about 7 squares)
  2 tablespoons barbecue sauce

1/4 teaspoon pepper
  1 egg
  5 teaspoons barbecue sauce
  5 whole-grain hamburger buns, split

Leaf lettuce, sliced tomatoes and sliced onions, if desired

1 Heat gas or charcoal grill. In large bowl, mix the beef, beans, cracker crumbs, 2 tablespoons barbecue sauce, the pepper and egg. Shape mixture into 5 patties, about 1/2 inch thick.

2 Carefully brush grill rack with canola oil. Place patties on grill over medium heat. Cover grill; cook 5 minutes. Turn patties; spread each patty with 1 teaspoon barbecue sauce. Cook 6 to 8 minutes longer or until meat thermometer inserted in center of patties reads 160°F.

3 Fill buns with lettuce, patties, tomatoes and onions.

High Altitude (3500-6500 ft): No change.

Nutritional Info: 1 Serving: Calories 320 (Calories from Fat 60); Total Fat 7g (Saturated Fat 2.5g, Trans Fat 0.5g); Cholesterol 70mg; Sodium 390mg; Total Carbohydrate 43g (Dietary Fiber 7g, Sugars 8g); Protein 21g. % Daily Value: Vitamin A 0%; Vitamin C 0%; Calcium 10%; Iron 30%. Exchanges: 2 Starch, 1 Other Carbohydrate, 2 Lean Meat. Carbohydrate Choices: 3.

Betty's Kitchen Tip

• Top these delicious burgers with your favorites: grilled onions, lettuce and tomato, relish or any veggies.

seafood bisque

Prep Time: 25 Minutes
Start to Finish: 25 Minutes
Servings: 8

QUICK

- 1/3 cup butter or margarine
- 1/3 cup Gold Medal® all-purpose flour
- 3-1/2 cups Progresso® chicken broth (from 32-oz carton)
- 4 cups (1 quart) half-and-half
- 1/2 cup dry white wine or water
- 1/2 cup chopped drained roasted red bell peppers (from 7-oz jar)
- 12 oz cod fillet, cut into 1-inch pieces
- 12 oz uncooked deveined peeled medium shrimp, thawed if frozen and tail shells removed
- 1/2 cup basil pesto
- 1/4 teaspoon salt
- 1/8 teaspoon freshly ground pepper

1. In 4-quart Dutch oven, melt butter over medium-high heat. Stir in flour. Gradually stir in broth, half-and-half and wine. Stir in bell peppers and cod. Heat to boiling, stirring occasionally.

2. Stir in shrimp. Reduce heat; simmer uncovered 2 to 3 minutes or until shrimp are pink. Stir in pesto, salt and pepper.

High Altitude (3500-6500 ft): No change.

Nutritional Info: 1 Serving: Calories 420 (Calories from Fat 280); Total Fat 31g (Saturated Fat 15g, Trans Fat 1g); Cholesterol 150mg; Sodium 860mg; Total Carbohydrate 11g (Dietary Fiber 0g, Sugars 6g); Protein 22g. % Daily Value: Vitamin A 35%; Vitamin C 20%; Calcium 20%; Iron 10%. Exchanges: 1/2 Starch, 3 Very Lean Meat, 6 Fat. Carbohydrate Choices: 1.

Betty's Kitchen Tips

Substitution: Cooked shrimp works great in this recipe, too. Just add the shrimp to the bisque and simmer until thoroughly heated.

Special Touch: As you dish up the soup, sprinkle chopped fresh basil leaves and a little freshly shredded Parmesan cheese on each serving. Or for a simple yet "showy" garnish for each serving, tie a chive around an additional cooked shrimp.

fish chowder

Prep Time: 30 Minutes
Start to Finish: 30 Minutes
Servings: 5 (1-1/2 cups each)

2 teaspoons canola oil	1 can (14 oz) reduced-sodium chicken broth
1 small onion, chopped (1/4 cup)	1-1/4 lb firm white fish fillets (such as cod or pollock), skin removed
1 medium stalk celery, chopped (1/2 cup)	1 cup fat-free (skim) milk
2 cups frozen potatoes O'Brien with onions and peppers	2 teaspoons cornstarch
1 can (14.75 oz) Green Giant® cream-style sweet corn	

1 In 3-quart saucepan, heat oil over medium heat. Add the onion and celery; cook 2 to 3 minutes, stirring occasionally, until tender.

2 Stir in potatoes, corn and broth. Heat to boiling; reduce heat. Simmer uncovered about 5 minutes or until potatoes are tender.

3 Add whole fish fillets. Cover; cook 5 to 7 minutes or until fish flakes easily with fork. In measuring cup, mix milk and cornstarch; stir into chowder. Heat just to boiling.

High Altitude (3500-6500 ft): No change.

Nutritional Info: 1 Serving: Calories 260 (Calories from Fat 35); Total Fat 4g (Saturated Fat 0.5g, Trans Fat 0g); Cholesterol 60mg; Sodium 500mg; Total Carbohydrate 28g (Dietary Fiber 2g, Sugars 7g); Protein 27g. % Daily Value: Vitamin A 4%; Vitamin C 10%; Calcium 10%; Iron 8%. Exchanges: 2 Starch, 3 Very Lean Meat. Carbohydrate Choices: 2.

Betty's Kitchen Tip

• Halibut is a bit more expensive than some fish, but it provides a wonderful flavor and texture to this chowder. If you like, any firm fish can be used.

greek turkey burgers with yogurt sauce

Prep Time: 20 Minutes
Start to Finish: 20 Minutes
Servings: 4

QUICK LOW FAT

Yogurt Sauce

1/2	cup plain fat-free yogurt
1/4	cup chopped red onion
1/4	cup chopped cucumber

Burgers

1	lb lean ground turkey
1/2	cup plain fat-free yogurt
1	teaspoon dried oregano leaves
1/2	teaspoon garlic powder
1/2	teaspoon salt
1/2	teaspoon pepper
4	whole wheat hamburger buns

1 In small bowl, mix all sauce ingredients; refrigerate until ready to serve.

2 Set oven control to broil. In medium bowl, mix all burger ingredients except buns. Shape mixture into 4 patties, each about 1/2 inch thick and 5 inches in diameter. Place on rack in broiler pan.

3 Broil burgers with tops about 6 inches from heat 8 to 10 minutes, turning after 5 minutes, until thermometer inserted in centers reads 165°F. Place burgers on buns. Serve with sauce.

High Altitude (3500-6500 ft): No change.

Nutritional Info: 1 Serving: Calories 310 (Calories from Fat 70); Total Fat 8g (Saturated Fat 2g, Trans Fat 0.5g); Cholesterol 75mg; Sodium 640mg; Total Carbohydrate 26g (Dietary Fiber 3g, Sugars 8g); Protein 33g. % Daily Value: Vitamin A 0%; Vitamin C 0%; Calcium 15%; Iron 15%. Exchanges: 1-1/2 Starch, 4 Very Lean Meat, 1 Fat. Carbohydrate Choices: 2.

Betty's Kitchen Tip

• This flavorful yogurt sauce tastes great on pita bread wedges or as a dip for veggies.

beef and pork barbecue sandwiches

Prep Time: 25 Minutes
Start to Finish: 8 Hours 40 Minutes
Servings: 15 sandwiches

1	boneless beef chuck roast (1-1/2 lb)	1	tablespoon chili powder
1	boneless pork loin rib end roast (1-1/2 lb)	1	teaspoon salt
1	large onion, chopped (1 cup)	1	teaspoon ground mustard
1	medium green bell pepper, chopped (1 cup)	2	teaspoons Worcestershire sauce
1/2	cup packed brown sugar	1	can (6 oz) tomato paste
1/4	cup cider vinegar	15	sandwich buns, split

1 Spray 4- to 5-quart slow cooker with cooking spray. Trim fat from beef and pork. Cut beef and pork into 3-inch pieces. In cooker, place beef, pork and remaining ingredients except tomato paste and buns.

2 Cover; cook on Low heat setting 8 to 10 hours.

3 Remove beef and pork from cooker, using slotted spoon; place on cutting board. Strain liquid in cooker; reserve. Return cooked vegetables to cooker. Shred meat,

using 2 forks. Return meat to cooker. Stir in tomato paste. Stir in 1 to 2 cups of strained liquid for desired moistness.

4 Increase heat setting to High. Cover; cook 10 to 15 minutes longer or until hot. To serve, spoon 1/3 cup meat mixture onto each bun. Meat mixture can be kept warm on Low heat setting up to 2 hours; stir occasionally.

High Altitude (3500-6500 ft): No change.

Nutritional Info: 1 Sandwich: Calories 320 (Calories from Fat 100); Total Fat 11g (Saturated Fat 4g, Trans Fat 0.5g); Cholesterol 55mg; Sodium 510mg; Total Carbohydrate 32g (Dietary Fiber 2g, Sugars 12g); Protein 23g. % Daily Value: Vitamin A 8%; Vitamin C 8%; Calcium 8%; Iron 20%. Exchanges: 1 Starch, 1 Other Carbohydrate, 3 Lean Meat. Carbohydrate Choices: 2.

Betty's Kitchen Tips

Success Hint: This is a great recipe for casual entertaining. Put the slow cooker, buns and accompaniments on a buffet and guests can serve themselves.

Do-Ahead: Make this recipe the day before your gathering, and put it in the fridge. Reheat it on the stove just before serving and transfer to the slow cooker to keep warm.

mexican chicken chili

Prep Time: 10 Minutes
Start to Finish: 7 Hours 10 Minutes
Servings: 6 (1-2/3 cups each)

EASY

1-3/4	lb boneless skinless chicken thighs
1	medium onion, chopped (1/2 cup)
2	medium stalks celery, sliced (3/4 cup)
2	cans (14.5 oz each) stewed tomatoes with garlic and onion, undrained
2	cans (15 to 16 oz each) pinto beans, undrained
1	can (10 oz) Old El Paso® enchilada sauce
2	teaspoons chili powder
1	teaspoon ground cumin
1	cup scoop-shaped corn chips, if desired
1/3	cup sour cream
2	tablespoons chopped fresh cilantro, if desired

1 Spray 4- to 5-quart slow cooker with cooking spray. In cooker, mix all ingredients except sour cream and cilantro.

2 Cover; cook on Low heat setting 7 to 8 hours.

3 Stir mixture to break up chicken. Top each serving with sour cream and cilantro.

High Altitude (3500-6500 ft): No change.

Nutritional Info: 1 Serving: Calories 410 (Calories from Fat 100); Total Fat 11g (Saturated Fat 4g, Trans Fat 0g); Cholesterol 60mg; Sodium 860mg; Total Carbohydrate 47g (Dietary Fiber 13g, Sugars 10g); Protein 31g. % Daily Value: Vitamin A 15%; Vitamin C 10%; Calcium 15%; Iron 30%. Exchanges: 2 Starch, 1 Other Carbohydrate, 3-1/2 Lean Meat. Carbohydrate Choices: 3.

Betty's Kitchen Tip

• In place of the stewed tomatoes with garlic and onion, use regular stewed tomatoes and add a teaspoon of finely chopped garlic.

muffuletta sandwiches

Prep Time: 20 Minutes
Start to Finish: 30 Minutes
Servings: 4 sandwiches

QUICK

2 cups Original Bisquick® mix	1/4 cup Italian dressing
1/2 teaspoon dried basil leaves	4 thin slices (about 4 oz) cooked ham (from deli)
1/4 cup grated Parmesan cheese	12 thin slices (about 4 oz) hard salami
1/2 cup water	4 slices (about 3 oz) provolone cheese
1/4 cup finely chopped pimiento-stuffed green olives	

1 Heat oven to 425°F. In medium bowl, stir Bisquick mix, basil, Parmesan cheese and water until soft dough forms. Place dough on surface sprinkled with Bisquick mix; roll in Bisquick mix to form ball. Knead 10 times. On ungreased cookie sheet, pat dough into 8-inch square. Cut into 4 squares; separate slightly.

2 Bake 8 to 10 minutes or until golden brown. Remove from cookie sheet to cooling rack; cool 5 minutes.

3 Meanwhile, in small bowl, mix olives and Italian dressing.

4 With serrated knife, split biscuits. On bottom halves, spread olive mixture. Layer ham, salami and provolone cheese on olive mixture. Top with biscuit tops.

High Altitude (3500-6500 ft): Bake 10 to 12 minutes.

Nutritional Info: 1 Sandwich: Calories 550 (Calories from Fat 280); Total Fat 31g (Saturated Fat 11g, Trans Fat 2.5g); Cholesterol 65mg; Sodium 2350mg; Total Carbohydrate 44g (Dietary Fiber 2g, Sugars 5g); Protein 25g. % Daily Value: Vitamin A 6%; Vitamin C 0%; Calcium 30%; Iron 15%. Exchanges: 2 Starch, 1 Other Carbohydrate, 2-1/2 High-Fat Meat, 2 Fat. Carbohydrate Choices: 3.

Betty's Kitchen Tips

Special Touch: Serve these deli-style. Wrap the sandwich in brown or white parchment paper. Top each with an olive and frilly toothpick.

Did You Know? Muffuletta refers to a New Orleans, hero-like sandwich created in 1906. The olive spread makes this sandwich unique.

Serve-With: Serve the sandwiches with cut-up fresh fruit, chips and lemonade.

tomato-lentil soup

Prep Time: 15 Minutes
Start to Finish: 50 Minutes
Servings: 4

EASY LOW FAT

1	tablespoon olive or canola oil
1	large onion, finely chopped (1 cup)
1	medium stalk celery, cut into 1/2-inch pieces (1/2 cup)
2	cloves garlic, finely chopped
2	medium carrots, cut into 1/2-inch pieces (1 cup)
1	cup dried lentils (8 oz), sorted, rinsed

4	cups water
2	teaspoons chicken or vegetable bouillon granules
1	teaspoon dried thyme leaves
1/4	teaspoon pepper
1	dried bay leaf
1	can (28 oz) diced tomatoes, undrained

1 In 3-quart saucepan, heat the oil over medium-high heat. Add onion, celery and garlic; cook about 5 minutes, stirring occasionally, until softened.

2 Stir in the remaining ingredients except tomatoes. Heat to boiling. Reduce heat; cover and simmer 15 to 20 minutes or until lentils and vegetables are tender.

3 Stir in tomatoes. Simmer uncovered about 15 minutes longer or until thoroughly heated. Remove bay leaf.

High Altitude (3500-6500 ft): No change.

Nutritional Info: 1 Serving: Calories 270 (Calories from Fat 40); Total Fat 4.5g (Saturated Fat 0.5g, Trans Fat 0g); Cholesterol 0mg; Sodium 710mg; Total Carbohydrate 43g (Dietary Fiber 11g, Sugars 9g); Protein 15g. % Daily Value: Vitamin A 110%; Vitamin C 20%; Calcium 10%; Iron 40%. Exchanges: 2 Starch, 1/2 Other Carbohydrate, 1 Vegetable, 1 Very Lean Meat, 1/2 Fat. Carbohydrate Choices: 3.

Betty's Kitchen Tip

• Packed with onion, celery, carrots, lentils and tomatoes, this delicious soup is wholesome and vegetarian.

asian chicken roll-ups

Prep Time: 15 Minutes
Start to Finish: 15 Minutes
Servings: 4

EASY QUICK

- 2 tablespoons crunchy peanut butter
- 2 tablespoons teriyaki baste and glaze (from 12-oz bottle)
- 1 tablespoon packed brown sugar
- 1 tablespoon hot water
- 1 teaspoon sesame or canola oil
- 4 Old El Paso® flour tortillas for burritos (8 inch; from 11.5-oz package)
- 8 slices (1 oz each) cooked deli chicken breast
- 1-1/2 cups shredded iceberg lettuce
- 1-1/2 cups shredded carrots
- 1/2 cup chopped fresh cilantro

1 In small bowl, beat peanut butter, teriyaki baste and glaze, brown sugar, water and oil with wire whisk until smooth.

2 Spread about 1-1/2 tablespoons peanut butter mixture over each tortilla. Top each with 2 slices chicken, about 1/3 cup lettuce, about 1/3 cup carrots and 2 tablespoons cilantro. Roll up tortillas.

High Altitude (3500-6500 ft) No change.

Nutritional Info: 1 Serving: Calories 340 (Calories from Fat 100); Total Fat 11g (Saturated Fat 2.5g, Trans Fat 0.5g); Cholesterol 50mg; Sodium 610mg; Total Carbohydrate 36g (Dietary Fiber 3g, Sugars 10g); Protein 24g. % Daily Value: Vitamin A 140%; Vitamin C 6%; Calcium 10%; Iron 15%. Exchanges: 1-1/2 Starch, 1/2 Other Carbohydrate, 1 Vegetable, 2-1/2 Lean Meat, 1/2 Fat. Carbohydrate Choices: 2-1/2.

Betty's Kitchen Tip

• Enjoy these flavor-packed roll-ups with an easy, refreshing salad and cut-up fresh pineapple sprinkled with flaked coconut.

philly cheese steak sandwiches

Prep Time: 15 Minutes
Start to Finish: 6 Hours 15 Minutes
Servings: 6 sandwiches

EASY

- 1 boneless beef round steak, 1 inch thick (2 lb), trimmed of fat, cut into bite-size strips
- 2 medium onions, sliced
- 1 tablespoon garlic-pepper blend
- 2 tablespoons water
- 1 tablespoon beef bouillon granules

- 2 large green bell peppers, cut into bite-size strips
- 6 slices (3/4 oz each) American cheese, cut in half
- 6 hoagie buns, split

1 Spray 3- to 4-quart slow cooker with cooking spray. In medium bowl, sprinkle beef and onions with garlic-pepper blend; stir to coat evenly. Spoon mixture into cooker.

2 In measuring cup, stir water and bouillon granules until dissolved. Pour over the mixture in cooker.

3 Cover; cook on Low heat setting 6 to 8 hours. About 20 minutes before serving, stir in bell peppers.

4 Place 2 cheese pieces on bottom of each bun. Using slotted spoon, spoon beef mixture over cheese. Cover with tops of buns. Beef mixture can be kept warm on Low heat setting up to 2 hours.

High Altitude (3500-6500 ft): No change.

Nutritional Info: 1 Sandwich: Calories 550 (Calories from Fat 130); Total Fat 14g (Saturated Fat 7g, Trans Fat 1g); Cholesterol 105mg; Sodium 1360mg; Total Carbohydrate 56g (Dietary Fiber 4g, Sugars 11g); Protein 49g. % Daily Value: Vitamin A 8%; Vitamin C 40%; Calcium 20%; Iron 35%. Exchanges: 2 Starch, 1 Other Carbohydrate, 1 Vegetable, 6 Very Lean Meat, 2 Fat. Carbohydrate Choices: 4.

Betty's Kitchen Tips

Substitution: Cheddar or mozzarella cheese can be used in place of the American cheese.

Variation: If you don't have hoagie buns, use crusty French or kaiser rolls instead.

italian chicken noodle soup

Prep Time: 35 Minutes
Start to Finish: 35 Minutes
Servings: 6 (1-1/2 cups each)

LOW FAT

1	tablespoon olive or canola oil
2	boneless skinless chicken breasts (about 1/2 lb), cut into 1/2-inch pieces
1	medium onion, chopped (1/2 cup)
2	cans (14 oz each) chicken broth
2	cups water
3	medium carrots, sliced (1-1/2 cups)
2	cups fresh broccoli florets
1-1/2	cups uncooked medium egg noodles
1	teaspoon dried basil leaves
1/2	teaspoon garlic-pepper blend
1/4	cup shredded Parmesan cheese

1 In 4-quart saucepan, heat oil over medium heat. Add chicken; cook 4 to 6 minutes, stirring occasionally, until no longer pink in center. Stir in onion. Cook 2 to 3 minutes, stirring occasionally, until onion is tender.

2 Stir in broth, water and carrots. Heat to boiling. Reduce heat to medium; cook 5 minutes. Stir in broccoli, noodles, basil and garlic-pepper blend. Heat to boiling.

3 Reduce heat; simmer uncovered 8 to 10 minutes, stirring occasionally, until vegetables and noodles are tender. Top each serving with cheese.

High Altitude (3500-6500 ft): No change.

Nutritional Info: 1 Serving: Calories 170 (Calories from Fat 60); Total Fat 6g (Saturated Fat 2g, Trans Fat 0g); Cholesterol 35mg; Sodium 730mg; Total Carbohydrate 14g (Dietary Fiber 2g, Sugars 3g); Protein 15g. % Daily Value: Vitamin A 110%; Vitamin C 25%; Calcium 10%; Iron 8%. Exchanges: 1/2 Starch, 1 Vegetable, 1-1/2 Very Lean Meat, 1 Fat. Carbohydrate Choices: 1.

Betty's Kitchen Tips

Substitution: You can easily use chicken thighs for part or all of the chicken breasts. Two boneless thighs usually equal one breast half.

Variation: Fresh vegetables are called for in this colorful soup, but if you keep frozen vegetables on hand, you can use them instead.

southwest chicken soup with baked tortilla strips

Prep Time: 15 Minutes
Start to Finish: 7 Hours 45 Minutes
Servings: 6

EASY   LOW FAT

Soup

- 1 lb boneless skinless chicken thighs, cut into 1-inch pieces
- 2 medium dark-orange sweet potatoes, peeled, cut into 1-inch pieces (2 cups)
- 1 large onion, chopped (1 cup)
- 2 cans (14.5 oz each) diced tomatoes with green chilies, undrained
- 1 can (14 oz) chicken broth
- 1 teaspoon dried oregano leaves
- 1/2 teaspoon ground cumin
- 1 cup Green Giant® Niblets® frozen whole kernel corn
- 1/2 cup chopped green bell pepper
- 2 tablespoons chopped fresh cilantro

Baked Tortilla Strips

- 8 yellow or blue corn tortillas (5 or 6 inch)

1   In 3-1/2- to 4-quart slow cooker, mix chicken, sweet potatoes, onion, tomatoes, broth, oregano and cumin. Cover; cook on Low heat setting 7 to 8 hours.

2   Stir in corn and bell pepper. Increase heat setting to High; cover and cook about 30 minutes or until chicken is no longer pink in center and vegetables are tender.

3   Meanwhile, heat oven to 450°F. Spray 2 cookie sheets with cooking spray. Cut each tortilla into strips; place in single layer on cookie sheets. Bake about 6 minutes or until crisp but not brown; cool.

4   Spoon soup into individual bowls. Top with tortilla strips. Sprinkle with cilantro.

High Altitude (3500-6500 ft): No change.

Nutritional Info: 1 Serving: Calories 310 (Calories from Fat 70); Total Fat 8g (Saturated Fat 2g, Trans Fat 0g); Cholesterol 45mg; Sodium 750mg; Total Carbohydrate 37g (Dietary Fiber 6g, Sugars 11g); Protein 23g. % Daily Value: Vitamin A 150%; Vitamin C 25%; Calcium 10%; Iron 15%. Exchanges: 2 Starch, 1-1/2 Vegetable, 2 Lean Meat. Carbohydrate Choices: 2-1/2.

Betty's Kitchen Tip

• Eating soups and stews is an easy—and delicious—way to include more vegetables in your diet. Other options: Snack on baby carrots, cucumber slices and celery sticks.

crab cake sandwiches

Prep Time: 20 Minutes
Start to Finish: 20 Minutes
Servings: 4 sandwiches

QUICK

1	cup soft bread crumbs (about 1-1/2 slices bread)
1/2	cup Original Bisquick® mix
2	teaspoons seafood seasoning (from 6-oz container)
2	medium green onions, finely chopped (2 tablespoons)
2	eggs, slightly beaten
2	cans (6 oz each) lump crabmeat, drained
2	tablespoons butter or margarine
4	whole wheat burger buns, split
1/2	cup shredded lettuce
4	slices tomato
4	tablespoons tartar sauce

1 In medium bowl, mix bread crumbs, Bisquick mix, seafood seasoning, onions, eggs and crabmeat until well blended. Shape mixture into 4 (3/4-inch-thick) patties.

2 In 12-inch nonstick skillet, melt 1 tablespoon of the butter over medium heat. Add patties; cook 4 minutes. Turn patties; add remaining 1 tablespoon butter to skillet. Cook about 4 minutes longer or until golden brown.

3 Fill buns with lettuce, patties, tomato and tartar sauce.

High Altitude (3500-6500 ft): No change.

Nutritional Info: 1 Sandwich: Calories 400 (Calories from Fat 170); Total Fat 19g (Saturated Fat 7g, Trans Fat 1g); Cholesterol 190mg; Sodium 1150mg; Total Carbohydrate 32g (Dietary Fiber 3g, Sugars 6g); Protein 24g. % Daily Value: Vitamin A 10%; Vitamin C 10%; Calcium 15%; Iron 15%. Exchanges: 2 Starch, 2-1/2 Lean Meat, 2 Fat. Carbohydrate Choices: 2.

Betty's Kitchen Tips

Success Hint: Compare the labels of different seafood seasoning brands, and select the one you prefer based on the spice mix. Remember that ingredient order starts with the largest amount first.

Purchasing: Look for bags of shredded lettuce in the produce case.

meatball mini sandwiches with roasted red pepper sauce

Prep Time: 15 Minutes
Start to Finish: 6 Hours 15 Minutes
Servings: 16 (3 meatballs each)

EASY

1-1/2 lb frozen meatballs (from two 1-lb bags), thawed
1 jar (7.25 oz) roasted red bell peppers, drained

1/4 cup grated Parmesan cheese
1/4 cup Italian dressing
1 jar (26 oz) marinara sauce
16 small sandwich buns, if desired

1 Spray 3- to 4-quart slow cooker with cooking spray. Place meatballs in cooker.

2 In blender, cover and blend bell peppers until smooth. Add cheese and Italian dressing; cover and blend until mixed. Add marinara sauce; pulse until just blended. Pour sauce over meatballs.

3 Cover; cook on Low heat setting 6 to 7 hours.

4 Stir before serving. Meatballs can be kept warm on Low heat setting up to 2 hours; stir occasionally. For mini sandwiches, serve meatballs on buns, or for appetizers, use appetizer picks to serve.

High Altitude (3500-6500 ft): No change.

Nutritional Info: 1 Serving (without bun): Calories 170 (Calories from Fat 80); Total Fat 9g (Saturated Fat 3g, Trans Fat 0g); Cholesterol 45mg; Sodium 530mg; Total Carbohydrate 14g (Dietary Fiber 1g, Sugars 6g); Protein 10g. % Daily Value: Vitamin A 20%; Vitamin C 20%; Calcium 6%; Iron 8%. Exchanges: 1/2 Starch, 1/2 Other Carbohydrate, 1 High-Fat Meat. Carbohydrate Choices: 1.

Betty's Kitchen Tips

Success Hint: Sprinkle freshly grated Parmesan cheese and chopped red or green bell pepper over the meatballs just before serving.

Did You Know? Small sandwich buns are sometimes called dollar buns.

two-bean minestrone

Prep Time: 10 Minutes
Start to Finish: 8 Hours 25 Minutes
Servings: 6 (1-1/2 cups each)

EASY LOW FAT

1   can (15 oz) Progresso® dark red kidney beans, drained

1   can (15 to 16 oz) garbanzo beans, drained

1   bag (1 lb) Green Giant® frozen mixed vegetables

1   can (14.5 oz) diced tomatoes with basil, garlic and oregano, undrained

1   large vegetarian vegetable bouillon cube

1   can (11.5 oz) vegetable juice

1   cup water

1/2 cup uncooked elbow macaroni

6   teaspoons refrigerated basil pesto (from 7-oz container)

1   Spray 3- to 4-quart slow cooker with cooking spray. In cooker, mix all ingredients except macaroni and pesto.

2   Cover; cook on Low heat setting 8 to 10 hours.

3   Stir in macaroni. Cover; cook on Low heat setting about 15 minutes longer or until macaroni is tender. Top each serving with teaspoon of pesto.

High Altitude (3500-6500 ft): In step 3, cook macaroni about 30 minutes.

Nutritional Info: 1 Serving: Calories 330 (Calories from Fat 45); Total Fat 5g (Saturated Fat 1g, Trans Fat 0g); Cholesterol 0mg; Sodium 510mg; Total Carbohydrate 55g (Dietary Fiber 12g, Sugars 7g); Protein 16g. % Daily Value: Vitamin A 80%; Vitamin C 20%; Calcium 10%; Iron 30%. Exchanges: 2-1/2 Starch, 1 Other Carbohydrate, 1 Vegetable, 1 Very Lean Meat, 1/2 Fat. Carbohydrate Choices: 3-1/2.

Betty's Kitchen Tips

Special Touch: Minestrone is traditionally served with a generous sprinkle of grated Parmesan cheese, so pass a dish of Parmesan cheese when you serve this hearty soup.

Serve-With: Italian gelato and biscotti cookies would be a sweet ending to this casual dinner.

smoked sausage and bean soup

Prep Time: 15 Minutes
Start to Finish: 8 Hours 45 Minutes
Servings: 7 (1-1/2 cups each)

EASY

- 1 lb small red potatoes, each cut into 8 pieces (about 3 cups)
- 4 medium carrots, sliced (2 cups)
- 1 medium onion, chopped (1/2 cup)
- 1 medium stalk celery, sliced (1/2 cup)
- 2 cans (15 oz each) navy or cannellini beans, drained, rinsed
- 2 cans (14 oz each) chicken broth
- 1 teaspoon dried thyme leaves
- 1/2 teaspoon seasoned salt
- 1 lb fully cooked kielbasa sausage, cut in half lengthwise, then into 1/4-inch slices
- 2 tablespoons chopped fresh parsley

1 Spray 3- to 4-quart slow cooker with cooking spray. In cooker, mix all ingredients except sausage and parsley.

2 Cover; cook on Low heat setting 8 to 9 hours.

3 Stir in sausage and parsley. Cover; cook on Low heat setting 30 minutes longer or until sausage is hot.

High Altitude (3500-6500 ft): No change.

Nutritional Info: 1 Serving: Calories 440 (Calories from Fat 170); Total Fat 19g (Saturated Fat 7g, Trans Fat 0.5g); Cholesterol 40mg; Sodium 1220mg; Total Carbohydrate 47g (Dietary Fiber 14g, Sugars 5g); Protein 20g. % Daily Value: Vitamin C 10%; Calcium 10%; Iron 25%. Exchanges: 2-1/2 Starch, 1 Vegetable, 1-1/2 High-Fat Meat, 1 Fat. Carbohydrate Choices: 3.

Betty's Kitchen Tips

Success Hint: If the red potatoes are very small, cut them in half to prevent overcooking.

Substitution: Diced cooked ham can be used in place of the sausage.

grilled blue cheese burgers

Prep Time: 25 Minutes
Start to Finish: 25 Minutes
Servings: 8 sandwiches

QUICK

2	cloves garlic, finely chopped
1/4	cup butter or margarine
2	teaspoons Worcestershire sauce
3	lb lean (at least 85%) ground beef
2	tablespoons Montreal steak grill seasoning
1	cup blue cheese crumbles (4 oz)
8	diagonal slices (1/2 to 1 inch thick) French bread
2	cups loosely packed baby salad greens

1 In 8-inch skillet, cook garlic in butter over low heat 2 to 3 minutes, stirring occasionally, until garlic is tender. Stir in Worcestershire sauce. Remove from heat.

2 Heat gas or charcoal grill. In large bowl, mix beef and grill seasoning. Shape the mixture into 8 oval patties, 1/2 inch thick.

3 Place patties on grill over medium heat. Cover grill; cook 10 to 12 minutes, turning once, until meat thermometer inserted in center of patties reads 160°F. Remove from grill to platter; top with cheese. Place the bread on grill. Cover; cook 2 to 4 minutes, turning once, until lightly toasted.

4 Spread one side of each toasted bread slice with butter mixture. Top bread slices with salad greens and burgers.

High Altitude (3500-6500 ft): No change.

Nutritional Info: 1 Sandwich: Calories 480 (Calories from Fat 250); Total Fat 27g (Saturated Fat 13g, Trans Fat 1.5g); Cholesterol 135mg; Sodium 1070mg; Total Carbohydrate 21g (Dietary Fiber 1g, Sugars 3g); Protein 38g. % Daily Value: Cholesterol 44%; Vitamin A 20%; Vitamin C 2%; Calcium 10%; Iron 25%. Exchanges: 1-1/2 Starch, 4-1/2 Medium-Fat Meat, 1/2 Fat. Carbohydrate Choices: 1-1/2.

Betty's Kitchen Tips

Success Hint: Shape the oval burgers slightly larger than the slices of French bread. They tend to shrink slightly as they cook.

Variation: Use your favorite small salad greens. Baby arugula or spinach provides a slightly bitter flavor that goes well with the grill flavor and blue cheese.

easy french dip sandwiches

Prep Time: 10 Minutes
Start to Finish: 8 Hours 10 Minutes
Servings: 8 sandwiches

EASY

1   (3 lb) fresh beef brisket (not corned beef)
1   package (1 oz) onion recipe and dip soup mix (from 2-oz box)

1   can (10-1/2 oz) condensed beef broth
8   mini baguettes or sandwich buns

1 Spray 3- to 4-quart slow cooker with cooking spray. Place beef in cooker. In small bowl, mix dry soup mix and broth; pour over beef.

2 Cover; cook on Low heat setting 8 to 10 hours.

3 Skim fat from liquid in cooker. Remove beef from cooker; place on cutting board. Cut beef across grain into thin slices or shred beef.

4 To serve, cut each baguette in half horizontally. Fill baguettes with beef; cut crosswise in half. Serve with broth for dipping. Beef mixture will hold on Low heat setting up to 2 hours; stir occasionally.

High Altitude (3500-6500 ft): No change.

Nutritional Info: 1 Sandwich: Calories 480 (Calories from Fat 130); Total Fat 14g (Saturated Fat 5g, Trans Fat 1g); Cholesterol 75mg; Sodium 1000mg; Total Carbohydrate 41g (Dietary Fiber 2g, Sugars 2g); Protein 48g. % Daily Value: Vitamin A 0%; Vitamin C 0%; Calcium 8%; Iron 30%. Exchanges: 2 Starch, 1/2 Other Carbohydrate, 6 Very Lean Meat, 2 Fat. Carbohydrate Choices: 3.

Betty's Kitchen Tip

- Make this recipe the day ahead; cover and refrigerate. Then, reheat it in the microwave or on the stove-top just before serving.

beef and barley soup

Prep Time: 20 Minutes
Start to Finish: 9 Hours 50 Minutes
Servings: 8 (about 1-1/2 cups each)

- 1-1/2   lb beef stew meat
- 3   medium carrots, sliced (1-1/2 cups)
- 1   large onion, chopped (1 cup)
- 2   cloves garlic, finely chopped
- 2/3   cup Green Giant® Niblets® frozen whole kernel corn, thawed
- 2/3   cup uncooked pearl barley
- 1/2   teaspoon salt
- 1/2   teaspoon pepper
- 1   can (14.5 oz) diced tomatoes, undrained
- 3   cans (14 oz each) beef broth
- 1   cup Green Giant® frozen sweet peas, thawed

1   Spray 5- to 6-quart slow cooker with cooking spray. In cooker, mix all ingredients except peas.

2   Cover; cook on Low heat setting 9 to 10 hours.

3   Stir in peas. Increase heat setting to High. Cover; cook 20 to 30 minutes longer or until peas are tender.

High Altitude (3500-6500 ft): No change.

Nutritional Info: 1 Serving: Calories 280 (Calories from Fat 100); Total Fat 11g (Saturated Fat 4g, Trans Fat 0g); Cholesterol 50mg; Sodium 930mg; Total Carbohydrate 25g (Dietary Fiber 5g, Sugars 5g); Protein 21g. % Daily Value: Vitamin A 90%; Vitamin C 8%; Calcium 6%; Iron 20%. Exchanges: 1 Starch, 1/2 Other Carbohydrate, 1 Vegetable, 2 Medium-Fat Meat. Carbohydrate Choices: 1-1/2.

Betty's Kitchen Tips

Sucess Hint: Pearl barley, which is the most common form, is the perfect grain to cook in the slow cooker. The long, slow cooking produces barley that is tender but not gummy.

Health Twist: Select lean beef to prevent having to trim excess fat before adding beef to the soup.

wild rice soup

Prep Time: 30 Minutes
Start to Finish: 30 Minutes
Servings: 4 (1-1/4 cups each)

QUICK

2 tablespoons butter or margarine	1/4 teaspoon dried thyme leaves, if desired
2 medium stalks celery, sliced (1 cup)	1 cup water
1 medium carrot, coarsely shredded (1 cup)	1 can (10-1/2 oz) condensed chicken broth
1 medium onion, chopped (1/2 cup)	1-1/2 cups canned or frozen cooked wild rice
1 small green bell pepper, chopped (1/2 cup)	1 cup half-and-half
1/4 cup Original Bisquick® or Bisquick Heart Smart® mix	1/3 cup slivered almonds, toasted
1/2 teaspoon salt	1/4 cup chopped fresh parsley
1/4 teaspoon pepper	

1 In 3-quart saucepan, melt butter over medium-high heat. Cook celery, carrot, onion and bell pepper in butter about 4 minutes, stirring occasionally, until tender.

2 Stir in Bisquick mix, salt, pepper and thyme. Stir in water, broth and wild rice.

Heat to boiling, stirring frequently; reduce heat to low. Cover and simmer 15 minutes, stirring occasionally.

3 Stir in half-and-half, almonds and parsley. Heat just until hot (do not boil).

High Altitude (3500-6500 ft): No change.

Nutritional Info: 1 Serving: Calories 320 (Calories from Fat 170); Total Fat 19g (Saturated Fat 9g, Trans Fat 1g); Cholesterol 40mg; Sodium 1150mg; Total Carbohydrate 26g (Dietary Fiber 4g, Sugars 7g); Protein 10g. % Daily Value: Vitamin A 110%; Vitamin C 20%; Calcium 15%; Iron 8%. Exchanges: 1-1/2 Starch, 1 Vegetable, 1/2 High-Fat Meat, 3 Fat. Carbohydrate Choices: 2.

Betty's Kitchen Tips

Health Twist: To cut down on fat and calories, spray saucepan with cooking spray before heating. Omit butter. Use Bisquick Heart Smart® mix, 1 cup evaporated fat-free milk for the half-and-half, and decrease almonds to 3 tablespoons.

How-To: To toast almonds, cook in ungreased heavy skillet over medium-low heat 5 to 7 minutes, stirring frequently until browning begins, then stirring constantly until golden brown.

SALADS&SIDE DISHES

p. 198

181

204

183

grilled garlic steak salad

Prep Time: 25 Minutes
Start to Finish: 25 Minutes
Servings: 6

Dressing

1/4	cup olive or canola oil
2	tablespoons chopped fresh parsley
3	tablespoons red wine vinegar
1	tablespoon lemon juice
1	teaspoon chopped fresh or 1/2 teaspoon dried oregano leaves
1/2	teaspoon crushed red pepper flakes
2	cloves garlic, finely chopped

Salad

1	lb boneless beef sirloin steak, 1 to 1-1/2 inches thick
1	large bell pepper, cut into strips
1	cup sliced fresh mushrooms (3 oz)
6	cups bite-size pieces salad greens

1 Heat gas or charcoal grill. In tightly covered container, shake the dressing ingredients; set aside.

2 Place beef on grill over medium heat. Cover grill; cook 10 to 14 minutes, turning once, until desired doneness.

3 Meanwhile, in medium bowl, toss bell pepper and mushrooms with 2 tablespoons of the dressing. Place vegetables in grill basket (grill "wok"). Place basket on grill. Cover grill; cook vegetables 5 minutes, shaking grill basket or stirring vegetables occasionally, until bell pepper is crisp-tender.

4 Season beef to taste with salt and pepper; cut into 1/4-inch slices. In large bowl, toss beef and 1/4 cup of the dressing. Add salad greens and vegetables. Drizzle with remaining dressing; toss.

Broil Directions: Make dressing as directed. Set oven setting to broil. Place beef on rack in broiler pan. Broil with top 4 to 6 inches from heat 6 minutes. Meanwhile, in medium bowl, toss bell pepper and mushrooms with 2 tablespoons of the dressing. Turn beef over; add vegetables. Broil 5 minutes longer or until beef is desired doneness and bell pepper is crisp-tender. Continue as directed in step 4.

High Altitude (3500-6500 ft): No change.

Nutritional Info: 1 Serving: Calories 200 (Calories from Fat 110); Total Fat 12g (Saturated Fat 2g, Trans Fat 0g); Cholesterol 45mg; Sodium 40mg; Total Carbohydrate 5g (Dietary Fiber 2g, Sugars 2g); Protein 19g. % Daily Value: Vitamin A 80%; Vitamin C 110%; Calcium 4%; Iron 15%. Exchanges: 1 Vegetable, 2-1/2 Lean Meat, 1 Fat. Carbohydrate Choices: 1/2.

Betty's Kitchen Tip

• Put a basket of crusty rolls on the table, and dinner is ready.

roasted butternut squash combo

Prep Time: 15 Minutes
Start to Finish: 45 Minutes
Servings: 8 (1/2 cup each)

EASY

- 1 medium butternut squash, peeled, seeded and cut into 1-inch chunks (about 4 cups)
- 1 medium red or green bell pepper, cut into 16 pieces
- 2 tablespoons olive or canola oil
- 1/2 teaspoon seasoned salt
- 1/2 teaspoon dried basil leaves
- 1/4 teaspoon garlic powder
- 1/4 teaspoon coarse ground black pepper

1 Heat oven to 425°F. Spray 13x9-inch pan with cooking spray. In large bowl, mix ingredients until squash and bell pepper are coated. Spread in pan.

2 Roast uncovered 25 to 30 minutes, stirring once, until squash is tender.

High Altitude (3500-6500 ft): No change.

Nutritional Info: 1 Serving: Calories 60 (Calories from Fat 30); Total Fat 3.5g (Saturated Fat 0g, Trans Fat 0g); Cholesterol 0mg; Sodium 90mg; Total Carbohydrate 7g (Dietary Fiber 1g, Sugars 3g); Protein 0g. % Daily Value: Vitamin A 140%; Vitamin C 30%; Calcium 2%; Iron 2%. Exchanges: 1/2 Starch, 1/2 Fat. Carbohydrate Choices: 1/2.

Betty's Kitchen Tips

Did You Know? Butternut is the variety of squash shaped like a peanut and is a great source of vitamins A and C.

Purchasing: When selecting butternut squash, look for those that have hard, tough rinds and are heavy for their size. Peeling the squash will be easier if you first microwave it on High for 3 minutes.

slow cooker wild rice with cranberries

Prep Time: 15 Minutes
Start to Finish: 4 Hours 30 Minutes
Servings: 6

EASY

1-1/2 cups uncooked wild rice
1 tablespoon butter or margarine, melted
1/2 teaspoon salt
1/4 teaspoon pepper
4 medium green onions, sliced (1/4 cup)

2 cans (14 oz each) vegetable broth
1 jar (4.5 oz) Green Giant® sliced mushrooms, undrained
1/2 cup slivered almonds
1/3 cup sweetened dried cranberries

1 In 3- to 4-quart slow cooker, mix all ingredients except almonds and cranberries.

2 Cover; cook on Low heat setting 4 to 5 hours.

3 Meanwhile, in ungreased heavy skillet, cook the almonds over medium-low heat 5 to 7 minutes, stirring frequently until browning begins, then stirring constantly until golden brown and fragrant; set aside.

4 Stir almonds and cranberries into rice mixture. Cover; cook on Low heat setting 15 minutes.

High Altitude (3500-6500 ft): No change.

Nutritional Info: 1 Serving: Calories 260 (Calories from Fat 65); Total Fat 7g (Saturated Fat 2g); Cholesterol 5mg; Sodium 900mg; Total Carbohydrate 45g (Dietary Fiber 5g); Protein 9g. % Daily Value: Vitamin A 10%; Vitamin C 2%; Calcium 4%; Iron 8%. Exchanges: 3 Starch, 1/2 Fat.

Betty's Kitchen Tips

Substitution: Many supermarkets now carry a wide variety of dried fruits. Dried blueberries or cherries are delicious substitutes for the cranberries.

Success Hint: Toasting the almonds not only enhances the flavor and color of the almonds but also helps prevent them from becoming soggy after they are stirred into the wild rice mixture. See Kitchen Tips on page 178 for directions.

christmas salad with balsamic vinaigrette

Prep Time: 20 Minutes
Start to Finish: 20 Minutes
Servings: 6

QUICK

. . . .

Vinaigrette
- 1/3 cup olive or vegetable oil
- 1/4 cup balsamic or red wine vinegar
- 2 tablespoons sugar
- 1 clove garlic, finely chopped
- 1 teaspoon Dijon mustard

Salad
- 1 bag (10 oz) mixed baby greens or Italian-blend salad greens
- 1 avocado, pitted, peeled and sliced
- 1/3 cup pistachio nuts
- 1/4 cup sweetened dried cranberries

. . . .

1 In large serving bowl, beat the dressing ingredients until well blended.

2 Just before serving, add salad ingredients; toss until well coated.

High Altitude (3500-6500 ft): No change.

Nutritional Info: 1 Serving: Calories 235 (Calories from Fat 125); Total Fat 20g (Saturated Fat 3g); Cholesterol 0mg; Sodium 35mg; Total Carbohydrate 14g (Dietary Fiber 3g); Protein 3g. % Daily Value: Vitamin A 30%; Vitamin C 18%; Calcium 4%; Iron 6%. Exchanges: 3 Vegetable, 3-1/2 Fat.

Betty's Kitchen Tip

• For a strawberry version, use 2 cups quartered strawberries, 1 package (4 oz) goat cheese crumbles and 1/3 cup slivered almonds, toasted, instead of the avocado, pistachio nuts and cranberries. Toss with the greens and vinaigrette.

chive-and-onion creamed corn

Prep Time: 20 Minutes
Start to Finish: 3 Hours
Servings: 8 (1/2 cup each)

4	slices bacon		1	teaspoon sugar
4-1/2	cups Green Giant® Niblets® frozen whole kernel corn (from two 1-lb bags), thawed		1/2	teaspoon salt
			1/8	teaspoon pepper
1/2	medium red bell pepper, chopped (1/2 cup)		1	container (8 oz) reduced-fat chive-and-onion cream cheese
1/2	cup milk			
1/4	cup butter or margarine, melted			

1 In 12-inch nonstick skillet, cook bacon over medium-high heat, turning occasionally, until crisp. Drain on paper towels. Crumble the bacon.

2 Spray 3- to 4-quart slow cooker with cooking spray. In cooker, mix corn, bell pepper, milk, butter, sugar, salt, pepper and half of the bacon. Refrigerate remaining bacon.

3 Cover; cook on High heat setting 2 hours to 2 hours 30 minutes.

4 Stir in cream cheese. Cook on High heat setting 10 minutes longer. Stir well; sprinkle with remaining bacon. Corn can be kept warm on Low heat setting up to 1 hour.

High Altitude (3500-6500 ft): No change.

Nutritional Info: 1 Serving: Calories 220 (Calories from Fat 110); Total Fat 12g (Saturated Fat 7g, Trans Fat 0g); Cholesterol 35mg; Sodium 460mg; Total Carbohydrate 21g (Dietary Fiber 2g, Sugars 6g); Protein 6g. % Daily Value: Vitamin A 20%; Vitamin C 15%; Calcium 6%; Iron 2%. Exchanges: 1-1/2 Starch, 2 Fat. Carbohydrate Choices: 1-1/2.

Betty's Kitchen Tips

Company coming? Serve this with baked ham and oven-fresh rolls.

Special Touch: Sprinkle with chopped fresh chives for an added burst of color.

pomegranate and citrus broccoli salad

Prep Time: 20 Minutes
Start to Finish: 20 Minutes
Servings: 9 (1/2 cup each)

QUICK

- 1/2 cup mayonnaise or salad dressing
- 1/4 cup orange juice
- 1 teaspoon sugar
- 1/2 teaspoon salt
  Dash pepper
- 3 cups coarsely chopped fresh broccoli florets (about 8 oz)
- 1 medium orange, peeled, cut into bite-size chunks (about 1 cup)
- 3/4 cup pomegranate seeds (from 1 pomegranate) or sweetened dried cranberries
- 1/3 cup roasted salted sunflower nuts
- 2 tablespoons sliced red onion

1 In large serving bowl, mix mayonnaise, orange juice, sugar, salt and pepper.

2 Add remaining ingredients; toss until well coated. Store covered in refrigerator.

High Altitude (3500-6500 ft): No change.

Nutritional Info: 1 Serving: Calories 150 (Calories from Fat 110); Total Fat 13g (Saturated Fat 2g, Trans Fat 0g); Cholesterol 5mg; Sodium 240mg; Total Carbohydrate 7g (Dietary Fiber 2g, Sugars 4g); Protein 2g. % Daily Value: Vitamin A 8%; Vitamin C 60%; Calcium 2%; Iron 4%. Exchanges: 1/2 Other Carbohydrate, 2-1/2 Fat. Carbohydrate Choices: 1/2.

Betty's Kitchen Tips

Do-Ahead: Make the salad a day ahead—it will taste just as good!

Did You Know? Bright red pomegranate seeds add a sparkling touch to any salad. Pomegranates are larger than apples and have a leathery, deep red to purplish red rind. Though not beautiful on the outside, they have a spectacular interior packed full of sparkling, juicy, ruby-colored seeds that are slightly sweet and refreshingly tart.

minted watermelon basket

Prep Time: 1 Hour
Start to Finish: 1 Hour
Servings: 16 (1/2 cup each)

LOW FAT

1 whole watermelon, about 17 inches long	2 tablespoons lemon juice
1 cup green grapes	1/4 cup sugar
3 cups cantaloupe balls	1 cup fresh strawberries
1/4 cup finely chopped fresh mint leaves	Additional fresh mint leaves

1 Using long sharp knife, cut a thin slice from end of watermelon, being careful not to cut into flesh of watermelon. Stand watermelon on cut end. Using a washable marker, mark handle at top of basket by drawing 2 parallel lines that are 2-1/2 inches apart, starting at top of watermelon and drawing lines about 6 inches down each side.

2 Using a sharp knife, cut out a wedge-shaped piece of watermelon from each side, leaving the handle intact. Using a large spoon, gently scoop out watermelon flesh, leaving about 4 inches of flesh at bottom of watermelon.

3 With a small knife or garnishing tool, make "V" or scallop cuts about 2 inches apart on cut sides and handle of watermelon basket.

4 Cut watermelon into 1-inch chunks or use melon ball tool to make balls of watermelon. Measure 3 cups of watermelon and place in large bowl. Refrigerate remaining watermelon for another use.

5 Add grapes and cantaloupe to watermelon in bowl. Gently mix in 1/4 cup mint, the lemon juice and sugar. Refrigerate fruit mixture and watermelon basket separately until ready to use. Just before serving, fill watermelon basket with fruit mixture. Garnish with strawberries and additional mint leaves.

High Altitude (3500-6500 ft): No change.

Nutritional Info: 1 Serving: Calories 45 (Calories from Fat 0); Total Fat 0g (Saturated Fat 0g, Trans Fat 0g); Cholesterol 0mg; Sodium 5mg; Total Carbohydrate 10g (Dietary Fiber 0g, Sugars 9g); Protein 0g. % Daily Value: Vitamin A 25%; Vitamin C 35%; Calcium 0%; Iron 0%. Exchanges: 1/2 Fruit. Carbohydrate Choices: 1/2.

Betty's Kitchen Tip

• Carve the watermelon and cut up the fruit a day ahead of time. Wrap the watermelon basket with plastic wrap to keep it moist and fresh.

tomato and herb salad

Prep Time: 20 Minutes
Start to Finish: 20 Minutes
Servings: 8

QUICK

· ·

Dressing

1/4	cup extra-virgin olive oil
3	tablespoons red wine vinegar
1	teaspoon salt
1/2	teaspoon freshly ground pepper

Salad

5	tomatoes (assorted varieties, including yellow and/or heirlooms), sliced or cut into wedges
1	cup small grape tomatoes, cut in half
1/4	cup thinly sliced sweet onion (such as Walla Walla or Maui)
2	tablespoons chopped fresh basil leaves
2	tablespoons chopped fresh Italian (flat-leaf) parsley
2	tablespoons chopped fresh oregano leaves

· ·

1 In small bowl, beat dressing ingredients with wire whisk until well blended.

2 On large platter, arrange tomatoes and onion. Drizzle dressing over tomatoes and onion. Sprinkle with basil, parsley and oregano.

High Altitude (3500-6500 ft): No change.

Nutritional Info: 1 Serving: Calories 90 (Calories from Fat 60); Total Fat 7g (Saturated Fat 1g, Trans Fat 0g); Cholesterol 0mg; Sodium 300mg; Total Carbohydrate 5g (Dietary Fiber 1g, Sugars 3g); Protein 1g. % Daily Value: Cholesterol 0%; Vitamin A 20%; Vitamin C 25%; Calcium 2%; Iron 4%. Exchanges: 1 Vegetable, 1-1/2 Fat. Carbohydrate Choices: 1/2.

Betty's Kitchen Tips

Success Hint: Make this simple, fresh salad when tomatoes are at their peak. Heirloom tomatoes provide unique flavors. They're often available at farmers' markets and at many grocery stores in the summer.

Substitution: Curly-leaf parsley can be used, but it usually has less flavor than flat-leaf parsley.

three-cheese mashed potato casserole

Prep Time: 25 Minutes
Start to Finish: 1 Hour 35 Minutes
Servings: 24 (1/2 cup each)

5	lb white potatoes, peeled, cut into 1-inch pieces (about 14 cups)	1/2	cup shredded Parmesan cheese (2 oz)
1	package (3 oz) cream cheese, softened	1	container (8 oz) sour cream
1	cup shredded Cheddar cheese (4 oz)	1	teaspoon garlic salt
		1/4	teaspoon paprika
		1	teaspoon chopped fresh chives, if desired

1 In 6-quart saucepan or Dutch oven, place potatoes. Add enough water to cover potatoes. Heat to boiling over high heat. Reduce heat to medium; cook uncovered 15 to 18 minutes or until tender. Drain. Mash potatoes in saucepan with potato masher or electric mixer on low speed.

2 Meanwhile, in large bowl, beat cream cheese, Cheddar cheese and Parmesan cheese with electric mixer on low speed until smooth. Beat in sour cream and garlic salt.

3 Heat oven to 350°F. Stir cheese mixture into mashed potatoes until well blended. If the potatoes are too stiff, stir in milk, 1 tablespoon at a time, until desired consistency. Spoon into ungreased 13x9-inch (3-quart) glass baking dish.

4 Bake uncovered 35 to 40 minutes or until hot and top is lightly browned. Sprinkle with paprika and chives.

High Altitude (3500-6500 ft): No change.

Nutritional Info: 1 Serving: Calories 130 (Calories from Fat 50); Total Fat 5g (Saturated Fat 3.5g, Trans Fat 0g); Cholesterol 15mg; Sodium 125mg; Total Carbohydrate 18g (Dietary Fiber 2g, Sugars 1g); Protein 4g. % Daily Value: Vitamin A 4%; Vitamin C 6%; Calcium 8%; Iron 2%. Exchanges: 1 Starch, 1 Fat. Carbohydrate Choices: 1.

Betty's Kitchen Tips

Do-Ahead: Up to two days ahead, you can make this dish up to the point of baking, then cover and refrigerate. Bake as directed.

Storage: Store potatoes in a cool, dark, well-ventilated place. Refrigerating potatoes causes them to become unnaturally sweet and turn dark. Warm temperatures encourage sprouting and shriveling.

spinach-mango salad

Prep Time: 10 Minutes
Start to Finish: 10 Minutes
Servings: 6 (1 cup each) **EASY QUICK LOW FAT**

- 1 tablespoon canola oil
- 2 tablespoons cider vinegar
- 1/3 cup peach or apricot preserves
- 1/2 teaspoon salt
- 1 bag (6 oz) baby spinach leaves
- 2 mangoes, cut lengthwise in half, seed removed and cut up (2 cups)
- 1/2 cup very thinly sliced red onion
- 1/2 cup golden raisins

1 In small bowl, beat oil, vinegar, preserves and salt with wire whisk or fork until blended.

2 In large bowl, toss remaining ingredients. Pour dressing over spinach mixture, tossing gently to coat.

High Altitude (3500-6500 ft): No change.

Nutritional Info: 1 Serving: Calories 170 (Calories from Fat 25); Total Fat 2.5g (Saturated Fat 0g, Trans Fat 0g); Cholesterol 0mg; Sodium 230mg; Total Carbohydrate 36g (Dietary Fiber 2g, Sugars 25g); Protein 2g. % Daily Value: Vitamin A 60%; Vitamin C 50%; Calcium 4%; Iron 6%. Exchanges: 1 Fruit, 1 Other Carbohydrate, 1 Vegetable, 1/2 Fat. Carbohydrate Choices: 2-1/2.

Betty's Kitchen Tips

Serve-With: This light and sweet salad partners nicely with baked fish, cooked carrots and crusty whole-grain rolls.

Health Twist: Spinach and mangoes make this recipe high in vitamins A and C. Try to get at least five or more 1/2-cup servings of fruits and veggies per day for optimal health.

granola-topped sweet potatoes

Prep Time: 25 Minutes
Start to Finish: 1 Hour 15 Minutes
Servings: 8 (1/2 cup each)

6   medium dark-orange sweet potatoes, peeled, cut into 1-1/2-inch pieces (7 to 8 cups)
1/2 cup evaporated milk (from 5-oz can)
1   tablespoon butter or margarine
1/4 cup real maple or maple-flavored syrup

1/2 teaspoon salt
6   Nature Valley® maple brown sugar crunchy granola bars (3 pouches from 8.9-oz box), crushed
1   tablespoon butter or margarine, melted

1   In 4-quart saucepan, place potato pieces. Add enough water to cover. Heat to boiling. Reduce heat to medium-low; cook uncovered 15 to 20 minutes or until tender. Drain; return to saucepan.

2   Heat oven to 350°F. Spray 8-inch square (2-quart) glass baking dish with cooking spray. To potatoes, add evaporated milk, 1 tablespoon butter, the maple syrup and salt. Mash with potato masher or electric mixer until smooth. Spoon into baking dish.

3   In small bowl, mix crushed granola bars and 1 tablespoon melted butter; sprinkle over potatoes.

4   Bake uncovered 25 to 30 minutes or until thoroughly heated and topping is crisp.

High Altitude (3500-6500 ft): No change.

Nutritional Info: 1 Serving: Calories 250 (Calories from Fat 50); Total Fat 6g (Saturated Fat 2.5g, Trans Fat 0g); Cholesterol 10mg; Sodium 290mg; Total Carbohydrate 44g (Dietary Fiber 5g, Sugars 23g); Protein 5g. % Daily Value: Vitamin A 450%; Vitamin C 20%; Calcium 10%; Iron 8%. Exchanges: 1-1/2 Starch, 1-1/2 Other Carbohydrate, 1 Fat. Carbohydrate Choices: 3.

Betty's Kitchen Tips

Do-Ahead: You can make this rich-tasting casserole up to eight hours ahead of time, but wait to sprinkle with the granola bar mixture until just before baking.

Success Hint: For the prettiest dish with the best flavor, use dark-orange or red sweet potatoes in this recipe.

pineapple-berry salad with honey-mint dressing

Prep Time: 15 Minutes
Start to Finish: 15 Minutes
Servings: 4 (3/4 cup each) **EASY QUICK LOW FAT**

- 3 tablespoons frozen (thawed) lemonade concentrate
- 2 tablespoons honey
- 1 tablespoon chopped fresh mint leaves
- 1/2 fresh pineapple, peeled, cored and cut into chunks (about 2 cups)
- 1/4 cup fresh blueberries
- 1/4 cup fresh raspberries
- 1/4 cup sliced fresh strawberries

1 In 1-cup measuring cup, mix lemonade concentrate, honey and mint.

2 In large bowl, gently stir together the remaining ingredients. Stir in lemonade mixture until fruits are coated. Serve immediately, or refrigerate up to 4 hours.

High Altitude (3500-6500 ft): No change.

Nutritional Info: 1 Serving: Calories 120 (Calories from Fat 0); Total Fat 0g (Saturated Fat 0g, Trans Fat 0g); Cholesterol 0mg; Sodium 0mg; Total Carbohydrate 28g (Dietary Fiber 2g, Sugars 23g); Protein 0g. % Daily Value: Vitamin A 0%; Vitamin C 70%; Calcium 0%; Iron 2%. Exchanges: 1/2 Fruit, 1-1/2 Other Carbohydrate. Carbohydrate Choices: 2.

Betty's Kitchen Tips

Success Hint: Go berry crazy and use 3/4 cup of any combination of your favorite berries.

Purchasing: Pineapples don't ripen after harvest, so select fresh-looking pineapples with a sweet aroma.

black beans and greens

Prep Time: 10 Minutes
Start to Finish: 10 Minutes
Servings: 6 (about 1 cup each)

EASY QUICK LOW FAT

3	tablespoons fat-free Italian dressing
1/2	teaspoon grated lime peel
1	tablespoon lime juice
1	tablespoon chopped fresh cilantro
1	can (15 oz) black beans, drained, rinsed

3-1/2	cups mixed salad greens (about half of 10-oz bag)
1	medium tomato, cut into wedges
1/2	avocado, pitted, peeled and chopped (1/3 cup)

1 In 1-cup measuring cup, mix dressing, lime peel, lime juice and cilantro.

2 In large bowl, toss beans, salad greens and tomato. Stir in dressing mixture until salad is coated. Top with avocado.

High Altitude (3500-6500 ft): No change.

Nutritional Info: 1 Serving: Calories 130 (Calories from Fat 25); Total Fat 3g (Saturated Fat 0g, Trans Fat 0g); Cholesterol 0mg; Sodium 95mg; Total Carbohydrate 20g (Dietary Fiber 8g, Sugars 2g); Protein 6g. % Daily Value: Vitamin A 35%; Vitamin C 15%; Calcium 6%; Iron 10%. Exchanges: 1 Starch, 1 Vegetable, 1/2 Fat. Carbohydrate Choices: 1.

Betty's Kitchen Tips

Special Touch: For added crunch, divide salad among six plates and arrange baked tortilla chips around the edge of each plate.

Health Twist: Avocados contain vitamin E, an antioxidant thought to help protect against heart disease and some types of cancer.

mushroom stuffing

Prep Time: 25 Minutes
Start to Finish: 1 Hour 10 Minutes
Servings: 16 (1/2 cup each)

- 2/3 cup butter or margarine
- 2 medium stalks celery, chopped (1 cup)
- 1 medium onion, finely chopped (1/2 cup)
- 1 lb fresh mushrooms, sliced (6 cups)
- 8 cups unseasoned croutons
- 1 tablespoon chopped fresh or 1 teaspoon dried sage, thyme or marjoram leaves
- 1 teaspoon poultry seasoning
- 1 teaspoon salt
- 1/2 teaspoon pepper

1. In 4-quart Dutch oven, melt butter over medium heat. Add the celery, onion and mushrooms; cook about 3 minutes, stirring occasionally, until tender.

2. Stir in half of the croutons. Cook, stirring frequently, until evenly mixed and croutons are softened. Stir in remaining croutons and ingredients.

3. Stuff turkey just before roasting. Or spoon stuffing into greased 3-quart casserole or 13x9-inch (3-quart) glass baking dish; cover and bake at 325°F 30 minutes, then uncover and bake 15 minutes longer or until thoroughly heated.

High Altitude (3500-6500 ft): No change.

Nutritional Info: 1 Serving: Calories 140 (Calories from Fat 80); Total Fat 9g (Saturated Fat 5g, Trans Fat 0.5g); Cholesterol 20mg; Sodium 310mg; Total Carbohydrate 13g (Dietary Fiber 1g, Sugars 1g); Protein 3g. % Daily Value: Vitamin A 6%; Vitamin C 0%; Calcium 0%; Iron 4%. Exchanges: 1 Starch, 1-1/2 Fat. Carbohydrate Choices: 1.

Betty's Kitchen Tips

Purchasing: Look for the croutons near the salad dressings or stocked in the produce department.

Did You Know? Poultry seasoning is a blend of herbs and spices such as thyme, sage, marjoram, rosemary, black pepper and nutmeg. Each of these seasonings goes well with poultry; mixed together, the combination provides a subtle, complex flavor the individual seasonings do not have on their own.

gorgonzola twice-baked potatoes with bacon

Prep Time: 15 Minutes
Start to Finish: 1 Hour 40 Minutes
Servings: 8

EASY

- 4 large baking potatoes (8 to 10 oz each)
- 4 slices bacon
- 2/3 cup milk
- 2 tablespoons butter or margarine
- 1/2 cup crumbled Gorgonzola or Roquefort cheese
- 4 medium green onions, sliced (1/4 cup)
- 1/2 teaspoon salt

1 Heat oven to 375°F. Gently scrub potatoes, but do not peel. Pierce potatoes several times with fork. Place on oven rack. Bake 1 hour to 1 hour 15 minutes or until tender when pierced in center with fork. Let stand until cool enough to handle.

2 Meanwhile, in 12-inch skillet, cook bacon over medium heat 5 to 6 minutes, turning occasionally, until crisp; drain on paper towel.

3 Cut each potato lengthwise in half; scoop out inside, leaving a thin shell. In medium bowl, mash potatoes, milk and butter with potato masher or electric mixer on low speed until no lumps remain (amount of milk needed will vary depending upon type of potato used). Stir in cheese, green onions and salt. Fill potato shells with mashed potato mixture; place on ungreased cookie sheet. Crumble bacon onto potatoes.

4 Bake about 20 minutes or until hot. If desired, garnish with additional sliced green onion tops.

High Altitude (3500-6500 ft): No change.

Nutritional Info: 1 Serving: Calories 160 (Calories from Fat 70); Total Fat 8g (Saturated Fat 4g, Trans Fat 0g); Cholesterol 20mg; Sodium 400mg; Total Carbohydrate 17g (Dietary Fiber 1g, Sugars 2g); Protein 5g. % Daily Value: Vitamin A 6%; Vitamin C 8%; Calcium 8%; Iron 2%. Exchanges: 1 Starch, 1-1/2 Fat. Carbohydrate Choices: 1.

Betty's Kitchen Tips

Success Hint: A grapefruit spoon is super for scraping the potato from the shell.

Time-Saver: You can cut down the baking time for the potatoes to about 30 minutes if you microwave them first for 6 minutes before putting them in the oven.

Do-Ahead: Assemble the potatoes up to 12 hours ahead, cover with plastic wrap or foil and put in the fridge. Then bake as directed in step 4.

noodles and peanut sauce salad bowl

Prep Time: 25 Minutes
Start to Finish: 25 Minutes
Servings: 4 (1-3/4 cups each)

QUICK

8 oz uncooked whole wheat linguine, broken in half	2 teaspoons canola oil
2 cups fresh broccoli florets	2 tablespoons rice vinegar or white vinegar
1 cup julienne-cut carrots (from 10-oz bag)	2 tablespoons reduced-sodium soy sauce
1 medium bell pepper, cut into bite-size pieces	1/2 teaspoon ground ginger
1/4 cup peanut butter	1/8 teaspoon ground red pepper (cayenne)
2 tablespoons water	3 medium green onions, chopped (3 tablespoons)
	3 tablespoons chopped fresh cilantro

1 Cook linguine as directed on package, adding broccoli, carrots and bell pepper during last minute of cooking; drain pasta and vegetables. Rinse with cold water until pasta and vegetables are cool; drain.

2 Place peanut butter in small bowl. With wire whisk, gradually beat water and oil into peanut butter until smooth. Beat in vinegar, soy sauce, ginger and ground red pepper.

3 In large serving bowl, stir together pasta mixture, peanut sauce, onions and cilantro until well mixed.

High Altitude (3500-6500 ft): No change.

Nutritional Info: 1 Serving: Calories 370 (Calories from Fat 100); Total Fat 12g (Saturated Fat 2g, Trans Fat 0g); Cholesterol 0mg; Sodium 570mg; Total Carbohydrate 51g (Dietary Fiber 8g, Sugars 6g); Protein 14g. % Daily Value: Vitamin A 120%; Vitamin C 110%; Calcium 8%; Iron 15%. Exchanges: 2 Starch, 1 Other Carbohydrate, 1 Vegetable, 1 High-Fat Meat, 1/2 Fat. Carbohydrate Choices: 3-1/2.

Betty's Kitchen Tip

• This recipe is an all-in-one. It's packed with all the nutrients you need for a meal (and more!); just add a glass of sparkling water. Flavor your water with fresh lemon or lime slices.

honey-lime fruit salad

Prep Time: 10 Minutes
Start to Finish: 10 Minutes
Servings: 8

EASY QUICK

- -

1/2	cup honey
1/2	cup frozen (thawed) limeade concentrate
1	tablespoon poppy seed, if desired
8	cups cut-up fresh fruit
1/2	cup slivered almonds, toasted

- -

1 In large bowl, mix the honey, limeade concentrate and poppy seed.

2 Carefully toss fruit with honey mixture. Sprinkle with almonds just before serving.

High Altitude (3500-6500 ft): No change.

Nutritional Info: 1 Serving: Calories 220 (Calories from Fat 45); Total Fat 5g (Saturated Fat 1g); Cholesterol 0mg; Sodium 10mg; Total Carbohydrate 45g (Dietary Fiber 4g); Protein 3g. Exchanges: 3 Fruit, 1 Fat.

Betty's Kitchen Tips

Special Touch: To arrange salad as pictured above, cut watermelon into 3- or 4-inch wedges, about 1/2 inch thick. Place wedges (points facing out) around the edge of large platter, stacking into 3 or 4 layers to form a star-like shape. Place the fruit salad in center. Garnish with sprigs of mint, if desired.

Success Hint: To toast nuts, bake uncovered in an ungreased shallow pan at 350°F for 6 to 10 minutes, stirring occasionally, until light brown.

tropical chicken salad

Prep Time: 25 Minutes
Start to Finish: 25 Minutes
Servings: 4

QUICK

1 lb boneless skinless chicken breasts, cut into 1/2-inch strips

2 tablespoons blackened seasoning blend

1 tablespoon canola oil

1 bag (5.5 oz) mixed baby salad greens (4 cups)

1 medium mango, seed removed, peeled and diced (1 cup)

1/2 medium red onion, sliced (3/4 cup)

1 small red bell pepper, chopped (1/2 cup)

2/3 cup raspberry vinaigrette

1 Place chicken in heavy-duty resealable food-storage plastic bag. Sprinkle seasoning blend over chicken; seal bag and shake until chicken is evenly coated.

2 Heat oil in 10-inch nonstick skillet over medium-high heat. Cook chicken in oil 7 to 10 minutes, stirring frequently, until no longer pink in center. Remove chicken from skillet; drain on paper towels.

3 In large bowl, toss salad greens, mango, onion and bell pepper; divide among 4 plates. Top with chicken. Drizzle with vinaigrette.

High Altitude (3500-6500 ft): No changes.

Nutritional Info: 1 Serving: Calories 280 (Calories from Fat 70); Total Fat 7g (Saturated Fat 1.5g, Trans Fat 0g); Cholesterol 70mg; Sodium 560mg; Total Carbohydrate 26g (Dietary Fiber 3g, Sugars 14g); Protein 26g. % Daily Value: Vitamin A 70%; Vitamin C 100%; Calcium 6%; Iron 10%. Exchanges: 1-1/2 Other Carbohydrate, 1 Vegetable, 3-1/2 Very Lean Meat, 1 Fat. Carbohydrate Choices: 2.

Betty's Kitchen Tip

• Loaded with mango and bell pepper, this salad is a tasty source of vitamins A and C. Vitamin A is vital for proper eyesight and healthy hair and skin; vitamin C helps promote healthy gums, blood vessels, bones and teeth.

country ranch smashed potatoes

Prep Time: 15 Minutes
Start to Finish: 5 Hours 15 Minutes
Servings: 12 (1/2 cup each)

EASY

- 3 lb small red potatoes
- 1/3 cup water
- 1 cup sour cream-and-chive potato topper (from 12-oz container)
- 2 tablespoons ranch dressing and seasoning mix (from 1-oz package)
- 1/3 cup half-and-half

1 Spray 5- to 6-quart slow cooker with cooking spray. Cut potatoes into halves or quarters as needed to make similar-size pieces. Place potatoes in cooker. Add water; mix well to coat all pieces.

2 Cover; cook on Low heat setting 5 to 6 hours.

3 Gently mash potatoes with fork or potato masher. Stir in potato topper and dry dressing mix. Stir in half-and-half until potatoes are soft consistency. Potatoes can be kept warm on Low heat setting up to 1 hour; stir occasionally.

High Altitude (3500-6500 ft): No change.

Nutritional Info: 1 Serving: Calories 140 (Calories from Fat 40); Total Fat 4g (Saturated Fat 2.5g, Trans Fat 0g); Cholesterol 5mg; Sodium 280mg; Total Carbohydrate 23g (Dietary Fiber 2g, Sugars 3g); Protein 3g. % Daily Value: Vitamin A 4%; Vitamin C 10%; Calcium 8%; Iron 10%. Exchanges: 1 Starch, 1/2 Other Carbohydrate, 1/2 Fat. Carbohydrate Choices: 1-1/2.

Betty's Kitchen Tips

Variation: For Cheesy Smashed Potatoes, fold in 1 cup shredded Cheddar cheese after stirring in the half-and-half.

Serve-With: Serve with sliced ham and steamed whole green beans.

chicken-gorgonzola pasta salad

Prep Time: 20 Minutes
Start to Finish: 20 Minutes
Servings: 12 (1-1/2 cups each)

QUICK

7 cups uncooked radiatore (nuggets) pasta (about 19 oz)	1 can (14.5 oz) Muir Glen® organic fire roasted diced tomatoes, drained
4-1/2 cups cubed cooked chicken breast (about 20 oz)	2 cups lightly packed fresh baby spinach leaves
1 package (2.1 oz) refrigerated precooked bacon (about 15 slices), cut into small pieces	1 jar (16 oz) refrigerated ranch dressing
	1 cup crumbled Gorgonzola cheese (4 oz)
	Bibb lettuce, if desired

1 Cook and drain pasta as directed on package.

2 In large bowl, mix cooked pasta, chicken, bacon, tomatoes and spinach. Pour dressing over pasta mixture; toss until coated. Fold in cheese. Cover and refrigerate until serving. To serve, line bowl with lettuce and spoon in salad.

High Altitude (3500-6500 ft): No change.

Nutritional Info: 1 Serving: Calories 530 (Calories from Fat 250); Total Fat 28g (Saturated Fat 7g, Trans Fat 0g); Cholesterol 70mg; Sodium 790mg; Total Carbohydrate 42g (Dietary Fiber 3g, Sugars 3g); Protein 28g. % Daily Value: Cholesterol 23%; Vitamin A 10%; Vitamin C 10%; Calcium 10%; Iron 15%. Exchanges: 2 Starch, 1 Other Carbohydrate, 3 Lean Meat, 3-1/2 Fat. Carbohydrate Choices: 3.

Betty's Kitchen Tips

Variation: Use cut-up cooked rotisserie or deli chicken for the cooked chicken breast.

Substitution: If you'd prefer, you can cook 15 slices of raw bacon until crisp and then crumble it instead of using the precooked bacon.

yummy fries

Prep Time: 10 Minutes
Start to Finish: 35 Minutes
Servings: 6

EASY

1	bag (22 oz) frozen waffle potato fries
1/4	cup chopped fresh parsley
1	teaspoon garlic powder
1/2	teaspoon seasoned salt
1/4	teaspoon pepper
6	tablespoons ranch dressing

1 Heat oven to 450°F. Arrange fries in single layer on cookie sheet. Bake 17 to 23 minutes or until desired crispness.

2 Meanwhile, in medium bowl, mix the remaining ingredients except ranch dressing. Add baked fries; toss to coat. Serve with dressing.

High Altitude (3500-6500 ft): No change.

Nutritional Info: 1 Serving: Calories 270 (Calories from Fat 150); Total Fat 16g (Saturated Fat 3g, Trans Fat 2.5g); Cholesterol 0mg; Sodium 570mg; Total Carbohydrate 27g (Dietary Fiber 2g, Sugars 2g); Protein 3g. % Daily Value: Vitamin A 4%; Vitamin C 4%; Calcium 0%; Iron 6%. Exchanges: 1 Starch, 1 Other Carbohydrate, 3 Fat. Carbohydrate Choices: 2.

Betty's Kitchen Tip

• Seasoned salt is a mixture of salt and spices, such as paprika, garlic, turmeric and onion, that jazzes up foods with a couple of shakes.

asparagus and corn with honey-mustard glaze

Prep Time: 10 Minutes
Start to Finish: 20 Minutes
Servings: 5 (1/2 cup each)

EASY QUICK LOW FAT

1 lb fresh asparagus spears	2 teaspoons honey
1 cup Green Giant® frozen whole kernel corn	1/4 teaspoon lemon-pepper seasoning
2 teaspoons Dijon mustard	

1 Snap off tough ends of asparagus; cut stalks into 1-inch pieces.

2 In 2-quart saucepan, heat 1/2 cup water to boiling. Add asparagus and corn; reduce heat. Simmer uncovered 5 to 8 minutes or until asparagus is crisp tender; drain.

3 In small bowl, mix mustard, honey and lemon-pepper seasoning. Stir into hot vegetables.

High Altitude (3500-6500 ft): No change.

Nutritional Info: 1 Serving: Calories 50 (Calories from Fat 0); Total Fat 0g (Saturated Fat 0g, Trans Fat 0g); Cholesterol 0mg; Sodium 75mg; Total Carbohydrate 11g (Dietary Fiber 1g, Sugars 4g); Protein 2g. % Daily Value: Vitamin A 10%; Vitamin C 4%; Calcium 0%; Iron 4%. Exchanges: 1/2 Other Carbohydrate, 1 Vegetable. Carbohydrate Choices: 1.

Betty's Kitchen Tips

Substitution: Green beans, cut into 1-inch pieces, can be substituted for the asparagus.

Serve-With: This colorful side goes well with grilled steaks or chicken and crusty rolls.

layered chicken salad

Prep Time: 20 Minutes
Start to Finish: 8 Hours 20 Minutes
Servings: 8

8	cups bite-size pieces salad greens
1	small red onion, thinly sliced, separated into rings
2	cups chopped deli rotisserie chicken (from 2- to 2-1/2-lb chicken)
2	small zucchini, thinly sliced (about 3 cups)
1	cup shredded Monterey Jack or Cheddar cheese (4 oz)
1/2	lb salami, thinly sliced, cut into fourths
2	cups cherry tomatoes, cut in half
1	cup reduced-calorie mayonnaise or salad dressing
1	tablespoon yellow mustard
1/2	teaspoon prepared horseradish

Parsley or watercress, if desired

1 In very large (5-quart) glass bowl, place about half of the lettuce. Layer with onion, chicken, zucchini, cheese, salami, remaining lettuce and the tomatoes.

2 In small bowl, mix mayonnaise, mustard and horseradish; spread over tomatoes, spreading to edge of bowl.

3 Cover; refrigerate at least 8 hours but no longer than 24 hours. If desired, garnish with additional cherry tomatoes and parsley or watercress.

High Altitude (3500-6500 ft): No change.

Nutritional Info: 1 Serving: Calories 370 (Calories from Fat 240); Total Fat 27g (Saturated Fat 8g, Trans Fat 0g); Cholesterol 75mg; Sodium 1020mg; Total Carbohydrate 9g (Dietary Fiber 3g, Sugars 4g); Protein 22g. % Daily Value: Vitamin A 50%; Vitamin C 40%; Calcium 15%; Iron 10%. Exchanges: 1 Vegetable, 3 Medium-Fat Meat, 2-1/2 Fat. Carbohydrate Choices: 1/2.

Betty's Kitchen Tips

Time-Saver: Keep convenient canned chicken on the shelf for supper salads in a flash. Three 5-3/4-ounce cans yield about 2 cups.

Special Touch: Dress up ordinary rolls with an easy herbed butter. Stir 1 teaspoon of your favorite chopped fresh herb into 1/2 cup margarine or butter, softened.

california citrus-broccoli slaw

Prep Time: 20 Minutes
Start to Finish: 20 Minutes
Servings: 12

QUICK

Slaw

- 1 bag (16 oz) broccoli slaw
- 1 small jicama, peeled, cut into julienne strips (2 cups)
- 3 oranges
- 1 small red onion, cut in half, thinly sliced (1 cup)
- 2/3 cup chopped fresh cilantro

Citrus Dressing

- 3 tablespoons canola oil
- 3 tablespoons lemon juice
- 4 teaspoons sugar
- 1-1/2 teaspoons grated orange peel
- 1/8 teaspoon salt

1 In large bowl, mix broccoli slaw and jicama. Peel oranges with sharp paring knife. Cut oranges into 1/4-inch slices; cut each slice into fourths. Add oranges, onion and cilantro to broccoli mixture.

2 In tightly covered container, shake dressing ingredients. Pour dressing over salad; toss. Serve immediately, or cover and refrigerate up to 24 hours.

High Altitude (3500-6500 ft): No change.

Nutritional Info: 1 Serving: Calories 80 (Calories from Fat 35); Total Fat 3.5g (Saturated Fat 0g, Trans Fat 0g); Cholesterol 0mg; Sodium 40mg; Total Carbohydrate 11g (Dietary Fiber 3g, Sugars 5g); Protein 2g. % Daily Value: Vitamin A 8%; Vitamin C 100%; Calcium 4%; Iron 2%. Exchanges: 1/2 Other Carbohydrate, 1 Vegetable, 1/2 Fat. Carbohydrate Choices: 1.

Betty's Kitchen Tips

Success Hint: Before peeling the orange, grate the orange peel for the dressing.

Did You Know? Jicama is a crunchy root vegetable with a sweet, nutty flavor that's popular in Mexican cuisine. Its pretty ivory color does not discolor, making it a natural to use in salads.

smoked turkey-jarlsberg salad supreme

Prep Time: 20 Minutes
Start to Finish: 20 Minutes
Servings: 8 (1 cup each)

QUICK

1-1/2	lb smoked turkey breast, cut into 1x1/4-inch strips (5 cups)
8	oz Jarlsberg or Swiss cheese, cut into 1x1/4-inch strips (2 cups)
2	cups seedless red grapes, whole or cut in half
1-1/2	cups slivered almonds, toasted
2/3	cup mayonnaise or salad dressing
2/3	cup sour cream
2	to 4 tablespoons milk

Salt and pepper to taste, if desired

Lettuce, if desired

1 In very large (4-quart) bowl, mix turkey, cheese, grapes and almonds.

2 In medium bowl, mix remaining ingredients except lettuce. Pour over turkey mixture; mix gently. Serve immediately, or cover and refrigerate until serving time. Serve on lettuce-lined plates.

High Altitude (3500-6500 ft): No change.

Nutritional Info: 1 Serving: Calories 575 (Calories from Fat 360); Total Fat 40g (Saturated Fat 11g); Cholesterol 120mg; Sodium 240mg; Total Carbohydrate 14g (Dietary Fiber 3g); Protein 40g. Exchanges: 1 Fruit, 6 Medium-Fat Meat. Carbohydrate Choices: 1.

Betty's Kitchen Tip

• Make the salad the night before. Just before serving, stir in a small amount of milk to make the dressing creamier.

cornbread stuffing

Prep Time: 20 Minutes
Start to Finish: 1 Hour 5 Minutes
Servings: 10 (1/2 cup each)

1/2	cup butter or margarine
1-1/2	cups chopped celery (3 medium stalks)
3/4	cup chopped onion (1-1/2 medium)
9	cups cubes (1/2 inch) cornbread or soft bread

1-1/2	teaspoons chopped fresh or 1/2 teaspoon dried sage leaves, crushed
1-1/2	teaspoons chopped fresh or 1/2 teaspoon dried thyme leaves
1	teaspoon salt
1/8	teaspoon pepper

1 In 10-inch skillet, melt butter over medium heat. Add celery and onion; cook about 2 minutes, stirring occasionally, until crisp-tender. Remove from heat.

2 In large bowl, stir together celery mixture and remaining ingredients.

3 Stuff 12-pound turkey just before roasting. Or spoon stuffing into greased 3-quart casserole; cover and bake at 325°F for 30 minutes, then uncover and bake 15 minutes longer or until thoroughly heated.

High Altitude (3500-6500 ft): No change.

Nutritional Info: 1 Serving: Calories 340 (Calories from Fat 160); Total Fat 17g (Saturated Fat 8g, Trans Fat 1g); Cholesterol 75mg; Sodium 930mg; Total Carbohydrate 40g (Dietary Fiber 4g, Sugars 13g); Protein 6g. % Daily Value: Vitamin A 10%; Vitamin C 0%; Calcium 8%; Iron 8%. Exchanges: 1-1/2 Starch, 1 Other Carbohydrate, 3-1/2 Fat. Carbohydrate Choices: 2-1/2.

Betty's Kitchen Tips

Did You Know? One 8-inch square pan of baked cornbread will yield about 9 cups of cornbread cubes.

Do-Ahead: You can make stuffing up to four hours ahead. Cover and refrigerate until it's time to bake. Add 5 to 10 minutes to the bake time since the stuffing will be cold.

asian tossed salad

Prep Time: 20 Minutes
Start to Finish: 20 Minutes
Servings: 5 (1 cup each)

QUICK

3	cups shredded romaine lettuce
1-1/2	cups (from 16-oz bag) coleslaw mix (shredded cabbage and carrots)
1	cup fresh sugar snap peas, trimmed
1/2	cup shredded carrots
1/4	cup very thinly sliced red onion
1/4	cup fat-free mayonnaise or salad dressing
1/4	cup Chinese chicken salad dressing
1	tablespoon honey
2	tablespoons slivered almonds

1 In large bowl, mix lettuce, coleslaw mix, peas, carrots and onion.

2 In small bowl, mix mayonnaise, salad dressing and honey with wire whisk until smooth.

3 Add dressing mixture to salad; toss to mix. Sprinkle with almonds.

High Altitude (3500-6500 ft): No change.

Nutritional Info: 1 Serving: Calories 110 (Calories from Fat 50); Total Fat 6g (Saturated Fat 1g, Trans Fat 0g); Cholesterol 0mg; Sodium 240mg; Total Carbohydrate 12g (Dietary Fiber 2g, Sugars 8g); Protein 2g. % Daily Value: Vitamin A 90%; Vitamin C 35%; Calcium 4%; Iron 4%. Exchanges: 1/2 Other Carbohydrate, 1 Vegetable, 1 Fat. Carbohydrate Choices: 1.

Betty's Kitchen Tips

Substitution: If you can't find Chinese dressing, you can make your own by mixing 1/4 cup mayonnaise, 3 tablespoons citrus vinaigrette dressing, 1 tablespoon soy sauce and 1 tablespoon honey.

Success Hint: For the best results, toss the dressing with the salad ingredients just before serving.

roasted vegetables with basil

Prep Time: 20 Minutes
Start to Finish: 1 Hour 20 Minutes
Servings: 12 (1/2 cup each)

3 cups ready-to-eat baby-cut carrots, cut in half lengthwise	1/2 cup zesty Italian dressing
2 medium red bell peppers, coarsely chopped (2 cups)	1 bag (22 oz) Green Giant Select® frozen whole green beans
1 cup Green Giant® Niblets® frozen whole kernel corn	2 medium green onions, sliced (2 tablespoons)
	1/4 cup shredded fresh basil leaves

1 Heat oven to 450°F. Spray 15x10x1-inch pan with cooking spray. In large bowl, mix carrots, bell peppers, corn and dressing. Spread in pan.

2 Roast uncovered 30 minutes. Add frozen green beans to vegetable mixture in pan; stir to mix. Roast uncovered 25 to 30 minutes longer or until vegetables are crisp-tender. Sprinkle with onions and basil; stir gently to mix.

High Altitude (3500-6500 ft): Do not add corn in step 1. Add corn with green beans in step 2.

Nutritional Info: 1 Serving: Calories 90 (Calories from Fat 40); Total Fat 4.5g (Saturated Fat 0g, Trans Fat 0g); Cholesterol 0mg; Sodium 105mg; Total Carbohydrate 10g (Dietary Fiber 3g, Sugars 5g); Protein 2g. % Daily Value: Vitamin A 150%; Vitamin C 45%; Calcium 4%; Iron 4%. Exchanges: 1 Vegetable, 1 Fat. Carbohydrate Choices: 1/2.

Betty's Kitchen Tips

Special Touch: Serve the vegetables on a pretty platter, and garnish with fresh basil sprigs.

Health Twist: To reduce fat and calories a bit, use reduced-fat Italian dressing.

fresh fruit medley

Prep Time: 20 Minutes
Start to Finish: 20 Minutes
Servings: 12 (about 1/2 cup each)

QUICK

Honey-Poppy Seed Dressing

1/4	cup vegetable oil
3	tablespoons honey
2	tablespoons lemon juice
1-1/2	teaspoons poppy seed

Fruits

2	nectarines or apricots, sliced
1	orange, peeled, sliced
1	medium pineapple, peeled, cored and cut into 1-inch pieces
1	small bunch seedless grapes, each cut in half (2 cups)

1 In tightly covered container, shake dressing ingredients. Shake again before pouring over fruits.

2 In large bowl, toss fruits and dressing. Cover; refrigerate until ready to serve.

High Altitude (3500-6500 ft): No change.

Nutritional Info: 1 Serving: Calories 110 (Calories from Fat 45); Total Fat 5g (Saturated Fat 0.5g, Trans Fat 0g); Cholesterol 0mg; Sodium 0mg; Total Carbohydrate 16g (Dietary Fiber 1g, Sugars 14g); Protein 0g. % Daily Value: Vitamin A 4%; Vitamin C 40%; Calcium 0%; Iron 0%. Exchanges: 1 Fruit, 1 Fat. Carbohydrate Choices: 1.

Betty's Kitchen Tips

Do-Ahead: Make this a day ahead of time to ease your entertaining or meal-planning schedule.

Special Touch: Use a mixture of red and green grapes to add color to the fruit medley.

baby peas with bacon and almonds

Prep Time: 15 Minutes
Start to Finish: 15 Minutes
Servings: 6 (1/2 cup each)

EASY QUICK

- -

4   cups Green Giant® Select® Le Sueur® frozen baby sweet peas

2   slices bacon, chopped

2   tablespoons finely chopped onion

1/4   cup slivered almonds

2   tablespoons butter or margarine

1/2   teaspoon salt

Dash pepper

- -

1 Cook the peas as directed on bag; drain.

2 In 10-inch nonstick skillet, cook bacon over medium-high heat 4 to 5 minutes, stirring occasionally, until crisp. Remove bacon; drain on paper towels. Reserve drippings in skillet.

3 Cook onion and almonds in bacon drippings over medium-high heat 3 to 4 minutes, stirring frequently, until onion is tender and almonds are lightly browned. Remove from skillet.

4 In same skillet, melt the butter over medium-high heat. Add peas, bacon, onion, almonds, salt and pepper; toss.

High Altitude (3500-6500 ft): No change.

Nutritional Info: 1 Serving: Calories 130 (Calories from Fat 70); Total Fat 8g (Saturated Fat 2.5g, Trans Fat 0g); Cholesterol 10mg; Sodium 310mg; Total Carbohydrate 11g (Dietary Fiber 3g, Sugars 4g); Protein 5g. % Daily Value: Vitamin A 10%; Vitamin C 6%; Calcium 2%; Iron 8%. Exchanges: 1 Starch, 1-1/2 Fat. Carbohydrate Choices: 1.

Betty's Kitchen Tip

• Use Green Giant® frozen whole green beans instead of the peas for a different side dish that is just as easy and flavorful.

TORTES&CAKES,CHEESECAKES

p. 230

217

216

239

honey bun cake

Prep Time: 15 Minutes
Start to Finish: 2 Hours 5 Minutes
Servings: 12

EASY

Cake

1	box Betty Crocker® SuperMoist® yellow cake mix
2/3	cup vegetable oil
4	eggs
1	container (8 oz) sour cream (1 cup)
1	cup packed brown sugar

1/3	cup chopped pecans
2	teaspoons ground cinnamon

Icing

1	cup powdered sugar
1	tablespoon milk
1	teaspoon vanilla

1 Heat oven to 350°F for shiny metal or glass pan (or 325°F for dark or nonstick pan). Spray bottom only of 13x9-inch pan with baking spray with flour.

2 In large bowl, beat cake mix, oil, eggs and sour cream with electric mixer on low speed 30 seconds; beat on medium speed 2 minutes, scraping bowl occasionally. Spread half of the batter in pan.

3 In small bowl, stir together brown sugar, pecans and cinnamon; sprinkle over batter in pan. Carefully spread remaining batter evenly over pecan mixture.

4 Bake 44 to 48 minutes or until deep golden brown.

5 In small bowl, stir icing ingredients until thin enough to spread. Prick surface of warm cake several times with fork. Spread icing over cake. Cool completely, about 1 hour. Store covered at room temperature.

High Altitude (3500-6500 ft): No change.

Nutritional Info: 1 Serving: Calories 480 (Calories from Fat 210); Total Fat 23g (Saturated Fat 6g, Trans Fat 1g); Cholesterol 85mg; Sodium 320mg; Total Carbohydrate 65g (Dietary Fiber 0g, Sugars 48g); Protein 4g. % Daily Value: Cholesterol 28%; Vitamin A 4%; Vitamin C 0%; Calcium 10%; Iron 8%. Exchanges: 1 Starch, 3-1/2 Other Carbohydrate, 4 Fat. Carbohydrate Choices: 4.

Betty's Kitchen Tips

How-To: Tackle spreading the batter over the pecan mixture with ease! Simply drizzle the batter over the pecan mixture from one end of the pan to the other, then spread to fill in the uncovered spaces.

Substitution: In a pinch, chopped walnuts or slivered almonds can be substituted for the pecans.

grasshopper fudge cake

Prep Time: 20 Minutes
Start to Finish: 1 Hour 55 Minutes
Servings: 15

1	box Betty Crocker® SuperMoist® white cake mix
1-1/4	cups water
1/3	cup vegetable oil
2	teaspoons mint extract
3	egg whites
12	drops green food color
2	jars (16 oz each) hot fudge topping
1	container (8 oz) frozen whipped topping, thawed
5	drops yellow food color

Thin rectangular crème de menthe chocolate candies, unwrapped and cut into pieces, if desired

1 Heat oven to 350°F for shiny metal or glass pan (or 325°F for dark or nonstick pan). Spray bottom only of 13x9-inch pan with baking spray with flour.

2 Make cake mix as directed on box, using water, oil, 1-1/2 teaspoons of the mint extract and the egg whites. Reserve 1 cup batter. Stir 3 drops of the green food color into reserved batter; set aside. Pour the remaining batter into pan.

3 Drop green batter by generous tablespoonfuls randomly in 12 to 14 mounds onto batter in pan. Cut through batters with metal spatula or knife in S-shaped curves in one continuous motion. Turn pan 1/4 turn; repeat cutting for swirled design.

4 Bake 28 to 33 minutes or until toothpick inserted in center comes out clean. Run knife around side of pan to loosen cake. Cool completely, about 1 hour.

5 Carefully spread fudge topping evenly over cake. In medium bowl, stir whipped topping, remaining 1/2 teaspoon extract, remaining 9 drops green food color and the yellow food color until blended. Spread whipped topping mixture evenly over fudge. Garnish with candy pieces. Store covered in refrigerator.

High Altitude (3500-6500 ft): No change.

Nutritional Info: 1 Serving: Calories 440 (Calories from Fat 150); Total Fat 16g (Saturated Fat 6g, Trans Fat 1g); Cholesterol 0mg; Sodium 450mg; Total Carbohydrate 68g (Dietary Fiber 2g, Sugars 46g); Protein 5g. % Daily Value: Cholesterol 0%; Vitamin A 0%; Vitamin C 0%; Calcium 10%; Iron 8%. Exchanges: 1-1/2 Starch, 3 Other Carbohydrate, 3 Fat. Carbohydrate Choices: 4-1/2.

Betty's Kitchen Tip

• Warm the foil-wrapped mints in your hands for a minute or two to make cutting them easier.

chocolate zucchini snack cake

Prep Time: 15 Minutes
Start to Finish: 1 Hour 50 Minutes
Servings: 6

EASY

1-3/4   cups Betty Crocker® SuperMoist® German chocolate cake mix (from 18.25-oz box)

1   cup shredded unpeeled zucchini (about 1 medium)

1/2   teaspoon ground cinnamon

1/8   teaspoon ground cloves

1/4   cup buttermilk

2   tablespoons vegetable oil

1   egg

1/4   cup chopped nuts

1/4   cup miniature semisweet chocolate chips

1   Heat oven to 350°F for shiny metal or glass pan (or 325°F for dark or nonstick pan). Spray bottom and side of 9- or 8-inch round cake pan with baking spray with flour.

2   In large bowl, beat cake mix, zucchini, cinnamon, cloves, buttermilk, oil and egg with electric mixer on low speed until moistened. Beat on medium speed 2 minutes, scraping bowl occasionally. Pour into pan. Sprinkle evenly with nuts and chocolate chips.

3   Bake 30 to 35 minutes or until toothpick inserted in center comes out clean. Cool completely, about 1 hour.

High Altitude (3500-6500 ft): No change.

Nutritional Info: 1 Serving: Calories 310 (Calories from Fat 120); Total Fat 14g (Saturated Fat 3.5g, Trans Fat 0.5g); Cholesterol 35mg; Sodium 350mg; Total Carbohydrate 42g (Dietary Fiber 2g, Sugars 26g); Protein 5g. % Daily Value: Cholesterol 12%; Vitamin A 0%; Vitamin C 4%; Calcium 6%; Iron 8%. Exchanges: 1 Starch, 2 Other Carbohydrate, 2-1/2 Fat. Carbohydrate Choices: 3.

Betty's Kitchen Tips

Special Touch: Bake and serve the cake in a pretty, oven-safe ceramic pan.

Substitution: Out of buttermilk? Use 3/4 teaspoon lemon juice or vinegar plus milk to make 1/4 cup. Let stand for about 5 minutes before using.

black forest cake

Prep Time: 25 Minutes
Start to Finish: 2 Hours 15 Minutes
Servings: 12

Cake

1 box Betty Crocker® SuperMoist® devil's food cake mix

Water, vegetable oil and eggs called for on cake mix box

Filling and Topping

1 pint (2 cups) whipping cream

1/2 cup powdered sugar

2 to 3 tablespoons brandy, if desired

1 can (21 oz) cherry pie filling

1/2 teaspoon almond extract

2 tablespoons sliced almonds

1 Heat oven to 350°F for shiny metal pans (or 325°F for dark or nonstick pans). Spray bottoms and sides of 2 (8- or 9-inch) round cake pans with baking spray with flour.

2 Make and bake cake as directed on box for 8- or 9-inch rounds, using water, oil and eggs. Cool 10 minutes; remove from pans to cooling rack. Cool completely, about 1 hour.

3 In medium bowl, beat whipping cream with electric mixer on high speed until slightly thickened. Gradually beat in powdered sugar until stiff peaks form. Fold in brandy. In another small bowl, mix pie filling and almond extract.

4 On serving plate, place 1 cake layer, bottom side up. Spread with 1 cup cherry mixture to within 1 inch of edge. Top with second cake layer, rounded side up. Frost top and side with whipped cream. Spoon remaining cherry mixture over top. Sprinkle with sliced almonds. Store covered in refrigerator.

High Altitude (3500-6500 ft): Follow High Altitude directions on cake mix box for 2 (8- or 9-inch) round cake pans.

Nutritional Info: 1 Serving: Calories 390 (Calories from Fat 150); Total Fat 16g (Saturated Fat 4.5g, Trans Fat 0.5g); Cholesterol 60mg; Sodium 370mg; Total Carbohydrate 55g (Dietary Fiber 2g, Sugars 39g); Protein 5. % Daily Value: Cholesterol 20%; Vitamin A 4%; Vitamin C 0%; Calcium 6%; Iron 10%. Exchanges: 1-1/2 Starch, 2 Other Carbohydrate, 3 Fat. Carbohydrate Choices: 3-1/2.

Betty's Kitchen Tips

Did You Know? "Black Forest" usually describes desserts made with chocolate, cherries and whipping cream.

Success Hint: If you start with a chilled bowl, the whipping cream will whip up much faster.

carrot-mandarin orange cake

Prep Time: 35 Minutes
Start to Finish: 2 Hours 50 Minutes
Servings: 15

Cake

1   box Betty Crocker® SuperMoist® yellow or golden vanilla cake mix
1   cup vegetable oil
2   teaspoons ground cinnamon
1   teaspoon ground allspice
3   eggs
1   can (11 oz) mandarin orange segments, undrained

1   cup finely shredded carrots (2 large)
1   cup flaked coconut

Topping

1   package (8 oz) cream cheese, softened
1   container (1 lb) Betty Crocker® Rich & Creamy vanilla frosting
1/2 cup finely chopped pecans, if desired

1 Heat oven to 350°F (or 325°F for dark or nonstick pan). Spray bottom only of 13x9-inch pan with baking spray with flour.

2 In large bowl, beat all cake ingredients except carrots and coconut with electric mixer on low speed 30 seconds. Beat on medium speed 2 minutes. Stir in carrots and coconut. Pour into pan.

3 Bake 40 to 45 minutes or until toothpick inserted in center comes out clean. Cool completely, about 1 hour.

4 In large bowl, beat cream cheese on medium speed until smooth and creamy. Stir in frosting until well mixed. Spread frosting over cake. Sprinkle with pecans (or top with additional mandarin orange segments just before serving). Refrigerate 30 minutes before serving. Store covered in refrigerator.

High Altitude (3500-6500 ft): Decrease oil to 1/2 cup.

Nutritional Info: 1 Serving: Calories 510 (Calories from Fat 290); Total Fat 32g (Saturated Fat 10g, Trans Fat 3.5g); Cholesterol 60mg; Sodium 370mg; Total Carbohydrate 53g (Dietary Fiber 0g, Sugars 38g); Protein 4g. % Daily Value: Cholesterol 20%; Vitamin A 35%; Vitamin C 6%; Calcium 8%; Iron 6%. Exchanges: 1 Starch, 2-1/2 Other Carbohydrate, 6 Fat. Carbohydrate Choices: 3-1/2.

Betty's Kitchen Tips

And the Winner Is: Judie Hampton of Shelly, Idaho, won a Betty Crocker gift basket with this recipe, which was inspired by her grandmother's beloved recipe.

Success Hint: Buy an extra can of mandarin orange segments for the garnish.

german chocolate picnic cake

Prep Time: 15 Minutes
Start to Finish: 1 Hour 25 Minutes
Servings: 9

EASY

- 1-3/4 cups Betty Crocker® SuperMoist® German chocolate cake mix (from 18.25-oz box)
- 1/2 cup water
- 2 tablespoons vegetable oil
- 1 egg
- 1/2 cup packed brown sugar
- 1/3 cup Gold Medal® all-purpose flour
- 1/3 cup quick-cooking or old-fashioned oats
- 3 tablespoons butter or margarine, softened
- 3/4 teaspoon ground cinnamon
- 1/4 teaspoon ground nutmeg

1 Heat oven to 350°F for shiny metal or glass pan (or 325°F for dark or nonstick pan). Spray bottom only of 8- or 9-inch square pan with baking spray with flour.

2 In large bowl, beat the cake mix, water, oil and egg with electric mixer on low speed 30 seconds. Beat on medium speed 2 minutes, scraping bowl occasionally. Pour batter into pan.

3 In medium bowl, stir remaining ingredients until well mixed; sprinkle evenly over batter in pan.

4 Bake 32 to 36 minutes or until toothpick inserted in center of cake comes out clean. Cool at least 30 minutes before serving. Serve warm or cool.

High Altitude (3500-6500 ft): Heat oven to 350°F for all pans. For 8-inch shiny pans, increase bake time to 35 to 41 minutes.

Nutritional Info: 1 Serving: Calories 260 (Calories from Fat 90); Total Fat 10g (Saturated Fat 4g, Trans Fat 0g); Cholesterol 35mg; Sodium 260mg; Total Carbohydrate 41g (Dietary Fiber 1g, Sugars 26g); Protein 3g. % Daily Value: Cholesterol 11%; Vitamin A 4%; Vitamin C 0%; Calcium 4%; Iron 6%. Exchanges: 1 Starch, 1-1/2 Other Carbohydrate, 2 Fat. Carbohydrate Choices: 3.

Betty's Kitchen Tip

• If you plan to tote this cake to a picnic, bake it in a disposable foil pan. Then you don't have to carry home the dirty pan.

strawberry-lime layer cake

Prep Time: 1 Hour
Start to Finish: 2 Hours 30 Minutes
Servings: 12

Cake

1   box Betty Crocker® SuperMoist® white
    cake mix
Water, vegetable oil and egg whites called for on
cake mix box
2   tablespoons grated fresh lime peel

Filling and Frosting

1   quart (4 cups) fresh strawberries
1/2   cup butter or margarine, softened
4   cups powdered sugar
1-1/3 cups whipping cream

1   Heat oven to 350°F for shiny metal pans
    (or 325°F for dark or nonstick pans).
    Generously spray bottoms and sides of
    2 (8- or 9-inch) round cake pans with
    baking spray with flour.

2   Make cake mix as directed on box, using
    water, oil and egg whites; stir lime peel
    into batter. Divide batter between pans.

3   Bake as directed on box for 8- or 9-inch
    rounds. Cool in pans 10 minutes. Remove
    from pans to cooling rack. Cool completely,
    about 1 hour.

4   Reserve 3 whole strawberries for garnish.
    Cut remaining strawberries into thin
    slices. Finely chop enough of the sliced
    strawberries to equal 1/2 cup.

5   In medium bowl, beat butter with electric
    mixer on low speed about 30 seconds to
    soften, then beat on high speed until fluffy.
    Add chopped strawberries and powdered
    sugar; beat on low speed until sugar has
    been incorporated. Increase speed to medium;
    beat until frosting is fluffy. Divide frosting
    into fourths.

6   With long, sharp knife, split each cooled
    cake layer horizontally in half. Place 1
    layer, cut side up, on serving plate. Spread
    with 1/4 of the frosting; top with half of
    the sliced strawberries. Add second layer,
    cut side down. Spread with 1/4 of the
    frosting. Add third layer, cut side up.
    Spread with 1/4 of the frosting; top with

remaining sliced strawberries. Add
remaining cake layer, cut side down.
Frost top of cake with remaining frosting.

7   In medium bowl, beat whipping cream
    with electric mixer on high speed until
    stiff peaks form. Frost side of cake with
    whipped cream. Refrigerate at least 1 hour
    before serving. Garnish top of cake with
    whole strawberries just before serving.
    Store covered in refrigerator.

High Altitude (3500-6500 ft): Follow High
Altitude cake mix directions for 2 (8- or 9-inch)
round cake pans.

Nutritional Info: 1 Serving: Calories 560 (Calories from Fat 240);
Total Fat 26g (Saturated Fat 12g, Trans Fat 1.5g); Cholesterol
50mg; Sodium 370mg; Total Carbohydrate 78g (Dietary Fiber 1g,
Sugars 60g); Protein 4g. % Daily Value: Cholesterol 17%;
Vitamin A 10%; Vitamin C 60%; Calcium 8%; Iron 6%.
Exchanges: 1 Starch, 4 Other Carbohydrate, 5 Fat. Carbohydrate
Choices: 5.

Betty's Kitchen Tips

Success Hint: It's easier to cut this cake if it is
chilled first.

How-To: To cut fresh strawberries into even
slices, use an egg slicer.

coconut cake with
white chocolate frosting

Prep Time: 25 Minutes
Start to Finish: 2 Hours
Servings: 15

1	can (14 oz) coconut milk (not cream of coconut)	3/4	cup flaked coconut
1	box Betty Crocker® SuperMoist® white cake mix	1	cup white vanilla baking chips (6 oz)
1/4	cup water	1-3/4	cups powdered sugar
3	egg whites	1/3	cup butter or margarine, softened
		1/2	teaspoon vanilla

1 Heat oven to 350°F for shiny metal or glass pan (or 325°F for dark or nonstick pan). Spray bottom only of 13x9-inch pan with baking spray with flour. Reserve 1/3 cup coconut milk for frosting.

2 In large bowl, beat cake mix, remaining coconut milk (1-1/3 cups), the water and egg whites with electric mixer on low speed 30 seconds. Beat on medium speed 2 minutes, scraping bowl occasionally. Stir in 1/2 cup of the coconut until well combined. Pour into pan.

3 Bake 28 to 33 minutes or until toothpick inserted in center comes out clean. Cool completely, about 1 hour.

4 Meanwhile, in 2-quart bowl, microwave vanilla baking chips uncovered on High 30 seconds or until melted. Stir; if chips are not completely melted, microwave 15 seconds longer, then stir until all chips are melted. Stir in powdered sugar, butter, reserved 1/3 cup coconut milk and the vanilla. Cover; refrigerate 30 to 60 minutes. (If frosting becomes too firm to spread, microwave uncovered on High 10 to 15 seconds to soften; stir until smooth.)

5 Spread frosting over cake. Immediately sprinkle top with 1/4 cup coconut. Store loosely covered at room temperature.

High Altitude (3500-6500 ft): No change.

Nutritional Info: 1 Serving: Calories 370 (Calories from Fat 150); Total Fat 16g (Saturated Fat 11g, Trans Fat 1g); Cholesterol 10mg; Sodium 320mg; Total Carbohydrate 51g (Dietary Fiber 0g, Sugars 37g); Protein 4g. % Daily Value: Cholesterol 4%; Vitamin A 2%; Vitamin C 0%; Calcium 4%; Iron 4%. Exchanges: 1 Starch, 2-1/2 Other Carbohydrate, 3 Fat. Carbohydrate Choices: 3-1/2.

Betty's Kitchen Tip

• Regular flaked coconut can be used instead of the large flakes.

mud slide ice cream cake

Prep Time: 30 Minutes
Start to Finish: 6 Hours
Servings: 15

- 1 box Betty Crocker® SuperMoist® chocolate fudge cake mix
- 1/2 cup butter or margarine, melted
- 2 eggs
- 2 tablespoons coffee-flavored liqueur or prepared strong coffee
- 4 cups vanilla ice cream
- 1 container (12 oz) Betty Crocker® Whipped chocolate frosting
- 2 tablespoons coffee-flavored liqueur, if desired

1 Heat oven to 350°F for shiny metal or glass pan (or 325°F for dark or nonstick pan). Spray bottom only of 13x9-inch pan with baking spray with flour.

2 In large bowl, beat cake mix, butter and eggs with electric mixer on medium speed until well blended. Spread batter in pan.

3 Bake 19 to 24 minutes or until center is set (top will appear dry and cracked). Cool completely, about 1 hour.

4 Brush 2 tablespoons liqueur over cake. Let ice cream stand at room temperature about 15 minutes to soften. Spread ice cream over cake. Freeze 3 hours or until firm.

5 In medium bowl, mix the frosting and 2 tablespoons liqueur; spread over ice cream. Freeze at least 1 hour. Store covered in the freezer.

High Altitude (3500-6500 ft): Decrease butter to 1/3 cup.

Nutritional Info: 1 Serving: Calories 390 (Calories from Fat 160); Total Fat 18g (Saturated Fat 9g, Trans Fat 1.5g); Cholesterol 60mg; Sodium 410mg; Total Carbohydrate 51g (Dietary Fiber 2g, Sugars 36g); Protein 4g. % Daily Value: Cholesterol 20%; Vitamin A 8%; Vitamin C 0%; Calcium 8%; Iron 10%. Exchanges: 1 Starch, 2-1/2 Other Carbohydrate, 3-1/2 Fat. Carbohydrate Choices: 3-1/2.

Betty's Kitchen Tips

Did You Know? Mud slide drinks are popular on menus across the country. Here the concoction is made into a frozen dessert with a brownie-like base.

Substitution: Coffee lovers can substitute coffee-flavored ice cream for the vanilla.

chocolate-orange cake

Prep Time: 25 Minutes
Start to Finish: 2 Hours 15 Minutes
Servings: 16

Cake

1	box Betty Crocker® SuperMoist® devil's food cake mix
2	tablespoons freshly grated orange peel
1-1/3	cups orange juice
1/2	cup vegetable oil
3	eggs

Frosting

1-1/2	containers (12 oz each) Betty Crocker® Whipped vanilla frosting
2	tablespoons freshly grated orange peel
1/2	teaspoon orange extract
1/3	cup orange marmalade

Garnishes, if desired

Orange peel strips, corn syrup and sugar

1 Heat oven to 350°F for shiny metal pans (or 325°F for dark or nonstick pans). Spray bottoms and sides of 2 (8- or 9-inch) round cake pans with baking spray with flour.

2 In large bowl, beat cake mix, 2 tablespoons orange peel, the orange juice, oil and eggs with electric mixer on low speed 30 seconds, scraping bowl frequently. Beat on medium speed 2 minutes, scraping bowl occasionally, until light and fluffy. Divide batter between pans.

3 Bake 8-inch pans 32 to 36 minutes, 9-inch pans 30 to 35 minutes, or until toothpick inserted in center comes out clean. Cool 10 minutes on cooling rack. Remove from pans to cooling rack. Cool completely, about 1 hour.

4 In medium bowl, stir frosting, 2 tablespoons orange peel and the orange extract until blended. On serving plate, place 1 cake layer, rounded side down. Spread 1/2 cup frosting over cake layer; spread marmalade over frosting. Add other cake layer, rounded side up. Frost side and top of cake with remaining frosting. For garnish, cut strips of orange peel. Brush strips with corn syrup and sprinkle with sugar. Top cake with sugared orange peel. Store loosely covered at room temperature.

High Altitude (3500-6500 ft): No change.

Nutritional Info: 1 Serving: Calories 370 (Calories from Fat 150); Total Fat 17g (Saturated Fat 4.5g, Trans Fat 2.5g); Cholesterol 40mg; Sodium 300mg; Total Carbohydrate 53g (Dietary Fiber 1g, Sugars 39g); Protein 3g. % Daily Value: Cholesterol 13%; Vitamin A 0%; Vitamin C 8%; Calcium 4%; Iron 8%. Exchanges: 1 Starch, 2-1/2 Other Carbohydrate, 3 Fat. Carbohydrate Choices: 3-1/2.

Betty's Kitchen Tip

• A pedestal plate makes any cake look pretty. For a special occasion, use a paper doily, too.

peppermint pattie poke cake

Prep Time: 25 Minutes
Start to Finish: 3 Hours 15 Minutes
Servings: 15

Cake

1   box Betty Crocker® SuperMoist® chocolate fudge cake mix

Water, vegetable oil and eggs called for on cake mix box

Filling

1   box (4-serving size) white chocolate instant pudding and pie filling mix

2   cups milk

1/2   teaspoon peppermint extract

Frosting

1/4   teaspoon peppermint extract

1   container (12 oz) Betty Crocker® Whipped milk chocolate frosting

3/4   cup coarsely chopped chocolate-covered peppermint patties (8 candies)

1   Heat oven to 350°F for shiny metal or glass pan (or 325°F for dark or nonstick pan). Spray bottom only of 13x9-inch pan with baking spray with flour. Make and bake cake mix as directed on box for 13x9-inch pan. Cool 15 minutes. With handle of wooden spoon, poke top of warm cake every 1/2 inch.

2   In medium bowl, beat filling ingredients with wire whisk about 2 minutes. Immediately pour over cake. Cover loosely; refrigerate about 2 hours or until chilled.

3   Stir 1/4 teaspoon peppermint extract into frosting. Spread frosting over top of cake. Sprinkle with peppermint patties. Store covered in refrigerator.

High Altitude (3500-6500 ft): Follow High Altitude directions on cake mix box for 13x9-inch pan.

Nutritional Info: 1 Serving: Calories 360 (Calories from Fat 130); Total Fat 15g (Saturated Fat 4.5g, Trans Fat 1.5g); Cholesterol 45mg; Sodium 440mg; Total Carbohydrate 54g (Dietary Fiber 1g, Sugars 38g); Protein 4g. % Daily Value: Cholesterol 15%; Vitamin A 2%; Vitamin C 0%; Calcium 8%; Iron 10%. Exchanges: 1 Starch, 2-1/2 Other Carbohydrate, 3 Fat. Carbohydrate Choices: 3-1/2.

Betty's Kitchen Tips

Success Hint: To keep candies from sticking together, sprinkle 1 tablespoon sugar over the cutting board. As you cut the candies, toss them with the sugar.

Substitution: Vanilla instant pudding and pie filling mix can be used instead of the white chocolate pudding mix.

praline mini bundt cakes

Prep Time: 20 Minutes
Start to Finish: 1 Hour 55 Minutes
Servings: 12 mini cakes

Cakes

1	box Betty Crocker® SuperMoist® yellow cake mix
1-1/4	cups water
1/3	cup vegetable oil
3	eggs
1/2	cup chopped pecans
1/2	cup toffee bits

Glaze and Garnish

1/4	cup butter (do not use margarine)
1/2	cup packed brown sugar
2	tablespoons corn syrup
2	tablespoons milk
1	cup powdered sugar
1	teaspoon vanilla
1/4	cup toffee bits

1 Heat oven to 350°F for shiny metal pans (or 325°F for dark or nonstick pans). Generously grease 12 mini fluted tube cake pans or 12 jumbo muffin cups with shortening (do not spray with cooking spray); lightly flour.

2 In large bowl, beat cake mix, water, oil and eggs with electric mixer on low speed 30 seconds. Beat on medium speed 2 minutes, scraping bowl occasionally. Fold in pecans and 1/2 cup toffee bits. Divide batter evenly among mini pans.

3 Bake 18 to 23 minutes or until toothpick inserted in center of cake comes out clean. Cool 10 minutes; remove from pans to cooling rack. Cool completely, about 1 hour.

4 In 1-quart saucepan, melt butter over medium-high heat. Stir in brown sugar, corn syrup and milk. Heat to rolling boil over medium-high heat, stirring frequently; remove from heat. Immediately beat in powdered sugar and vanilla with wire whisk until smooth. Immediately drizzle about 1 tablespoon glaze over each cake; sprinkle each with 1 teaspoon toffee bits. Store loosely covered at room temperature.

High Altitude (3500-6500 ft): No change.

Nutritional Info: 1 Mini Cake: Calories 480 (Calories from Fat 200); Total Fat 23g (Saturated Fat 8g, Trans Fat 1g); Cholesterol 75mg; Sodium 390mg; Total Carbohydrate 66g (Dietary Fiber 0g, Sugars 48g); Protein 3g. % Daily Value: Cholesterol 24%; Vitamin A 4%; Vitamin C 0%; Calcium 8%; Iron 6%. Exchanges: 1/2 Starch, 4 Other Carbohydrate, 4-1/2 Fat. Carbohydrate Choices: 4-1/2.

Betty's Kitchen Tips

Substitution: Almond lovers can get a nut fix by substituting almonds for the pecans and almond extract for the vanilla.

Success Hint: To keep the cakes from sticking to the cake pans, be sure to grease and flour the pans generously.

creamy orange cake

Prep Time: 25 Minutes
Start to Finish: 2 Hours
Servings: 12

- 1 cup boiling water
- 1 box (4-serving size) orange-flavored gelatin
- 1 box Betty Crocker® SuperMoist® white cake mix
- 3/4 cup frozen (thawed) orange juice concentrate
- 1/3 cup vegetable oil
- 1/4 cup water
- 4 egg whites
- 1 container (12 oz) Betty Crocker® Whipped vanilla frosting
- 1 container (8 oz) frozen whipped topping, thawed

1 Heat oven to 350°F for shiny metal or glass pan (or 325°F for dark or nonstick pan). Spray bottom only of 13x9-inch pan with baking spray with flour. In small bowl, mix boiling water and gelatin until gelatin is completely dissolved. Cool slightly, about 5 minutes.

2 In large bowl, beat cake mix, 1/4 cup of the gelatin mixture, 1/4 cup of the orange juice concentrate, the oil, water and egg whites with electric mixer on low speed 30 seconds. Beat on medium speed 2 minutes, scraping bowl occasionally. Pour into pan. Reserve remaining gelatin mixture and orange juice concentrate.

3 Bake 30 to 35 minutes or until toothpick inserted in center comes out clean. Poke warm cake every inch with fork. Place 1 tablespoon of the reserved gelatin mixture in microwavable custard cup or small bowl; set aside. Into remaining gelatin mixture, stir remaining 1/2 cup orange juice concentrate; pour slowly over cake. Cool cake completely, about 1 hour.

4 In medium bowl, gently stir together frosting and whipped topping; frost cake. Microwave 1 tablespoon gelatin mixture uncovered on High 10 seconds to liquefy. Using 1/4 teaspoon measuring spoon, place small drops of gelatin mixture over frosting. With spoon or toothpick, swirl gelatin into frosting. Store covered in refrigerator.

High Altitude (3500-6500 ft): Follow High Altitude directions on cake mix box for 13x9-inch pan.

Nutritional Info: 1 Serving: Calories 470 (Calories from Fat 180); Total Fat 20g (Saturated Fat 7g, Trans Fat 3g); Cholesterol 0mg; Sodium 370mg; Total Carbohydrate 69g (Dietary Fiber 0g, Sugars 49g); Protein 5g. % Daily Value: Cholesterol 0%; Vitamin A 0%; Vitamin C 20%; Calcium 6%; Iron 4%. Exchanges: 1-1/2 Starch, 3 Other Carbohydrate, 4 Fat. Carbohydrate Choices: 4-1/2.

Betty's Kitchen Tip

- Pour the leftover thawed frozen orange juice concentrate over a cup of fresh fruit for a snack.

strawberry-rhubarb angel torte

Prep Time: 25 Minutes
Start to Finish: 3 Hours 10 Minutes
Servings: 12

Cake

1	box Betty Crocker® white angel food cake mix
1-1/4	cups cold water
2	teaspoons grated orange peel

Filling

2	cups sliced fresh rhubarb
1/2	cup granulated sugar
2	tablespoons orange juice

1-1/2	cups sliced fresh strawberries
4	drops red food color, if desired

Frosting and Garnish

1-1/2	cups whipping cream
3	tablespoons granulated or powdered sugar
1	container (15 oz) ricotta cheese
1/4	cup powdered sugar
1/2	cup sliced fresh strawberries

1 Move oven rack to lowest position (remove other racks). Heat oven to 350°F.

2 In extra-large glass or metal bowl, beat cake mix, water and orange peel with electric mixer on low speed 30 seconds. Beat on medium speed 1 minute. Pour into ungreased 10-inch angel food (tube) cake pan. (Do not use fluted tube cake pan or 9-inch angel food pan or batter will overflow.)

3 Bake 37 to 47 minutes or until top is dark golden brown and cracks feel very dry and not sticky. Do not underbake. Immediately turn pan upside down onto glass bottle until cake is completely cool, about 2 hours.

4 Meanwhile, in 2-quart saucepan, mix rhubarb, 1/2 cup granulated sugar and the orange juice. Cook over medium heat 10 minutes, stirring occasionally. Cool 15 minutes. Stir in 1-1/2 cups strawberries. Stir in 4 drops food color if deeper red color is desired. Refrigerate about 1 hour.

5 In medium bowl, beat whipping cream and 3 tablespoons sugar on high speed until soft peaks form. In large bowl, beat ricotta cheese and 1/4 cup powdered sugar on medium speed until fluffy. Fold in whipped cream.

6 Run knife around side of pan to loosen cake; remove from pan. Cut cake horizontally to make 3 layers. Fill layers with strawberry-rhubarb filling. Frost side and top of cake with frosting. Arrange 1/2 cup strawberries over top of cake. Store covered in refrigerator.

High Altitude (3500-6500 ft): Follow High Altitude directions on cake mix box for 10-inch angel food (tube) cake pan, adding orange peel with water in step 2.

Nutritional Info: 1 Serving: Calories 350 (Calories from Fat 110); Total Fat 12g (Saturated Fat 8g, Trans Fat 0g); Cholesterol 45mg; Sodium 380mg; Total Carbohydrate 51g (Dietary Fiber 0g, Sugars 40g); Protein 8g. Exchanges: 2-1/2 Starch, 1 Other Carbohydrate, 2 Fat. Carbohydrate Choices: 3-1/2.

Betty's Kitchen Tips

Variation: For Blueberry-Rhubarb Angel Torte, substitute 1-1/2 cups fresh or frozen (thawed) blueberries for the strawberries in the filling. Omit food color and garnish.

Substitution: Use 2 containers (12 oz each) Betty Crocker® Whipped whipped cream or vanilla frosting instead of the ricotta frosting.

deep dark mocha torte

Prep Time: 50 Minutes
Start to Finish: 2 Hours 40 Minutes
Servings: 12 to 16

Torte

1	box Betty Crocker® SuperMoist® chocolate fudge cake mix

Water, vegetable oil and eggs called for on cake mix box

1/3	cup granulated sugar
1/3	cup rum or water
1-1/4	teaspoons instant espresso coffee granules

Filling

2	packages (8 oz each) cream cheese, softened
1	cup powdered sugar
1	teaspoon vanilla
2	to 3 teaspoons milk

Ganache

1-1/2	cups semisweet chocolate chips
6	tablespoons butter (do not use margarine)
1/3	cup whipping cream

1 Heat oven to 350°F for shiny metal pans (or 325°F for dark or nonstick pans). Spray bottoms only of 2 (8- or 9-inch) round cake pans with baking spray with flour. Make cake mix as directed on box, using water, oil and eggs. Pour batter into pans. Bake as directed on box for 8- or 9-inch round pans. Cool 10 minutes; remove from pans to cooling rack. Cool completely, about 1 hour.

2 Meanwhile, in 1-quart saucepan, stir granulated sugar, rum and coffee granules until coffee is dissolved. Heat to boiling, stirring occasionally; remove from heat. Cool completely.

3 In medium bowl, beat filling ingredients with electric mixer on low speed just until blended, adding enough milk for spreading consistency; set aside.

4 In 1-quart saucepan, heat ganache ingredients over low heat, stirring frequently, until chips are melted and mixture is smooth. Refrigerate about 30 minutes, stirring occasionally, until slightly thickened.

5 Cut each cake layer horizontally to make 2 layers. (To cut, mark side of cake with toothpicks and cut with long, thin knife.) Brush about 1 tablespoon of the rum mixture over cut side of each layer; let stand 1 minute to soak into cake. Fill each layer with about 2/3 cup filling. Spread ganache over side and top of torte. Store loosely covered in refrigerator.

Nutrition Info: 1 Serving: Calories 660 (Calories from Fat 370); Total Fat 41g (Saturated Fat 20g); Cholesterol 115mg; Sodium 520mg; Total Carbohydrate 64g (Dietary Fiber 2g); Protein 7g.

Betty's Kitchen Tip

• Garnish cake by piping on sweetened whipped cream and adding chocolate-covered coffee beans.

no-cholesterol carrot cake

Prep Time: 30 Minutes
Start to Finish: 2 Hours 40 Minutes
Servings: 16

- 1 box Betty Crocker® SuperMoist® yellow cake mix
- 2 teaspoons ground cinnamon
- 1 cup fat-free egg product
- 2/3 cup applesauce
- 1/3 cup vegetable oil
- 3 cups freshly shredded carrots (4 to 5 large)
- 1/2 cup raisins
- 1 container (12 oz) Betty Crocker® Whipped cream cheese frosting (no cholesterol)
- 2 drops red food color
- 1 drop yellow food color
- 2 drops green food color

1 Heat oven to 350°F for shiny metal or glass pan (or 325°F for dark or nonstick pan). Spray bottom only of 13x9-inch pan with baking spray with flour.

2 In medium bowl, beat cake mix, cinnamon, egg product, applesauce and oil with electric mixer on low speed 30 seconds, scraping bowl frequently. Beat on medium speed 2 minutes, scraping bowl occasionally. Add carrots; beat about 1 minute or until well blended. Stir in raisins. Pour batter into pan; spread evenly.

3 Bake 33 to 38 minutes or until center of cake feels firm or toothpick inserted in center comes out clean. Cool cake in pan on cooling rack at least 1 hour.

4 Reserve 1/2 cup of the frosting. Spread remaining frosting over top of cake. Spoon 1/4 cup of the reserved frosting into small resealable freezer plastic bag; spoon remaining frosting into second bag. Add red and yellow food colors to one bag; add green food color to other bag. Seal bags; squeeze bags to tint frosting evenly.

5 Pull tip of knife through frosting on top of the cake to score 16 serving pieces (4 rows by

4 rows). Cut 1/8-inch tip off 1 bottom corner of bag with orange frosting. Diagonally on each scored cake piece, pipe a carrot by squeezing frosting in a thick line, letting up on pressure at end to draw to a point. Cut off tiny corner of bag with green frosting. At top of each carrot, pipe loops of green frosting for carrot tops. Refrigerate until frosting is firm before serving, about 30 minutes. Store loosely covered in refrigerator.

High Altitude (3500-6500 ft): No change.

Nutritional Info: 1 Serving: Calories 300 (Calories from Fat 110); Total Fat 12g (Saturated Fat 3g, Trans Fat 2g); Cholesterol 0mg; Sodium 290mg; Total Carbohydrate 47g (Dietary Fiber 1g, Sugars 31g); Protein 3g. % Daily Value: Cholesterol 0%; Vitamin A 70%; Vitamin C 0%; Calcium 6%; Iron 6%. Exchanges: 1 Starch, 2 Other Carbohydrate, 2-1/2 Fat. Carbohydrate Choices: 3.

Betty's Kitchen Tip

• This version is healthier for you than traditional ones. There's no cholesterol in the cake or frosting — really!

banana turtle torte

Prep Time: 30 Minutes
Start to Finish: 5 Hours 15 Minutes
Servings: 16

- 1 box Betty Crocker® SuperMoist® German chocolate cake mix

Water, vegetable oil and eggs called for on cake mix box

- 1-1/2 cups whipping cream
- 3 bananas
- 1 cup butterscotch caramel topping
- 6 tablespoons chopped pecans, toasted

1 Heat oven to 350°F (325°F for dark or nonstick pans). Grease bottoms only of 2 (9-inch) round cake pans with shortening or cooking spray. Make cake mix as directed on box, using water, oil and eggs. Pour into pans.

2 Bake as directed on box for 9-inch pans or until toothpick inserted in center comes out clean. Cool 10 minutes. Run knife around sides of pans to loosen cakes. Place cooling rack upside down over each pan; turn rack and pan over. Remove pans. Cool completely, about 1 hour. If desired, freeze cakes uncovered about 1 hour for easier cutting and frosting.

3 In chilled medium bowl, beat whipping cream with electric mixer on high speed until stiff peaks form.

4 Split each cake horizontally into 2 layers. On serving plate, place top layer of first cake, cut side up. Spread 2/3 cup whipped cream over layer to within 1/4 inch of edge. Slice 1 banana; arrange on whipped cream, overlapping slices if necessary. Drizzle 1/4 cup butterscotch caramel topping over banana, spreading to coat slices. Sprinkle with 2 tablespoons pecans. Top with bottom layer of first cake, cut side down.

5 Top first cake with 2/3 cup whipped cream, 1 sliced banana, 1/4 cup butterscotch caramel topping and 2 tablespoons pecans. Top with bottom layer of second cake, cut

side up. Repeat filling. Top with top layer of second cake, cut side down.

6 Frost top of torte with remaining whipped cream. Spoon remaining butterscotch caramel topping over whipped cream. Swirl caramel into whipped cream with tip of knife.

7 Cover torte; refrigerate about 2 hours or until ready to serve. For best results, serve torte the same day. Store covered in refrigerator.

High Altitude (3500-6500 ft): No change.

Nutritional Info: 1 Serving: Calories 370 (Calories from Fat 170); Total Fat 19g (Saturated Fat 7g, Trans Fat 0.5g); Cholesterol 65mg; Sodium 340mg; Total Carbohydrate 46g (Dietary Fiber 2g, Sugars 30g); Protein 4g. % Daily Value: Vitamin A 6%; Vitamin C 0%; Calcium 6%; Iron 4%. Exchanges: 1 Starch, 2 Other Carbohydrate, 3-1/2 Fat. Carbohydrate Choices: 3.

Betty's Kitchen Tips

Special Touch: For a jazzy presentation, drizzle caramel topping on each plate. Center a slice of torte on the plate, then place a dollop of whipped cream topped with a pecan half next to it.

How-To: To toast pecans, heat oven to 350°F. Spread pecans in ungreased shallow pan. Bake uncovered 6 to 10 minutes, stirring occasionally, until light brown.

key lime pie poke cake

Prep Time: 20 Minutes
Start to Finish: 1 Hour 55 Minutes
Servings: 15

Cake

- 1 box Betty Crocker® SuperMoist® white cake mix
- 1-1/4 cups water
- 1 tablespoon vegetable oil
- 4 eggs

Key Lime Filling

- 1 can (14 oz) sweetened condensed milk (not evaporated)
- 3/4 cup whipping cream

- 1/2 cup Key lime juice or regular lime juice
- 1 teaspoon grated lime peel
- 4 drops yellow food color
- 1 drop green food color

Frosting

- 1 container (12 oz) Betty Crocker® Whipped vanilla frosting
- 2 teaspoons grated lime peel

Garnishes, if desired

Fresh strawberries, Key lime slices and lemon leaves

1 Heat oven to 350°F for shiny metal or glass pan (or 325°F for dark or nonstick pan). Spray bottom only of 13x9-inch pan with baking spray with flour.

2 In large bowl, beat cake ingredients with electric mixer on low speed 30 seconds. Beat on medium speed 2 minutes, scraping bowl occasionally. Pour into pan.

3 Bake 26 to 30 minutes or until toothpick inserted in center comes out clean. Cool 5 minutes. With handle of wooden spoon (1/4 to 1/2 inch in diameter), poke holes almost to bottom of cake every 1/2 inch, wiping spoon handle occasionally to reduce sticking.

4 In medium bowl, stir together filling ingredients (mixture will thicken). Pour over cake; spread evenly over surface, working back and forth to fill holes. (Some filling should remain on top of cake.) Refrigerate 1 hour.

5 Spread frosting over cake; sprinkle with lime peel. Garnish with strawberries, lime slices and lemon leaves. Store loosely covered in refrigerator.

High Altitude (3500-6500 ft): No change.

Nutritional Info: 1 Serving: Calories 390 (Calories from Fat 150); Total Fat 16g (Saturated Fat 7g, Trans Fat 2.5g); Cholesterol 80mg; Sodium 310mg; Total Carbohydrate 56g (Dietary Fiber 0g, Sugars 41g); Protein 6g. % Daily Value: Cholesterol 26%; Vitamin A 6%; Vitamin C 2%; Calcium 10%; Iron 4%. Exchanges: 1/2 Starch, 3 Other Carbohydrate, 1/2 High-Fat Meat, 2-1/2 Fat. Carbohydrate Choices: 4.

Betty's Kitchen Tip

- If Key limes aren't available in your grocery store, look for bottled Key lime juice near the other bottled lime juices.

lemon-ginger bundt cake

Prep Time: 25 Minutes
Start to Finish: 2 Hours 20 Minutes
Servings: 16

Cake

1	box Betty Crocker® SuperMoist® lemon cake mix
3/4	cup water
1/2	cup vegetable oil
1/2	cup sour cream
1	teaspoon ground ginger
3	eggs
1/2	cup finely chopped crystallized ginger (about 2-1/2 oz)

Frosting

1	cup powdered sugar
1/2	teaspoon grated fresh lemon peel
4	teaspoons fresh lemon juice

1 Heat oven to 350°F for shiny metal pan (or 325°F for dark or nonstick pan). Generously spray 12-cup fluted tube cake pan with baking spray with flour.

2 In medium bowl, beat cake mix, water, oil, sour cream, ground ginger and eggs with electric mixer on low speed 30 seconds. Beat on medium speed 2 minutes, scraping bowl occasionally. Stir in crystallized ginger. Pour batter into pan.

3 Bake 40 to 45 minutes or until toothpick inserted in center comes out clean. Cool 10 minutes. Place cooling rack or heatproof serving plate upside down on pan; turn rack and pan over. Remove pan. Cool completely, about 1 hour.

4 In small bowl, stir frosting ingredients until well blended. Spoon over cake. Store loosely covered at room temperature.

High Altitude (3500-6500 ft): Increase water to 1 cup; decrease oil to 1/3 cup.

Nutritional Info: 1 Serving: Calories 270 (Calories from Fat 110); Total Fat 12g (Saturated Fat 3g, Trans Fat 1g); Cholesterol 45mg; Sodium 230mg; Total Carbohydrate 38g (Dietary Fiber 0g, Sugars 23g); Protein 2g. % Daily Value: Cholesterol 15%; Vitamin A 2%; Vitamin C 0%; Calcium 6%; Iron 4%. Exchanges: 1/2 Starch, 2 Other Carbohydrate, 2-1/2 Fat. Carbohydrate Choices: 2-1/2.

Betty's Kitchen Tips

Purchasing: Check your produce department for clear plastic bags of crystallized ginger. Buying ginger this way costs much less than buying it in a jar from the spice section.

Special Touch: Garnish with additional crystallized ginger. (If you purchase a 3-oz package, there will be 2 tablespoons left over for this.)

yule log

Prep Time: 35 Minutes
Start to Finish: 2 Hours 5 Minutes
Servings: 12

Cake

3	eggs
1-3/4	cups Betty Crocker® SuperMoist® devil's food cake mix (from 18.25-oz box)
1/3	cup water
2	tablespoons vegetable oil
1	tablespoon powdered sugar

Rich Chocolate Frosting

1/2	cup whipping cream
1	cup semisweet chocolate chips (6 oz)
1	tablespoon corn syrup
1/4	teaspoon vanilla

Filling

1	container (12 oz) Betty Crocker® Whipped vanilla frosting

1 Heat oven to 375°F for shiny metal pan (or 350°F for dark or nonstick pan). Line bottom only of 15x10x1-inch pan with foil or waxed paper; spray with baking spray with flour.

2 In large bowl, beat eggs with electric mixer on high speed about 5 minutes or until thick and lemon colored. Add cake mix, water and oil; beat on low speed 30 seconds, then on medium speed 1 minute, scraping bowl occasionally. Pour into pan.

3 Bake 11 to 14 minutes or until cake springs back when lightly touched in center. If necessary, run knife around edges of pan to loosen cake. Turn cake upside down onto clean kitchen towel sprinkled generously with powdered sugar; carefully remove foil. While hot, carefully roll up cake and towel from narrow end. Cool completely on cooling rack, about 1 hour.

4 Meanwhile, in medium microwavable bowl, microwave whipping cream uncovered on High 1 minute to 1 minute 30 seconds or until it just starts to boil. Stir in chocolate chips and corn syrup; let stand 3 minutes. Beat gently with wire whisk until smooth. Beat in vanilla. Refrigerate about 1 hour, stirring every 15 minutes, until spreading consistency.

5 Unroll cake carefully and remove towel. Spread filling evenly over cake; roll up cake. Place cooling rack on sheet of waxed paper. Place cake roll on cooling rack; frost cake. Using fork, drag tines through frosting to resemble log. Let stand 15 minutes. Transfer cake to serving platter. Store loosely covered in refrigerator. Let stand at room temperature 30 minutes before serving.

High Altitude (3500-6500 ft): No change.

Nutritional Info: 1 Serving: Calories 360 (Calories from Fat 160); Total Fat 18g (Saturated Fat 8g, Trans Fat 2g); Cholesterol 65mg; Sodium 220mg; Total Carbohydrate 46g (Dietary Fiber 1g, Sugars 35g); Protein 3g. % Daily Value: Cholesterol 21%; Vitamin A 4%; Vitamin C 0%; Calcium 4%; Iron 8%. Exchanges: 1 Starch, 2 Other Carbohydrate, 3-1/2 Fat. Carbohydrate Choices: 3.

Betty's Kitchen Tips

Special Touch: For a garnish, brush cranberries with water and roll in coarse white or gold sugar. Add fresh mint leaves.

Leftover Cake Mix: See page 256 for another recipe that uses half a box of devil's food cake mix.

lemon pound cake

Prep Time: 15 Minutes
Start to Finish: 2 Hours 25 Minutes
Servings: 1 loaf cake (12 slices)

EASY

1 box Betty Crocker® SuperMoist® yellow cake mix	1 tablespoon grated lemon peel
1 package (3 oz) cream cheese, softened	3 eggs
3/4 cup water	1/4 cup Betty Crocker® Rich & Creamy lemon frosting (from 1-lb container)

1 Heat oven to 325°F for shiny metal or glass pan (or 300°F for dark or nonstick pan). Generously spray bottom only of 9x5-inch loaf pan with baking spray with flour.

2 In medium bowl, beat cake mix, cream cheese, water, grated lemon peel and eggs with electric mixer on low speed 1 minute, scraping bowl frequently. Beat on medium speed 2 minutes, scraping bowl occasionally. Pour into pan.

3 Bake 55 to 60 minutes or until toothpick inserted in center comes out clean. Cool in pan 10 minutes. Remove from pan to cooling rack or heatproof serving plate. Cool completely, about 1 hour.

4 In small microwavable bowl, microwave frosting uncovered on High 10 to 15 seconds or until frosting is thin enough to drizzle; stir. Spoon the frosting evenly over cake, allowing frosting to drip down sides.

High Altitude (3500-6500 ft): Heat oven to 350°F. Increase water to 1 cup.

Nutritional Info: 1 Slice: Calories 240 (Calories from Fat 70); Total Fat 8g (Saturated Fat 3g, Trans Fat 1.5g); Cholesterol 60mg; Sodium 330mg; Total Carbohydrate 38g (Dietary Fiber 0g, Sugars 22g); Protein 4g. % Daily Value: Cholesterol 20%; Vitamin A 4%; Vitamin C 0%; Calcium 8%; Iron 6%. Exchanges: 1 Starch, 1-1/2 Other Carbohydrate, 1-1/2 Fat. Carbohydrate Choices: 2-1/2.

Betty's Kitchen Tip

• If you have leftover cake, cut it into slices and place individually in sandwich-size food-storage plastic bags. Seal bags and freeze. You'll have a quick treat when you need it!

spice cake with raspberry filling and cream cheese frosting

Prep Time: 35 Minutes
Start to Finish: 2 Hours 20 Minutes
Servings: 16

- -

1	box Betty Crocker® SuperMoist® spice cake mix

Water, vegetable oil and eggs called for on cake mix box

1	package (8 oz) cream cheese, softened
1/2	cup butter or margarine, softened
3-1/2	cups powdered sugar
1	teaspoon vanilla
2	cups fresh raspberries
1/4	cup red currant jelly, if desired

Fresh mint leaves, if desired

- -

1 Heat oven to 350°F for shiny metal pans (or 325°F for dark or nonstick pans). Spray bottoms and sides of 2 (8- or 9-inch) round cake pans with baking spray with flour.

2 Make and bake cake mix as directed on box for 8- or 9-inch rounds, using water, oil and eggs. Cool 10 minutes. Run knife around side of pans to loosen cakes; remove from pans to cooling rack. Cool completely, about 1 hour.

3 In medium bowl, beat cream cheese and butter with electric mixer on medium speed until fluffy. Beat in powdered sugar and vanilla.

4 On serving plate, place 1 cake, rounded side down. Spread with 1 cup frosting. Sprinkle 1 cup of the raspberries over frosting. Top with second cake, rounded side up.

5 Frost side and top of cake with remaining frosting. Arrange remaining 1 cup raspberries on top of cake along edge.

6 In 1-quart saucepan, heat jelly over medium heat, stirring constantly, until melted. Brush melted jelly over berries. Garnish with mint leaves. Store covered in refrigerator.

High Altitude (3500-6500 ft): No change.

Nutritional Info: 1 Serving: Calories 410 (Calories from Fat 170); Total Fat 19g (Saturated Fat 8g, Trans Fat 1g); Cholesterol 70mg; Sodium 310mg; Total Carbohydrate 57g (Dietary Fiber 1g, Sugars 44g); Protein 3g. % Daily Value: Cholesterol 24%; Vitamin A 8%; Vitamin C 4%; Calcium 8%; Iron 6%. Exchanges: 1 Starch, 3 Other Carbohydrate, 3-1/2 Fat. Carbohydrate Choices: 4.

Betty's Kitchen Tip

• You can save time by using Betty Crocker® Rich & Creamy cream cheese frosting instead of making the frosting from scratch.

mojito cake

Prep Time: 30 Minutes
Start to Finish: 2 Hours 20 Minutes
Servings: 15

Cake

1	box Betty Crocker® SuperMoist® white cake mix
1	cup unflavored carbonated water
1/3	cup vegetable oil
1/4	cup rum or 1 teaspoon rum extract plus 1/4 cup water
3	tablespoons chopped fresh mint leaves
2	teaspoons grated lime peel
3	egg whites

Glaze

1/2	cup butter or margarine
1/4	cup water
1	cup granulated sugar
1/2	cup rum or 2 teaspoons rum extract plus 1/2 cup water

Garnish

1	cup whipping cream
2	tablespoons powdered sugar

Mint leaves and shredded lime peel, if desired

1 Heat oven to 350°F for shiny metal or glass pan (or 325°F for dark or nonstick pan). Spray bottom only of 13x9-inch pan with baking spray with flour.

2 In large bowl, beat cake ingredients with electric mixer on low speed 30 seconds. Beat on medium speed 2 minutes, scraping bowl occasionally. Pour batter into pan.

3 Bake 28 to 33 minutes or until toothpick inserted in center comes out clean. Cool 15 minutes.

4 Meanwhile, in 2-quart saucepan, mix glaze ingredients. Heat to boiling over high heat, stirring frequently. Reduce heat to medium; continue to boil 3 minutes, stirring frequently, until glaze has thickened slightly.

5 Poke warm cake every inch with fork tines. Pour glaze slowly over cake. Cool completely, about 1 hour.

6 In small bowl, beat whipping cream and powdered sugar on high speed until soft peaks form. Garnish each serving with whipped cream, mint leaf and shredded lime peel. Store loosely covered at room temperature.

High Altitude (3500-6500 ft): Follow High Altitude cake mix directions for 13x9-inch pan.

Nutritional Info: 1 Serving: Calories 350 (Calories from Fat 170); Total Fat 19g (Saturated Fat 8g, Trans Fat 1g); Cholesterol 35mg; Sodium 290mg; Total Carbohydrate 41g (Dietary Fiber 0g, Sugars 29g); Protein 3g. % Daily Value: Cholesterol 11%; Vitamin A 8%; Vitamin C 0%; Calcium 4%; Iron 4%. Exchanges: 1 Starch, 1-1/2 Other Carbohydrate, 4 Fat. Carbohydrate Choices: 3.

Betty's Kitchen Tip

• In a pinch, use purchased frozen whipped topping, thawed, instead of making your own whipped cream.

cream cheese pound cake

Prep Time: 15 Minutes
Start to Finish: 2 Hours 20 Minutes
Servings: 10

EASY

3	cups Original Bisquick® mix
1-1/2	cups granulated sugar
3/4	cup butter or margarine, softened
1/2	cup Gold Medal® all-purpose flour
1	teaspoon vanilla
1/8	teaspoon salt
6	eggs
1	package (8 oz) cream cheese, softened

Powdered sugar, if desired

1 Heat oven to 350°F. Grease and flour 12-cup fluted tube cake pan or 2 (9x5-inch) loaf pans.

2 In large bowl, beat all ingredients except powdered sugar with electric mixer on low speed 30 seconds, scraping bowl frequently. Beat on medium speed 4 minutes, scraping bowl occasionally. Pour into pan.

3 Bake 55 to 60 minutes or until toothpick inserted near center comes out clean. Cool 5 minutes. Turn pan upside down onto cooling rack or heatproof serving plate; remove pan. Cool cake completely, about 1 hour. Sprinkle with powdered sugar.

High Altitude (3500-6500 ft): Heat oven to 375°F. Do not use loaf pans. Use 2-1/2 cups Bisquick mix, 1-1/4 cups granulated sugar and 1 cup Gold Medal flour. Bake 45 to 50 minutes.

Nutritional Info: 1 Serving: Calories 540 (Calories from Fat 270); Total Fat 29g (Saturated Fat 16g, Trans Fat 2g); Cholesterol 190mg; Sodium 670mg; Total Carbohydrate 59g (Dietary Fiber 1g, Sugars 32g); Protein 9g. % Daily Value: Vitamin A 20%; Vitamin C 0%; Calcium 8%; Iron 10%. Exchanges: 2 Starch, 2 Other Carbohydrate, 1/2 Medium-Fat Meat, 5 Fat. Carbohydrate Choices: 4.

Betty's Kitchen Tip

• This cake makes a fabulous base for strawberry shortcake. Drizzle crushed sweetened berries over individual slices and top with whipped cream.

peanut butter tandy cake

Prep Time: 20 Minutes
Start to Finish: 1 Hour 25 Minutes
Servings: 24

1	box Betty Crocker® SuperMoist® yellow cake mix
1-1/4	cups water
1/3	cup vegetable oil
3	eggs

1-1/2	cups creamy peanut butter
1/2	cup semisweet chocolate chips
2	tablespoons butter or margarine
1	container (1 lb) Betty Crocker® Rich & Creamy chocolate frosting

1 Heat oven to 350°F for shiny metal pan (or 325°F for dark or nonstick pan). Spray bottom and sides of 15x10x1-inch pan with baking spray with flour.

2 In large bowl, beat cake mix, water, oil and eggs with electric mixer on low speed 30 seconds. Beat on medium speed 2 minutes, scraping bowl occasionally. Pour batter into pan.

3 Bake 22 to 28 minutes or until toothpick inserted in center comes out clean. Cool in pan on cooling rack 30 minutes.

4 In small microwavable bowl, microwave peanut butter uncovered on High 20 seconds or until softened and spreadable. Drop by

teaspoonfuls onto surface of warm cake; spread carefully to cover top. Refrigerate cake to harden the peanut butter, about 15 minutes.

5 Meanwhile, in medium microwavable bowl, microwave chocolate chips and butter uncovered on High 30 seconds. Stir; continue to microwave on High 10 to 20 seconds longer, stirring after 10 seconds until chips are melted. Stir in frosting.

6 Spread frosting over peanut butter layer on cake.

High Altitude (3500-6500 ft): No change.

Nutritional Info: 1 Serving: Calories 330 (Calories from Fat 170); Total Fat 18g (Saturated Fat 5g, Trans Fat 1.5g); Cholesterol 30mg; Sodium 280mg; Total Carbohydrate 35g (Dietary Fiber 1g, Sugars 23g); Protein 5g. % Daily Value: Cholesterol 10%; Vitamin A 0%; Vitamin C 0%; Calcium 4%; Iron 6%. Exchanges: 1/2 Starch, 2 Other Carbohydrate, 1/2 High-Fat Meat, 2-1/2 Fat. Carbohydrate Choices: 2.

Betty's Kitchen Tips

Did You Know? This is our version of a "Tandy Kake," a white cake made with peanut butter and chocolate that was popular in the 1930s.

Substitution: For a flavor reminiscent of a popular candy bar, use milk chocolate chips for the semisweet.

FUN CAKES & CUPCAKES

p. 245

244

248

242

lemon-blueberry cupcakes

Prep Time: 25 Minutes
Start to Finish: 1 Hour 55 Minutes
Servings: 24 cupcakes

Cupcakes

1	box Betty Crocker® SuperMoist® lemon cake mix
3/4	cup water
1/3	cup vegetable oil
1	tablespoon grated lemon peel
2	eggs
1	package (3 oz) cream cheese, softened
1-1/2	cups fresh blueberries

Frosting and Garnish

2-1/2	cups powdered sugar
3/4	cup unsalted butter, softened
1	teaspoon grated lemon peel
1/2	teaspoon kosher (coarse) salt
1-1/4	teaspoons vanilla
1	tablespoon milk
1	cup fresh blueberries

Lemon peel, if desired

Fresh mint leaves, if desired

1 Heat oven to 375°F for shiny metal pans (or 350°F for dark or nonstick pans). Place paper baking cup in each of 24 regular-size muffin cups.

2 In large bowl, beat all cupcake ingredients except blueberries with electric mixer on low speed 30 seconds. Beat on medium speed 2 minutes, scraping bowl occasionally. Fold 1-1/2 cups blueberries into batter. Divide batter evenly among muffin cups.

3 Bake 18 to 22 minutes or until tops are light golden brown. Cool 5 minutes; remove from pan to cooling rack. Cool completely, about 1 hour.

4 In medium bowl, beat powdered sugar, butter, 1 teaspoon lemon peel, the salt, vanilla and 1 tablespoon milk on high speed about 4 minutes or until smooth and well blended, adding more milk by teaspoonfuls if needed. Frost cupcakes with frosting. Garnish with 1 cup blueberries, the lemon peel and mint leaves, if desired. Store in an airtight container at room temperature.

High Altitude (3500-6500 ft): No change.

Nutritional Info: 1 Cupcake: Calories 250 (Calories from Fat 110); Total Fat 12g (Saturated Fat 6g, Trans Fat 1g); Cholesterol 35mg; Sodium 210mg; Total Carbohydrate 32g (Dietary Fiber 0g, Sugars 23g); Protein 2g. % Daily Value: Cholesterol 12%; Vitamin A 6%; Vitamin C 0%; Calcium 4%; Iron 2%. Exchanges: 1/2 Starch, 1-1/2 Other Carbohydrate, 2-1/2 Fat. Carbohydrate Choices: 2.

Betty's Kitchen Tip

• Unsalted butter tastes a little sweeter than the more common salted butter. We added the coarse salt for small bursts of saltiness to complement the sweetness of the other ingredients and to bring out the lemon flavor. If you don't have unsalted butter, salted butter can be used and omit the kosher salt.

adorable applesauce cupcakes

Prep Time: 30 Minutes
Start to Finish: 1 Hour 25 Minutes
Servings: 24 cupcakes

. . . .

Cupcakes

1	box Betty Crocker® SuperMoist® yellow cake mix
1/2	teaspoon ground cinnamon
1	cup apple juice
1/3	cup unsweetened applesauce
3	eggs

Frosting

1/2	teaspoon red paste food color
1	container (1 lb) Betty Crocker® Rich & Creamy vanilla frosting

Decorations

12	thin pretzel sticks, broken into pieces
16	spearmint leaf gumdrops
12	gummy worm candies, cut in half, if desired

. . . .

1 Heat oven to 350°F for shiny metal pans (or 325°F for dark or nonstick pans). Place paper baking cup in each of 24 regular-size muffin cups.

2 In large bowl, beat cupcake ingredients with electric mixer on low speed 30 seconds. Beat on medium speed 2 minutes, scraping bowl occasionally. Divide batter evenly among muffin cups.

3 Bake 18 to 22 minutes or until tops spring back when lightly touched. Cool 10 minutes; carefully remove from pan to cooling rack. Cool completely, about 30 minutes.

4 Stir paste food color into frosting in container. Spread frosting over cupcakes.

5 To decorate cupcakes, poke 1 pretzel piece into each cupcake for stem. Cut each gumdrop leaf into 3 slices. Poke 2 gumdrop leaves into top of each cupcake on either side of pretzel stem. Poke half of gummy worm into each cupcake.

High Altitude (3500-6500 ft): No change.

Nutritional Info: 1 Cupcake: Calories 200 (Calories from Fat 60); Total Fat 6g (Saturated Fat 2g, Trans Fat 2g); Cholesterol 25mg; Sodium 200mg; Total Carbohydrate 34g (Dietary Fiber 0g, Sugars 24g); Protein 1g. % Daily Value: Cholesterol 9%; Vitamin A 0%; Vitamin C 0%; Calcium 4%; Iron 2%. Exchanges: 1/2 Starch, 2 Other Carbohydrate, 1 Fat. Carbohydrate Choices: 2.

Betty's Kitchen Tip

• If you don't have unsweetened applesauce on hand, the regular kind will taste great in these cupcakes, too.

chocolate cupcakes with penuche filling

Prep Time: 40 Minutes
Start to Finish: 2 Hours 10 Minutes
Servings: 24 cupcakes

Cupcakes

1	box Betty Crocker® SuperMoist® chocolate fudge cake mix
1-1/3	cups water
1/2	cup vegetable oil
3	eggs
1	teaspoon vanilla

Filling and Garnish

1	cup butter or margarine
2	cups packed brown sugar
1/2	cup milk
4	cups powdered sugar
1	oz grated semisweet baking chocolate, if desired

1 Heat oven to 350°F for shiny metal pans (or 325°F for dark or nonstick pans). Spray bottoms only of 24 regular-size muffin cups with baking spray with flour.

2 In large bowl, beat cake mix, water, oil, eggs and vanilla with electric mixer on low speed 30 seconds. Beat on medium speed 2 minutes, scraping bowl occasionally. Divide batter evenly among muffin cups.

3 Bake 18 to 24 minutes or until toothpick inserted in center comes out clean. Cool 15 minutes; remove from pan to cooling rack. Cool completely, about 30 minutes.

4 Meanwhile, in 2-quart saucepan, melt butter over medium heat. Stir in brown sugar. Heat to boiling, stirring constantly; reduce heat to low. Boil and stir 2 minutes. Stir in milk. Heat to boiling; remove from heat. Pour mixture into medium bowl; refrigerate about 30 minutes or until lukewarm.

5 Beat powdered sugar into cooled brown sugar mixture on low speed until smooth. If frosting becomes too stiff, stir in additional milk, 1 teaspoon at a time.

6 Using serrated knife, cut each cupcake in half horizontally, being careful not to break either half. Place 1 heaping tablespoon filling on each cupcake base. Replace rounded cupcake tops. Pipe or spoon rounded 1 tablespoon frosting onto cupcake tops. Garnish with grated chocolate. Store in airtight container at room temperature.

High Altitude (3500-6500 ft): Follow High Altitude directions on cake mix box for cupcakes, adding vanilla to batter.

Nutritional Info: 1 Cupcake: Calories 360 (Calories from Fat 130); Total Fat 15g (Saturated Fat 6g, Trans Fat 0.5g); Cholesterol 45mg; Sodium 240mg; Total Carbohydrate 56g (Dietary Fiber 0g, Sugars 48g); Protein 2g. % Daily Value: Cholesterol 16%; Vitamin A 6%; Vitamin C 0%; Calcium 4%; Iron 6%. Exchanges: 1/2 Starch, 3 Other Carbohydrate, 3 Fat. Carbohydrate Choices: 4.

Betty's Kitchen Tip

• The word penuche comes from a Mexican word meaning "raw sugar" or "brown sugar." It is used to describe a fudgelike candy made from brown sugar, butter, milk or cream and vanilla.

lemon burst cupcakes

Prep Time: 30 Minutes
Start to Finish: 1 Hour 15 Minutes
Servings: 24 cupcakes

. . . .

1   box Betty Crocker SuperMoist®
    white cake mix

Water, vegetable oil and egg whites called for on cake
mix box

1   jar (10 to 12 oz) lemon curd
1   container (12 oz) Betty Crocker® Whipped
    fluffy white frosting
1/4 cup Betty Crocker® yellow candy sprinkles
1/4 cup Betty Crocker® white candy sprinkles

. . . .

1 Heat oven to 350°F for shiny metal pans
  (or 325°F for dark or nonstick pans). Place
  paper baking cup in each of 24 regular-size
  muffin cups.

2 In large bowl, make cake mix as directed on
  box, using water, oil and egg whites. Divide
  batter evenly among muffin cups.

3 Bake as directed on box or until toothpick
  inserted in center comes out clean. Cool 10
  minutes; remove from pan to cooling rack.
  Cool completely, about 30 minutes.

4 Spoon lemon curd into corner of resealable
  heavy-duty food-storage plastic bag. Cut
  about 1/4 inch off corner of bag. Gently push
  cut corner of bag into center of cupcake.
  Squeeze about 2 teaspoons lemon curd into
  center of each cupcake for filling, being
  careful not to split cupcake.

5 Frost cupcakes with frosting. To decorate,
  roll edge of each cupcake in candy sprinkles.
  Store loosely covered at room temperature.

High Altitude (3500-6500 ft): No change.

Nutritional Info: 1 Cupcake: Calories 240 (Calories from Fat 90);
Total Fat 10g (Saturated Fat 3g, Trans Fat 1.5g); Cholesterol
10mg; Sodium 180mg; Total Carbohydrate 36g (Dietary Fiber 0g,
Sugars 26g); Protein 1g. % Daily Value: Cholesterol 3%; Vitamin A
0%; Vitamin C 0%; Calcium 2%; Iron 2%. Exchanges: 1/2 Fruit,
2 Other Carbohydrate, 2 Fat. Carbohydrate Choices: 2-1/2.

Betty's Kitchen Tips

Purchasing: Look for lemon curd near the jams
and preserves or by canned pie filling.

Substitution: Canned lemon filling can be
substituted for the lemon curd.

roller coaster cake

Prep Time: 40 Minutes
Start to Finish: 2 Hours 10 Minutes
Servings: 24

Cake

1	box Betty Crocker® SuperMoist® butter recipe yellow cake mix
1-1/4	cups water
1/2	cup butter, softened
3	eggs

Frosting and Decorations

1	container (12 oz) Betty Crocker® Whipped vanilla frosting

Blue food color

1	roll Betty Crocker® Fruit by the Foot® chewy fruit snack (from 4.5-oz box)

21	thin pretzel sticks
3	fruit slice candies (flat)
6	miniature brown candy-coated semisweet chocolate baking bits
1	tablespoon Betty Crocker® Rich & Creamy chocolate frosting (from 1-lb container)
3	thin candy wafers (1 inch diameter)
1/2	teaspoon Betty Crocker® candy sprinkles
3	miniature red candy-coated semisweet chocolate baking bits
6	oblong (1 inch) candy-coated licorice pieces

1 Heat oven to 350°F for shiny metal pan (or 325°F for dark or nonstick pan). Spray bottom only of 15x10x1-inch pan with baking spray with flour.

2 In large bowl, make cake mix as directed on box, using water, butter and eggs. Pour into pan. Bake 23 to 28 minutes or until toothpick inserted in center comes out clean. Cool completely, about 1 hour.

3 Frost cake with vanilla frosting. With toothpick, lightly draw shape of roller coaster on cake (see photo). Squeeze drops of food color in several places on frosting above roller coaster outline; use knife to swirl into frosting for sky.

4 Tear or cut fruit snack in half lengthwise; place strips on cake to make track of roller coaster. Add pretzels for supports. Add fruit slice candies just above track for cars; place 2 brown baking bits under each car for wheels.

5 In small microwavable bowl, microwave chocolate frosting uncovered on Medium (50%) 15 seconds; stir. Dip top third of each candy wafer into melted frosting; top with sprinkles for hair. Place 1 wafer "face" on top of each car.

6 Place remaining melted frosting in small resealable food-storage plastic bag; seal bag. Cut small hole in bottom corner of bag. Add dot of frosting to each red baking bit; add to wafers for mouths. Add licorice candies on both sides of each wafer candy for arms.

High Altitude (3500-6500 ft): No change.

Nutritional Info: 1 Serving (Cake and Frosting): Calories 190 (Calories from Fat 80); Total Fat 9g (Saturated Fat 4g, Trans Fat 1.5g); Cholesterol 35mg; Sodium 190mg; Total Carbohydrate 26g (Dietary Fiber 0g, Sugars 18g); Protein 1g. % Daily Value: Cholesterol 12%; Vitamin A 4%; Vitamin C 0%; Calcium 4%; Iron 2%. Exchanges: 1-1/2 Other Carbohydrate, 2 Fat. Carbohydrate Choices: 2.

Betty's Kitchen Tip

• To add eyes to the people, use blue or green balls from a bottle of multi-colored, ball-shaped sprinkles (non-pareils).

pirate's hidden treasure cupcakes

Prep Time: 50 Minutes
Start to Finish: 1 Hour 55 Minutes
Servings: 24 cupcakes

1 box Betty Crocker® SuperMoist® chocolate fudge cake mix	2 rolls (from 4.5-oz box) Betty Crocker® Fruit by the Foot® chewy fruit snack (any red color)
1 cup water	24 pieces Cheerios® cereal or small ring-shaped candies (about 4 teaspoons)
1/2 cup vegetable oil	
3 eggs	3 tablespoons miniature candy-coated semisweet chocolate baking bits
24 miniature chocolate-covered peanut butter cup candies (from 12-oz bag), unwrapped	1 tablespoon semisweet chocolate chips
1 container (1 lb) Betty Crocker® Rich & Creamy vanilla frosting	2 pieces black string licorice (each 34 inches long)

1 Heat oven to 350°F for shiny metal pans (or 325°F for dark or nonstick pans). Place paper baking cup in each of 24 regular-size muffin cups.

2 In large bowl, make cake mix as directed on box—except use 1 cup water, the oil and eggs. Divide batter evenly among muffin cups. Place 1 candy in top of batter for each cupcake (candies will sink as cupcakes bake).

3 Bake 17 to 22 minutes or until toothpick inserted in cake comes out clean. Cool 10 minutes; remove from pan to cooling rack. Cool completely, about 30 minutes.

4 Frost cupcakes with frosting. Cut 12-inch piece from 1 fruit snack roll; set aside. From remaining fruit snack, cut 24 (2-inch)

pieces; cut crescent-shaped piece from each. Peel off paper backing; add 1 piece to each cupcake for top of kerchief.

5 Cut reserved fruit snack into 12 (1-inch) pieces; peel off paper backing. Cut each piece in half lengthwise. Twist each piece in middle; add to 1 end of crescent-shaped fruit snack on each cupcake, forming tie of kerchief. Add 1 piece of cereal under each tie for earring. Use baking bits, chocolate chips and licorice to make facial features and eye patches.

High Altitude (3500-6500 ft): Bake 19 to 22 minutes.

Nutritional Info: 1 Frosted Cupcake (Undecorated): Calories 250 (Calories from Fat 110); Total Fat 12g (Saturated Fat 3g, Trans Fat 1.5g); Cholesterol 25mg; Sodium 240mg; Total Carbohydrate 33g (Dietary Fiber 0g, Sugars 24g); Protein 2g. % Daily Value: Cholesterol 9%; Vitamin A 0%; Vitamin C 0%; Calcium 2%; Iron 4%. Exchanges: 1/2 Starch, 1-1/2 Other Carbohydrate, 2-1/2 Fat. Carbohydrate Choices: 2.

Betty's Kitchen Tip

• These cupcakes are great to serve at kids' birthday parties. Complete the theme by having eye patches and red kerchiefs available for the kids to wear.

sports party cake

Prep Time: 35 Minutes
Start to Finish: 3 Hours 25 Minutes
Servings: 15

- -

    1   box Betty Crocker® SuperMoist® cake mix
          (any flavor)
Water, vegetable oil and eggs called for on cake mix box
Tray or cardboard (15x12 inch), covered
    2   cups Betty Crocker® Whipped fluffy white
          frosting (from two 12-oz containers)
Food colors

- -

1 Heat oven to 350°F for shiny metal or glass pan (or 325°F for dark or nonstick pan). Spray bottom only of 13x9-inch pan with baking spray with flour.

2 Make and bake cake as directed on box for 13x9-inch pan, using water, oil and eggs. Cool 10 minutes; remove from pan to cooling rack. Cool completely, about 1 hour.

3 Use toothpicks to mark sections of cake to be cut (see diagram below). Cut cake into sections with serrated knife. Cut neck hole from top of cake.

4 On tray, place largest piece of cake. Using frosting attach 2 small rectangular pieces on each side of top of cake to form sleeves. Position sleeves in place. Cover; freeze cake 1 hour or until firm.

5 Tint 1-1/2 cups of the frosting with food color as desired for your favorite team's jersey color. Remove cake from freezer; frost sides and top of cake with jersey frosting. Tint remaining 1/2 cup frosting as desired; pipe onto cake to create numbers, name and trim. Store loosely covered at room temperature.

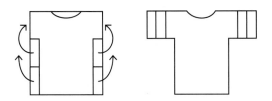

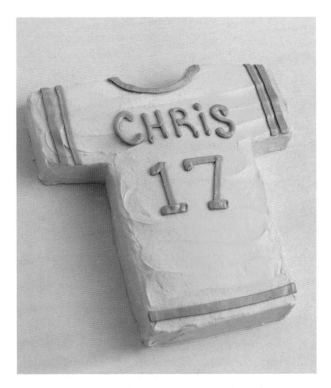

High Altitude (3500-6500 ft): Follow High Altitude cake mix directions for 13x9-inch pan.

Nutritional Info: 1 Serving: Calories 310 (Calories from Fat 130); Total Fat 14g (Saturated Fat 4g, Trans Fat 2.5g); Cholesterol 40mg; Sodium 260mg; Total Carbohydrate 44g (Dietary Fiber 0g, Sugars 30g); Protein 2g. % Daily Value: Cholesterol 14%; Vitamin A 0%; Vitamin C 0%; Calcium 6%; Iron 4%. Exchanges: 3 Other Carbohydrate, 3 Fat. Carbohydrate Choices: 3.

Betty's Kitchen Tip

- If your jersey signifies a pro team, put the team name across the chest rather than a person's name.

polka dot cake

Prep: 25 Minutes
Start to Finish: 2 Hours 5 Minutes
Servings: 12

- -

1   box Betty Crocker® SuperMoist® white cake mix

Water, vegetable oil and egg whites called for on cake mix box

1   container (12 oz) Betty Crocker® Whipped fluffy white frosting

Red food color

1/2   cup round pink and orange candy melts or coating wafers (3 oz)

- -

1 Heat oven to 350°F for shiny metal pans (or 325°F for dark or nonstick pans). Spray bottoms and sides of 2 (9- or 8-inch) round cake pans with baking spray with flour.

2 Make and bake cake mix as directed on box for 2 (9- or 8-inch) round pans, using water, oil and egg whites. Cool 10 minutes; remove from pans to cooling racks. Cool completely, about 1 hour.

3 Tint 1/3 cup of the frosting with 1 or 2 drops food color for desired shade of pink.

4 On serving plate, place 1 cake layer, rounded side down; spread pink frosting over layer almost to edge. Top with second layer, rounded side up. Frost side and top of cake with remaining frosting.

5 Insert candies into frosting on side and top of cake as desired.

High Altitude (3500-6500 ft): Follow High Altitude directions on cake mix box for 2 (9- or 8-inch) round cake pans.

Nutritional Info: 1 Serving: Calories 380 (Calories from Fat 140); Total Fat 16g (Saturated Fat 3.5g, Trans Fat 3g); Cholesterol 0mg; Sodium 330mg; Total Carbohydrate 57g (Dietary Fiber 0g, Sugars 38g); Protein 3g. % Daily Value: Vitamin A 0%; Vitamin C 0%; Calcium 4%; Iron 4%. Exchanges: 1 Starch, 3 Other Carbohydrate, 3 Fat. Carbohydrate Choices: 4

Betty's Kitchen Tip

• Look for colored candy melts in the cake-decorating section of craft stores or in the baking aisle at some supermarkets and cooking specialty stores.

turkey cupcakes

Prep Time: 30 Minutes
Start to Finish: 1 Hour 30 Minutes
Servings: 24 cupcakes

- 1 box Betty Crocker® SuperMoist® devil's food cake mix

Water, vegetable oil and eggs called for on cake mix box

- 2 containers (1 lb each) Betty Crocker® Rich & Creamy milk chocolate frosting
- 1 tube (4.25 oz) Betty Crocker® white decorating icing
- 1 bag (11 oz) candy corn (1-2/3 cups)
- 1/4 cup Betty Crocker® chocolate candy sprinkles

1 Heat oven to 350°F for shiny metal pans (or 325°F for dark or nonstick pans). Make and bake 24 cupcakes as directed on box, using water, oil and eggs. Cool in pan 10 minutes; remove from pan to cooling rack. Cool completely, about 30 minutes.

2 Frost cupcakes with frosting. Place remaining frosting in corner of resealable freezer plastic bag; seal bag. Cut small tip off 1 bottom corner of bag.

3 To decorate each cupcake, pipe 1-inch mound of frosting on 1 side of cupcake for head of turkey. Make eyes with white decorating icing. Using a toothpick add a dot of chocolate frosting to each eye. Add candy corn for beak. To make feathers, pipe frosting on opposite side from "head" to hold candy corn; place candy corn upright on frosting to look like feathers. Sprinkle chocolate candy sprinkles near head and at base of feathers. If desired, add candy corn at base of cupcake for feet. Store loosely covered at room temperature.

High Altitude (3500-6500 ft): Follow High Altitude directions on cake mix box for cupcakes.

Nutritional Info: 1 Cupcake: Calories 290 (Calories from Fat 110); Total Fat 13g (Saturated Fat 3.5g, Trans Fat 2.5g); Cholesterol 25mg; Sodium 280mg; Total Carbohydrate 42g (Dietary Fiber 0g, Sugars 32g); Protein 2g. % Daily Value: Cholesterol 9%; Vitamin A 0%; Vitamin C 0%; Calcium 0%; Iron 10%. Exchanges: 1/2 Starch, 2 Other Carbohydrate, 2-1/2 Fat. Carbohydrate Choices: 3.

Betty's Kitchen Tip

- If you don't need all 24 frosted and decorated cupcakes, freeze the remaining unfrosted ones for a later use. Tightly covered, they'll keep up to 2 months. Besides, frozen cupcakes are easier to frost!

easter bunny cake

Prep Time: 30 Minutes
Start to Finish: 2 Hours 20 Minutes
Servings: 6

- 2 cups Betty Crocker® SuperMoist® yellow cake mix (from 18.25-oz box)
- 1/2 cup water
- 3 tablespoons vegetable oil
- 1 egg

Tray or cardboard covered with foil

- 1 container (12 oz) Betty Crocker® Whipped fluffy white frosting
- 1 cup shredded coconut

Decorative paper

- 3 jelly beans or small gumdrops
- 6 chocolate candy sprinkles, if desired

1 Heat oven to 350°F for shiny metal pan (or 325°F for dark or nonstick pan). Spray bottom and side of 8- or 9-inch round cake pan with baking spray with flour.

2 Make cake mix as directed on box, using water, oil and egg. Pour into pan. Bake as directed for 8- or 9-inch rounds. Cool 10 minutes; remove from pan to cooling rack. Cool completely, about 1 hour.

3 Cut cake in half as shown in diagram. Attach halves together with some of the frosting to form body. On tray, place cake upright on cut edge.

4 Cut out a notch about 1/3 of the way up one end of body to form head (small end) as shown in diagram. Attach cutout piece with toothpicks for tail. (If desired, freeze cake 1 hour to make frosting cake easier.)

5 Frost cake with remaining frosting, rounding body on sides. Sprinkle coconut over frosting. Cut ears from paper; pleat bottoms. Press ears into top of head. Use 3 jelly beans for eyes and nose. Add candy sprinkles for eyelashes. Store loosely covered at room temperature.

High Altitude (3500-6500 ft): No change.

Nutritional Info: 1 Serving: Calories 580 (Calories from Fat 260); Total Fat 28g (Saturated Fat 11g, Trans Fat 4.5g); Cholesterol 35mg; Sodium 390mg; Total Carbohydrate 76g (Dietary Fiber 0g, Sugars 54g); Protein 3g. % Daily Value: Cholesterol 12%; Vitamin A 0%; Vitamin C 0%; Calcium 6%; Iron 6%. Exchanges: 1 Starch, 4 Other Carbohydrate, 5-1/2 Fat. Carbohydrate Choices: 5.

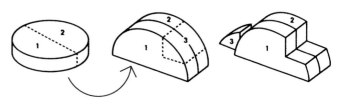

molten chocolate cupcakes

Prep Time: 30 Minutes
Start to Finish: 2 Hours 5 Minutes
Servings: 18 cupcakes

- -

1/2	cup whipping cream
1	cup semisweet chocolate chips (6 oz)
1	box Betty Crocker® SuperMoist® devil's food cake mix
1	cup water
1/3	cup vegetable oil
3	eggs
1	container (1 lb) Betty Crocker® Rich & Creamy chocolate frosting

Powdered sugar, if desired

Sliced strawberries, if desired

- -

1 In 1-quart saucepan, heat whipping cream over medium-high heat until hot but not boiling. Stir in chocolate chips until melted and mixture is smooth. Refrigerate about 1 hour, stirring occasionally, until thick.

2 Heat oven to 350°F (325°F for dark or nonstick pans). Spray 18 large muffin cups, 2-3/4x1-1/4 inches, with baking spray with flour. In large bowl, beat cake mix, water, oil and eggs with electric mixer on low speed 30 seconds; beat on medium speed 2 minutes, scraping bowl constantly. Place 1/4 cup batter in each muffin cup. Spoon 1 tablespoon cold chocolate mixture on top of batter in center of each cup.

3 Bake 18 to 22 minutes or until top springs back when lightly touched. Cool 1 minute. Carefully remove from pan; place on cooking parchment paper. Cool 10 minutes. Frost with chocolate frosting. Just before serving, dust with powdered sugar; garnish with strawberry slices. Serve warm.

High Altitude (3500-6500 ft): Heat oven to 400°F (375°F for dark or nonstick pans). Increase water to 1-1/4 cups, decrease oil to 1/4 cup and add 2 tablespoons Gold Medal® all-purpose flour to dry cake mix. Place paper baking cups in 24 large muffin cups. Bake 15 to 18 minutes.

Nutritional Info: 1 Cupcake: Calories 340 (Calories from Fat 150); Total Fat 17g (Saturated Fat 6g, Trans Fat 2.5g); Cholesterol 45mg; Sodium 320mg; Total Carbohydrate 43g (Dietary Fiber 1g, Sugars 31g); Protein 3g. % Daily Value: Vitamin A 2%; Vitamin C 0%; Calcium 4%; Iron 10%. Exchanges: 1/2 Starch, 2-1/2 Other Carbohydrate, 3-1/2 Fat. Carbohydrate Choices: 3.

Betty's Kitchen Tip

• These warm, gooey cakes are delicious served with a small scoop of vanilla ice cream.

sparkling fourth of july cake

Prep Time: 40 Minutes
Start to Finish: 2 Hours 20 Minutes
Servings: 15

- -

1	box Betty Crocker® SuperMoist® white cake mix
1-1/4	cups water
1/3	cup vegetable oil
3	egg whites
1/2	teaspoon red food color
1/2	teaspoon blue food color

1	container (12 oz) Betty Crocker® Whipped fluffy white or whipped cream frosting
1	tablespoon Betty Crocker® blue sugar
2	tablespoons Betty Crocker® red sugar

White star candies, if desired

Fourth of July candles

- -

1 Heat oven to 350°F for metal or glass pan (or 325°F for dark or nonstick pan). Spray bottom only of 13x9-inch pan with baking spray with flour. Place paper baking cup in 1 regular-size muffin cup.

2 Make cake mix as directed on box, using water, oil and egg whites. In small bowl, place 1/2 cup batter; stir in red food color. In another small bowl, place 1/2 cup batter; stir in blue food color.

3 Fill muffin cup with 1/4 cup white batter; set aside. Pour remaining white batter into 13x9-inch pan. Randomly drop generous teaspoonfuls of red and blue batters over white batter in pan. For swirled design, cut through batters with knife in S-shaped curves in one continuous motion; turn pan 1/4 turn and repeat.

4 Place muffin pan and cake pan in oven. Bake muffin cup 12 to 13 minutes or until toothpick inserted in center comes out clean; place pan on cooling rack. Continue baking 13x9-inch cake 14 to 18 minutes longer or until toothpick inserted in center comes out clean. Cool cake in pan 10 minutes. Remove cake and cupcake from pans to cooling rack. Cool completely, about 1 hour.

5 Reserve 2 tablespoons frosting. Frost cake with remaining frosting. In upper left-hand corner of cake, lightly score 5x3-1/2-inch rectangle in frosting for blue area of flag; sprinkle with blue sugar. Cut 2 strips of clean white paper, 13 inches long and 1-1/2 inches wide. Cut a third strip, 8 inches long and 1-1/2 inches wide. Place strips lightly on cake to cover area for white stripes. Sprinkle red sugar on cake for red stripes. Remove paper strips. Top blue sugar with candy stars.

6 Frost cupcake with reserved frosting; place in center of cake. Arrange candles in and/or around cupcake.

High Altitude (3500-6500 ft): Beat cake batter on low speed 30 seconds, then on medium speed 3 minutes. Bake cupcake 13 to 14 minutes.

Nutritional Info: 1 Serving: Calories 300 (Calories from Fat 110); Total Fat 13g (Saturated Fat 3g, Trans Fat 2g); Cholesterol 0mg; Sodium 270mg; Total Carbohydrate 43g (Dietary Fiber 0g, Sugars 29g); Protein 2g. % Daily Value: Cholesterol 0%; Vitamin A 0%; Vitamin C 0%; Calcium 4%; Iron 4%. Exchanges: 1/2 Starch, 2-1/2 Other Carbohydrate, 2-1/2 Fat. Carbohydrate Choices: 3.

Betty's Kitchen Tip

- The star candies pictured at right are available on www.shopbakersnook.com.

hot chocolate cupcakes

Prep Time: 20 Minutes
Start to Finish: 1 Hour 25 Minutes
Servings: 12 cupcakes

1-3/4 cups Betty Crocker® SuperMoist® devil's
 food cake mix (from 18.25-oz box)
 1/2 cup water
  3 tablespoons vegetable oil
  1 egg

1 cup Betty Crocker® Whipped vanilla frosting
 (from 12-oz container)
1/2 cup marshmallow creme
1/4 teaspoon unsweetened baking cocoa
  6 miniature pretzel twists, broken in half

---

1 Heat oven to 350°F for shiny metal pan
 (or 325°F for dark or nonstick pan). Place
 paper baking cup in each of 12 regular-size
 muffin cups.

2 In large bowl, beat cake mix, water, oil and
 egg with electric mixer on low speed 30
 seconds. Beat on medium speed 2 minutes,
 scraping bowl occasionally. Divide batter
 evenly among muffin cups.

3 Bake 17 to 22 minutes or until toothpick
 inserted in center comes out clean. Cool in
 pan 10 minutes; remove from pan to cooling
 rack. Cool completely, about 30 minutes.

4 In small bowl, mix frosting and marshmallow
 creme. Spoon into small resealable food-
 storage plastic bag; seal bag. Cut 3/8-inch tip
 off 1 corner of bag. (Or spoon mixture onto
 cupcakes instead of piping.)

5 Pipe 3 small dollops of frosting mixture
 on top of each cupcake to resemble melted
 marshmallows. Sprinkle with cocoa. Press
 pretzel half into side of each cupcake for
 cup handle.

High Altitude (3500-6500 ft): Heat oven to
350°F for all pans.

Nutritional Info: 1 Cupcake: Calories 240 (Calories from Fat 80);
Total Fat 9g (Saturated Fat 2.5g, Trans Fat 1.5g); Cholesterol
20mg; Sodium 300mg; Total Carbohydrate 37g (Dietary Fiber 0g,
Sugars 22g); Protein 2g. % Daily Value: Cholesterol 6%; Vitamin A
0%; Vitamin C 0%; Calcium 0%; Iron 6%. Exchanges: 2-1/2 Other
Carbohydrate, 2 Fat. Carbohydrate Choices: 2-1/2.

Betty's Kitchen Tips

Using Up Cake Mix: Turn to page 234 for another
recipe using 1/2 box of devil's food cake mix.

Variation: If you like peppermint, frost these fun
cupcakes with the frosting mixture, and sprinkle
the tops with crushed candy canes.

teddy-at-the-beach cupcakes

Prep Time: 30 Minutes
Start to Finish: 1 Hour 35 Minutes
Servings: 12 cupcakes

- 1 box Betty Crocker® SuperMoist® cake mix (any flavor)
- Water, vegetable oil and eggs called for on cake mix box
- 2 drops blue food color
- 1 cup Betty Crocker® Whipped vanilla frosting (from 12-oz container)
- 1 roll (from 4.5-oz box) Betty Crocker® Fruit by the Foot® chewy fruit snack (any flavor)
- 1/2 cup teddy bear-shaped graham snacks, crushed, or brown sugar
- 1 tablespoon blue sugar or edible glitter, if desired
- 12 teddy bear-shaped graham snacks
- 6 paper drink umbrellas or small plastic umbrellas, if desired
- 6 ring-shaped gummy candies
- 6 multi-colored fish-shaped crackers

1. Heat oven to 350°F for shiny metal pans (or 325°F for dark or nonstick pans). Place paper baking cup in each of 24 regular-size muffin cups.

2. In large bowl, make cake mix as directed on box, using water, oil and eggs. Divide batter evenly among muffin cups.

3. Bake as directed on box or until toothpick inserted in center comes out clean. Cool 10 minutes; remove from pan to cooling rack. Cool completely, about 30 minutes. Tightly wrap 12 cupcakes; freeze for a later use.

4. Stir blue food color into frosting until blended. Frost cupcakes with frosting.

5. Cut 6 (1-1/2-inch) pieces from fruit snack roll; peel off paper backing. Use fruit snack, crushed graham snacks, blue sugar, teddy bear-shaped snacks, umbrellas, gummy candies and fish-shaped crackers to decorate cupcakes as shown in photo or as desired.

High Altitude (3500-6500 ft): Follow High Altitude directions on cake mix box for cupcakes.

Nutritional Info: 1 Frosted Cupcake (Undecorated): Calories 190 (Calories from Fat 80); Total Fat 9g (Saturated Fat 2.5g, Trans Fat 1.5g); Cholesterol 25mg; Sodium 160mg; Total Carbohydrate 28g (Dietary Fiber 0g, Sugars 19g); Protein 1g. % Daily Value: Cholesterol 9%; Vitamin A 0%; Vitamin C 0%; Calcium 4%; Iron 2%. Exchanges: 1/2 Starch, 1-1/2 Other Carbohydrate, 1-1/2 Fat. Carbohydrate Choices: 2.

Betty's Kitchen Tips

How-To: If you have Betty Crocker® decorating icing (in 4.25-oz tubes), use the writing tip to pipe swimsuits on the bears.

Purchasing: The small plastic umbrellas can be found at fancyflours.com.

chai latte cupcakes

Prep Time: 25 Minutes
Start to Finish: 1 Hour 50 Minutes
Servings: 24 cupcakes

Cake

1	box Betty Crocker® SuperMoist® French vanilla cake mix
1-1/2	cups water
1/3	cup vegetable oil
3	eggs
1	package (1.1 oz) instant chai tea latte mix (or 3 tablespoons from larger container)

Frosting & Garnish

4	oz white chocolate baking bars (from 6-oz package), chopped
1/3	cup butter or margarine, softened
4	cups powdered sugar
1/4	cup milk
1/2	teaspoon vanilla

Ground cinnamon, if desired

1 Heat oven to 350°F for shiny metal pans (or 325°F for dark or nonstick pans). Place paper baking cup in each of 24 regular-size muffin cups.

2 In large bowl, beat cake ingredients with electric mixer on low speed 30 seconds. Beat on medium speed 2 minutes, scraping bowl occasionally. Divide batter evenly among muffin cups.

3 Bake 18 to 23 minutes or until toothpick inserted in center comes out clean. Cool 10 minutes; remove from pan to cooling rack. Cool completely, about 1 hour.

4 In medium microwavable bowl, microwave baking bars on High 30 seconds; stir until melted. If necessary, microwave 15 seconds longer or until melted and smooth. Stir in butter until smooth. Add powdered sugar, milk and vanilla; stir until well blended.

5 Frost cupcakes with frosting. Sprinkle with cinnamon. Store loosely covered at room temperature.

High Altitude (3500-6500 ft): Decrease water to 1-1/4 cups.

Nutritional Info: 1 Cupcake: Calories 260 (Calories from Fat 90); Total Fat 10g (Saturated Fat 3.5g, Trans Fat 0.5g); Cholesterol 35mg; Sodium 180mg; Total Carbohydrate 41g (Dietary Fiber 0g, Sugars 33g); Protein 2g. % Daily Value: Cholesterol 11%; Vitamin A 2%; Vitamin C 0%; Calcium 6%; Iron 2%. Exchanges: 1/2 Starch, 2 Other Carbohydrate, 2 Fat. Carbohydrate Choices: 3.

Betty's Kitchen Tips

Did You Know? Chai is the Hindi word for a tea made with milk and spices such as cardamom, cinnamon, cloves, ginger, nutmeg and pepper.

Variation: Instant chai tea mix comes in a variety of flavors. Experiment to find your favorite.

cookies
GALORE

p. 281

287

282

260

browned butter cookies with caramel frosting

Prep Time: 1 Hour 10 Minutes
Start to Finish: 1 Hour 40 Minutes
Servings: About 4 dozen cookies

Cookies

1/2	cup butter (do not use margarine)
1	cup packed brown sugar
1/4	cup milk
1	teaspoon vanilla
1	egg
1-3/4	cups Gold Medal® all-purpose flour
1/2	teaspoon baking soda
1/2	teaspoon salt
1/2	cup chopped cashews

Caramel Frosting

1/2	cup butter
1	cup packed brown sugar
1/4	cup milk
1	teaspoon vanilla
2	cups powdered sugar

Decoration

48	cashew halves (about 1/2 cup)

1 Heat oven to 375°F. In heavy 2-quart saucepan, melt 1/2 cup butter over medium heat. Cook, stirring constantly, until butter is light brown; pour into large bowl. Cool 5 minutes.

2 Stir in 1 cup brown sugar, 1/4 cup milk, 1 teaspoon vanilla and 1 egg with spoon. Stir in flour, baking soda, salt and 1/2 cup chopped cashews. On ungreased cookie sheets, drop dough by rounded teaspoonfuls 2 inches apart.

3 Bake 8 to 10 minutes or until almost no indentation remains when touched in center. Cool 1 to 2 minutes. Remove from the cookie sheets to cooling rack. Cool completely, about 30 minutes.

4 Meanwhile, in 2-quart saucepan, melt 1/2 cup butter over medium heat. Stir in 1 cup brown sugar. Heat to boiling, stirring constantly. Stir in 1/4 cup milk. Heat to boiling; remove from heat. Stir in 1 teaspoon vanilla. Cool to lukewarm, about 30 minutes. Gradually stir in powdered sugar.

5 Spread about 1 tablespoon frosting on each cookie; top with cashew half.

High Altitude (3500-6500 ft): No change.

Nutritional Info: 1 Cookie: Calories 130 (Calories from Fat 50); Total Fat 5g (Saturated Fat 2.5g, Trans Fat 0g); Cholesterol 15mg; Sodium 70mg; Total Carbohydrate 18g (Dietary Fiber 0g, Sugars 14g); Protein 1g. % Daily Value: Vitamin A 2%; Vitamin C 0%; Calcium 0%; Iron 4%. Exchanges: 1/2 Starch, 1/2 Other Carbohydrate, 1 Fat. Carbohydrate Choices: 1.

Betty's Kitchen Tip

• For richer frosting, substitute whipping cream for the milk.

rich peanut butter cookies

Prep Time: 40 Minutes
Start to Finish: 40 Minutes
Servings: About 2 dozen cookies

1	cup packed brown sugar
1/2	cup peanut butter
1/2	cup butter or margarine, softened
1	egg
1-1/4	cups Gold Medal® all-purpose flour
3/4	teaspoon baking soda
1/2	teaspoon baking powder
1/4	teaspoon salt
1	cup peanut butter chips (6 oz)

Granulated sugar

1 Heat oven to 375°F. In large bowl, beat brown sugar, peanut butter, butter and egg with electric mixer on medium speed until creamy. On low speed, beat in flour, baking soda, baking powder and salt. Stir in peanut butter chips.

2 Shape dough into 1-1/2-inch balls. Dip tops of balls into granulated sugar. On ungreased cookie sheets, place balls, sugared sides up, about 3 inches apart (do not flatten).

3 Bake 9 to 10 minutes or until light brown. Cool 5 minutes; remove from cookie sheet to cooling racks.

High Altitude (3500-6500 ft): Use 1/2 teaspoon baking soda.

Nutritional Info: 1 Cookie: Calories 170 (Calories from Fat 80); Total Fat 9g (Saturated Fat 3g, Trans Fat 0g); Cholesterol 20mg; Sodium 150mg; Total Carbohydrate 19g (Dietary Fiber 0g, Sugars 13g); Protein 3g. % Daily Value: Vitamin A 4%; Vitamin C 0%; Calcium 2%; Iron 4%. Exchanges: 1 Starch, 1/2 Other Carbohydrate, 1-1/2 Fat. Carbohydrate Choices: 1.

Betty's Kitchen Tip

• For best results, if you use margarine in this recipe, select one that contains at least 80 percent vegetable oil.

heart sandwich cookies

Prep Time: 1 Hour 30 Minutes
Start to Finish: 2 Hours 30 Minutes
Servings: 3 dozen sandwich cookies

Cookies

1/2	cup butter, softened
1/2	cup granulated sugar
1	egg
1	tablespoon milk
1	teaspoon vanilla
1-1/2	cups Gold Medal® all-purpose flour

1/2	teaspoon baking powder
1	teaspoon red edible glitter

Cinnamon Filling

1/4	cup red cinnamon candies
1/3	cup water
3	tablespoons butter, softened
3	cups powdered sugar

1 In medium bowl, beat 1/2 cup butter, granulated sugar and egg with electric mixer on medium speed until creamy. Beat in milk and vanilla, scraping bowl frequently, until well mixed. On low speed, beat in flour and baking powder until well mixed, scraping bowl frequently.

2 Shape dough into 2 equal halves; wrap in plastic wrap. Flatten each to 1/2-inch thickness. Refrigerate until firm, about 1 hour.

3 Heat oven to 400°F. On generously floured surface, roll out 1 half of dough 1/8 inch thick. Cut with small (2-inch) heart-shaped cookie cutter. On ungreased cookie sheets, place cookies 1 inch apart. Sprinkle glitter on cookies. Bake 5 to 8 minutes or until edges are lightly browned. Repeat with remaining half of dough, except do not sprinkle with glitter. Remove from cookie sheets to cooling rack. Cool completely, about 10 minutes.

4 Meanwhile, in 2-quart saucepan, heat candies and water to boiling over medium-high heat, stirring constantly. Reduce heat to medium-low; simmer uncovered about 3 minutes, stirring frequently, until candies are melted. Remove from heat. Using wire whisk, stir in butter and powdered sugar, 1/3 cup at a time, until smooth.

5 Spread or pipe heaping teaspoon filling in center of flat side of each undecorated cookie. Press decorated cookie over filling; press firmly to secure.

High Altitude (3500-6500 ft): No change.

Nutritional Info: 1 Cookie: Calories 110 (Calories from Fat 35); Total Fat 3.5g (Saturated Fat 2.5g, Trans Fat 0g); Cholesterol 15mg; Sodium 35mg; Total Carbohydrate 18g (Dietary Fiber 0g, Sugars 14g); Protein 0g. % Daily Value: Vitamin A 2%; Vitamin C 0%; Calcium 0%; Iron 0%. Exchanges: 1 Other Carbohydrate, 1 Fat. Carbohydrate Choices: 1.

Betty's Kitchen Tip

• In the winter months, make these cookies using a mitten-shaped cookie cutter.

iced molasses cookies

Prep Time: 55 Minutes
Start to Finish: 1 Hour 15 Minutes
Servings: 3 dozen cookies

....

Cookies

1/2	cup packed brown sugar
1/4	cup shortening
1/2	cup molasses
2	eggs
3-1/2	cups Original Bisquick® mix
1	teaspoon ground ginger
1	teaspoon ground cinnamon
1/2	teaspoon ground nutmeg
1/8	teaspoon ground cloves

Icing

1	cup powdered sugar
1	tablespoon plus 1 teaspoon milk
1/4	teaspoon vanilla

....

1 Heat oven to 350°F. Spray cookie sheets with cooking spray. In large bowl, beat brown sugar, shortening and molasses with electric mixer on medium speed until well blended. Beat in eggs. Stir in remaining cookie ingredients until well blended. (Dough will be sticky.)

2 Drop dough by rounded teaspoonfuls about 1 inch apart onto cookie sheets.

3 Bake 7 to 9 minutes or until light golden brown. Remove from cookie sheets to cooling racks. Cool completely, about 20 minutes.

4 In small bowl, mix icing ingredients until smooth. Drizzle icing over cookies.

High Altitude (3500-6500 ft): Bake 11 to 13 minutes.

Nutritional Info: 1 Cookie: Calories 120 (Calories from Fat 40); Total Fat 4.5g (Saturated Fat 1.5g, Trans Fat 1g); Cholesterol 10mg; Sodium 150mg; Total Carbohydrate 18g (Dietary Fiber 0g, Sugars 9g); Protein 1g. % Daily Value: Vitamin A 0%; Vitamin C 0%; Calcium 2%; Iron 4%. Exchanges: 1/2 Starch, 1/2 Other Carbohydrate, 1 Fat. Carbohydrate Choices: 1.

Betty's Kitchen Tips

Success Hint: You can choose how strong you want the molasses flavor of these cookies to be. Look for the lighter-colored mild-flavor molasses or the darker full-flavor molasses in the baking aisle of your grocery store.

How-To: If the icing is too thick to drizzle, stir in additional milk, 1/2 teaspoon at a time, until easy to drizzle.

crisp chocolate-espresso ribbon cookies

Prep Time: 1 Hour 20 Minutes
Start to Finish: 3 Hours 20 Minutes
Servings: 4 dozen cookies

- -

1   pouch (1 lb 1.5 oz) Betty Crocker® sugar cookie mix

1   tablespoon Gold Medal® all-purpose flour

1/2 cup butter or margarine, softened

1   teaspoon almond extract

1   egg, slightly beaten

1/3 cup bittersweet chocolate chips, melted

1/2 cup coarsely to finely crushed chocolate-covered espresso coffee beans

1/3 cup coarsely chopped toasted almonds

- -

1 Line bottom and sides of 9x5-inch loaf pan with plastic wrap. In large bowl, stir cookie mix, flour, butter, almond extract and egg until soft dough forms. Divide dough in half; place half of dough in another bowl. Stir melted chocolate into half of dough. To remaining half of dough, mix in espresso beans and almonds.

2 Firmly press half of chocolate dough evenly in bottom of loaf pan. Evenly press half of espresso dough over chocolate dough in pan. Repeat with remaining chocolate dough and espresso dough. Fold plastic wrap over dough to cover. Refrigerate until firm, about 2 hours.

3 Heat oven to 350°F. Remove dough from pan; unwrap. Place dough on cutting board. Cut dough crosswise into 4 equal pieces. Cut each piece crosswise into 12 slices. On ungreased cookie sheets, place slices 2 inches apart.

4 Bake 9 to 10 minutes or until edges are light golden brown. Cool 1 minute; remove from cookie sheets to cooling rack.

High Altitude (3500-6500 ft): Add 2 tablespoons Gold Medal® all-purpose flour to dry cookie mix. Bake 11 to 12 minutes.

Nutritional Info: 1 Cookie: Calories 80 (Calories from Fat 40); Total Fat 4.5g (Saturated Fat 2g, Trans Fat 0g); Cholesterol 10mg; Sodium 45mg; Total Carbohydrate 10g (Dietary Fiber 0g, Sugars 6g); Protein 1g. % Daily Value: Vitamin A 0%; Vitamin C 0%; Calcium 0%; Iron 0%. Exchanges: 1/2 Starch, 1 Fat. Carbohydrate Choices: 1/2.

Betty's Kitchen Tips

Do-Ahead: Cookie dough can be stored in the fridge for up to 24 hours or in the freezer for up to two months before cutting and baking.

Prize-Winner: This prize-winning recipe from the 2008 Bake Life Sweeter™ Cookie Mix Recipe Contest is from Barbara Estabrook of Wisconsin.

fruit and nut chews

Prep Time: 45 Minutes
Start to Finish: 45 Minutes
Servings: About 4 dozen cookies

- 1 bag (12 oz) white vanilla baking chips (2 cups)
- 1 bag (7 oz) flaked coconut (about 2-2/3 cups)
- 1 bag (6 oz) dried cherries or cranberries, coarsely chopped (about 1-1/2 cups)
- 1 bag (7 oz) dried apricots, chopped (about 1-1/2 cups)
- 1 bag (6 oz) roasted, salted and shelled pistachio nuts, chopped (about 1-1/2 cups)
- 1 can (14 oz) sweetened condensed milk (not evaporated)

1 Heat oven to 325°F. Spray 2 large cookie sheets with cooking spray.

2 In large bowl, mix all ingredients except milk with spoon to combine. Pour milk over dry ingredients; stir gently to evenly coat.

3 Spoon heaping teaspoonfuls mixture onto cookie sheets. Moisten fingers with water, and gently form cookies into tighter mounds on cookie sheets.

4 Bake 10 to 12 minutes or until cookies just begin to brown. Cool 1 minute; remove from cookie sheets to waxed paper. Cool completely, about 10 minutes.

High Altitude (3500-6500 ft): Heat oven to 350°F.

Nutritional Info: 1 Cookie: Calories 130 (Calories from Fat 50); Total Fat 6g (Saturated Fat 3.5g, Trans Fat 0g); Cholesterol 0mg; Sodium 50mg; Total Carbohydrate 17g (Dietary Fiber 1g, Sugars 15g); Protein 2g. % Daily Value: Vitamin A 4%; Vitamin C 0%; Calcium 4%; Iron 2%. Exchanges: 1 Starch, 1 Fat. Carbohydrate Choices: 1.

Betty's Kitchen Tips

Did You Know? This recipe is based on an old family favorite of Kathy Eich, our kitchen tester. She updated the recipe with pistachio nuts and white vanilla baking chips.

Special-Touch: For a pretty presentation, serve these treats in small foil cups.

mocha latte logs

Prep Time: 1 Hour 30 Minutes
Start to Finish: 2 Hours
Servings: 48 cookies

Cookies

1	cup butter, softened
3/4	cup granulated sugar
1/4	cup packed brown sugar
2	oz unsweetened baking chocolate, melted, cooled slightly
1	teaspoon vanilla

1	egg
1	tablespoon instant espresso coffee powder
2-1/2	cups Gold Medal® all-purpose flour

Glaze

2	tablespoons whipping cream or milk
2	teaspoons instant espresso coffee powder
1	cup powdered sugar

1. Heat oven to 350°F. In large bowl, beat butter with electric mixer on medium speed until fluffy. Beat in sugars until well blended. Beat in melted chocolate, vanilla, egg and 1 tablespoon coffee powder. Gradually beat flour into butter mixture until well blended.

2. Roll dough into ball; flatten ball slightly. Cut dough into 8 equal wedges; roll each into 18-inch long rope. Cut each rope into 6 (3-inch) pieces. On ungreased cookie sheets, place pieces 2 inches apart. Using tines of fork, make lines along each log by pulling gently down length of each piece.

3. Bake 10 to 12 minutes or until firm but not browned. Remove from cookie sheets to cooling rack. Cool completely, about 10 minutes.

4. Place waxed paper on counter under cooling rack. In small, deep microwavable bowl or measuring cup, microwave cream uncovered on High about 15 seconds or until warm. Stir in 2 teaspoons coffee powder until dissolved. Using wire whisk, beat in powdered sugar until no lumps remain. Dip one end of each log into glaze. Place on cooling rack, allowing glaze to drip through rack, until glaze is dry, about 30 minutes.

High Altitude (3500-6500 ft): No change.

Nutritional Info: 1 Cookie: Calories 100 (Calories from Fat 45); Total Fat 5g (Saturated Fat 3g, Trans Fat 0g); Cholesterol 15mg; Sodium 30mg; Total Carbohydrate 12g (Dietary Fiber 0g, Sugars 7g); Protein 1g. % Daily Value: Vitamin A 2%; Vitamin C 0%; Calcium 0%; Iron 4%. Exchanges: 1 Other Carbohydrate, 1 Fat. Carbohydrate Choices: 1.

Betty's Kitchen Tip

• To melt baking chocolate in microwave, cut chocolate into 4 pieces; place in small microwavable bowl. Microwave uncovered on High 1 minute; stir. If needed, microwave an additional 10 seconds at a time and stirring after each time, just until chocolate is melted.

wild blue energy chews

Prep Time: 1 Hour 5 Minutes
Start to Finish: 1 Hour 5 Minutes
Servings: About 2-1/2 dozen cookies

- -

1	pouch (1 lb 1.5 oz) Betty Crocker® oatmeal cookie mix
1/4	cup toasted wheat germ
3	tablespoons butter or margarine, softened
3	tablespoons canola oil
3	tablespoons water
1	egg white
1/2	cup dried blueberries
1/4	cup whole almonds, chopped
2	oz bittersweet baking chocolate, chopped

- -

1 Heat oven to 350°F. In large bowl, stir cookie mix, wheat germ, butter, oil, water and egg white until soft dough forms. Stir in blueberries, almonds and chocolate.

2 On ungreased cookie sheets, drop dough by rounded tablespoonfuls 2 inches apart.

3 Bake 11 to 13 minutes or until edges are light golden brown. Cool 5 minutes; remove from cookie sheets to cooling rack.

High Altitude (3500-6500 ft): No change.

Nutritional Info: 1 Cookie: Calories 120 (Calories from Fat 45); Total Fat 4.5g (Saturated Fat 1.5g, Trans Fat 0g); Cholesterol 0mg; Sodium 75mg; Total Carbohydrate 17g (Dietary Fiber 1g, Sugars 8g); Protein 2g. % Daily Value: Vitamin A 0%; Vitamin C 0%; Calcium 0%; Iron 4%. Exchanges: 1/2 Starch, 1/2 Other Carbohydrate, 1 Fat. Carbohydrate Choices: 1.

Betty's Kitchen Tip

• These cookies get their name from the dried blueberries. They are great to pack for hikes, picnics and other outdoor events.

pecan-shortbread trees

Prep Time: 30 Minutes
Start to Finish: 1 Hour 15 Minutes
Servings: 32 cookies

1 cup butter, softened	1/2 cup coarsely chopped pecans
2/3 cup powdered sugar	32 pecan halves
1/2 teaspoon vanilla	3/4 cup white vanilla baking chips
5 drops green food color	Granulated sugar, if desired
1-3/4 cups Gold Medal® all-purpose flour	32 yellow decorating stars, if desired

1 Heat oven to 325°F. Spray or lightly grease 2 large cookie sheets. In large bowl, beat butter and powdered sugar with electric mixer on medium speed until light and fluffy. Beat in vanilla and food color. On low speed, beat in flour just until mixed. Stir in chopped pecans.

2 Divide dough into 4 equal parts; shape each into ball. Place 2 balls of dough on each cookie sheet, on opposite ends. With rolling pin or floured fingers, gently flatten and shape each ball into 6-inch circle. With large knife, divide and cut each round into 8 wedges, slightly separating each cut with knife. Poke tops of wedges with fork, and place 1 pecan half in middle of each outer edge to make tree trunk.

3 Bake 15 to 18 minutes or until firm but not brown. While still warm, cut into wedges again. Cool completely on cookie sheets, about 30 minutes.

4 Place cooled tree wedges on cooling racks or waxed paper. Place baking chips in small resealable freezer plastic bag. Microwave on High 40 to 60 seconds, turning bag over after 30 seconds. Squeeze bag gently until chips are melted and smooth. Cut small tip off one corner of bag, and drizzle side to side over wedges to make tree garland. Sprinkle with sugar. Top each tree with star.

High Altitude (3500-6500 ft): No change.

Nutritional Info: 1 Cookie: Calories 160 (Calories from Fat 100); Total Fat 11g (Saturated Fat 6g, Trans Fat 0g); Cholesterol 15mg; Sodium 65mg; Total Carbohydrate 15g (Dietary Fiber 0g, Sugars 9g); Protein 1g. % Daily Value: Vitamin A 4%; Vitamin C 0%; Calcium 0%; Iron 2%. Exchanges: 1 Starch, 2 Fat. Carbohydrate Choices: 1.

Betty's Kitchen Tips

Special Touch: After the holiday season, make these great-tasting cookies without the food color, pecan "trunks" and stars.

Success Hint: If using paste food color, you need only a small amount to get a nice green color.

italian pignoli nut cookies

Prep Time: 1 Hour
Start to Finish: 1 Hour 30 Minutes
Servings: 3 dozen cookies

- 1 pouch (1 lb 1.5 oz) Betty Crocker® sugar cookie mix
- 1/2 cup granulated sugar
- 1/2 cup butter or margarine, softened
- 1 package (7 or 8 oz) almond paste (not marzipan)
- 1 egg
- 2 cups pine nuts (8 oz)
- 1 tablespoon powdered sugar

1 Heat oven to 350°F. Spray cookie sheets with cooking spray. In large bowl, beat cookie mix, granulated sugar, butter, almond paste and egg with electric mixer on low speed until soft dough forms.

2 Shape dough into 1-1/4-inch balls; roll each ball in pine nuts, pressing to coat. Place balls 2 inches apart on cookie sheets.

3 Bake 13 to 17 minutes or just until edges are light golden brown. Cool 5 minutes; remove from cookie sheets to cooling rack. Cool completely, about 15 minutes. Before serving, sprinkle with powdered sugar.

High Altitude (3500-6500 ft): Follow High Altitude directions on cookie mix pouch, adding sugar and almond paste. Bake 12 to 15 minutes.

Nutritional Info: 1 Cookie: Calories 170 (Calories from Fat 90); Total Fat 10g (Saturated Fat 2.5g, Trans Fat 0.5g); Cholesterol 15mg; Sodium 60mg; Total Carbohydrate 18g (Dietary Fiber 0g, Sugars 12g); Protein 2g. % Daily Value: Vitamin A 0%; Vitamin C 0%; Calcium 0%; Iron 4%. Exchanges: 1/2 Starch, 1/2 Other Carbohydrate, 2 Fat. Carbohydrate Choices: 1.

Betty's Kitchen Tips

Purchasing: Look for pine nuts in the grocery store near the other nuts. Budget-priced pine nuts can be found in the bulk-foods section of the store or in club stores.

Prize-Winner: This recipe was one of 15 finalists in the 2008 Bake Life Sweeter™ Cookie Mix Recipe Contest. It's from Gina DeSilva of New York.

decorate-before-you-bake cookies

Prep Time: 50 Minutes
Start to Finish: 1 Hour 40 Minutes
Servings: 6 dozen cookies

Cookies

3/4	cup butter or margarine, softened
1/2	cup sugar
1	egg
1-3/4	cups Gold Medal® all-purpose flour
1/2	teaspoon baking soda
1/4	teaspoon cream of tartar
1/4	teaspoon salt
2	tablespoons sugar

Decorating Mixture

1/2	cup butter or margarine, softened
3	teaspoons milk
1/2	cup Gold Medal® all-purpose flour
4	drops red food color
4	drops green food color

1 In large bowl, beat 3/4 cup butter and 1/2 cup sugar with electric mixer on medium speed until light and fluffy. Add egg; beat well. Stir in 1-3/4 cups flour, the baking soda, cream of tartar and salt. Knead dough into smooth ball. Wrap in plastic wrap; refrigerate until firm, about 1 hour.

2 Meanwhile, in small bowl, mix 1/2 cup butter, the milk and 1/2 cup flour with fork until well mixed. Divide mixture in half. Stir red food color into 1 half and green food color into other half. Spoon each mixture into decorating bag fitted with small writing tip; set aside.

3 Heat oven to 375°F. Shape 1 half of the cookie dough into 3/4-inch balls. Place balls 2 inches apart on ungreased cookie sheets. In small bowl, measure 2 tablespoons sugar. Dip bottom of glass into sugar, and use to flatten each ball into 1-1/2-inch round. Pipe colored mixture from decorating bags on each cookie in various holiday designs. Repeat with remaining half of dough.

4 Bake 7 to 9 minutes or until set. Immediately remove to cooling rack.

High Altitude (3500-6500 ft): No change.

Nutritional Info: 1 Cookie: Calories 50 (Calories from Fat 30); Total Fat 3.5g (Saturated Fat 2g, Trans Fat 0g); Cholesterol 10mg; Sodium 40mg; Total Carbohydrate 5g (Dietary Fiber 0g, Sugars 2g); Protein 0g. % Daily Value: Vitamin A 2%; Vitamin C 0%; Calcium 0%; Iron 0%. Exchanges: 1/2 Other Carbohydrate, 1/2 Fat. Carbohydrate Choices: 1/2.

Betty's Kitchen Tip

• If you don't have decorating bags and tips, use small resealable food-storage plastic bags. Cut off the tip of one corner for piping.

candy-topped blossom cookies

Prep Time: 1 Hour 35 Minutes
Start to Finish: 2 Hours 5 Minutes
Servings: 48 cookies

- -

1 can (14 oz) sweetened condensed milk (not evaporated)

1 cup creamy peanut butter

2 cups Original Bisquick® mix

1 teaspoon vanilla

3 tablespoons sugar

48 round chewy caramels in milk chocolate (from 12-oz bag), unwrapped

- -

1 Heat oven to 375°F. In large bowl, beat condensed milk and peanut butter with electric mixer on medium speed until well blended.

2 Stir in Bisquick mix and vanilla until well blended.

3 Shape dough into 48 (1-1/4-inch) balls. Measure sugar into small bowl. Dip top of each ball into sugar. On ungreased cookie sheets, place balls 2 inches apart.

4 Bake 7 to 9 minutes. Firmly press 1 caramel into center of each cookie. Bake about 1 minute or until chocolate begins to soften and cookie begins to turn light golden brown. Cool 2 to 3 minutes. Remove from cookie sheets to cooling rack. Cool completely, about 30 minutes.

High Altitude (3500-6500 ft): No change.

Nutritional Info: 1 Cookie: Calories 110 (Calories from Fat 50); Total Fat 5g (Saturated Fat 2g, Trans Fat 0g); Cholesterol 0mg; Sodium 110mg; Total Carbohydrate 14g (Dietary Fiber 0g, Sugars 9g); Protein 2g. % Daily Value: Vitamin A 0%; Vitamin C 0%; Calcium 4%; Iron 0%. Exchanges: 1/2 Starch, 1/2 Other Carbohydrate, 1 Fat. Carbohydrate Choices: 1.

Betty's Kitchen Tips

Special Touch: Get the kids involved in making this recipe. Simple steps and kid-friendly ingredients make for great holiday memories.

Do-Ahead: These cookies freeze well. Make them early in the season, cool completely and freeze in an airtight container.

season's best sugar cookies

Prep Time: 1 Hour
Start to Finish: 3 Hours
Servings: About 5 dozen cookies

LOW FAT

Cookies

1-1/2	cups powdered sugar
1	cup butter or margarine, softened
1	teaspoon vanilla
1/2	teaspoon almond extract
1	egg
2-1/2	cups Gold Medal® all-purpose flour
1	teaspoon baking soda

1	teaspoon cream of tartar

White Glaze

2	cups powdered sugar
2	tablespoons milk
1/4	teaspoon almond extract

Sprinkles

Red edible glitter or red sugar

1 In large bowl, beat 1-1/2 cups powdered sugar and the butter with electric mixer on medium speed, or mix with spoon. Stir in vanilla, 1/2 teaspoon almond extract and the egg. Stir in flour, baking soda and cream of tartar. Cover and refrigerate about 2 hours or until firm.

2 Heat oven to 375°F. On lightly floured cloth-covered surface, roll half of dough at a time 1/8 inch thick. Cut into desired shapes. On ungreased cookie sheets, place 2 inches apart.

3 Bake 7 to 8 minutes or until light brown. Remove from cookie sheet to cooling rack. Cool completely.

4 Mix glaze ingredients until smooth and desired spreading consistency, adding a few extra drops milk if needed. Spread glaze over cookies. Sprinkle with edible glitter or sugar.

High Altitude (3500-6500 ft): No change.

Nutritional Info: 1 Cookie: Calories 80 (Calories from Fat 30); Total Fat 3g (Saturated Fat 2g, Trans Fat 0g); Cholesterol 10mg; Sodium 45mg; Total Carbohydrate 11g (Dietary Fiber 0g, Sugars 7g); Protein 0g. % Daily Value: Vitamin A 2%; Vitamin C 0%; Calcium 0%; Iron 0%. Exchanges: 1 Other Carbohydrate, 1/2 Fat. Carbohydrate Choices: 1.

Betty's Kitchen Tips

Success Hint: When you're making cutout cookies, always work with well-chilled dough. Cold dough rolls out smoothly, with less sticking. The cookies are easy to cut, remove, and transfer to baking sheets, and they hold their shape in the oven.

Purchasing: To purchase edible glitter, visit the cake-decorating aisle at craft stores.

apricot pinwheels

Prep Time: 1 Hour 20 Minutes
Start to Finish: 1 Hour 50 Minutes
Servings: 4 dozen cookies

- 1 package (3 oz) cream cheese, softened
- 1 cup butter or margarine, softened
- 1/4 cup sugar
- 1 teaspoon vanilla
- 2-1/4 cups Gold Medal® all-purpose flour
- 1/8 teaspoon salt
- 1/4 cup apricot jam or preserves
- 1/4 chopped unblanched almonds

1 In large bowl, beat cream cheese, butter, sugar and vanilla with electric mixer on medium speed, or mix with spoon, until light and fluffy. Stir in flour and salt. Cover and refrigerate about 30 minutes or until firm.

2 Heat oven to 350°F. Lightly grease cookie sheets with shortening. On generously floured surface, roll dough into 16x12-inch rectangle. Cut rectangle into 48 (2-inch) squares, 8 rows by 6 rows. Use a metal spatula to place squares 1 inch apart on cookie sheets.

3 Spread each square with about 1/4 teaspoon jam. On each square, cut from each corner to 1/4 inch from center. Bring every other point to center and press together to form pinwheel. Sprinkle each with almonds.

4 Bake 8 to 10 minutes or until lightly browned. Immediately remove from cookie sheet to cooling rack; cool.

High Altitude (3500-6500 ft): Bake 13 to 15 minutes.

Nutritional Info: 1 Cookie: Calories 80 (Calories from Fat 45); Total Fat 5g (Saturated Fat 3g, Trans Fat 0g); Cholesterol 10mg; Sodium 40mg; Total Carbohydrate 7g (Dietary Fiber 0g, Sugars 2g); Protein 1g. % Daily Value: Vitamin A 2%; Vitamin C 0%; Calcium 0%; Iron 0%. Exchanges: 1/2 Starch, 1 Fat. Carbohydrate Choices: 1/2.

Betty's Kitchen Tips

Success Hint: Use a floured cloth-covered rolling pin to make rolling easier.

Substitution: Any flavor jam can be substituted for the apricot jam. Raspberry would be pretty for the holidays.

ginger-ski men

Prep Time: 1 Hour
Start to Finish: 1 Hour
Servings: 10 servings

---

30 fruit-flavored ring-shaped gummy candies (from 7-oz package)

10 (2-1/2-inch) gingerbread man cookies (from 5-oz package)

1 roll Betty Crocker® Fruit by the Foot® chewy fruit-flavored snack (from 6-roll box)

20 pretzel sticks

1 cup white vanilla baking chips

20 red cinnamon candies

20 miniature chocolate chips

10 gingersnap cookies (from 16-oz box)

20 (3-inch) candy canes

---

1 Cover work space with large sheet of waxed paper. Gently stretch 1 candy ring, and pull over top of 1 gingerbread man's head to make hat; repeat 9 times. Unroll fruit snack; cut into 5-inch pieces, separating along perforations. Wrap 1 (5-inch) piece around neck, twisting in center of each, to make scarf. Gently press to stick. Place 1 candy ring near 1 end of each pretzel stick to make ski poles.

2 Place white vanilla baking chips in small resealable freezer plastic bag. Microwave on High 45 seconds, turning bag over after 30 seconds. Squeeze bag until chips are melted and smooth (if necessary, continue microwaving, 15 seconds at a time, until smooth). Cut small tip off one corner of bag.

3 Using melted chips as glue, for each ski man squeeze small dot in middle of face; attach 1 cinnamon candy to make nose. Squeeze 2 small dots above nose; attach 2 miniature chocolate chips to make eyes. Squeeze small amount to hold candy rings onto pretzels at bottom. Squeeze small amount on top of head to hold candy ring; place cinnamon candy on top. Squeeze small amount to make each hand, and attach pretzel ski poles, setting outward to fit outside skis. Drizzle over top of round

gingersnap cookie, and set 2 miniature candy canes 1/2 inch apart, with hook ends standing up. Repeat for remaining ski men. Allow to set, about 30 minutes.

4 When set, microwave chips in bag to melt again, about 30 seconds or until smooth. For each ski man, squeeze small amount on top of candy cane skis; stand gingerbread man on each; allow to set, about 30 minutes.

High Altitude (3500-6500 ft): No change.

Nutritional Info: 1 Serving: Calories 390 (Calories from Fat 110); Total Fat 12g (Saturated Fat 6g, Trans Fat 1.5g); Cholesterol 0mg; Sodium 270mg; Total Carbohydrate 66g (Dietary Fiber 1g, Sugars 43g); Protein 4g. % Daily Value: Vitamin A 0%; Vitamin C 2%; Calcium 4%; Iron 6%. Exchanges: 1 Starch, 3 1/2 Other Carbohydrate, 2 Fat. Carbohydrate Choices: 4-1/2.

Betty's Kitchen Tip

• This no-bake idea is great to make with kids. The ski men look cute atop a cake covered with white frosting and coconut.

truffle-filled orange thumbprint cookies

Prep Time: 45 Minutes
Start to Finish: 45 Minutes
Servings: About 2-1/2 dozen cookies

Cookies

3/4	cup butter, softened
1/2	cup sugar
2	egg yolks
1	teaspoon vanilla
1	tablespoon grated orange peel
1-3/4	cups Gold Medal® all-purpose flour
1-1/2	teaspoons baking powder
1/4	teaspoon salt
2	tablespoons sugar

Truffle Filling

1/2	cup dark chocolate chips
2	tablespoons whipping cream
1	tablespoon butter
1	teaspoon light corn syrup

Garnish

Sugared orange peel, if desired

1 Heat oven to 350°F. Spray or lightly grease 2 large cookie sheets.

2 In large bowl, beat 3/4 cup butter with electric mixer on medium speed until fluffy. Beat in 1/2 cup sugar, the egg yolks, vanilla and orange peel until light and fluffy. In medium bowl, mix flour, baking powder and salt until well blended. On low speed, beat flour mixture into butter mixture.

3 Shape dough into 1-1/4-inch balls. Measure 2 tablespoons sugar into small bowl. Dip top of each ball into sugar. On cookie sheets, place balls 2 inches apart. Make large indentation in center of each cookie with thumb or end of wooden spoon or thumb.

4 Bake 12 to 14 minutes or until set. If necessary, make another indentation in center of each cookie with thumb or end of wooden spoon or thumb. Cool 2 minutes; remove from cookie sheets to cooling rack.

5 Meanwhile, in small microwavable bowl, microwave chocolate chips, cream and 1 tablespoon butter uncovered on High 40 seconds; stir. Continue heating and stirring 15 seconds at a time until smooth. Stir in corn syrup. Spoon generous 1/2 teaspoon filling into indentation of each cookie. Top each cookie with piece of sugared orange peel.

High Altitude (3500-6500 ft): Bake 15 to 17 minutes.

Nutritional Info: 1 Cookie: Calories 110 (Calories from Fat 60); Total Fat 7g (Saturated Fat 4g, Trans Fat 0g); Cholesterol 30mg; Sodium 80mg; Total Carbohydrate 12g (Dietary Fiber 0g, Sugars 6g); Protein 1g. % Daily Value: Vitamin A 4%; Vitamin C 0%; Calcium 0%; Iron 2%. Exchanges: 1/2 Other Carbohydrate, 1-1/2 Fat. Carbohydrate Choices: 1.

Betty's Kitchen Tip

• Crank up the orange flavor by gently stirring 1 tablespoon orange-flavored liqueur into filling.

cherry meringue puffs

Prep Time: 1 Hour 20 Minutes
Start to Finish: 2 Hours
Servings: About 5 dozen cookies **LOW FAT**

. . . .

3	egg whites
1	teaspoon white vinegar
1/8	teaspoon salt
3/4	cup sugar
1/2	box (4-serving size) cherry-flavored gelatin (about 3 tablespoons)
1	bag (12 oz) white vanilla baking chips (2 cups)

. . . .

1 In medium bowl, place egg whites; set aside until room temperature, about 30 minutes. Meanwhile, line 2 large cookie sheets with cooking parchment paper or foil; set aside.

2 Heat oven to 300°F. Beat egg whites, vinegar and salt with electric mixer on high speed until soft peaks form. Gradually beat in sugar and gelatin until stiff peaks form, scraping bowl occasionally. Spoon half of the mixture into large decorating bag fitted with large star tip #824 (at least 1/2-inch opening). Pipe puffs about 1 inch wide and 1 inch high onto cookie sheets, about 1 inch apart. Repeat with remaining mixture.

3 Bake 18 to 20 minutes or until dry but not brown. Turn off oven; let stand in oven 15 minutes.

4 In small microwavable bowl, microwave 1-1/3 cups of the baking chips uncovered on High 45 to 60 seconds, stirring after 35 seconds, until melted and smooth. Peel cookies from paper or foil; dip bottoms into melted chocolate, and place on waxed paper. Cool completely, about 20 minutes.

5 Place remaining baking chips in small resealable freezer plastic bag. Microwave on High 45 to 50 seconds, turning bag over after 25 seconds. Squeeze bag until

chips are melted and smooth. Cut small tip off one corner of bag, and drizzle over cooled puffs. Let stand until drizzle hardens, about 10 minutes.

High Altitude (3500-6500 ft): No change.

Nutritional Info: 1 Cookie: Calories 40 (Calories from Fat 15); Total Fat 1.5g (Saturated Fat 1g, Trans Fat 0g); Cholesterol 0mg; Sodium 20mg; Total Carbohydrate 7g (Dietary Fiber 0g, Sugars 7g); Protein 0g. % Daily Value: Vitamin A 0%; Vitamin C 0%; Calcium 0%; Iron 0%. Exchanges: 1/2 Other Carbohydrate. Carbohydrate Choices: 1/2.

Betty's Kitchen Tip

• To change the flavor of these treats, try making them with lemon- or orange-flavored gelatin.

turtle tassies

Prep Time: 1 Hour 40 Minutes
Start to Finish: 1 Hour 40 Minutes
Servings: 48 cookies

1   pouch (17.5 oz) Betty Crocker® sugar
    cookie mix
Butter and egg called for on cookie mix pouch
2   bags (14 oz each) caramels, unwrapped

1/3   cup whipping cream
3/4   cup dark chocolate chips
1/2   cup chopped pecans

1 Heat oven to 375°F. Lightly spray 48 mini muffin cups with cooking spray.

2 Make dough as directed on cookie pouch. Shape dough into 48 (1-inch) balls. Press 1 ball into bottom of each muffin cup, pressing up sides to fill cups.

3 Bake 8 to 9 minutes or until edges begin to brown. Meanwhile, in 3-quart saucepan, heat caramels and cream over medium heat, stirring frequently, until melted. Reduce heat to low.

4 Remove pans from oven; gently press end of wooden spoon into bottoms and against sides of cookie cups to flatten, being careful not to make holes in dough.

5 Bake 2 to 3 minutes longer or until edges are light golden brown. Immediately spoon 1/2 teaspoon (about 4) chocolate chips into each cookie cup.

6 Spoon about 1 tablespoon caramel mixture into each cookie cup. Immediately top with chopped pecans. Cool 5 minutes; remove from pans with narrow spatula.

High Altitude (3500-6500 ft): Heat oven to 350°F.

Nutritional Info: 1 Cookie: Calories 150 (Calories from Fat 60); Total Fat 6g (Saturated Fat 2.5g, Trans Fat 0g); Cholesterol 15mg; Sodium 85mg; Total Carbohydrate 22g (Dietary Fiber 0g, Sugars 14g); Protein 1g. % Daily Value: Vitamin A 0%; Vitamin C 0%; Calcium 2%; Iron 0%. Exchanges: 1/2 Starch, 1 Other Carbohydrate, 1 Fat. Carbohydrate Choices: 1-1/2.

Betty's Kitchen Tips

Do-Ahead: These tasty tassies can be made ahead. Store them in an airtight container in the freezer for up to one month.

Special Touch: For a festive look, roll the unbaked balls in colored sugar.

cinna-spin cookies

Prep Time: 1 Hour 10 Minutes
Start to Finish: 1 Hour 10 Minutes
Servings: 2-1/2 dozen cookies

Cookies

1	pouch (1 lb 1.5 oz) Betty Crocker® sugar cookie mix
1/2	teaspoon ground cinnamon
1/2	cup butter or margarine, softened
1	egg, slightly beaten
1	tablespoon ground cinnamon

Glaze

1	cup powdered sugar
2	tablespoons milk
1/4	teaspoon vanilla

1 Heat oven to 375°F. In large bowl, mix cookie mix and 1/2 teaspoon cinnamon. Stir in butter and egg until soft dough forms.

2 On piece of waxed paper, shape 1 tablespoon cinnamon into a line about 5 inches long. Using floured fingers, shape 1 tablespoon of dough into a rope 5 inches long. Press one side of dough rope into cinnamon.

3 Coil dough rope tightly, cinnamon side facing center, into cinnamon-roll shape. Press end of rope into roll to seal. Repeat with remaining dough. Place cookies 2 inches apart on ungreased cookie sheets.

4 Bake 7 to 10 minutes or until edges are light golden brown. Cool 1 minute; remove from cookie sheets to cooling rack. Cool completely, about 15 minutes.

5 In small bowl, mix glaze ingredients until smooth. Drizzle over cookies.

High Altitude (3500-6500 ft): Decrease butter to 1/3 cup.

Nutritional Info: 1 Cookie: Calories 110 (Calories from Fat 45); Total Fat 5g (Saturated Fat 2.5g, Trans Fat 0.5g); Cholesterol 15mg; Sodium 70mg; Total Carbohydrate 17g (Dietary Fiber 0g, Sugars 11g); Protein 1g. % Daily Value: Vitamin A 2%; Vitamin C 0%; Calcium 0%; Iron 0%. Exchanges: 1 Other Carbohydrate, 1 Fat. Carbohydrate Choices: 1.

Betty's Kitchen Tips

Success Hint: Shiny, smooth-surface or textured aluminum cookie sheets provide the best baking results for cookies.

Prize-Winner: This prize-winning recipe from the 2008 Bake Life Sweeter™ Cookie Mix Recipe Contest is from Lynette Spence of Minnesota.

cinnamon cardinal cookies

Prep Time: 1 Hour
Start to Finish: 1 Hour 50 Minutes
Servings: 4 dozen cookies

LOW FAT

1/2	cup butter, softened	1-1/2	teaspoons ground cinnamon or cardamom
1/2	cup packed light brown sugar	1/3	cup whipping cream
1	teaspoon vanilla	48	miniature chocolate chips
2	cups Gold Medal® all-purpose flour		Red, black and yellow decorator sugar crystals
1/4	teaspoon baking soda		

1 In large bowl, beat butter and brown sugar with electric mixer on medium speed until light and fluffy; stir in vanilla. In small bowl, stir together flour, soda and cinnamon. On low speed, beat flour mixture into butter mixture alternately with cream. Divide dough in half. Wrap halves in plastic wrap. Refrigerate until firm, about 30 minutes.

2 Heat oven to 350°F. Lightly spray or grease 2 large cookie sheets. On lightly floured surface, roll half of dough at a time about 1/8 inch thick. Using 3-inch lightly floured cardinal-shaped cookie cutter, cut out cookies and place on cookie sheets.

3 Place miniature chocolate chip on each for eye. Sprinkle top of back, crown, tail and wing of each bird with red sugar crystals, neck and eye with black sugar crystals, and beak with yellow sugar crystals. Leave bottom breast of bird without sugar.

4 Bake 6 to 8 minutes or until light brown and set.

High Altitude (3500-6500 ft): No change.

Nutritional Info: 1 Cookie: Calories 50 (Calories from Fat 25); Total Fat 2.5g (Saturated Fat 1.5g, Trans Fat 0g); Cholesterol 5mg; Sodium 20mg; Total Carbohydrate 6g (Dietary Fiber 0g, Sugars 2g); Protein 0g. % Daily Value: Vitamin A 0%; Vitamin C 0%; Calcium 0%; Iron 0%. Exchanges: 1/2 Other Carbohydrate, 1/2 Fat. Carbohydrate Choices: 1/2.

Betty's Kitchen Tips

Success Hint: If you don't have a cardinal-shaped cookie cutter, trace the outline of a cardinal from a coloring book, bird book or find one online and cut it out. Use a small paring knife in the dough to cut around outline to form the bird.

How-To: For helpful tips on making cutout cookies, visit bettycrocker.com, click on "How-To" then "Baking Basics" then "Rolled Cookies."

chocolate-cherry tea cookies

Prep Time: 1 Hour 25 Minutes
Start to Finish: 2 Hours 5 Minutes
Servings: About 4 dozen cookies

- 1 cup butter, softened
- 1/2 cup powdered sugar
- 1/2 teaspoon almond extract
- 2 cups Gold Medal® all-purpose flour
- 1/4 teaspoon salt
- 1 cup (8 oz) candied cherries, finely chopped
- 1/2 cup powdered sugar
- 1/2 cup dark chocolate chips

1 Heat oven to 400°F. In large bowl, beat butter with electric mixer on medium speed until fluffy. Gradually beat in 1/2 cup powdered sugar until light and fluffy. Stir in almond extract. In medium bowl, mix flour and salt. On low speed, beat flour mixture into butter mixture until well blended. Stir in cherries.

2 Shape dough into 1-inch balls. On ungreased cookie sheet, place balls 2 inches apart.

3 Bake 9 to 11 minutes or until edges just begin to brown. Cool slightly. Measure 1/2 cup powdered sugar into small bowl. Roll each cookie in powdered sugar. Place on cooling rack to cool completely.

4 Place chocolate chips in small resealable freezer plastic bag. Microwave on High 45 to 60 seconds, turning bag over every 20 seconds. Squeeze bag until chips are melted and smooth. Cut small tip off one corner of bag, and drizzle over cooled cookies. Let stand at room temperature at least 30 minutes until chocolate hardens before storing.

High Altitude (3500-6500 ft): Heat oven to 375°F.

Nutritional Info: 1 Cookie: Calories 90 (Calories from Fat 40); Total Fat 4.5g (Saturated Fat 3g, Trans Fat 0g); Cholesterol 10mg; Sodium 45mg; Total Carbohydrate 11g (Dietary Fiber 0g, Sugars 6g); Protein 0g. % Daily Value: Vitamin A 2%; Vitamin C 0%; Calcium 0%; Iron 0%. Exchanges: 1 Other Carbohydrate, 1 Fat. Carbohydrate Choices: 1.

Betty's Kitchen Tips

Success Hint: To make it easier to chop the cherries, dip knife in water or use a kitchen scissors sprayed with cooking spray.

Time-Saver: Refrigerate cookies 10 minutes to reduce cooling time and set the chocolate faster.

glazed eggnog spritz

Prep Time: 45 Minutes
Start to Finish: 45 Minutes
Servings: About 6 dozen cookies

LOW FAT

Cookies

3/4	cup granulated sugar
1	cup butter or margarine, softened
2	teaspoons vanilla
2	teaspoons rum extract
1	egg
2-1/4	cups Gold Medal® all-purpose flour
1	teaspoon ground nutmeg

Rum Drizzle

2	tablespoons butter or margarine, melted
1	cup powdered sugar
1	teaspoon rum extract
1	tablespoon water
1/2	teaspoon ground nutmeg, if desired

1 Heat oven to 350°F (if using dark or nonstick cookie sheet, heat oven to 325°F). In large bowl, beat granulated sugar and 1 cup butter with electric mixer on medium speed until fluffy. Beat in vanilla, 2 teaspoons rum extract and the egg until smooth. Beat in flour and 1 teaspoon nutmeg.

2 Place 1/4 of the dough at a time in cookie press. On ungreased cookie sheet, form desired shapes with dough.

3 Bake 6 to 10 minutes until edges are lightly browned. Cool 1 minute; remove from cookie sheet to cooling rack.

4 In small bowl, stir all glaze ingredients except nutmeg with spoon until smooth and thin enough to drizzle. Pour mixture into small resealable food-storage plastic bag; cut off tiny corner of bag. Squeeze bag to drizzle glaze on cookies. Before glaze is set, sprinkle 1/2 teaspoon nutmeg over cookies.

High Altitude (3500-6500 ft): No change.

Nutritional Info: 1 Cookie: Calories 60 (Calories from Fat 25); Total Fat 3g (Saturated Fat 2g, Trans Fat 0g); Cholesterol 10mg; Sodium 20mg; Total Carbohydrate 7g (Dietary Fiber 0g, Sugars 4g); Protein 0g. % Daily Value: Vitamin A 0%; Vitamin C 0%; Calcium 0%; Iron 0%. Exchanges: 1/2 Other Carbohydrate, 1/2 Fat. Carbohydrate Choices: 1/2.

Betty's Kitchen Tip

• These cookies will keep in the freezer, tightly wrapped, for six months.

almond-oatmeal crispies

Prep Time: 1 Hour
Start to Finish: 1 Hour
Servings: About 2 dozen cookies

. . . .

Cookies

1/2	cup butter or margarine, softened
1	package (7 or 8 oz) almond paste (not marzipan)
1	egg
1	pouch (1 lb 1.5 oz) Betty Crocker® oatmeal cookie mix
1	tablespoon water
24	unblanched whole almonds

Icing

1/2	cup powdered sugar
1/4	teaspoon almond extract
1	tablespoon water

. . . .

1 Heat oven to 375°F. In large bowl, beat butter and almond paste with electric mixer on medium speed until well blended. Beat in egg until well blended. Stir in cookie mix and 1 tablespoon water until soft dough forms.

2 Using cookie scoop (2-tablespoon size), drop dough by level scoopfuls 2 inches apart onto ungreased cookie sheets. Press 1 almond in center of each mound of dough.

3 Bake 12 to 14 minutes or until edges are light golden brown. Cool 1 minute; remove from cookie sheets to cooling racks. Cool completely, about 15 minutes.

4 In small bowl, mix icing ingredients until smooth. Drizzle icing over cookies.

High Altitude (3500-6500 ft): Bake 10 to 12 minutes.

Nutrition Info: Calories 170 (Calories from Fat 70); Total Fat 8g (Saturated Fat 2.5g, Trans Fat 0g); Cholesterol 20mg; Sodium 110mg; Total Carbohydrate 24g (Dietary Fiber 1g, Sugars 15g); Protein 3g. Exchanges: 1/2 Starch, 1 Other Carbohydrate, 1-1/2 Fat. Carbohydrate Choices: 1-1/2.

Betty's Kitchen Tips

Purchasing: Almond paste comes in a tube or a can. You can use either one in this recipe.

Did You Know? This recipe was one of 15 finalists in the 2008 Bake Life Sweeter™ Cookie Mix Recipe Contest.

café coffee cookies

Prep Time: 1 Hour 10 Minutes
Start to Finish: 1 Hour 20 Minutes
Servings: About 15 cookies

Cookies

1/2	cup granulated sugar
1/2	cup packed brown sugar
1/2	cup butter or margarine, softened
1	egg
1-1/2	cups Gold Medal® all-purpose flour
1	tablespoon instant coffee or instant espresso coffee granules or crystals
1	teaspoon baking soda
1/4	teaspoon salt
1/2	cup chopped pecans
1	bag (11.5 or 12 oz) semisweet chocolate chunks (2 cups)

Coffee Drizzle

1/2	teaspoon instant coffee or instant espresso coffee granules or crystals
1	tablespoon water
1/2	cup powdered sugar

1 Heat oven to 350°F. In large bowl, beat granulated and brown sugars, butter and egg with electric mixer on medium speed until creamy. On low speed, beat in flour, 1 tablespoon coffee granules, the baking soda and salt. Stir in pecans and chocolate chunks.

2 On ungreased large cookie sheets, drop dough by 1/4 cupfuls about 2 inches apart.

3 Bake 12 to 15 minutes or until golden brown and edges are set. Cool 4 minutes; remove from cookie sheets to cooling racks. Cool completely, about 30 minutes.

4 Meanwhile, in small bowl, dissolve 1/2 teaspoon coffee granules in water. Stir in powdered sugar until smooth and thin enough to drizzle. Drizzle over cooled cookies.

High Altitude (3500-6500 ft): Bake 13 to 16 minutes.

Nutritional Info: 1 Cookie: Calories 330 (Calories from Fat 140); Total Fat 16g (Saturated Fat 7g, Trans Fat 0g); Cholesterol 30mg; Sodium 170mg; Total Carbohydrate 42g (Dietary Fiber 2g, Sugars 30g); Protein 3g. % Daily Value: Vitamin A 6%; Vitamin C 0%; Calcium 2%; Iron 8%. Exchanges: 1 Starch, 2 Other Carbohydrate, 3 Fat. Carbohydrate Choices: 3.

Betty's Kitchen Tips

Special Touch: Sprinkle cookies with additional chopped pecans just after drizzling.

Storage: Allow coffee drizzle to set before storing cookies between layers of waxed paper, plastic wrap or foil.

chocolate spritz reindeer

Prep Time: 1 Hour
Start to Finish: 1 Hour 15 Minutes
Servings: 5 dozen cookies

1	cup butter, softened
1/2	cup powdered sugar
1/2	cup packed brown sugar
1/4	cup unsweetened baking cocoa
3	tablespoons milk
1	teaspoon vanilla
1	egg yolk
2	cups Gold Medal® all-purpose flour
60	large pretzel twists
120	miniature candy-coated chocolate baking bits
60	semisweet chocolate chips

1 Heat oven to 375°F. In large bowl, beat butter with electric mixer on medium speed until light and fluffy. Beat in sugars and cocoa until well blended. Beat in milk, vanilla and egg yolk. On low speed, slowly beat in flour until well blended, scraping bowl occasionally.

2 Fit heart template in cookie press; fill cookie press with dough. Place pretzels onto lightly floured surface. Force dough through template on top of flat, bottom end of each pretzel twist (two rounds at top of pretzel will form the antlers). Press 2 baking bits at upper part of heart to make eyes, and 1 chocolate chip to make nose on each reindeer. Place reindeer on ungreased cookie sheet.

3 Bake 8 to 10 minutes or until cookies are firm, but not browned. Remove from pans to cooling rack. Cool completely, about 15 minutes.

High Altitude (3500-6500 ft): No change.

Nutritional Info: 1 Cookie: Calories 130 (Calories from Fat 40); Total Fat 4.5g (Saturated Fat 2.5g, Trans Fat 0g); Cholesterol 10mg; Sodium 240mg; Total Carbohydrate 21g (Dietary Fiber 1g, Sugars 5g); Protein 2g. % Daily Value: Vitamin A 2%; Vitamin C 0%; Calcium 0%; Iron 6%. Exchanges: 1/2 Starch, 1 Other Carbohydrate, 1 Fat. Carbohydrate Choices: 1-1/2.

Betty's Kitchen Tips

Success Hint: If you don't have a cookie press, shape dough into 1-1/4-inch balls. Press 1 ball over bottom of 1 pretzel, pinching bottom in to form nose.

Did You Know? These cookies get their name from the word "spritzen," which is German for "to squirt or spray."

baked hazelnut truffles

Prep Time: 1 Hour
Start to Finish: 2 Hours
Servings: 3-1/2 dozen cookies

4 oz semisweet baking chocolate	1/2 cup chopped hazelnuts (filberts)
1/4 cup butter or margarine	About 40 milk chocolate stars
1 can (14 oz) sweetened condensed milk (not evaporated)	1/2 cup white vanilla baking chips
2 tablespoons hazelnut liqueur	1 teaspoon vegetable oil
2-1/2 cups Gold Medal® all-purpose flour	Candy sprinkles or coarse white sparkling sugar, if desired

1 Heat oven to 350°F. In large microwavable bowl, microwave baking chocolate and butter uncovered on Medium (50%) 2 to 3 minutes, stirring once, until softened. Stir in condensed milk, liqueur, flour and hazelnuts. Cover and refrigerate until firm, about 30 minutes.

2 Shape dough by tablespoonfuls around each chocolate star. On ungreased cookie sheet, place 1 inch apart.

3 Bake 7 to 8 minutes or until dough is shiny and set but still soft. Cool 5 minutes; remove from cookie sheet to cooling rack. Cool about 30 minutes.

4 In small microwavable bowl, microwave white vanilla baking chips and oil uncovered on Medium (50%) 1 minute to 1 minute 15 seconds, stirring once, until softened. Stir until smooth. Dip top of each cookie into melted mixture; immediately top each with candy sprinkles while mixture is still soft. Let stand until coating is set.

High Altitude (3500-6500 ft): Bake 9 to 10 minutes.

Nutritional Info: 1 Cookie: Calories 100 (Calories from Fat 45); Total Fat 5g (Saturated Fat 2.5g, Trans Fat 0g); Cholesterol 0mg; Sodium 20mg; Total Carbohydrate 13g (Dietary Fiber 0g, Sugars 6g); Protein 1g. % Daily Value: Vitamin A 0%; Vitamin C 0%; Calcium 2%; Iron 4%. Exchanges: 1 Other Carbohydrate, 1 Fat. Carbohydrate Choices: 1.

Betty's Kitchen Tips

Special Touch: For a gift, tuck single cookies in small tissue-lined holiday boxes.

Did You Know? Frangelico is one brand of hazelnut liqueur.

double-chocolate cherry cookies

Prep Time: 1 Hour
Start to Finish: 1 Hour
Servings: 4 dozen cookies

• •

1-1/4   cups sugar
1   cup butter or margarine, softened
1/4   cup milk
1/4   teaspoon almond extract
1   egg
1-3/4   cups Gold Medal® all-purpose flour
1   cup quick-cooking oats
1/3   cup unsweetened baking cocoa
1/2   teaspoon baking soda
1   cup semisweet chocolate chips (6 oz)
1   cup dried cherries

• •

1 Heat oven to 350°F. In large bowl, beat sugar, butter, milk, almond extract and egg with electric mixer on medium speed until smooth. On low speed, beat in flour, oats, cocoa and baking soda. Stir in chocolate chips and cherries.

2 Onto ungreased cookie sheets, drop dough by rounded tablespoonfuls about 2 inches apart.

3 Bake 10 to 12 minutes or until almost no indentation remains when touched in center and surface is no longer shiny. Immediately remove from cookie sheets to cooling racks.

High Altitude (3500-6500 ft): No change.

Nutritional Info: 1 Cookie: Calories 110 (Calories from Fat 45); Total Fat 5g (Saturated Fat 3g, Trans Fat 0g); Cholesterol 15mg; Sodium 45mg; Total Carbohydrate 15g (Dietary Fiber 0g, Sugars 9g); Protein 1g. % Daily Value: Vitamin A 4%; Vitamin C 0%; Calcium 0%; Iron 2%. Exchanges: 1/2 Starch, 1/2 Other Carbohydrate, 1 Fat. Carbohydrate Choices: 1.

Betty's Kitchen Tips

Variation: Try using 1 teaspoon vanilla instead of the almond extract.

Success Hint: To make all the cookies similar in size, use a spring-handled ice cream scoop to drop the dough onto the cookie sheet.

maple-nut biscotti

Prep Time: 30 Minutes
Start to Finish: 1 Hour 45 Minutes
Servings: 2-1/2 dozen cookies

1/2 cup packed brown sugar	2 teaspoons baking powder
1/4 cup granulated sugar	3/4 cup chopped walnuts
1/2 cup butter or margarine, softened	1 teaspoon vegetable oil
1 teaspoon maple flavor	4 oz vanilla-flavored candy coating (almond bark), melted
3 eggs	
3 cups Gold Medal® all-purpose flour	

1 Heat oven to 350°F. Lightly grease cookie sheet with shortening or cooking spray.

2 In large bowl, beat sugars and butter with electric mixer on medium speed about 3 minutes or until creamy. Beat in maple flavor and eggs. Stir in flour and baking powder. Stir in walnuts. Divide dough in half. Shape each half into 10-inch roll. Place rolls 5 inches apart on cookie sheet; flatten to 3-inch width.

3 Bake 20 to 30 minutes or until set and edges begin to brown. Remove from cookie sheet to cooling rack. Cool 10 minutes. With serrated knife, cut rolls diagonally into 1/2-inch slices. Place slices cut side down on ungreased cookie sheets.

4 Bake 5 to 10 minutes or until lightly browned and dry. Turn cookies over; bake 5 to 8 minutes longer or until lightly browned and dry. Remove from cookie sheets to cooling racks. Cool completely, about 15 minutes.

5 Stir oil into melted candy coating; drizzle over biscotti. Let stand until coating is dry. Store in tightly covered container.

High Altitude (3500-6500 ft): Decrease baking powder to 1-1/2 teaspoons.

Nutritional Info: 1 Cookie: Calories 150 (Calories from Fat 60); Total Fat 7g (Saturated Fat 2.5g, Trans Fat 0g); Cholesterol 30mg; Sodium 65mg; Total Carbohydrate 19g (Dietary Fiber 0g, Sugars 9g); Protein 3g. % Daily Value: Vitamin A 2%; Vitamin C 0%; Calcium 4%; Iron 4%. Exchanges: 1 Starch, 1-1/2 Fat. Carbohydrate Choices: 1.

Betty's Kitchen Tips

Variation: Instead of drizzling the biscotti, dip one end into the melted candy coating.

Serve-With: These dunkable cookies are great with a cup of hot apple cider or cinnamon-spiced tea.

chai-spiced almond celebration cookies

Prep Time: 1 Hour 25 Minutes
Start to Finish: 1 Hour 25 Minutes
Servings: 3 dozen cookies

- -

1   pouch (1 lb 1.5 oz) Betty Crocker® sugar cookie mix
3/4 cup finely chopped toasted almonds
3/4 teaspoon ground allspice
3/4 teaspoon ground cardamom
1/2 teaspoon ground cinnamon
1/2 cup butter or margarine, softened
1   teaspoon vanilla
1/2 teaspoon almond extract
1   cup powdered sugar

- -

1 Heat oven to 350°F. In large bowl, stir together cookie mix, almonds, allspice, cardamom and cinnamon. Stir in butter, vanilla and almond extract until soft dough forms.

2 Shape level tablespoonfuls of dough into balls. On ungreased cookie sheets, place balls 2 inches apart.

3 Bake 12 to 14 minutes or until set. Cool 5 minutes; remove from cookie sheets to cooling rack.

4 Place powdered sugar in shallow bowl. Gently roll warm cookies in powdered sugar to coat; place on cooling rack. Cool completely, about 15 minutes. Roll in sugar again.

High Altitude (3500-6500 ft): No change.

Nutritional Info: 1 Cookie: Calories 110 (Calories from Fat 45); Total Fat 5g (Saturated Fat 2g, Trans Fat 0.5g); Cholesterol 5mg; Sodium 60mg; Total Carbohydrate 14g (Dietary Fiber 0g, Sugars 9g); Protein 1g. % Daily Value: Vitamin A 0%; Vitamin C 0%; Calcium 0%; Iron 0%. Exchanges: 1 Other Carbohydrate, 1 Fat. Carbohydrate Choices: 1.

Betty's Kitchen Tips

How-To: To toast nuts, heat oven to 350°F. Spread nuts in ungreased shallow pan. Bake uncovered 6 to 10 minutes, stirring occasionally, until light brown.

Did You Know? Chai spices add a new twist to an old favorite, Mexican Wedding Cakes.

Prize-Winner: This recipe was one of 15 finalists in the 2008 Bake Life Sweeter™ Cookie Mix Recipe Contest. It's from Lori Welander of Virginia.

gingerbread cookies with royal icing

Prep Time: 1 Hour 40 Minutes
Start to Finish: 3 Hours 40 Minutes
Servings: 5 dozen cookies

LOW FAT

Cookies

- 1/2 cup butter or margarine, softened
- 1/2 cup packed brown sugar
- 1/2 cup mild-flavor or full-flavor molasses
- 1/3 cup cold water
- 3-1/2 cups Gold Medal® all-purpose flour
- 2 teaspoons baking soda
- 2 teaspoons ground ginger
- 1/2 teaspoon ground allspice
- 1/2 teaspoon ground cinnamon
- 1/4 teaspoon salt
- 1/4 teaspoon ground cloves

Royal Icing

- 1 tablespoon meringue powder
- 2 tablespoons cold water
- 1 cup powdered sugar

Granulated sugar, if desired

1 In large bowl, beat butter, brown sugar, molasses and cold water with electric mixer on medium speed (or with wooden spoon) until well mixed. Mixture may look curdled. With wooden spoon, stir in remaining cookie ingredients until soft dough forms. Wrap with plastic wrap; refrigerate until firm, at least 2 hours.

2 Heat oven to 350°F. Lightly spray cookie sheets with cooking spray. On floured surface, roll dough 1/8 inch thick.

3 Cut dough with floured 3-1/2- by 2-1/2-inch gingerbread boy or girl cookie cutter or other cookie cutter. Place on cookie sheets 2 inches apart. Reroll dough, and cut additional cookies.

4 Bake 10 to 12 minutes or until no indentation remains when touched. Immediately remove from cookie sheets to cooling rack. Cool cookie sheets 10 minutes between batches. Cool cookies completely, about 30 minutes.

5 In medium bowl, beat meringue powder and cold water with electric mixer on medium speed until peaks form. Gradually beat in powdered sugar until soft peaks form, about 1 minute. Spoon icing into decorating bag fitted with medium round tip, and pipe over cookies. Sprinkle with sugar. Let stand about 5 minutes or until icing is set.

High Altitude (3500-6500 ft): Bake 8 to 10 minutes.

Nutritional Info: 1 Cookie: Calories 60 (Calories from Fat 15); Total Fat 1.5g (Saturated Fat 1g, Trans Fat 0g); Cholesterol 0mg; Sodium 65mg; Total Carbohydrate 12g (Dietary Fiber 0g, Sugars 5g); Protein 0g. % Daily Value: Vitamin A 0%; Vitamin C 0%; Calcium 0%; Iron 2%. Exchanges: 1 Other Carbohydrate. Carbohydrate Choices: 1.

Betty's Kitchen Tip

- Look for meringue powder in the baking aisle of the grocery store.

coconut-fudge cups

Prep Time: 25 Minutes
Start to Finish: 50 Minutes
Servings: 24 cookies

Cookies

1/4	cup butter or margarine, softened
1	package (3 oz) cream cheese, softened
3/4	cup Gold Medal® all-purpose flour
1/4	cup powdered sugar
2	tablespoons unsweetened baking cocoa
1/2	teaspoon vanilla

Coconut-Fudge Filling

2/3	cup granulated sugar
2/3	cup flaked coconut

1/3	cup unsweetened baking cocoa
2	tablespoons butter or margarine, softened
1	egg

Garnish, if desired

1/4	cup semisweet chocolate chips
2	teaspoons whipping cream
1/2	cup flaked coconut
1	drop red food color
1	drop green food color

1 Heat oven to 350°F. In large bowl, beat butter and cream cheese with electric mixer on medium speed, or mix with spoon. Stir in remaining cookie ingredients.

2 Shape dough into 24 (1-inch) balls. Press 1 ball into bottom and up side of each of 24 ungreased mini muffin cups, 1-3/4x1 inch. Mix filling ingredients until spreadable. Spoon about 2 teaspoons filling into each cup.

3 Bake 18 to 20 minutes or until almost no indentation remains when filling is touched lightly. Cool slightly; carefully remove from muffin cups to cooling rack.

4 In 1-cup microwavable measuring cup, microwave chocolate chips and whipping cream on High 30 seconds; stir until smooth. Microwave 15 seconds longer if necessary to melt chips. Frost tops of fudge cups with chocolate.

5 In small resealable food-storage plastic bag, toss 1/4 cup coconut with red food color. In another small bag, toss remaining 1/4 cup coconut with green food color. Garnish each fudge cup with red or green coconut.

High Altitude (3500-6500 ft): Bake 19 to 21 minutes.

Nutritional Info: 1 Cookie: Calories 100 (Calories from Fat 50); Total Fat 5g (Saturated Fat 3.5g, Trans Fat 0g); Cholesterol 20mg; Sodium 40mg; Total Carbohydrate 12g (Dietary Fiber 0g, Sugars 8g); Protein 1g. % Daily Value: Vitamin A 2%; Vitamin C 0%; Calcium 0%; Iron 2%. Exchanges: 1 Other Carbohydrate, 1 Fat. Carbohydrate Choices: 1.

Betty's Kitchen Tip

• Replace the coconut in the filling with 2/3 cup chopped nuts to make a fudge-nut filling. Garnish with nuts, if desired.

raspberry poinsettia blossoms

Prep Time: 25 Minutes
Start to Finish: 1 Hour 50 Minutes
Servings: 3 dozen cookies

- 3/4 cup butter or margarine, softened
- 1/2 cup sugar
- 1 teaspoon vanilla
- 1 box (4-serving size) raspberry-flavored gelatin
- 1 egg
- 2 cups Gold Medal® all-purpose flour
- 2 tablespoons yellow candy sprinkles

1. In large bowl, beat butter, sugar, vanilla, gelatin and egg with electric mixer on medium speed, or mix with spoon. On low speed, beat in flour.

2. Shape dough into 1-1/4-inch balls. Cover and refrigerate 1 hour.

3. Heat oven to 375°F. On ungreased cookie sheets, place balls about 2 inches apart. With sharp knife, make 6 cuts in top of each ball about three-fourths of the way through to make 6 wedges. Spread wedges apart slightly to form flower petals (cookies will separate and flatten as they bake). Sprinkle about 1/8 teaspoon yellow candy sprinkles into center of each cookie.

4. Bake 9 to 11 minutes or until set and edges begin to brown. Cool 2 to 3 minutes. Remove from cookie sheets to cooling rack. Cool completely, about 15 minutes.

High Altitude (3500-6500 ft): No change.

Nutritional Info: 1 Cookie: Calories 90 (Calories from Fat 40); Total Fat 4g (Saturated Fat 2.5g, Trans Fat 0g); Cholesterol 15mg; Sodium 40mg; Total Carbohydrate 11g (Dietary Fiber 0g, Sugars 5g); Protein 1g. % Daily Value: Vitamin A 2%; Vitamin C 0%; Calcium 0%; Iron 0%. Exchanges: 1 Other Carbohydrate, 1 Fat. Carbohydrate Choices: 1.

Betty's Kitchen Tips

Special Touch: During the holidays, time can be the greatest gift. Why not get together with a few friends and host a cookie exchange? This is a great recipe to share.

Variation: For a flavor twist, use strawberry-, cranberry- or cherry-flavored gelatin instead of the raspberry.

sparkling lemon snowflakes

Prep Time: 50 Minutes
Start to Finish: 1 Hour 40 Minutes
Servings: 6 dozen cookies

LOW FAT

Cookies

3/4	cup butter, softened
3/4	cup granulated sugar
2	teaspoons grated lemon peel
1	egg
2-1/4	cups Gold Medal® all-purpose flour

1/4	teaspoon salt

Glaze

2	cups powdered sugar
2	tablespoons lemon juice
2	tablespoons water
1/4	cup coarse white sparkling sugar

1 In large bowl, beat butter and granulated sugar with electric mixer on medium speed until light and fluffy. Add lemon peel and egg; beat until well blended. On low speed, gradually beat in flour and salt until well blended.

2 Heat oven to 350°F. On floured surface, roll dough 1/8 inch thick. Cut with lightly floured 2-1/2- to 3-inch snowflake-shaped cookie cutter. On ungreased cookie sheets, place 2 inches apart.

3 Bake 8 to 10 minutes or until cookies just begin to brown. Remove from cookie sheets to cooling racks. Cool completely, about 10 minutes.

4 In small bowl, mix powdered sugar, lemon juice and water. Using small metal spatula, spread glaze on tops of cookies; sprinkle with sparkling sugar. When glaze is dry, store in airtight container.

High Altitude (3500-6500 ft): Bake 9 to 11 minutes.

Nutritional Info: 1 Cookie: Calories 60 (Calories from Fat 20); Total Fat 2g (Saturated Fat 1g, Trans Fat 0g); Cholesterol 10mg; Sodium 25mg; Total Carbohydrate 9g (Dietary Fiber 0g, Sugars 6g); Protein 0g. % Daily Value: Vitamin A 0%; Vitamin C 0%; Calcium 0%; Iron 0%. Exchanges: 1/2 Other Carbohydrate, 1/2 Fat. Carbohydrate Choices: 1/2.

Betty's Kitchen Tips

Success Hint: If you don't have a snowflake-shaped cookie cutter, you can use either a star-shaped or scalloped-edge cutter, and cut small triangles and pieces out of the center to form snowflakes.

Purchasing: Look for coarse sugar in the baking aisle of the supermarket or in the cake-decorating aisle at craft stores.

ginger-almond biscotti

Prep Time: 30 Minutes
Start to Finish: 1 Hour 25 Minutes
Servings: 34 cookies

- -

1/2	cup butter or margarine, melted
1	teaspoon grated orange peel
1/4	cup fresh orange juice
2	eggs
1	pouch (1 lb 1.5 oz) Betty Crocker® sugar cookie mix
1	cup Gold Medal® all-purpose flour
1/2	cup slivered almonds
1/2	cup white vanilla baking chips
1/4	cup finely chopped crystallized ginger

- -

1 Heat oven to 350°F. In large bowl, beat melted butter, orange peel, orange juice and eggs with wire whisk. Stir in remaining ingredients until soft dough forms.

2 Divide dough in half. Shape each half into 12x2-inch roll. On ungreased cookie sheet, place rolls 5 inches apart.

3 Bake 25 to 30 minutes or until edges are golden brown. Cool on cookie sheet 10 minutes. Place rolls on cutting board. Cut crosswise into 3/4-inch slices. Place slices cut sides down on ungreased cookie sheets.

4 Bake 15 minutes. Immediately remove from cookie sheets to cooling racks. Cool completely. Store loosely covered.

High Altitude (3500-6500 ft): Increase flour in dough to 1-1/4 cups, and add up to 1/4 cup additional flour as needed when shaping dough into rolls.

Nutritional Info: 1 Cookie: Calories 140 (Calories from Fat 60); Total Fat 6g (Saturated Fat 3g, Trans Fat 0.5g); Cholesterol 20mg; Sodium 65mg; Total Carbohydrate 18g (Dietary Fiber 0g, Sugars 10g); Protein 2g. % Daily Value: Vitamin A 2%; Vitamin C 0%; Calcium 0%; Iron 2%. Exchanges: 1/2 Starch, 1/2 Other Carbohydrate, 1-1/2 Fat. Carbohydrate Choices: 1.

Betty's Kitchen Tips

Did You Know? This recipe was one of 15 finalists in the 2006 Mix It Up with Betty! Cookie Mix Recipe Contest.

Success Hint: You'll need one medium juice orange, like a Valencia, to get enough juice and peel for this recipe.

peppermint swirls

Prep Time: 1 Hour
Start to Finish: 1 Hour
Servings: 4 dozen cookies

1	cup butter or margarine, softened		1/2	teaspoon peppermint extract
1/3	cup powdered sugar		1/4	teaspoon red food color
1	teaspoon vanilla		2	tablespoons granulated sugar
2	cups Gold Medal® all-purpose flour			

1 Heat oven to 350°F. In large bowl, beat butter, powdered sugar and vanilla with electric mixer on medium speed, or mix with spoon. Stir in flour. Divide dough in half. Stir peppermint extract and food color into 1 half of dough. Divide each color of dough in half.

2 On surface generously sprinkled with flour, shape each piece of dough into rope 12 inches long. Place 2 ropes, 1 red and 1 white, side by side. Twist ropes. Repeat with remaining 2 pieces of dough.

3 Cut twisted ropes into 1/2-inch pieces; shape each into ball. On ungreased cookie sheet, place balls about 1 inch apart. Flatten to about 1/4-inch thickness with greased bottom of glass dipped in granulated sugar.

4 Bake 7 to 9 minutes or until set. Remove from cookie sheet to cooling rack; cool.

High Altitude (3500-6500 ft): No change.

Nutritional Info: 1 Cookie: Calories 60 (Calories from Fat 35); Total Fat 4g (Saturated Fat 2.5g, Trans Fat 0g); Cholesterol 10mg; Sodium 25mg; Total Carbohydrate 5g (Dietary Fiber 0g, Sugars 1g); Protein 0g. % Daily Value: Vitamin A 2%; Vitamin C 0%; Calcium 0%; Iron 0%. Exchanges: 1/2 Other Carbohydrate, 1 Fat. Carbohydrate Choices: 1/2.

Betty's Kitchen Tip

• For a fun change of color, tint 1 half of the dough green instead of red. Or tint 1 half red and 1 half green.

CANDIES&BARS

p. 298

304

318

320

pumpkin streusel cheesecake bars

Prep Time: 45 Minutes
Start to Finish: 3 Hours
Servings: 24 bars

Cookie Crust

- 1   pouch (1 lb 1.5 oz) Betty Crocker® oatmeal cookie mix
- 1/2 cup crushed gingersnap cookies
- 1/2 cup finely chopped pecans
- 1/2 cup cold butter or margarine

Filling

- 2   packages (8 oz each) cream cheese, softened
- 1   cup sugar
- 1   cup canned pumpkin (not pumpkin pie mix)
- 2   tablespoons Gold Medal® all-purpose flour
- 1   tablespoon pumpkin pie spice
- 2   tablespoons whipping cream
- 2   eggs

Topping

- 1/3 cup chocolate topping
- 1/3 cup caramel topping

1 Heat oven to 350°F. In large bowl, stir together cookie mix, crushed cookies and pecans. Cut in butter, using pastry blender or fork, until mixture is crumbly. Reserve 1 cup mixture for topping. Press remaining mixture in bottom of ungreased 13x9-inch pan. Bake 10 minutes. Cool 10 minutes.

2 Meanwhile, in large bowl, beat cream cheese and sugar with electric mixer on medium speed until smooth. Add remaining filling ingredients; beat until well blended. Pour over warm cookie crust. Sprinkle with reserved topping.

3 Bake 35 to 40 minutes or until center is set. Cool 30 minutes. Refrigerate about 2 hours or until chilled.

4 Before serving, drizzle with chocolate and caramel toppings. For bars, cut into 6 rows by 4 rows. Store covered in refrigerator.

High Altitude (3500-6500 ft): Bake 40 to 45 minutes.

Nutritional Info: 1 Bar: Calories 280 (Calories from Fat 130); Total Fat 14g (Saturated Fat 7g, Trans Fat 0g); Cholesterol 50mg; Sodium 200mg; Total Carbohydrate 35g (Dietary Fiber 1g, Sugars 22g); Protein 4g. % Daily Value: Vitamin A 40%; Vitamin C 0%; Calcium 4%; Iron 6%. Exchanges: 1 Starch, 1-1/2 Other Carbohydrate, 2-1/2 Fat. Carbohydrate Choices: 2.

Betty's Kitchen Tip

• A food processor can be used for even easier preparation. Place cookie crust ingredients in processor bowl; pulse until crumbly. Reserve 1 cup for topping. Press remaining cookie crust mixture in pan. Place filling ingredients in processor bowl; pulse until well blended. Continue recipe as directed.

chocolate-peppermint creams

Prep Time: 45 Minutes
Start to Finish: 1 Hour
Servings: 75 pieces

- 1 bag (12 oz) semisweet chocolate chips (2 cups)
- 1 bag (12 oz) dark chocolate chips (2 cups)
- 1/3 cup whipping cream
- 1 cup butter
- 1/4 cup dry pudding mix from 1 box (4-serving size) vanilla pudding and pie filling mix (not instant)
- 1/2 cup whipping cream
- 1/2 teaspoon peppermint extract
- 1/2 teaspoon vanilla
- 1 bag (2 lb) powdered sugar
- 1/2 cup coarsely chopped peppermint candy canes

1 Spray 15x10x1-inch pan with cooking spray. Reserve 1/2 cup of the semisweet chocolate chips. In 2-quart saucepan, heat remaining semisweet chocolate chips, the dark chocolate chips and 1/3 cup cream over medium-low heat, stirring constantly, until melted. Pour into pan; spread evenly. Refrigerate.

2 Meanwhile, in 3-quart saucepan, heat butter, pudding mix and 1/2 cup cream to boiling over medium heat, stirring constantly. Remove from heat; stir in peppermint extract, vanilla and powdered sugar, beating well, until mixture is smooth. Spread evenly over cooled chocolate layer; freeze until firm, 15 to 20 minutes.

3 Place reserved 1/2 cup chocolate chips in small resealable freezer plastic bag. Microwave on High 45 to 55 seconds, turning bag over after 30 seconds. Squeeze bag until chips are melted and smooth. Cut small tip off one corner of bag, and drizzle over top. Immediately sprinkle with chopped candy. Cut into 15 rows by 5 rows.

High Altitude (3500-6500 ft): No change.

Nutritional Info: 1 Piece: Calories 140 (Calories from Fat 50); Total Fat 6g (Saturated Fat 3.5g, Trans Fat 0g); Cholesterol 10mg; Sodium 25mg; Total Carbohydrate 21g (Dietary Fiber 0g, Sugars 19g); Protein 0g. % Daily Value: Vitamin A 2%; Vitamin C 0%; Calcium 0%; Iron 0%. Exchanges: 1-1/2 Other Carbohydrate, 1 Fat. Carbohydrate Choices: 1-1/2.

Betty's Kitchen Tips

Kitchen Tips: To easily crush peppermint candies, place them in a resealable plastic freezer bag, seal the bag, and pound with a rolling pin or meat mallet.

Special Touch: Use red and green colored peppermint candy canes for special color during the holidays. If candy canes are not available, use round peppermint candies.

oatmeal brownies

Prep Time: 25 Minutes
Start to Finish: 3 Hours 10 Minutes
Servings: 48 brownies

Crust and Topping

2-1/2	cups quick-cooking or old-fashioned oats
3/4	cup Gold Medal® all-purpose flour
3/4	cup packed brown sugar
1/2	teaspoon baking soda
3/4	cup butter or margarine, melted

Filling

4	oz unsweetened baking chocolate
2/3	cup butter or margarine
2	cups granulated sugar
1	teaspoon vanilla
4	eggs
1-1/4	cups Gold Medal® all-purpose flour
1	teaspoon baking powder
1	teaspoon salt

1 Heat oven to 350°F. Spray bottom and sides of 13x9-inch pan with cooking spray.

2 In large bowl, mix oats, 3/4 cup flour, the brown sugar and baking soda. Stir in melted 3/4 cup butter. Reserve 3/4 cup oat mixture for topping. Press remaining oat mixture in pan. Bake 10 minutes. Cool 5 minutes.

3 Meanwhile, in 3-quart saucepan, heat chocolate and 2/3 cup butter over low heat, stirring occasionally, until melted; remove from heat. Stir in granulated sugar, vanilla and eggs. Stir in 1-1/4 cups flour, the baking powder and salt.

4 Spread filling over baked crust. Sprinkle with reserved oat mixture. Bake about 30 minutes longer or until center is set and oat mixture turns golden brown (do not overbake). Cool completely, about 2 hours. Cut into 8 rows by 6 rows.

High Altitude (3500-6500 ft): In filling, decrease 2/3 cup butter to 1/2 cup and baking powder to 3/4 teaspoon. In step 2, bake 13 minutes. In step 4, bake 33 minutes.

Nutritional Info: 1 Brownie: Calories 150 (Calories from Fat 70); Total Fat 7g (Saturated Fat 4.5g, Trans Fat 0g); Cholesterol 30mg; Sodium 120mg; Total Carbohydrate 19g (Dietary Fiber 1g, Sugars 12g); Protein 2g. % Daily Value: Vitamin A 4%; Vitamin C 0%; Calcium 0%; Iron 6%. Exchanges: 1-1/2 Other Carbohydrate, 1-1/2 Fat. Carbohydrate Choices: 1.

Betty's Kitchen Tips

Did You Know? Unsweetened baking chocolate is bitter in flavor and used primarily in baking.

Storage: To keep brownies longer, wrap tightly, label and freeze up to 6 months.

holiday eggnog bars

Prep Time: 15 Minutes
Start to Finish: 2 Hours 5 Minutes
Servings: 36 bars

EASY

1/2	cup butter, softened
1/2	cup sugar
1	cup Gold Medal® all-purpose flour
5	egg yolks
1/4	cup sugar
1-1/4	cups whipping cream
1	tablespoon rum or 1 teaspoon rum extract
1/4	teaspoon ground nutmeg
1/2	teaspoon ground nutmeg

1 Heat oven to 350°F. Line bottom and sides of 9-inch square pan with foil, leaving 1 inch of foil overhanging at 2 opposite sides of pan. In small bowl, stir together butter, 1/2 cup sugar and the flour. Press in bottom and 1/2 inch up sides of foil-lined pan. Bake 20 minutes.

2 Reduce oven temperature to 300°F. In small bowl, beat egg yolks and 1/4 cup sugar with electric mixer on medium-high speed until thick. Gradually beat in cream, rum and 1/4 teaspoon nutmeg. Pour over baked layer.

3 Bake 40 to 50 minutes at 300°F until custard is set and knife inserted in center comes out clean. Cool completely, about 1 hour.

4 Sprinkle tops of bars evenly with 1/2 teaspoon nutmeg. Using foil handles, lift cooled bars from pan to cutting board; remove foil from sides of bars. With sharp knife, cut into 6 rows by 6 rows. Cover; store in refrigerator.

High Altitude (3500-6500 ft): In step 2, reduce oven temperature to 325°F; in step 3, bake at 325°F.

Nutritional Info: 1 Bar: Calories 80 (Calories from Fat 50); Total Fat 6g (Saturated Fat 3.5g, Trans Fat 0g); Cholesterol 45mg; Sodium 20mg; Total Carbohydrate 7g (Dietary Fiber 0g, Sugars 4g); Protein 1g. % Daily Value: Vitamin A 4%; Vitamin C 0%; Calcium 0%; Iron 0%. Exchanges: 1 Starch, 2 Fat. Carbohydrate Choices: 1/2.

Betty's Kitchen Tips

Special Touch: Don't like to drink plain eggnog but like the flavor? Then you are sure to love these squares for a holiday dessert.

How-To: Use an egg separator to easily separate the yolk from the egg white.

salty nutty peanut bars

Prep Time: 30 Minutes
Start to Finish: 2 Hours 10 Minutes
Servings: 60 bars

- -

Cookie Crust

1   pouch (1 lb 1.5 oz) Betty Crocker® peanut butter cookie mix
3   tablespoons vegetable oil
1   tablespoon water
1   egg
2   cups dry-roasted or honey-roasted peanuts

Topping

1   bag (10 oz) miniature marshmallows
1/2   cup butter or margarine
1/2   cup peanut butter
1   can (14 oz) sweetened condensed milk (not evaporated)
1   bag (10 oz) peanut butter chips (1-2/3 cups)
2   cups dry-roasted or honey-roasted peanuts

- -

1 Heat oven to 350°F. Spray bottom and sides of 13x9-inch pan with cooking spray.

2 In large bowl, stir all cookie crust ingredients except peanuts until soft dough forms. Press dough in bottom of pan. Sprinkle evenly with 2 cups peanuts; press lightly into dough. Bake 12 to 15 minutes until light golden brown. Cool 30 minutes.

3 In 3-quart saucepan, heat marshmallows and butter over medium-low heat, stirring frequently, until melted. Stir in peanut butter, milk and peanut butter chips until smooth.

4 Immediately pour marshmallow mixture over cookie crust; spread evenly. Sprinkle evenly with 2 cups peanuts; press gently into marshmallow mixture. Refrigerate about 1 hour or until firm. For bars, cut into 10 rows by 6 rows. Store covered in refrigerator.

High Altitude (3500-6500 ft): No change.

Nutritional Info: 1 Bar: Calories 190 (Calories from Fat 100); Total Fat 11g (Saturated Fat 3g, Trans Fat 0g); Cholesterol 10mg; Sodium 150mg; Total Carbohydrate 19g (Dietary Fiber 1g, Sugars 12g); Protein 4g. % Daily Value: Vitamin A 0%; Vitamin C 0%; Calcium 2%; Iron 2%. Exchanges: 1 Starch, 1/2 Other Carbohydrate, 2 Fat. Carbohydrate Choices: 1.

Betty's Kitchen Tips

Success Hint: Skip the cooking spray, and instead line the pan with quick-release foil for easy cleanup and removal of bars from the pan.

Special Touch: Serve bars in mini paper or metallic cups for a dessert buffet.

dark chocolate-hazelnut truffles

Prep Time: 30 Minutes
Start to Finish: 2 Hours 40 Minutes
Servings: 3 dozen truffles

4	oz bittersweet baking chocolate, chopped
4	oz semisweet baking chocolate, chopped
1/4	cup whipping cream
5	tablespoons cold butter, cut into pieces
2	tablespoons hazelnut liqueur
4	oz (about 1 cup) hazelnuts (filberts)

1 In 1-quart heavy saucepan, heat both chocolates and whipping cream over low heat, stirring constantly, until chocolate is melted and smooth. Remove from heat. Stir in butter, a few pieces at a time. Stir in liqueur. Place plastic wrap over surface of chocolate. Refrigerate about 2 hours, stirring once, until firm enough to hold its shape.

2 Meanwhile, heat oven to 350°F. Place hazelnuts in ungreased shallow pan. Bake 6 to 10 minutes, stirring occasionally, until light brown. Rub with towel to remove skins. Cool 10 minutes. Place nuts in food processor. Cover; process with on-and-off pulses 20 to 30 seconds or until finely ground. Place on sheet of waxed paper.

3 Scoop rounded teaspoonfuls of chocolate mixture onto nuts. Roll lightly to coat and shape into 1-inch balls (truffles do not need to be smooth; they should be a little rough). Place on plate; cover loosely. Store loosely covered in refrigerator. Let stand at room temperature 15 minutes before serving.

High Altitude (3500-6500 ft): No change.

Nutritional Info: 1 Truffle: Calories 80 (Calories from Fat 60); Total Fat 7g (Saturated Fat 3g, Trans Fat 0g); Cholesterol 5mg; Sodium 15mg; Total Carbohydrate 4g (Dietary Fiber 1g, Sugars 2g); Protein 1g. % Daily Value: Vitamin A 0%; Vitamin C 0%; Calcium 0%; Iron 4%. Exchanges: 1-1/2 Fat. Carbohydrate Choices: 0.

Betty's Kitchen Tips

How-To: A 1-inch cookie or ice cream scoop (#100 size) comes in handy for scooping the truffles. Order one on bettycrocker.com.

Special Touch: For added "aah," place each truffle in a small paper candy cup.

peanut-mallow fudge

Prep Time: 20 Minutes
Start to Finish: 2 Hours
Servings: 48 candies

1/2   cup creamy peanut butter
2/3   cup powdered sugar
1/2   cup butter
  3   cups granulated sugar
  1   cup evaporated milk (from 12-oz can)
  1   bag (10.5 oz) miniature marshmallows

  1   cup semisweet chocolate chips
  8   oz sweet baking chocolate, chopped
  1   oz unsweetened baking chocolate, chopped
  1   teaspoon vanilla
2/3   cup dry-roasted peanuts

1 Line bottom and sides of 13x9-inch pan with foil, leaving 1 inch of foil overhanging at 2 opposite sides of pan; grease foil with butter. In medium bowl, stir peanut butter and powdered sugar until well blended. Shape into 24 (1-inch) balls. Place balls evenly in foil-lined pan.

2 In 5- to 6-quart saucepan, cook the butter, granulated sugar and evaporated milk over medium-high heat, stirring constantly, until sugar is dissolved. Heat to full boil, stirring constantly. Reduce heat to medium. Boil uncovered without stirring 3 minutes. Remove from heat.

3 Stir in 3 cups of the marshmallows until melted. Add chocolate chips, sweet chocolate and unsweetened chocolate, stirring rapidly until all chocolate is melted and mixture is smooth. Stir in vanilla. Quickly pour mixture over peanut butter balls in pan. Press peanuts and remaining marshmallows into top of fudge. Cool completely, about 1-1/2 hours.

4 Using foil handles, lift fudge from pan to cutting board; remove foil from sides of fudge. Cut into 8 rows by 6 rows.

High Altitude (3500-6500 ft): In step 2, after reducing heat to medium, boil uncovered 4 to 5 minutes.

Nutritional Info: 1 Candy: Calories 180 (Calories from Fat 70); Total Fat 7g (Saturated Fat 3.5g, Trans Fat 0g); Cholesterol 5mg; Sodium 55mg; Total Carbohydrate 26g (Dietary Fiber 1g, Sugars 23g); Protein 2g. % Daily Value: Vitamin A 0%; Vitamin C 0%; Calcium 2%; Iron 2%. Exchanges: 1/2 Starch, 1 Other Carbohydrate, 1-1/2 Fat. Carbohydrate Choices: 2.

Betty's Kitchen Tips

Did You Know? Sweet baking chocolate is also often called German baking chocolate and can be found in the baking section of your local grocery store.

Special Touch: Homemade fudge makes a memorable gift. Arrange fudge in a decorative tin and tie with holiday ribbon.

tiramisu cheesecake dessert

Prep Time: 20 Minutes
Start to Finish: 2 Hours 25 Minutes
Servings: 24

. . . .

2	cups crushed vanilla wafer cookies (about 60 cookies)
1/3	cup butter or margarine, melted
2	tablespoons whipping cream
2	tablespoons instant espresso coffee granules
3	packages (8 oz each) cream cheese, softened
3/4	cup sugar
3	eggs
1	oz bittersweet baking chocolate, grated

Chocolate-covered espresso beans, if desired

. . . .

1 Heat oven to 350°F. Line 13x9-inch pan with foil; spray with cooking spray. In small bowl, mix crushed cookies and melted butter with fork. Press mixture in bottom of pan. Refrigerate while continuing with recipe.

2 In small bowl, mix whipping cream and coffee granules with fork until coffee is dissolved; set aside.

3 In large bowl, beat cream cheese with electric mixer on medium speed 2 to 3 minutes, scraping bowl occasionally, until smooth and creamy. On low speed, beat in sugar, eggs and coffee mixture, about 30 seconds. Beat on medium speed about 2 minutes longer or until ingredients are well blended. Using rubber spatula, spread cream cheese filling over crust. Bake 25 to 35 minutes or until center is set.

4 Cool 30 minutes. Sprinkle with grated chocolate, or top with espresso beans. Refrigerate about 1 hour or until completely chilled. For servings, cut into 6 rows by 4 rows, using sharp knife dipped in water.

High Altitude (3500-6500 ft): No change.

Nutritional Info: 1 Square: Calories 200 (Calories from Fat 140); Total Fat 15g (Saturated Fat 9g, Trans Fat 0.5g); Cholesterol 65mg; Sodium 140mg; Total Carbohydrate 12g (Dietary Fiber 0g, Sugars 9g); Protein 4g. % Daily Value: Vitamin A 10%; Vitamin C 0%; Calcium 4%; Iron 4%. Exchanges: 1/2 Starch, 1/2 Other Carbohydrate, 1/2 High-Fat Meat, 2 Fat. Carbohydrate Choices: 1.

Betty's Kitchen Tip

• Dress up these dessert bars by serving them in colorful paper baking cups.

almond streusel-cherry cheesecake bars

Prep Time: 45 Minutes
Start to Finish: 4 Hours
Servings: 24 bars

Cookie Base and Topping

1	pouch (1 lb 1.5 oz) Betty Crocker® sugar cookie mix
1/4	cup cold butter or margarine
4	oz (half of 8-oz package) cream cheese
1/2	cup sliced almonds

Filling

2-1/2	packages (8 oz each) cream cheese (20 oz), softened
1/2	cup sugar
2	tablespoons Gold Medal® all-purpose flour
1	teaspoon almond extract
2	eggs
1	can (21 oz) cherry pie filling

1 Heat oven to 350°F. Spray bottom and sides of 13x9-inch pan with cooking spray. Place cookie mix in large bowl. Cut in butter and 4 oz cream cheese, using pastry blender or fork, until mixture is crumbly. Reserve 1-1/2 cups mixture for topping. Press remaining mixture in bottom of pan. Bake 12 minutes.

2 Meanwhile, in large bowl, beat 20 oz cream cheese, the sugar, flour, almond extract and eggs with electric mixer on medium speed until smooth.

3 Spread cream cheese mixture evenly over partially baked cookie base. Spoon pie filling evenly over cream cheese mixture. Sprinkle with reserved topping and almonds.

4 Bake 40 to 45 minutes or until light golden brown. Cool 30 minutes. Refrigerate about 2 hours or until chilled. For bars, cut into 6 rows by 4 rows. Store covered in refrigerator.

High Altitude (3500-6500 ft): In step 1, bake cookie base 15 minutes. In step 4, bake 45 to 50 minutes.

Nutritional Info: 1 Bar: Calories 270 (Calories from Fat 140); Total Fat 15g (Saturated Fat 8g, Trans Fat 1g); Cholesterol 55mg; Sodium 160mg; Total Carbohydrate 28g (Dietary Fiber 0g, Sugars 20g); Protein 4g. % Daily Value: Vitamin A 10%; Vitamin C 0%; Calcium 4%; Iron 4%. Exchanges: 1 Starch, 1 Other Carbohydrate, 3 Fat. Carbohydrate Choices: 2.

Betty's Kitchen Tips

Success Hint: You'll need a total of three 8-ounce packages of cream cheese for this recipe.

Prize-Winner: This prize-winning recipe from the 2008 Bake Life Sweeter™ Cookie Mix Recipe Contest is from Brenda Watts of South Carolina.

festive cake bars

Prep Time: 25 Minutes
Start to Finish: 1 Hour 30 Minutes
Servings: 24 bars

- 1 pouch (1 lb 1.5 oz) Betty Crocker® sugar cookie mix
- 1/4 cup butter, melted
- 1/4 cup milk
- 2 eggs
- 1 jar (10 oz) maraschino cherries, drained, stems removed, coarsely chopped (about 2/3 cup)
- 1/2 teaspoon almond extract
- 1 tub (12 oz) Betty Crocker® Whipped fluffy white frosting
- 2 tablespoons Betty Crocker® red sugar

1 Heat oven to 350°F. Spray 13x9-inch pan with baking spray with flour. In medium bowl, beat cookie mix, butter, milk and eggs with electric mixer on medium speed about 20 seconds or until well mixed. Stir in cherries and almond extract. Spread in pan.

2 Bake 20 to 25 minutes or until top is golden brown and toothpick inserted in center comes out clean. Cool completely on cooling rack, about 45 minutes. Frost with frosting. Cut into 6 rows by 4 rows.

3 Measure red sugar into bowl. Press 2-inch cookie cutter lightly into frosting of bar to make imprint of design; remove cutter. Dip cutter into sugar; place on imprint in frosting to make design.

High Altitude (3500-6500 ft): Heat oven to 375°F.

Nutritional Info: 1 Bar: Calories 180 (Calories from Fat 60); Total Fat 7g (Saturated Fat 2.5g, Trans Fat 1.5g); Cholesterol 25mg; Sodium 95mg; Total Carbohydrate 28g (Dietary Fiber 0g, Sugars 20g); Protein 1g. % Daily Value: Vitamin A 0%; Vitamin C 0%; Calcium 0%; Iron 0%. Exchanges: 2 Other Carbohydrate, 1-1/2 Fat. Carbohydrate Choices: 2.

Betty's Kitchen Tips

How-To: Chop maraschino cherries easily by snipping them with kitchen scissors. Drain on paper towels to absorb moisture.

Success Hint: Cake bars store well, tightly covered, in the freezer. Remove from freezer about two hours before serving.

frosted brownies

Prep Time: 20 Minutes
Start to Finish: 1 Hour 55 Minutes
Servings: 36 brownies

Brownies

6	oz unsweetened baking chocolate
3/4	cup butter or margarine, softened
2	cups granulated sugar
1-1/2	cups Original Bisquick® mix
2	teaspoons vanilla
3	eggs

Frosting

2	oz unsweetened baking chocolate
1/4	cup butter or margarine, softened
2	cups powdered sugar
2	tablespoons milk
1	teaspoon vanilla

1 Heat oven to 350°F. Spray bottom only of 13x9-inch pan with cooking spray. In small microwavable bowl, microwave 6 oz chocolate and 3/4 cup butter uncovered on High 1 to 2 minutes, stirring every 30 seconds, until melted. Stir until smooth.

2 In medium bowl, stir granulated sugar, Bisquick mix, 2 teaspoons vanilla, eggs and melted chocolate mixture until well blended. Spread in pan.

3 Bake 25 to 30 minutes or until edges begin to pull away from sides of pan. Cool completely, about 1 hour.

4 In medium microwavable bowl, microwave 2 oz chocolate uncovered on High 30 seconds to 1 minute, stirring after 30 seconds, until melted. Stir until smooth; cool 5 minutes. Stir in butter. Stir in remaining frosting ingredients until smooth and spreadable; if necessary, add more milk, 1 teaspoon at a time. Spread frosting over brownies. Let stand until set. For brownies, cut into 6 rows by 6 rows.

High Altitude (3500-6500 ft): In brownies, decrease butter to 1/2 cup; decrease granulated sugar to 1-1/2 cups.

Nutritional Info: 1 Brownie: Calories 190 (Calories from Fat 90); Total Fat 10g (Saturated Fat 6g, Trans Fat 0g); Cholesterol 30mg; Sodium 105mg; Total Carbohydrate 23g (Dietary Fiber 1g, Sugars 18g); Protein 1g. % Daily Value: Vitamin A 4%; Vitamin C 0%; Calcium 0%; Iron 8%. Exchanges: 1/2 Starch, 1 Other Carbohydrate, 2 Fat. Carbohydrate Choices: 1-1/2.

Betty's Kitchen Tip

• Unsweetened baking chocolate contains 50 to 58 percent cocoa butter. Bitter in flavor, it's used primarily in baking. You'll find it in the supermarket in a rectangular box containing packages of one-ounce squares or bars.

toffee bars

Prep Time: 15 Minutes
Start to Finish: 1 Hour 20 Minutes
Servings: 32 bars

EASY

1	cup butter or margarine, softened
1	cup packed brown sugar
1	teaspoon vanilla
1	egg yolk
2	cups Gold Medal® all-purpose flour
1/4	teaspoon salt
2/3	cup milk chocolate chips
1/2	cup chopped nuts, if desired

1 Heat oven to 350°F. Spray 13x9-inch pan with cooking spray. In large bowl, mix butter, brown sugar, vanilla and egg yolk. Stir in flour and salt. Press in pan.

2 Bake 25 to 30 minutes or until very light brown (crust will be soft). Immediately sprinkle chocolate chips on hot crust. Let stand about 5 minutes or until chocolate is soft; spread evenly. Sprinkle with nuts.

3 Cool 30 minutes in pan on cooling rack. For bars, cut into 8 rows by 4 rows.

High Altitude (3500-6500 ft): No change.

Nutritional Info: 1 Bar: Calories 130 (Calories from Fat 60); Total Fat 7g (Saturated Fat 4g, Trans Fat 0g); Cholesterol 20mg; Sodium 65mg; Total Carbohydrate 15g (Dietary Fiber 0g, Sugars 9g); Protein 1g. % Daily Value: Vitamin A 4%; Vitamin C 0%; Calcium 0%; Iron 4%. Exchanges: 1 Other Carbohydrate, 1-1/2 Fat. Carbohydrate Choices: 1.

Betty's Kitchen Tips

Substitution: Three bars (1.55 oz each) milk chocolate candy, broken into small pieces, can be substituted for the milk chocolate chips.

Success Hint: For easiest cutting, cut the bars while they're still warm.

strawberry-almond paste shortbread bars

Prep Time: 25 Minutes
Start to Finish: 1 Hour 15 Minutes
Servings: 32 bars

1 cup butter, softened	1/4 cup sliced almonds
3/4 cup granulated sugar	1 jar (12 oz) strawberry preserves
2 cups Gold Medal® all-purpose flour	1 teaspoon powdered sugar
1/4 teaspoon salt	
1/4 cup packed almond paste (from 7-oz roll), crumbled (not marzipan)	

1 Heat oven to 350°F. Line bottom and sides of 9-inch square pan with foil, leaving 1 inch of foil overhanging at 2 opposite sides of pan; spray foil with cooking spray.

2 In large bowl, beat butter and granulated sugar with electric mixer on medium-high speed until well mixed. Beat in flour and salt on medium speed just until blended. Press 3-1/2 cups mixture into pan. Bake about 20 minutes or until top begins to brown.

3 Meanwhile, in same bowl, mix remaining crumb mixture and crumbled almond paste with fork until small clumps form; stir in almonds.

4 Spread preserves evenly over hot base. Crumble almond paste mixture evenly over preserves; press slightly.

5 Bake 25 to 30 minutes or until top and edges are golden brown and preserves are bubbly. Using foil handles, lift bars from pan; remove foil from sides of bars. Cool completely on cooling rack before cutting. Sprinkle powdered sugar on top. Cut into 4 rows by 4 rows. Cut each square in half diagonally.

High Altitude (3500-6500 ft): In step 2, bake about 25 minutes or until golden.

Nutritional Info: 1 Bar: Calories 140 (Calories from Fat 60); Total Fat 7g (Saturated Fat 3.5g, Trans Fat 0g); Cholesterol 15mg; Sodium 65mg; Total Carbohydrate 19g (Dietary Fiber 0g, Sugars 11g); Protein 1g. % Daily Value: Vitamin A 4%; Vitamin C 0%; Calcium 0%; Iron 2%. Exchanges: 1/2 Starch, 1/2 Other Carbohydrate, 1-1/2 Fat. Carbohydrate Choices: 1.

Betty's Kitchen Tip

• You'll find the almond paste packaged in tubes with the other baking ingredients at the grocery store.

white chocolate chunk blonde brownies

Prep Time: 20 Minutes
Start to Finish: 2 Hours 55 Minutes
Servings: 36 brownies

. . . .

Brownies

2	cups packed brown sugar
1/2	cup butter or margarine, softened
2	teaspoons vanilla
1/2	teaspoon rum extract
2	eggs
2	cups Gold Medal® all-purpose flour
1	teaspoon baking powder
1/4	teaspoon salt
12	oz white chocolate baking bars, chopped
1	cup chopped walnuts

Glaze

1/4	cup semisweet chocolate chunks (from 12-oz bag)
1	teaspoon vegetable oil

. . . .

1 Heat oven to 350°F. In large bowl, beat brown sugar, butter, vanilla, rum extract and eggs with electric mixer on medium speed until light and fluffy.

2 On low speed, beat in flour, baking powder and salt until well blended. Stir in white chocolate pieces and walnuts. In ungreased 13x9-inch pan, spread batter evenly.

3 Bake 25 to 35 minutes or until top is golden brown and set. Cool completely, about 2 hours.

4 In small microwavable bowl, microwave glaze ingredients uncovered on High 30 to 60 seconds, stirring every 15 seconds, until melted; stir well. Spread glaze over brownies. If desired, place glaze in small food-storage plastic bag and cut small tip from one corner of bag; drizzle glaze in diagonal lines over brownies. Let stand until glaze is set. For brownies, cut into 6 rows by 6 rows.

High Altitude (3500-6500 ft): Spread batter in pan up to 1/2 inch of sides (batter will flow to sides during baking). Bake 30 to 35 minutes.

Nutritional Info: 1 Brownie: Calories 180 (Calories from Fat 80); Total Fat 9g (Saturated Fat 3.5g, Trans Fat 0g); Cholesterol 20mg; Sodium 65mg; Total Carbohydrate 24g (Dietary Fiber 0g, Sugars 18g); Protein 2g. % Daily Value: Vitamin A 2%; Vitamin C 0%; Calcium 4%; Iron 4%. Exchanges: 1-1/2 Other Carbohydrate, 2 Fat. Carbohydrate Choices: 1-1/2.

Betty's Kitchen Tips

Variation: You could use pecans instead of the walnuts, or you can make the brownies without the nuts, if you like.

Success Hint: For easy cutting, line the pan with foil. When the brownies are cool, use the foil to lift them from the pan and place on a flat surface for cutting.

raspberry mousse brownies

Prep Time: 20 Minutes
Start to Finish: 4 Hours 10 Minutes
Servings: 24 servings

1 box (1 lb 6.5 oz) Betty Crocker® Original Supreme brownie mix (with chocolate syrup pouch)

Water, oil and eggs called for on brownie mix box

1 bag (10 oz) raspberry-flavored or semisweet chocolate chips

1-1/4 cups whipping cream

1 container (1 lb) Betty Crocker® Rich & Creamy cream cheese frosting

1 tablespoon whipping cream

Fresh raspberries, if desired

1. Heat oven to 350°F. Grease bottom only of 13x9-inch pan with cooking spray or shortening (for easier cutting, line pan with foil, then grease foil on bottom only of pan). Make brownies as directed on box for 13x9-inch pan. Cool completely, about 1 hour.

2. Reserve 1/4 cup chocolate chips for drizzle. In large microwavable bowl, place remaining chocolate chips and 1-1/4 cups whipping cream. Microwave uncovered on High 2 to 3 minutes, stirring once every minute, until chocolate is melted. Stir until mixture is smooth. Refrigerate about 20 minutes or until slightly thickened.

3. Add frosting to chocolate mixture. Beat with electric mixer on high speed 1 to 2 minutes or until well blended and soft peaks form. Spread over cooled brownies, smoothing top.

4. In small microwavable bowl, microwave reserved 1/4 cup chocolate chips and 1 tablespoon whipping cream uncovered on High 30 to 45 seconds, stirring once, until mixture can be stirred smooth. Drizzle over frosting mixture. Refrigerate 1 to 2 hours or until set.

5. Cut into 12 squares; cut each square diagonally in half to make triangles. Garnish with raspberries.

High Altitude (3500-6500 ft): Follow High Altitude directions on brownie mix box for 13x9-inch pan.

Nutritional Info: 1 Serving: Calories 330 (Calories from Fat 150); Total Fat 16g (Saturated Fat 7g, Trans Fat 2g); Cholesterol 30mg; Sodium 140mg; Total Carbohydrate 42g (Dietary Fiber 2g, Sugars 34g); Protein 2g. % Daily Value: Vitamin A 4%; Vitamin C 0%; Calcium 4%; Iron 8%. Exchanges: 1/2 Starch, 2-1/2 Other Carbohydrate, 3 Fat. Carbohydrate Choices: 3.

Betty's Kitchen Tip

• Fresh strawberries or chocolate-covered coffee beans can be used as a garnish instead of the raspberries.

oatmeal-cranberry-sour cream bars

Prep Time: 20 Minutes
Start to Finish: 3 Hours 25 Minutes
Servings: 16 bars

1	pouch (1 lb 1.5 oz) Betty Crocker® oatmeal cookie mix
1/4	teaspoon ground cinnamon
1/2	cup butter or margarine, softened
1	egg
3/4	cup sour cream
3	tablespoons sugar
2	teaspoons grated lemon peel
1/4	teaspoon vanilla
1	egg yolk
1	cup sweetened dried cranberries
1/2	cup coarsely chopped pecans

1 Heat oven to 350°F. Line bottom and sides of 9-inch square pan with foil, leaving 1 inch of foil overhanging at 2 opposite sides of pan; spray foil with cooking spray.

2 In large bowl, stir cookie mix, cinnamon, butter and egg until stiff dough forms. Reserve 1/4 of the dough. Press remaining dough in bottom of foil-lined pan. Bake 15 minutes.

3 In small bowl, stir sour cream, sugar, lemon peel, vanilla and egg yolk until well blended. Stir in cranberries. Spread over crust. Stir pecans into reserved oatmeal dough; crumble over cranberry mixture.

4 Bake 18 to 20 minutes or until top is light brown. Cool 30 minutes. Refrigerate 2 hours. Using foil handles, lift cooled bars from pan to cutting board; remove foil from sides of bars. Cut into 4 rows by 4 rows. Store covered in refrigerator.

High Altitude (3500-6500 ft): In step 2, bake 20 minutes.

Nutritional Info: 1 Bar: Calories 260 (Calories from Fat 110); Total Fat 12g (Saturated Fat 5g, Trans Fat 0g); Cholesterol 50mg; Sodium 170mg; Total Carbohydrate 34g (Dietary Fiber 1g, Sugars 21g); Protein 3g. % Daily Value: Vitamin A 6%; Vitamin C 0%; Calcium 0%; Iron 4%. Exchanges: 1 Starch, 1 Other Carbohydrate, 2-1/2 Fat. Carbohydrate Choices: 2.

Betty's Kitchen Tips

Variation: Dried cherries and walnuts can be used instead of dried cranberries and pecans.

Success Hint: Lining the baking pan with foil eliminates sticking and makes for easy cleanup.

cardamom-cashew bars

Prep Time: 20 Minutes
Start to Finish: 1 Hour 5 Minutes
Servings: 48 bars

LOW FAT

Crust

1/2	package (8-oz size) 1/3-less-fat cream cheese (Neufchâtel)
1/2	cup powdered sugar
1/4	cup packed brown sugar
2	teaspoons vanilla
1	egg yolk
1-1/2	cups Gold Medal® all-purpose flour

Filling

1-1/2	cups packed brown sugar

1/2	cup fat-free egg product or 2 eggs
3	tablespoons Gold Medal® all-purpose flour
2	teaspoons vanilla
1/2	teaspoon ground cardamom or cinnamon
1/4	teaspoon salt
1-1/2	cups cashew pieces and halves

Orange Drizzle

3/4	cup powdered sugar
1	tablespoon orange juice

1 Heat oven to 350°F. Grease 13x9-inch pan. To make crust, beat cream cheese and sugars in medium bowl with electric mixer on medium speed until fluffy. Beat in vanilla and egg yolk. Gradually stir in flour to make a soft dough. Press dough evenly in pan. Bake 15 to 20 minutes or until very light brown.

2 In medium bowl, beat all filling ingredients except cashews with electric mixer on medium speed about 2 minutes or until thick. Stir in cashews. Spread over baked crust.

3 Bake 19 to 22 minutes or until top is golden brown and bars are set around edges. Cool completely.

4 Mix icing ingredients until smooth and spreadable. Spread over bars. For bars, cut into 8 rows by 6 rows.

High Altitude (3500-6500 ft): In step 1, add up to 1 tablespoon water to dough if needed. In step 3, bake 22 to 25 minutes.

Nutritional Info: 1 Bar: Calories 90 (Calories from Fat 25); Total Fat 2.5g (Saturated Fat 0.5g, Trans Fat 0g); Cholesterol 5mg; Sodium 30mg; Total Carbohydrate 16g (Dietary Fiber 0g, Sugars 11g); Protein 1g. % Daily Value: Vitamin A 0%; Vitamin C 0%; Calcium 0%; Iron 4%. Exchanges: 1 Other Carbohydrate, 1/2 Fat. Carbohydrate Choices: 1.

Betty's Kitchen Tip

• No cardamom? It's a unique aromatic spice, a member of the ginger family and a bit pricey. Cinnamon is a good substitute in this recipe.

triple-chocolate brownies

Prep Time: 20 Minutes
Start to Finish: 3 Hours 5 Minutes
Servings: 24 brownies

Brownies

5	oz unsweetened baking chocolate
2/3	cup butter or margarine
1-3/4	cups granulated sugar
2	teaspoons vanilla
3	eggs
1	cup Gold Medal® all-purpose flour
1	cup chopped nuts
1	cup semisweet chocolate chips (6 oz)

Chocolate Frosting

2	oz unsweetened baking chocolate
2	tablespoons butter or margarine
2	cups powdered sugar
2	to 4 tablespoons hot water

1 Heat oven to 350°F. Grease bottom and sides of 9-inch square pan with shortening or cooking spray. In 1-quart saucepan, melt 5 oz chocolate and 2/3 cup butter over low heat, stirring frequently; remove from heat. Cool slightly.

2 In large bowl, beat granulated sugar, vanilla and eggs with electric mixer on high speed 5 minutes. On low speed, beat in chocolate mixture. Beat in flour just until blended. Stir in nuts and chocolate chips. Spread in pan.

3 Bake 40 to 45 minutes or just until brownies begin to pull away from sides of pan. Cool completely, about 2 hours.

4 In 2-quart saucepan, melt 2 oz chocolate and 2 tablespoons butter over low heat, stirring frequently; remove from heat. Stir in powdered sugar and hot water until smooth and spreadable. (If frosting is too thick, add more water, 1 tablespoon at a time.) Spread over brownies. For brownies, cut into 6 rows by 4 rows.

High Altitude (3500-6500 ft): Bake 45 to 50 minutes.

Nutritional Info: 1 Brownie: Calories 300 (Calories from Fat 150); Total Fat 17g (Saturated Fat 8g, Trans Fat 0g); Cholesterol 45mg; Sodium 50mg; Total Carbohydrate 36g (Dietary Fiber 2g, Sugars 28g); Protein 3g. % Daily Value: Vitamin A 6%; Vitamin C 0%; Calcium 0%; Iron 6%. Exchanges: 1 Starch, 1-1/2 Other Carbohydrate, 3 Fat. Carbohydrate Choices: 2-1/2.

Betty's Kitchen Tips

Success Hint: Be sure not to overbake brownies because the edges will get hard and dry.

Special Touch: Package these beautiful brownies for a bake sale. Bake brownies in a 12x8-inch disposable foil pan about 35 minutes. Cover with see-through wrap, and attach a plastic knife.

chocolate-peanut butter dream bars

Prep Time: 30 Minutes
Start to Finish: 2 Hours 5 Minutes
Servings: 24 bars

Cookie Crust
- 1 pouch (1 lb 1.5 oz) Betty Crocker® double chocolate chunk cookie mix
- 1/4 cup vegetable oil
- 2 tablespoons cold strong brewed coffee or water
- 1 egg

Filling
- 1 package (8 oz) cream cheese, softened
- 1/4 cup sugar

- 1 container (8 oz) frozen whipped topping, thawed
- 1 bag (9 oz) miniature chocolate-covered peanut butter cup candies, chopped

Topping
- 1/4 cup creamy peanut butter
- 1/4 cup milk
- 2 tablespoons sugar
- 3 oz bittersweet baking chocolate, melted
- 1 cup unsalted dry-roasted peanuts

1 Heat oven to 350°F. In large bowl, stir cookie crust ingredients until soft dough forms. Spread dough in bottom of ungreased 13x9-inch pan. Bake 12 to 15 minutes or just until set. Cool completely, about 30 minutes.

2 In large bowl, beat cream cheese and 1/4 cup sugar with electric mixer on medium speed until smooth. Fold in whipped topping and candies. Spread over cooled cookie crust.

3 In small microwavable bowl, beat peanut butter, milk and 2 tablespoons sugar with wire whisk until smooth. Microwave uncovered on High 30 to 60 seconds, stirring after 30 seconds, to thin for drizzling. Drizzle mixture over filling. Drizzle with melted chocolate. Sprinkle with peanuts. Refrigerate about 1 hour or until set. For bars, cut into 6 rows by 4 rows. Store covered in refrigerator.

High Altitude (3500-6500 ft): No change.

Nutritional Info: 1 Bar: Calories 320 (Calories from Fat 170); Total Fat 19g (Saturated Fat 8g, Trans Fat 0g); Cholesterol 20mg; Sodium 170mg; Total Carbohydrate 31g (Dietary Fiber 2g, Sugars 20g); Protein 5g. % Daily Value: Vitamin A 4%; Vitamin C 0%; Calcium 4%; Iron 8%. Exchanges: 1/2 Starch, 1-1/2 Other Carbohydrate, 1/2 High-Fat Meat, 3 Fat. Carbohydrate Choices: 2.

Betty's Kitchen Tips

Do-Ahead: Make these chilly dessert bars up to 24 hours before serving.

Did You Know? This recipe was one of 15 finalists in the 2008 Bake Life Sweeter™ Cookie Mix Recipe Contest.

luscious chocolate truffles

Prep Time: 20 Minutes
Start to Finish: 1 Hour 15 Minutes
Servings: 15 truffles

- 1 bag (12 oz) semisweet chocolate chips (2 cups)
- 2 tablespoons butter or margarine
- 1/4 cup whipping cream
- 2 tablespoons liqueur (almond, cherry, coffee, hazelnut, Irish cream, orange, raspberry, etc.), if desired
- 1 tablespoon shortening

Finely chopped nuts, if desired
Finely chopped dried apricots, if desired
White chocolate baking bar, chopped, if desired

1 Line cookie sheet with foil or parchment paper. In 2-quart saucepan, melt 1 cup of the chocolate chips over low heat, stirring constantly; remove from heat. Stir in butter. Stir in whipping cream and liqueur. Refrigerate 10 to 15 minutes, stirring frequently, just until thick enough to hold a shape.

2 Drop mixture by teaspoonfuls onto cookie sheet. Shape into balls. (If mixture is too sticky, refrigerate until firm enough to shape.) Freeze 30 minutes.

3 In 1-quart saucepan, heat shortening and remaining 1 cup chocolate chips over low heat, stirring constantly, until chocolate is melted and mixture is smooth; remove from heat. Dip truffles, one at a time, into chocolate. Return to cookie sheet. Immediately sprinkle nuts and apricots over some of the truffles. Reheat chocolate dipping mixture, if necessary. Refrigerate truffles about 10 minutes or until coating is set.

4 In 1-quart saucepan, heat baking bar over low heat, stirring constantly, until melted. Drizzle over some of the truffles. Refrigerate just until set. Store in airtight container in refrigerator. Remove truffles from refrigerator about 30 minutes before serving; serve at room temperature.

High Altitude (3500-6500 ft): No change.

Nutritional Info: 1 Truffle: Calories 160 (Calories from Fat 90); Total Fat 10g (Saturated Fat 6g, Trans Fat 0g); Cholesterol 10mg; Sodium 15mg; Total Carbohydrate 14g (Dietary Fiber 1g, Sugars 12g); Protein 1g. % Daily Value: Vitamin A 0%; Vitamin C 0%; Calcium 0%; Iron 4%. Exchanges: 1 Other Carbohydrate, 2 Fat. Carbohydrate Choices: 1.

Betty's Kitchen Tips

Do-Ahead: You can make these delightful truffles up to a week ahead—just take them out of the fridge about half an hour before serving for better flavor and texture.

Substitution: Milk chocolate chips can be substituted for the semisweet chocolate chips.

tiramisu cheesecake bars

Prep Time: 40 Minutes
Start to Finish: 4 Hours 30 Minutes
Servings: 36 bars

Cookie Base

- 1 pouch (1 lb 1.5 oz) Betty Crocker® sugar cookie mix
- 2 tablespoons Gold Medal® all-purpose flour
- 1/3 cup butter or margarine, softened
- 1 egg, slightly beaten

Filling

- 2 packages (8 oz each) cream cheese, softened
- 1 can (14 oz) sweetened condensed milk (not evaporated)

- 1 tablespoon instant coffee granules or crystals
- 2 teaspoons vanilla
- 2 eggs
- 1 cup miniature semisweet chocolate chips

Topping

- 6 oz cream cheese, softened
- 1/2 cup whipping cream

Chocolate curls, if desired

1 Heat oven to 350°F. Spray bottom and sides of 13x9-inch pan with cooking spray. In large bowl, stir cookie base ingredients until soft dough forms. Press dough in bottom of pan. Bake 15 to 18 minutes or until light golden brown. Cool 15 minutes.

2 Meanwhile, in another large bowl, beat 2 packages (8 oz each) cream cheese with electric mixer on medium speed until smooth. Add condensed milk; beat until well blended. Add coffee, vanilla and eggs; beat until well blended. Stir in chocolate chips. Pour over cookie base.

3 Bake 35 to 40 minutes or until set. Cool at room temperature 30 minutes. Refrigerate 30 minutes to cool completely.

4 In small bowl, beat 6 oz cream cheese on medium speed until smooth. Gradually beat in whipping cream; beat about 2 minutes longer or until fluffy. Spread mixture over cooled bars. Sprinkle chocolate curls over topping.

5 Refrigerate until chilled, about 2 hours. For bars, cut into 9 rows by 4 rows. Store covered in refrigerator.

High Altitude (3500-6500 ft): No change.

Nutritional Info: 1 Bar: Calories 210 (Calories from Fat 120); Total Fat 13g (Saturated Fat 7g, Trans Fat 1g); Cholesterol 50mg; Sodium 125mg; Total Carbohydrate 20g (Dietary Fiber 0g, Sugars 15g); Protein 3g. % Daily Value: Vitamin A 8%; Vitamin C 0%; Calcium 6%; Iron 4%. Exchanges: 1/2 Starch, 1 Other Carbohydrate, 2-1/2 Fat. Carbohydrate Choices: 1.

Betty's Kitchen Tip

Prize-Winner: This prize-winning recipe from the 2008 Bake Life Sweeter™ Cookie Mix Recipe Contest is from Kurt Wait of California.

just
DESSERTS

p. 336

322   327   342

peach cobbler

Prep Time: 25 Minutes
Start to Finish: 50 Minutes
Servings: 6

· ·

1/3	cup sugar		2	teaspoons lemon juice
1	tablespoon cornstarch		1	cup Original Bisquick® mix
1/4	teaspoon ground cinnamon		2	tablespoons sugar
6	peaches, peeled, cut into 1/2-inch slices (6 cups)		1/3	cup milk
2	tablespoons water		1	tablespoon butter or margarine, melted

Sweetened whipped cream, if desired

· ·

1 Heat oven to 400°F. In 4-quart saucepan, mix 1/3 cup sugar, the cornstarch and cinnamon. Stir in peaches, water and lemon juice. Heat to boiling, stirring constantly; boil and stir 1 minute. Pour into ungreased 8- or 9-inch square (2-quart) glass baking dish.

2 In medium bowl, stir the Bisquick mix, 1 tablespoon of the sugar, the milk and melted butter until soft dough forms.

3 Drop dough by 6 tablespoonfuls onto hot peach mixture. Sprinkle remaining 1 tablespoon sugar over dough.

4 Bake 20 to 25 minutes or until golden brown. Serve with whipped cream.

High Altitude (3500-6500 ft): No change.

Nutritional Info: 1 Serving: Calories 240 (Calories from Fat 45); Total Fat 5g (Saturated Fat 2g, Trans Fat 1g); Cholesterol 5mg; Sodium 260mg; Total Carbohydrate 45g (Dietary Fiber 3g, Sugars 29g); Protein 3g. % Daily Value: Vitamin A 10%; Vitamin C 8%; Calcium 4%; Iron 6%. Exchanges: 1 Starch, 1 Fruit, 1 Other Carbohydrate, 1 Fat. Carbohydrate Choices: 3.

Betty's Kitchen Tips

Did You Know? Cobbler comes from "cobble up" which means to mix in a hurry. And what could be quicker than a cobbler made with Bisquick® mix?

Substitution: You can substitute frozen peach slices, thawed, for the fresh peaches.

cappuccino crème brûlée

Prep Time: 15 Minutes
Start to Finish: 2 Hours 20 Minutes
Servings: 8

EASY

- 1-1/2 cups sugar
- 2 cups half-and-half
- 1 tablespoon instant espresso coffee granules
- 1 teaspoon vanilla
- 2 whole eggs
- 6 egg yolks
- 3 oz bittersweet baking chocolate

1 Heat oven to 350°F. In large bowl, beat all ingredients except chocolate with wire whisk until smooth.

2 Pour mixture into 8 ungreased 6-ounce ramekins. Place ramekins in shallow roasting pan. Fill pan with hot water to halfway up sides of ramekins.

3 Bake 30 to 35 minutes or just until set. Remove ramekins to cooling rack. Cool for 30 minutes. Meanwhile, in small microwavable bowl, microwave chocolate uncovered on High 30 to 40 seconds, stirring every 15 seconds, until melted and smooth.

4 Spoon about 2 teaspoons melted chocolate over top of each custard, spreading evenly to form a thin layer. Cover; refrigerate at least 1 hour until well chilled.

High Altitude (3500-6500 ft): Bake 40 to 45 minutes.

Nutritional Info: 1 Serving: Calories 360 (Calories from Fat 150); Total Fat 17g (Saturated Fat 9g, Trans Fat 0g); Cholesterol 230mg; Sodium 50mg; Total Carbohydrate 44g (Dietary Fiber 2g, Sugars 40g); Protein 7g. % Daily Value: Vitamin A 10%; Vitamin C 0%; Calcium 10%; Iron 15%. Exchanges: 3 Other Carbohydrate, 1 Medium-Fat Meat, 2 Fat. Carbohydrate Choices: 3.

Betty's Kitchen Tips

Variation: For a more intense coffee flavor, add an additional 2 teaspoons coffee granules.

Success Hint: Use 6-ounce custard cups if you don't have ramekins.

Special Touch: Garnish with sifted baking cocoa, if desired.

apple-raspberry crumb pie

Prep Time: 15 Minutes
Start to Finish: 1 Hour 35 Minutes
Servings: 8

EASY

Crust

1	Pillsbury® refrigerated pie crust (from 15-oz box), softened as directed on box

Filling

3	cups thinly sliced peeled cooking apples (3 medium)
1/2	cup sugar
2	tablespoons Gold Medal® all-purpose flour
1/2	teaspoon ground cinnamon

2	cups fresh or frozen (thawed and drained) raspberries
1/2	cup cubed or crumbled pure almond paste (from 7- or 8-oz package)

Topping

1/2	cup Gold Medal® all-purpose flour
1/4	cup sugar
1/4	cup butter or margarine
1/2	cup sliced almonds

1 Heat oven to 350°F. Place pie crust in 9-inch glass pie plate as directed on box for One-Crust Filled Pie.

2 In large bowl, stir together apples, 1/2 cup sugar, 2 tablespoons flour and the cinnamon. Spoon into crust-lined pie plate. Sprinkle with raspberries. Sprinkle almond paste over raspberries.

3 In medium bowl, mix 1/2 cup flour and 1/4 cup sugar. Cut in butter, using pastry blender (or pulling 2 table knives through ingredients in opposite directions), until particles are size of small peas. Stir in almonds. Sprinkle evenly over the almond paste.

4 Bake 1 hour to 1 hour 20 minutes, covering edge of crust with foil after about 30 minutes, until apples are tender in center and topping is golden brown. Serve warm or cool.

High Altitude (3500-6500 ft): Use deep-dish glass pie plate. Bake 1 hour 10 minutes to 1 hour 20 minutes.

Nutritional Info: 1 Serving: Calories 420 (Calories from Fat 180); Total Fat 20g (Saturated Fat 7g, Trans Fat 0g); Cholesterol 20mg; Sodium 150mg; Total Carbohydrate 57g (Dietary Fiber 4g, Sugars 31g); Protein 4g. % Daily Value: Vitamin A 4%; Vitamin C 8%; Calcium 4%; Iron 8%. Exchanges: 1 Starch, 3 Other Carbohydrate, 4 Fat. Carbohydrate Choices: 4.

Betty's Kitchen Tips

Do-Ahead: You can make the pie several hours before serving. To warm it up, microwave slices on individual microwavable plates on High for about 10 seconds.

Purchasing: Look for almond paste near the baking chocolate and nuts. Check the label to make sure it lists almonds as the first ingredient.

red, white and blueberry sundaes

Prep Time: 10 Minutes
Start to Finish: 10 Minutes
Servings: 8   **EASY QUICK**

- 1/3   cup seedless strawberry jam
- 2   tablespoons light corn syrup
- 2   teaspoons balsamic vinegar, if desired
- 1   cup fresh blueberries
- 1   cup quartered small to medium fresh strawberries
- 1   quart (4 cups) vanilla ice cream

White chocolate curls, if desired

1 In medium bowl, beat jam, corn syrup and vinegar with wire whisk until smooth. Fold in blueberries and strawberries until coated.

2 Scoop ice cream into 8 dessert bowls. Top with the berry mixture. Garnish with white chocolate.

High Altitude (3500-6500 ft): No change.

Nutritional Info: 1 Serving: Calories 220 (Calories from Fat 70); Total Fat 8g (Saturated Fat 5g, Trans Fat 0g); Cholesterol 30mg; Sodium 65mg; Total Carbohydrate 35g (Dietary Fiber 1g, Sugars 24g); Protein 3g. % Daily Value: Cholesterol 11%; Vitamin A 6%; Vitamin C 15%; Calcium 10%; Iron 0%. Exchanges: 2 Other Carbohydrate, 1/2 Low-Fat Milk, 1 Fat. Carbohydrate Choices: 2.

Betty's Kitchen Tips

Special Touch: To make the white chocolate curls, melt 1/2 cup chips with 1 teaspoon oil in microwave or over low heat. Pour into a small bowl lined with foil. Refrigerate 20 minutes or until set. Peel off foil. Use vegetable peeler to make curls.

Did You Know? Blueberries pack a huge nutritional punch. One cup of fresh blueberries gives you 3.5 grams of fiber and is an excellent source of vitamin C.

white chocolate bread pudding

Prep Time: 30 Minutes
Start to Finish: 2 Hour 20 Minutes
Servings: 10

2 cups whipping cream	8 egg yolks
2 cups half-and-half	1 teaspoon vanilla
8 oz white baking bars (white chocolate), cut into 1/4- to 1/2-inch pieces	1/4 teaspoon salt
1-1/2 cups sugar	1 baguette (about 25 inches), thinly sliced
	1 bag (12 oz) frozen raspberries, thawed

1 Heat oven to 325°F. Grease shallow 3-quart casserole with shortening or cooking spray. In 3-quart saucepan, heat whipping cream and half-and-half to boiling over medium-high heat, stirring constantly. Stir in baking bar pieces; remove from heat.

2 In large bowl, beat sugar, egg yolks, vanilla and salt with electric mixer on medium speed until creamy. Gradually add cream mixture, beating constantly, until smooth.

3 Line bottom and side of casserole with some of the baguette slices. Pour 2 cups of the cream mixture over bread. Let stand a few minutes until bread absorbs mixture. Add the remaining baguette slices. Pour remaining cream mixture, 2 cups at a time, over bread; let stand a few minutes until bread absorbs mixture. Place casserole in roasting pan; place in oven. Pour boiling water into roasting pan until 1 inch deep.

4 Bake uncovered 45 minutes. Cover with foil; bake about 1 hour 5 minutes longer or until knife inserted 1 inch from edge comes out clean.

5 Place raspberries in blender. Cover and blend on high speed until smooth; strain seeds. Serve warm bread pudding with raspberry sauce and, if desired, fresh raspberries.

High Altitude (3500-6500 ft): Bake uncovered 45 minutes. Cover; bake 1 hour 15 minutes.

Nutritional Info: 1 Serving: Calories 640 (Calories from Fat 300); Total Fat 34g (Saturated Fat 19g, Trans Fat 1g); Cholesterol 240mg; Sodium 390mg; Total Carbohydrate 74g (Dietary Fiber 4g, Sugars 51g); Protein 10g. % Daily Value: Vitamin A 20%; Vitamin C 8%; Calcium 20%; Iron 10%. Exchanges: 3 Starch, 2 Other Carbohydrate, 6-1/2 Fat. Carbohydrate Choices: 5.

Betty's Kitchen Tips

Special Touch: At Christmas time, serve this cozy pudding spooned into holiday mugs.

Serve-With: Add a scoop of vanilla ice cream to each serving before drizzling with raspberry sauce.

raspberry-pear-granola crisp

Prep Time: 25 Minutes
Start to Finish: 1 Hour 30 Minutes
Servings: 9

- 5 cups sliced peeled pears (5 to 6 pears)
- 1 bag (12 oz) frozen raspberries, thawed
- 1 cup granulated sugar
- 1/4 cup Gold Medal® all-purpose flour
- 6 Nature Valley® roasted almond crunchy granola bars (3 pouches from 8.9-oz box), finely crushed
- 1/2 cup Gold Medal® all-purpose flour
- 1/4 cup packed brown sugar
- 1/4 cup butter or margarine, melted

Whipped cream or ice cream, if desired

1 Heat oven to 350°F. Spray 8-inch square (2-quart) glass baking dish with cooking spray.

2 In large bowl, mix pears, raspberries, granulated sugar and 1/4 cup flour. Spoon evenly into baking dish.

3 In medium bowl, mix crushed granola bars, 1/2 cup flour, the brown sugar and butter until crumbly. Sprinkle over pear mixture.

4 Bake 55 to 65 minutes or until top is golden brown and fruit is tender (mixture will be bubbly). Cool slightly. Serve warm or cool with whipped cream or ice cream.

High Altitude (3500-6500 ft): No change.

Nutritional Info: 1 Serving: Calories 340 (Calories from Fat 70); Total Fat 8g (Saturated Fat 3.5g, Trans Fat 0g); Cholesterol 15mg; Sodium 95mg; Total Carbohydrate 64g (Dietary Fiber 6g, Sugars 43g); Protein 3g. % Daily Value: Vitamin A 4%; Vitamin C 10%; Calcium 4%; Iron 8%. Exchanges: 1 Starch, 1/2 Fruit, 2-1/2 Other Carbohydrate, 1-1/2 Fat. Carbohydrate Choices: 4.

Betty's Kitchen Tips

How-To: Use the flat side of a meat mallet to crush the granola bars right in their pouches.

Success Hint: If your pears are not quite ripe, let them stand at room temperature for one or two days.

decadent chocolate tart

Prep Time: 40 Minutes
Start to Finish: 3 Hours 10 Minutes
Servings: 12 servings

Crust

1/3	cup butter or margarine, softened
1/4	cup powdered sugar
1/2	cup Gold Medal® all-purpose flour
2	tablespoons unsweetened baking cocoa

Filling

1/4	cup butter or margarine
4	oz semisweet baking chocolate
1/4	cup granulated sugar

2	eggs
1/4	cup sour cream
2	tablespoons Gold Medal® all-purpose flour

Topping

2	oz semisweet baking chocolate
1	tablespoon butter or margarine
1	tablespoon honey
2	kiwifruit, peeled, cut up
1	can (11 oz) mandarin orange segments, drained

1 Heat oven to 350°F. Grease 9-inch tart pan with removable bottom with shortening or cooking spray. In medium bowl, beat 1/3 cup butter and the powdered sugar with electric mixer on medium speed until blended. Beat in 1/2 cup flour and the cocoa until coarse crumbs form. With floured fingers, press in bottom of tart pan. Bake 5 to 7 minutes or until set.

2 Meanwhile, in 1-quart saucepan, heat 1/4 cup butter and 4 oz chocolate over low heat 2 to 3 minutes, stirring constantly, until melted and smooth. Set aside to cool.

3 In large bowl, beat granulated sugar and eggs with electric mixer on high speed 3 to 4 minutes, scraping bowl frequently, until foamy and light in color. Add sour cream, 2 tablespoons flour and the chocolate mixture; continue beating 1 to 2 minutes, scraping bowl frequently, until well blended. Spread filling over crust.

4 Bake 20 to 25 minutes or until firm to the touch. Cool 15 minutes. Remove side of pan. Cool completely, about 30 minutes.

5 In 1-quart saucepan, heat 2 oz chocolate, 1 tablespoon butter and the honey over low heat 2 to 3 minutes, stirring constantly, until melted and smooth. Spread chocolate mixture over tart. Lightly press kiwifruit and orange segments around edge of tart. Refrigerate about 1 hour or until firm. Let stand at room temperature about 20 minutes before serving.

High Altitude (3500-6500 ft): No change.

Nutritional Info: 1 Serving: Calories 260 (Calories from Fat 150); Total Fat 16g (Saturated Fat 10g, Trans Fat 0g); Cholesterol 65mg; Sodium 85mg; Total Carbohydrate 26g (Dietary Fiber 2g, Sugars 19g); Protein 3g. % Daily Value: Vitamin A 15%; Vitamin C 30%; Calcium 2%; Iron 6%. Exchanges: 1-1/2 Other Carbohydrate, 1/2 High-Fat Meat, 2-1/2 Fat. Carbohydrate Choices: 2.

Betty's Kitchen Tips

Success Hint: The tart filling might bubble up during baking, but it will settle during cooling.

Substitution: Use 2 cups fresh raspberries instead of the kiwifruit and oranges.

baked apples with rum-caramel sauce

Prep Time: 5 Minutes
Start to Finish: 15 Minutes
Servings: 4

EASY QUICK LOW FAT

4 medium baking apples	1/4 cup fat-free caramel topping
2 tablespoons water	1 tablespoon rum or apple cider
1 cup vanilla low-fat ice cream	Dash ground cinnamon

1 Cut thin slice off bottom and top of each apple. Using paring knife or apple corer, remove core from each apple.

2 In 8- or 9-inch square microwavable dish, place apples upright. Pour 2 tablespoons water over apples. Cover with microwavable plastic wrap, folding back one edge or corner 1/4 inch to vent steam. Microwave on High 8 to 10 minutes or until apples are tender. Reserve 1 tablespoon cooking liquid. Cut each apple in half.

3 Place 2 apple halves in each individual serving bowl. For each serving, spoon 1/4 cup ice cream between apple halves. In small bowl, stir caramel topping, 1 tablespoon cooking liquid and the rum; pour over apples. Sprinkle with cinnamon.

High Altitude (3500-6500 ft): No change.

Nutritional Info: 1 Serving: Calories 200 (Calories from Fat 25); Total Fat 3g (Saturated Fat 1.5g, Trans Fat 0g); Cholesterol 10mg; Sodium 100mg; Total Carbohydrate 41g (Dietary Fiber 3g, Sugars 31g); Protein 2g. % Daily Value: Vitamin A 4%; Vitamin C 6%; Calcium 6%; Iron 0%. Exchanges: 1/2 Starch, 1 Fruit, 1 Other Carbohydrate, 1 Fat. Carbohydrate Choices: 3.

CHOOSING THE BEST APPLES

• Try to select apples that are in season for their variety. If the apples are out of season, they may have been in storage and will not be as flavorful and juicy as fresh-picked apples.

• Look for apples that are bruise-free, have no bug holes and are firm to the touch.

• Apples should look fresh, be bright in color and have a fresh apple aroma.

• Don't choose under-ripe apples that are hard and have too much green or yellow color for the specific variety.

plum and walnut crisp

Prep Time: 15 Minutes
Start to Finish: 1 Hour 10 Minutes
Servings: 6

EASY

6	medium red or purple plums, sliced (about 5 cups)
3/4	cup sugar
3	tablespoons cornstarch
1/2	cup crushed gingersnap cookies (about 15 cookies)
1/2	cup chopped walnuts
1/2	cup Original Bisquick® mix
1/4	cup butter or margarine, softened

1 Heat oven to 350°F. Spray 8-inch square (2-quart) glass baking dish with cooking spray.

2 In large bowl, stir sliced plums, 1/2 cup of the sugar and the cornstarch until combined. Spread in baking dish.

3 In medium bowl, mix the crushed cookies, walnuts, Bisquick mix, butter and remaining 1/4 cup sugar with fork until crumbly. Sprinkle over plum mixture.

4 Bake 45 to 55 minutes or until mixture is hot and bubbly and topping is lightly browned. Serve warm.

High Altitude (3500-6500 ft): No change.

Nutritional Info: 1 Serving: Calories 410 (Calories from Fat 150); Total Fat 17g (Saturated Fat 6g, Trans Fat 1g); Cholesterol 20mg; Sodium 260mg; Total Carbohydrate 60g (Dietary Fiber 3g, Sugars 44g); Protein 4g. % Daily Value: Vitamin A 15%; Vitamin C 10%; Calcium 4%; Iron 6%. Exchanges: 1 Starch, 1 Fruit, 2 Other Carbohydrate, 3-1/2 Fat. Carbohydrate Choices: 4.

Betty's Kitchen Tips

Serve-With: Be sure to serve this crisp warm with a scoop of vanilla or caramel-ribbon ice cream.

Substitution: Crushed cinnamon-sugar graham crackers can be substituted for the gingersnap cookies.

mexican chocolate-raspberry parfaits

Prep Time: 15 Minutes
Start to Finish: 15 Minutes
Servings: 4

EASY   QUICK   LOW FAT

1-1/4   cups light chocolate-flavored soymilk

1   box (4-serving size) chocolate instant pudding and pie filling mix

1/4   teaspoon ground cinnamon

1   slice (4x1-inch) angel food cake, torn into pieces

1/2   cup frozen (thawed) fat-free whipped topping

1/2   cup fresh or frozen (thawed and drained) raspberries

Grated semisweet chocolate, if desired

1 In medium bowl, beat soymilk, pudding mix and cinnamon with wire whisk until mixture is blended and thickened.

2 To assemble, spoon 2 tablespoons pudding into each of 4 small parfait glasses. Layer each with 1/4 of the cake, 1 tablespoon whipped topping and 2 tablespoons of the raspberries. Top each with remaining pudding and whipped topping. Garnish with grated chocolate.

High Altitude (3500-6500 ft): No change.

Nutritional Info: 1 Serving: Calories 150 (Calories from Fat 10); Total Fat 1g (Saturated Fat 0g, Trans Fat 0g); Cholesterol 0mg; Sodium 440mg; Total Carbohydrate 32g (Dietary Fiber 2g, Sugars 23g); Protein 3g. % Daily Value: Vitamin A 4%; Vitamin C 6%; Calcium 10%; Iron 6%. Exchanges: 1 Starch, 1 Other Carbohydrate. Carbohydrate Choices: 2.

Betty's Kitchen Tip

• To make Mexican Chocolate-Orange Parfaits, substitute 1/2 cup well-drained mandarin orange segments for the raspberries.

country fruit cobbler

Prep Time: 10 Minutes
Start to Finish: 1 Hour 10 Minutes
Servings: 6

EASY

- 1/4 cup butter or margarine
- 1 cup all-purpose flour
- 1 cup sugar
- 2 teaspoons baking powder
- 1/4 teaspoon salt
- 3/4 cup milk
- 4 cups fresh or frozen (thawed and drained) blueberries, raspberries, sliced peaches or strawberries (or combination of fruit)

1 Heat oven to 350°F. In 1-1/2-quart casserole, melt butter in oven.

2 Meanwhile, in medium bowl, mix flour, sugar, baking powder, salt and milk. Pour batter into casserole onto butter without mixing with butter. Spread fruit over batter.

3 Bake about 1 hour or until top is golden brown. Serve warm.

High Altitude (3500-6500 ft): Decrease baking powder to 1-1/4 teaspoons.

Nutritional Info: 1 Serving: Calories 415 (Calories from Fat 100); Total Fat 11g (Saturated Fat 6g); Cholesterol 30mg; Sodium 400mg; Total Carbohydrate 78g (Dietary Fiber 4g).

Betty's Kitchen Tip

• Berries contain natural antioxidants that may help protect the body from certain diseases, such as cancer and heart disease. Orange-colored fruits such as peaches and apricots are rich in beta-carotene and a good source of folic acid.

apricot petits fours

Prep Time: 1 Hour 20 Minutes
Start to Finish: 4 Hours 20 Minutes
Servings: 54 petits fours

Cake

1	box Betty Crocker® SuperMoist® yellow cake mix
1	cup apricot nectar or juice
1/3	cup vegetable oil
1	teaspoon grated orange peel
2	eggs
2	tablespoons orange-flavored liqueur or apricot nectar

Icing

9	cups powdered sugar
3/4	cup apricot nectar or water
1/2	cup light corn syrup
1/3	cup butter or margarine, melted
2	teaspoons almond extract

Sliced almonds and sugared orange peels for garnish, if desired

1 Heat oven to 350°F for shiny metal pan (or 325°F for dark or nonstick pan). Spray bottom and sides of 15x10x1-inch pan with baking spray with flour.

2 In large bowl, beat all cake ingredients except liqueur with electric mixer on low speed 30 seconds. Beat on medium speed 2 minutes, scraping bowl occasionally. Pour batter into pan.

3 Bake 22 to 28 minutes or until cake springs back when touched lightly in center. Brush liqueur over top of cake. Cool completely, about 20 minutes. To avoid cake crumbs when adding icing, freeze cake 1 hour before cutting.

4 In large bowl, beat icing ingredients on low speed until powdered sugar is moistened. Beat on high speed until smooth. If

necessary, add 2 to 3 teaspoons more apricot nectar until icing is pourable.

5 Place cooling rack on cookie sheet or waxed paper to catch icing drips. Cut cake into 9 rows by 6 rows. Working with 6 pieces at a time, remove cake pieces from pan and place on cooling rack. Spoon icing evenly over top and sides of cake pieces, letting icing coat sides. (Icing that drips off can be reused.) Let stand until icing is set, about 2 hours.

6 Decorate with almonds and orange peel if desired. Store in single layer in airtight plastic container at room temperature.

High Altitude (3500-6500 ft): Decrease nectar in cake to 3/4 cup and add 1/4 cup water.

Nutritional Info: 1 Petit Four: Calories 160 (Calories from Fat 30); Total Fat 3.5g (Saturated Fat 1.5g, Trans Fat 0g); Cholesterol 10mg; Sodium 75mg; Total Carbohydrate 31g (Dietary Fiber 0g, Sugars 26g); Protein 0g. % Daily Value: Cholesterol 4%; Vitamin A 4%; Vitamin C 0%; Calcium 0%; Iron 0%. Exchanges: 2 Other Carbohydrate, 1 Fat. Carbohydrate Choices: 2.

Betty's Kitchen Tip

• To top the cakes with butterflies, place 4 almond slices around a piece of sugared orange peel.

brownie 'n berries dessert pizza

Prep Time: 20 Minutes
Start to Finish: 2 Hours 50 Minutes
Servings: 16

- 1 box (1 lb 6.5 oz) Betty Crocker® Original Supreme brownie mix
- Water, vegetable oil and eggs called for on brownie mix box
- 1 package (8 oz) cream cheese, softened
- 1/3 cup sugar
- 1/2 teaspoon vanilla
- 2 cups sliced fresh strawberries
- 1 cup fresh blueberries
- 1 cup fresh raspberries
- 1/2 cup apple jelly

1. Heat oven to 350°F (or 325°F for dark or nonstick pan). Grease bottom only of 12-inch pizza pan with cooking spray or shortening.

2. In medium bowl, stir brownie mix, pouch of chocolate syrup, water, oil and eggs until well blended. Spread in pan.

3. Bake 28 to 30 minutes or until toothpick inserted 2 inches from side of pan comes out clean or almost clean. Cool completely, about 1 hour.

4. In small bowl, beat cream cheese, sugar and vanilla with electric mixer on medium speed until smooth. Spread mixture evenly over brownie base. Arrange berries over cream cheese mixture. Stir jelly until smooth; brush over berries. Refrigerate about 1 hour or until chilled. Cut into wedges. Store covered in refrigerator.

High Altitude (3500-6500 ft): Follow High Altitude directions on brownie mix box. Use 14-inch pizza pan.

Nutritional Info: 1 Serving: Calories 310 (Calories from Fat 110); Total Fat 12g (Saturated Fat 4.5g, Trans Fat 0g); Cholesterol 40mg; Sodium 180mg; Total Carbohydrate 47g (Dietary Fiber 2g, Sugars 34g); Protein 3g. % Daily Value: Cholesterol 14%; Vitamin A 4%; Vitamin C 25%; Calcium 2%; Iron 10%. Exchanges: 1 Starch, 2 Other Carbohydrate, 2-1/2 Fat. Carbohydrate Choices: 3.

Betty's Kitchen Tips

Success Hint: For easy cleanup, bake the brownie in a 12-inch disposable foil pizza pan. Slide the pan onto a cookie sheet when you remove the brownie from the oven. Place the brownie dessert on a tray when you take it to the table.

Variation: Any cut-up fresh fruit can be used for this dessert. Substitute 4 cups cut-up fresh fruit for the berries.

dulce de leche-banana pie

Prep Time: 20 Minutes
Start to Finish: 1 Hour 5 Minutes
Servings: 8

Crust

1	cup Gold Medal® all-purpose flour
1/2	teaspoon salt
1/3	cup plus 1 tablespoon shortening
2	to 3 tablespoons cold water

Filling

1	can (13.4 oz) dulce de leche (caramelized sweetened condensed milk)
3	ripe medium bananas
1	cup whipping cream
1/4	cup powdered sugar
1/2	cup semisweet chocolate chips
1	teaspoon vegetable oil

1 Heat oven to 450°F. In medium bowl, mix flour and salt. Cut in shortening, using pastry blender (or pulling 2 table knives through ingredients in opposite directions), until particles are size of small peas. Sprinkle with water, 1 tablespoon at a time, tossing with fork until all flour is moistened and dough almost leaves side of bowl (1 to 2 teaspoons more water can be added if necessary).

2 On lightly floured surface, shape dough into a ball. Flatten ball to 1/2-inch thickness, rounding and smoothing edges. With floured rolling pin, roll dough into 11-inch round, rolling from center to edge. Fold dough in half; place in 9-inch glass pie plate. Unfold; gently press in bottom and up side of plate, being careful not to stretch dough.

3 Fold and roll edge of dough under, even with plate; flute edge. Prick bottom and side of dough generously with fork. Bake 9 to 12 minutes or until light golden brown. Cool completely, about 30 minutes.

4 Spoon contents of can of dulce de leche into center of cooled crust; gently spread to edge. Thinly slice bananas; arrange over dulce de leche.

5 In medium bowl, beat whipping cream and powdered sugar with electric mixer on high speed until stiff peaks form. Spread over bananas.

6 In small resealable freezer plastic bag, place chocolate chips and oil; seal bag. Microwave on High 30 seconds; knead bag to mix melted chips and unmelted chips. Microwave 15 to 30 seconds longer or until all chips are melted and smooth. Snip off tiny corner of bag. Pipe melted chocolate mixture over whipped cream. Store pie in refrigerator.

High Altitude (3500-6500 ft): No change.

Nutritional Info: 1 Serving: Calories 500 (Calories from Fat 230); Total Fat 26g (Saturated Fat 12g, Trans Fat 2g); Cholesterol 35mg; Sodium 210mg; Total Carbohydrate 60g (Dietary Fiber 2g, Sugars 38g); Protein 7g. % Daily Value: Vitamin A 10%; Vitamin C 4%; Calcium 15%; Iron 6%. Exchanges: 1 Starch, 3 Other Carbohydrate, 1/2 High-Fat Meat, 4 Fat. Carbohydrate Choices: 4.

Betty's Kitchen Tip

• Dulce de leche is a traditional Spanish confection made from milk. It's a popular culinary reference to rich caramel flavors. Look for canned dulce de leche in the Hispanic section of the supermarket.

peach-raspberry streusel tart

Prep Time: 15 Minutes
Start to Finish: 2 Hours 40 Minutes
Servings: 8

EASY

Crust

1	cup Gold Medal® all-purpose flour
1/2	cup butter or margarine, softened
2	tablespoons packed brown sugar
1	egg yolk

Filling

1	can (21 oz) peach pie filling
1	cup frozen unsweetened raspberries

Topping

1/2	cup quick-cooking oats
1/2	cup Gold Medal® all-purpose flour
1/2	cup packed brown sugar
1/4	cup butter or margarine
1/4	cup chopped pecans

1 Heat oven to 400°F. In small bowl, mix crust ingredients with spoon or electric mixer on low speed until dough forms. In ungreased 9-inch tart pan with removable bottom, press dough firmly and evenly against bottom and side. Place pan on cookie sheet. Bake 15 to 20 minutes or until light brown. Cool 10 minutes before filling.

2 Reduce oven temperature to 350°F. Spread pie filling over bottom of partially baked crust. Top with raspberries. In medium bowl, mix topping ingredients with pastry blender or fork until crumbly; sprinkle over raspberries and pie filling.

3 Bake 20 to 25 minutes or until filling is hot and topping is golden brown. Cool completely, about 1 hour 30 minutes, before serving.

High Altitude (3500-6500 ft): Not recommended.

Nutritional Info: 1 Serving: Calories 500 (Calories from Fat 245); Total Fat 27g (Saturated Fat 15g); Cholesterol 90mg; Sodium 160mg; Total Carbohydrate 60g (Dietary Fiber 5g); Protein 5g. Exchanges: 2 Starch, 1 Fruit, 1 Other Carbohydrate, 5 Fat. Carbohydrate Choices: 4.

Betty's Kitchen Tip

• Using pie filling saves you the time needed to peel and slice fresh fruit, and combining the filling with frozen fruit adds a fresh taste while still being convenient. You can make this memorable tart with other fruit combinations. Try apple or cherry pie filling in place of the peach.

chocolate mousse

Prep Time: 30 Minutes
Start to Finish: 2 Hours 40 Minutes
Servings: 8

. . . .

Mousse

4	egg yolks
1/4	cup sugar
1	cup whipping cream
8	oz semisweet baking chocolate, chopped
1-1/2	cups whipping cream

Chocolate Piping

1/2	cup semisweet chocolate chips
1/2	teaspoon shortening

. . . .

1 In small bowl, beat egg yolks with electric mixer on high speed about 3 minutes or until thickened and lemon colored. Gradually beat in sugar.

2 In 2-quart saucepan, heat 1 cup whipping cream over medium heat just until hot. Gradually stir at least half of the hot cream into egg yolk mixture, then stir egg mixture back into hot cream in saucepan. Cook over low heat about 5 minutes, stirring constantly, until mixture thickens (do not boil).

3 Stir in baking chocolate until melted. Cover; refrigerate about 2 hours, stirring occasionally, just until chilled.

4 In chilled medium bowl, beat 1-1/2 cups whipping cream on high speed until stiff peaks form. Fold chocolate mixture into whipped cream.

5 In 1-cup microwavable measuring cup, microwave chocolate chips and shortening uncovered on Medium (50%) 30 seconds. Stir; microwave in 10-second increments, stirring after each, until melted and smooth. Place in small resealable food-storage plastic bag; seal bag. Cut off tiny corner of bag. Squeeze bag to pipe designs or swirls inside parfait glasses. Refrigerate 10 minutes to set chocolate.

6 Spoon mousse into glasses. Refrigerate until serving. Store covered in refrigerator.

High Altitude (3500-6500 ft): No change.

Nutritional Info: 1 Serving: Calories 490 (Calories from Fat 330); Total Fat 37g (Saturated Fat 22g, Trans Fat 1g); Cholesterol 185mg; Sodium 35mg; Total Carbohydrate 33g (Dietary Fiber 2g, Sugars 29g); Protein 5g. % Daily Value: Vitamin A 20%; Vitamin C 0%; Calcium 8%; Iron 8%. Exchanges: 1/2 Starch, 1-1/2 Other Carbohydrate, 1/2 High-Fat Meat, 6-1/2 Fat. Carbohydrate Choices: 2.

Betty's Kitchen Tips

Success Hint: The cream will whip up faster if you chill the bowl and beaters in the freezer for about 15 minutes before whipping.

Do-Ahead: Make this mousse up to 24 hours ahead. Just spoon it into individual serving dishes, cover and refrigerate.

two-berry crisp with pecan streusel topping

Prep Time: 15 Minutes
Start to Finish: 55 Minutes
Servings: 6

EASY

Topping

3/4	cup quick-cooking oats
1/2	cup Gold Medal® all-purpose flour
1/2	cup packed brown sugar
1/2	cup cold butter or margarine, cut into pieces
1/4	cup chopped pecans

Filling

1	can (21 oz) blueberry pie filling
2	cups frozen unsweetened raspberries
3	tablespoons granulated sugar
1	tablespoon Gold Medal® all-purpose flour

1 Heat oven to 400°F. Spray 8-inch square (2-quart) glass baking dish with cooking spray.

2 In large bowl, mix oats, 1/2 cup flour and the brown sugar. Cut in butter, using pastry blender or fork, until crumbly. Stir in pecans. Set aside.

3 In large bowl, combine and stir filling ingredients. Pour into baking dish. Sprinkle with topping.

4 Bake 30 to 40 minutes or until mixture is bubbly and topping is golden brown. Serve warm.

High Altitude (3500-6500 ft): No change.

Nutritional Info: 1 Serving: Calories 490 (Calories from Fat 180); Total Fat 20g (Saturated Fat 8g, Trans Fat 1g); Cholesterol 40mg; Sodium 110mg; Total Carbohydrate 74g (Dietary Fiber 9g, Sugars 52g); Protein 4g. Exchanges: 1 Starch, 4 Other Carbohydrate, 4 Fat. Carbohydrate Choices: 5.

Betty's Kitchen Tips

Variation: If you like, use another flavor of fruit pie filling for the blueberry. Try raspberry, cherry, blackberry, strawberry or peach for a different twist.

Special Touch: Top each serving with whipped cream or ice cream and a few pecan halves.

peachy pear-coconut crumble

Prep Time: 20 Minutes
Start to Finish: 1 Hour 5 Minutes
Servings: 10

- -

1	cup Gold Medal® all-purpose flour
3/4	cup sugar
1/4	cup butter or margarine, softened
1	egg, beaten
1	can (29 oz) sliced peaches in heavy syrup, drained, 1/2 cup syrup reserved
1	can (29 oz) sliced pears in syrup, drained, 1/2 cup syrup reserved
3	tablespoons cornstarch
1/2	teaspoon almond extract
1/2	cup maraschino cherries, cut in half, drained
1/4	cup flaked coconut

- -

1 Heat oven to 400°F. In medium bowl, mix flour and sugar. Cut in butter, using pastry blender or fork, until crumbly. Stir in egg; set aside.

2 In 1-quart saucepan, mix reserved peach and pear syrups and the cornstarch. Cook over medium heat, stirring constantly, until mixture boils and thickens. Stir in almond extract.

3 In ungreased 12x8- or 11x7-inch (2-quart) glass baking dish, mix peaches, pears and cherries. Stir in syrup mixture. Crumble and spoon flour mixture over fruit mixture.

4 Bake 40 to 45 minutes, sprinkling with coconut for last 10 minutes of baking, until topping is deep golden brown and fruit is bubbly.

High Altitude (3500-6500 ft): No change.

Nutritional Info: 1 Serving: Calories 360 (Calories from Fat 60); Total Fat 6g (Saturated Fat 3g, Trans Fat 0g); Cholesterol 35mg; Sodium 50mg; Total Carbohydrate 74g (Dietary Fiber 3g, Sugars 56g); Protein 3g. % Daily Value: Vitamin A 10%; Vitamin C 2%; Calcium 0%; Iron 6%. Exchanges: 1 Starch, 2 Fruit, 2 Other Carbohydrate, 1 Fat. Carbohydrate Choices: 5.

Betty's Kitchen Tips

Did You Know? A crumble is a British dessert in which fruit is topped with a crumbly pastry mixture and baked.

Special Touch: Spoon into stemmed dessert cups for a beautiful presentation.

caramel apple dessert

Prep Time: 20 Minutes
Start to Finish: 1 Hour 20 Minutes
Servings: 6

1-1/2	cups Original Bisquick® mix
2/3	cup granulated sugar
1/2	cup milk
2	medium cooking apples, peeled and sliced (2 cups)

1	tablespoon lemon juice
3/4	cup packed brown sugar
1/2	teaspoon ground cinnamon
1	cup boiling water

Ice cream or sweetened whipped cream, if desired

1. Heat oven to 350°F. In medium bowl, stir together Bisquick mix and granulated sugar. Stir in milk until blended.

2. Pour into ungreased 9-inch square pan. Top with apples; sprinkle with lemon juice. Stir together brown sugar and cinnamon; sprinkle over apples. Pour boiling water over apples.

3. Bake 50 to 60 minutes or until toothpick inserted in center comes out clean. Spoon into small bowls. Serve warm with ice cream.

High Altitude (over 3500 ft): Not recommended.

Nutritional Info: 1 Serving: Calories 350 (Calories from Fat 40); Total Fat 4g (Saturated Fat 1.5g, Trans Fat 1g); Cholesterol 0mg; Sodium 390mg; Total Carbohydrate 74g (Dietary Fiber 1g, Sugars 54g); Protein 3g. % Daily Value: Vitamin A 0%; Vitamin C 0%; Calcium 8%; Iron 8%. Exchanges: 1 Starch, 4 Other Carbohydrate, 1/2 Fat. Carbohydrate Choices: 5.

THE RIGHT APPLE VARIETY

- Choose a variety of apple that is appropriate for what you want to use it for.

- For the best pies, crisps and other baked items, apples should be firm enough to hold their shape and have great flavor.

- Top pie choices that are slightly tart and crisp include Braeburn, Cortland and Newtown Pippin.

- For a crisp and sweet choice, try Fuji. For crisp but only slightly sweet, use Gala.

- Top pie choices that are tart and crisp include Granny Smith and Haralson.

- For general baking, such as cakes and sauces, chopped and sliced apples can be less firm than those used in pies. Golden Delicious apples are sweet and tender. Jonathan and McIntosh are slightly tart and tender.

banana-chocolate mousse tart

Prep Time: 20 Minutes
Start to Finish: 3 Hours 10 Minutes
Servings: 10

Pastry

1-1/3	cups Gold Medal® all-purpose flour
1/2	teaspoon salt
1/2	cup shortening
3	to 4 tablespoons cold water

Filling

1-1/2	cups milk
1	package (4-serving size) chocolate pudding and pie filling mix (not instant)
2	oz semisweet baking chocolate, chopped
1-1/2	cups frozen (thawed) whipped topping
3	bananas, sliced

1 Heat oven to 400°F. In medium bowl, mix flour and salt. Cut in shortening, using pastry blender (or pulling 2 table knives through ingredients in opposite directions), until particles are size of small peas. Sprinkle with cold water, 1 tablespoon at a time, tossing with fork until all flour is moistened and pastry almost leaves side of bowl (1 to 2 teaspoons more water can be added if necessary).

2 On lightly floured surface, roll pastry into 13-inch circle, about 1/8 inch thick. In 10-inch tart pan with removable bottom, press in bottom and up side. Trim pastry even with top edge of pan. Prick bottom and side of pastry with fork.

3 Bake 15 to 20 minutes or until golden brown. Cool completely, about 30 minutes.

4 Meanwhile, in 2-quart saucepan, heat milk and pudding mix over medium heat, stirring occasionally, until mixture boils. Stir in chopped chocolate until melted. Pour into medium bowl; place plastic wrap directly on surface of pudding mixture. Refrigerate about 1 hour or until completely cooled.

5 Fold 1/2 cup of the whipped topping into cooled chocolate mixture. Arrange banana slices in single layer in bottom of baked crust. Spoon chocolate mixture over bananas. Refrigerate about 1 hour or until thoroughly chilled. Garnish with remaining 1 cup whipped topping and, if desired, additional banana slices.

High Altitude (3500-6500 ft): No change.

Nutritional Info: 1 Serving: Calories 310 (Calories from Fat 140); Total Fat 16g (Saturated Fat 6g, Trans Fat 2g); Cholesterol 0mg; Sodium 190mg; Total Carbohydrate 38g (Dietary Fiber 2g, Sugars 17g); Protein 4g. % Daily Value: Vitamin A 0%; Vitamin C 6%; Calcium 6%; Iron 8%. Exchanges: 1 Starch, 1/2 Fruit, 1 Other Carbohydrate, 3 Fat. Carbohydrate Choices: 2-1/2.

Betty's Kitchen Tip

• Short on time? Use a refrigerated pie crust instead of making the crust from scratch.

impossibly easy pear-custard pie

Prep Time: 15 Minutes
Start to Finish: 1 Hour 25 Minutes
Servings: 8

EASY

- -

Streusel

1/2	cup Original Bisquick® mix
1/4	cup old-fashioned or quick-cooking oats
1/4	cup packed brown sugar
1/2	teaspoon ground nutmeg
1	tablespoon cold butter or margarine

Pie

1/2	cup Original Bisquick® mix
1/3	cup granulated sugar
1/2	cup milk
2	tablespoons butter or margarine, softened
2	eggs
3	medium fresh pears, peeled, sliced (about 3 cups)

- -

1 Heat oven to 350°F. Spray 9-inch glass pie plate with cooking spray. In small bowl, stir 1/2 cup Bisquick mix, the oats, brown sugar and nutmeg. Cut in 1 tablespoon butter, using pastry blender (or pulling 2 table knives through ingredients in opposite directions), until crumbly. Set aside.

2 In medium bowl, stir all pie ingredients except pears with wire whisk or fork until blended. Pour into pie plate. Arrange pears evenly over top.

3 Bake 25 minutes. Sprinkle streusel over top. Bake 12 to 15 minutes longer or until knife inserted in center comes out clean. Cool 30 minutes. Serve warm. Store in refrigerator.

High Altitude (3500-6500 ft): No change.

Nutritional Info: 1 Serving: Calories 230 (Calories from Fat 70); Total Fat 8g (Saturated Fat 4g, Trans Fat 1g); Cholesterol 65mg; Sodium 240mg; Total Carbohydrate 36g (Dietary Fiber 2g, Sugars 21g); Protein 4g. % Daily Value: Vitamin A 4%; Vitamin C 0%; Calcium 6%; Iron 4%. Exchanges: 1 Starch, 1-1/2 Other Carbohydrate, 1-1/2 Fat. Carbohydrate Choices: 2-1/2.

Betty's Kitchen Tip

- Unlike many types of fruits, pears improve in both texture and flavor after they're picked. Choose pears that are free of blemishes and soft spots, and store them at room temperature until ripe.

peach and blueberry crisp with crunchy nut topping

Prep Time: 20 Minutes
Start to Finish: 50 Minutes
Servings: 6

- 4   medium peaches, peeled, sliced
- 1   cup fresh or frozen (thawed and drained) blueberries
- 2   tablespoons packed brown sugar
- 2   tablespoons orange juice
- 1   teaspoon ground cinnamon
- 1/4   teaspoon ground nutmeg
- 1   cup Honey Nut Clusters® or Total® cereal, slightly crushed
- 1/3   cup chopped pecans

1. Heat oven to 375°F. Spray bottom and sides of square baking dish, 8x8x2 inches, or rectangular baking dish, 11x7x1-1/2 inches, with cooking spray.

2. Place peaches and blueberries in baking dish. Stir together brown sugar, orange juice, cinnamon and nutmeg in small bowl; drizzle over fruit.

3. Bake 15 minutes. Sprinkle with crushed cereal and pecans. Bake 10 to 15 minutes longer or until peaches are tender when pierced with fork.

High Altitude (3500-6500 ft): No changes.

Nutritional Info: 1 Serving: Calories 150 (Calories from Fat 45); Total Fat 5g (Saturated Fat 0g, Trans Fat 0g); Cholesterol 0mg; Sodium 50mg; Total Carbohydrate 24g (Dietary Fiber 3g, Sugars 16g); Protein 2g. % Daily Value: Vitamin A 4%; Vitamin C 8%; Calcium 2%; Iron 8%. Exchanges: 1/2 Starch, 1/2 Fruit, 1/2 Other Carbohydrate, 1 Fat. Carbohydrate Choices: 1-1/2.

Betty's Kitchen Tips

Health Twist: If you like fruit crisps with streusel topping, you'll love this recipe. Instead of the traditional crumble, crushed cereal and nuts give this topping the same great crunch for fewer calories and carbs.

Serve-With: Enjoy this fruity dessert with a scoop of vanilla ice cream or frozen yogurt.

general index

alphabetical index

*star pattern is for apricot-chipotle-cream cheese star recipe on page 44